SOVIET RELIGIOUS POLICY
IN ESTONIA AND LATVIA

SOVIET RELIGIOUS POLICY IN ESTONIA AND LATVIA

Playing Harmony in the Singing Revolution

Robert F. Goeckel

Indiana University Press

This book is a publication of

Indiana University Press
Office of Scholarly Publishing
Herman B Wells Library 350
1320 East 10th Street
Bloomington, Indiana 47405 USA

iupress.indiana.edu

© 2018 by Robert F. Goeckel

All rights reserved
No part of this book may be reproduced or utilized in any form or
by any means, electronic or mechanical, including photocopying
and recording, or by any information storage and retrieval
system, without permission in writing from the publisher.

The paper used in this publication meets the minimum requirements of
the American National Standard for Information Sciences—Permanence
of Paper for Printed Library Materials, ANSI Z39.48-1992.

Manufactured in the United States of America

Cataloging information is available from the Library of Congress.

ISBN 978-0-253-03615-5 (cloth)
ISBN 978-0-253-03611-7 (paperback)
ISBN 978-0-253-03613-1 (ebook)

1 2 3 4 5   22 21 20 19 18

To my wife, Gay, for her unstinting support and understanding during my years of research and many trips to the Baltics and Moscow.
And to the many archivists who kindly assisted this particular effort at glasnost.

Contents

	Preface	ix
	List of Abbreviations	xiii
	Introduction: Studying Soviet Policy toward Religion and the Church in Latvia and Estonia	1
1	The Early Stalinization Process: 1944–1949	9
2	The Period of High Stalinism: 1949–1953	45
3	The Post-Stalin Thaw: 1953–1957	78
4	Renewed Repression and International Opening Under Khrushchev: 1958–1964	109
5	Détente and Stagnation During the Brezhnev Era: 1964–1985	142
6	Perestroika and Religious Policy in the Baltics: Playing Harmony in the Singing Revolution, 1985–1991	172
	Conclusion: The Contours of Baltic Exceptionalism in Soviet Religious Policy—and Its Limits	200
	Glossary	211
	Bibliography	213
	Index	247

Preface

THIS BOOK EXAMINES the policy of the Soviet regime toward churches and religion in two of the three Baltic republics, Estonia and Latvia. The Baltic republics posed a unique challenge for the regime: they represented the only republics with primarily Western religious traditions and churches. In the remaining republics, various forms of eastern Orthodoxy and Islam were predominant, historically and culturally. The Bolsheviks who assumed power in 1917 had experienced Protestants and Catholics only as tiny minority religions until 1944. With the Communist takeovers in Eastern Europe, the Soviets would also encounter societies that were largely Catholic (such as Poland and Hungary), Lutheran (such as East Germany), and confessionally mixed (such as Yugoslavia and Czechoslovakia). But in these Eastern European cases, adoption of the Soviet model of religious policy was not automatically or rigorously expected of these nominally sovereign states. Having been incorporated as constituent units in the USSR, however, the Baltic republics were expected to adopt Soviet religious policy in its entirety. Using in-depth description and analysis of two of these Baltics cases, Estonia and Latvia, my aim here is to investigate the extent to which this was the case over time and the factors in the church-state relationship that may explain any divergence from Soviet policy.

As author, I should clarify what did *not* motivate the writing of this book. When I began the research on which it is based, the Berlin Wall had recently fallen, and Germany had been reunited. I had recently completed a related book on the role of the GDR's relationship with the Lutheran Church, which eventually played an instrumental role in the democratic revolution and end of communism in 1989. During my on-site research in 1990–1991, many of my Baltic interlocutors good-naturedly asked me to quickly write my second book so that it might have the same effect in the case of the USSR! Little did we know that the USSR would collapse long before my book would be complete. On the other hand, today's interested observers often assume my goal was to explain why so few Estonians believe in God, looking for answers in the almost fifty years of Soviet atheistic policies. This book was obviously not written in the heat of the system collapse of the USSR, with the intent to explain the churches' role in that regime change. Nor has it been written to explain why this region is among the most secularized in Europe, however intriguing the correlation might be.

Rather, my intention has been to shed light on variation in Soviet religious policy, yielding generalizations regarding church-state relations in communist political systems. Some of the variation occurred over time, based on leadership changes and underlying shifts in policy, explaining the periodization in the structure of the chapters. Spanning the periods is a continuous official atheism, but pursued with varying tactics and levels of commitment. Embedded in the periods are also variations by confession—Lutheran and Catholic in particular—and contrasts between these institutionalized national churches and various minority churches. Driving my research, as with my previous work, was also the goal of weighing the impact of international and transnational ties of the churches, particularly those with German churches and the Vatican, on the churches' leverage with the Soviet regime, both in Moscow and at the republic level. Finally, informing the analysis of variation is also a concern with the distinctiveness of local and republic interests, reflective of national culture and bureaucratic political interests.

In the former USSR as recipient of an IREX award, and later under the auspices of the SUNY-Moscow State University exchange and the Fulbright program in the Russian Federation, I was fortunate to use the documentary materials of the Council for Religious Affairs shortly after portions had been declassified. In addition, the research benefited from limited access to materials of the Communist Party regarding religion. The following archives proved invaluable for this project and I wish to give them well-deserved credit for their scholarly access and assistance: the State Archive of the Russian Federation (GARF), Russian State Archive for Social and Political History (RGASPI), Russian State Archive for Contemporary History (RGANI), Estonian State Archive (ERA and ERAF), Latvian State Archive (LVA), and Lithuanian Central State Archive (LCVA). Also, I wish to give credit to the archive of the Finnish National Committee of the Lutheran World Federation. In the initial stage of research, I also utilized the samizdat archive of Keston College.

I wish to extend my heartfelt thanks to Baltic scholars and policy makers who, in the frenetic and fraught days of 1991, assisted and supported my archival research, including Andra Veidemann and Alfreds Kublinskis (heads of the transitional offices of religious questions in Estonia and Latvia, respectively, in 1991), as well as Latvian scholars Solveiga Krumina and the late Nikandrs Gills.

I thank those who have read and commented on the manuscript or my related work. To Norman Naimark, my mentor since graduate school, as well as Sabrina Ramet, my energetic collaborator on various projects on church-state relations, many thanks for advice and support on this project. In particular, I benefited greatly from the comments of my co-panelists at numerous panels on church and state in Communist Europe at Association for Slavic, East European, and Eurasian Studies, including James Felak, David Doellinger, Sean Brennan, David Curp, Jonathan Huener, Jennifer Garza, and Jerry Pankhurst.

Early versions of portions of my work benefited from conference presentation and eventual publication in *Kirchliche Zeitgeschichte* in 1993. I am also grateful for the support and shared interest over many years of Dr. Joachim Heise of the Institut für Staat-Kirche Forschung in Berlin.

The editors at Indiana University Press deserve great credit for their invaluable assistance with revision of the original manuscript and facilitating the process of publication. In particular, I thank Jennika Baines and Kate Schramm. In this regard, I also extend my gratitude to the two readers of the manuscript for their careful reading and very helpful comments, which assisted me in making final revisions.

Finally, I wish to also thank my colleagues in the Department of Political Science and International Relations, in particular Chair Jeffrey Koch, and to State University of New York at Geneseo for creating a supportive environment for such research.

I gratefully acknowledge the financial support over the years—from acquisition of Russian language facility to final manuscript—of the NEH (Summer Seminar 1988 on the Russian Orthodox Church by Gregory Freeze), the International Research and Exchanges Board, the Hoover Institution and Title VIII program, State University of New York-Moscow State University exchange, Fulbright scholar exchange programs in Germany and Russia, and SUNY Geneseo sabbatical support.

Portions of Chapter Four appeared earlier as "Soviet Religious Policy in the Baltics under Khrushchev, 1957–1964: Domestic Repression and International Engagement," in *Religion and Politics*, August 2010.

A word of explanation is in order regarding the system of archival references.

In the chapter endnotes, an abbreviated format for archival documents is utilized: archive.fond.opis.delo (file), list (page number).

The more complete form of each archival document is found in the bibliography, including additional information identifying the number and date, source and recipient, and title or description of the document. To facilitate cross-reference between the abbreviated endnote and the bibliography, documents in the bibliography are sequenced by archive; within each archive, by delo (file); and within each delo, by list (page number).

An example of a document from the State Archive of the Russian Federation (GARF), in abbreviated format: GARF.6991.3.129, l. 40-46; in full format: GARF.6991.3.129, n. 10-110c (27 Feb. 1956), Polyanski—Mikoyan (Chair CM USSR), l. 40-46.

All translations from Russian are my own. Likewise I alone assume responsibility for the accuracy of the account and validity of the interpretation.

Robert F. Goeckel
Geneseo, NY

Abbreviations

AUCECB	All-Union Council of Evangelical Christians and Baptists
CARC	Council for the Affairs of Religious Cults
CC	Central Committee, Communist Party
CEC	Conference of European Churches
CM	Council of Ministers
CPC	Christian Peace Conference
CPE	Communist Party of Estonia
CPL	Communist Party of Latvia
CPSU	Communist Party of the Soviet Union
CRA	Council for Religious Affairs (merged CARC and CROC, after 1965)
CROC	Council for the Affairs of the Russian Orthodox Church
EELC	Estonian Evangelical Lutheran Church
EKD	Evangelical Church in Germany
ELCL	Evangelical Lutheran Church of Latvia
ELKRAS	Evangelical Lutheran Church in Russia and Other States
ESSR	Estonian Soviet Socialist Republic
FRG	Federal Republic of Germany (West)
GDR	German Democratic Republic (East)
HCA	Higher Church Administration (ELCL executive)
KGB	Committee for State Security
LSSR	Latvian Soviet Socialist Republic
LWF	Lutheran World Federation
MFA	Ministry of Foreign Affairs
NCC	National Council of Churches
ROC	Russian Orthodox Church
RWF	Reformed World Federation
WCC	World Council of Churches

SOVIET RELIGIOUS POLICY
IN ESTONIA AND LATVIA

Introduction: Studying Soviet Policy toward Religion and the Church in Latvia and Estonia

ALTHOUGH QUITE SMALL in population—Estonia numbers 1.25 million and Latvia only 1.94 million—these two polities have punched above their weight class since independence.¹ They managed to gain accession to the EU in the first round—ahead of several east European countries—and NATO in the second round. Despite intense economic shocks from the global financial crisis and eurozone recession, both states have weathered the economic austerity with remarkable political stability. Estonia even managed to join the eurozone at the height of the crisis. Yet in terms of religiosity and secularization, they offer an ominous warning to the old Christian Europe: Estonia and Latvia have become two of the most de-Christianized countries in Europe, a distinction they share with the former Communist East Germany, also an historically Lutheran region like Estonia and Latvia.² Could the roots for both these striking phenomena lie in a Baltic cultural distinctiveness, particularly the interaction of Lutheran cultures with fifty years of antireligious Communism?

This Baltic exceptionalism was also arguably in evidence even earlier, namely during the period of the USSR and its collapse. The Baltics led the struggle for independence from the USSR, ahead of other Soviet republics. Even though Ukraine provided the knockout blow to the Soviet project with its December 1991 referendum, the Baltic republics, especially Lithuania, were the vanguard for pushing perestroika to the point of revising the political community. Even though they sailed in Lithuania's wake to a great extent, Latvia and Estonia mounted growing if more restrained demands for greater national autonomy. Indeed it was the coherent stance of the three Baltic republics and their respective Popular Fronts that led to the volte-face of their own Communist Party organizations and eventually of the Kremlin. Before the recent color revolutions in the former USSR, there were singing revolutions in the Baltics; investigating the role of religion and the churches seems essential to providing a full explanation of these social movements.

Additional significance stems from the USSR's self-conception as a multinational federation. Some have described it as an "affirmative action empire," claiming to transcend nationality while in fact legally and politically entrenching it.[3] The effort to inculcate supranational Soviet norms seems to have been more effective in the Slavic republics than the non-Slavic ones. To the extent that religious identification is often a marker for nationality, a study of the Soviet religious policy in the Baltics will shed light on the efforts of the Soviets to erode national consciousness—as manifested in religious adherence—and replace it with a Soviet consciousness, or at least secular-socialist Estonian and Latvian identities. The study will test the effectiveness of antireligious policy in creating this official political culture. To what extent did the unofficial milieu of cultural Christianity and Baltic distinctiveness remain resistant to these efforts?

Moreover, a study of Estonia and Latvia will permit one to analyze the effect of confession as an independent variable in church-state relations. After early Catholicization, Estonia became primarily Lutheran as a result of the Reformation and the influence of German nobility; by contrast, Latvia remained confessionally mixed as a result of these historical forces.[4] The Lutheran preponderance in Estonia, contrasted with the balance of Catholics and Lutherans in Latvia, provides a good basis for comparison. Both countries also have small Protestant minority churches, along with Orthodox churches, a result of conversions to Orthodoxy under imperial Russian rule as well as Russian immigration since 1944. The different theological tenets and organizational principles may be expected to yield contrasting approaches to the state, despite a uniform position of tension with Soviet atheism. Some churches might be more vulnerable to co-optation, even subversion by the totalitarian state. This exploration will also facilitate conclusions regarding the role of the predominant Russian Orthodox Church (ROC) in the USSR in mixed confessional settings. This kind of comparative work is not viable in other Soviet republics or regions due to the particular heterogeneity found in the Baltics.

A study of these two Baltic republics will also allow testing of the validity of the totalitarian model. After serving as the mainstream approach in the 1950s, it was sidelined by scholars' application of interest group analysis and developmental approaches in the 1960s and 1970s, only to see a renaissance among scholars after the end of Communism due to greater appreciation for the role of the secret police, coercion, and collaboration. This model posits the subordination of society to the all-encompassing state, particularly employing its mass organizations, universalistic ideology, and monopoly of force (especially the secret police) to atomize individuals. In this system, there is room only for transmission belts, not for intermediary organizations with any real autonomy, such as churches. The growing emphasis on social history since 1991 would be augmented greatly by a detailed look at religious policy, particularly in the Baltics. The religious question is a key test of the state-society relationship in any political system, especially in a Communist one. Was the totalitarian model only aspirational and largely unrealized, or was it achieved, if only partially?

Thus Estonian and Latvian exceptionalism since 1991, their role in the collapse of the USSR, their particular confessional composition, and the possibility of testing the totalitarian model all seem to make a study of these two cases promising. Yet little work has been done on them, despite the new openness of archival materials and accessibility to decision-makers and church leaders.

Many studies have focused on the ROC, the dominant church historically in imperial Russia and the USSR and doubtless the key religious institution from the perspective of the Soviet regime. Dimitry Pospielovsky, for example, has written extensively on the Soviet campaign to suborn the ROC.[5] Most work on the international role of Soviet churches has focused on the ROC as well. William Fletcher and J. A. Hebly both looked at the interaction between the ROC and Soviet foreign policy.[6]

Research on the early Soviet period has been particularly extensive since 1991. Gregory Freeze and Edward Roslof have done in-depth work on the Renovationist challenges to the ROC in the 1920s.[7] William Husband and Daniel Peris have analyzed the regime's failed efforts during this period to erode religion and inculcate atheism.[8] Glennys Young's study of village life underscores the resistance to atheism by local religious activists.[9]

Russian and Finnish scholars are understandably well represented among researchers of the history of church and state, but they again have tended to focus on the ROC. Mikhail Shkarovski's inquiry of Soviet policy in the 1920s and 1930s has been informed by his familiarity with and careful application of archival sources.[10] Arto Luukkanen, a Finnish scholar, has insightfully investigated the reach and limits of the Bolshevik bureaucratic apparatus on religion under Stalin.[11]

A number of scholars have addressed the atheistic campaigns, particularly under Khrushchev.[12] Solid work has been done on the Khrushchev period by John Anderson, focusing primarily on the politics of the bureaucratic struggles between the Communist Party of the Soviet Union (CPSU) and the state officials in Moscow.[13] Also using new archival sources on the Khrushchev period are Tatiana Chumachenko and Shkarovski, but again their work deals primarily with the ROC.[14]

Most works addressing the Baltics do not address Lutherans or do not reflect the archival sources newly available since 1990. Stanley Vardys, among others, focused exclusively on Lithuania and its Catholic Church.[15] Both Alexander Veinbergs's contribution in the collection edited by Richard Marshall, Thomas Bird, and Andrew Blane and the historical study of Lutheranism by Edgar Duin sketch the broad outlines of the regime's policy but were unable to document the tactics and shifts in policy using party and state records.[16] Exceptions are the well-documented monographs by Juoko Talonen analyzing the Latvian Lutheran Church in the early postwar period and the work of Riho Altnurme and Atko

Remmel on the case of Estonia.[17] Recently Mikko Ketola has contributed considerably to understanding Estonian Lutheranism in the interwar period.[18] The Estonian Baptists and the small yet internationally connected Methodist Church in Estonia have also received some exploration by theological scholars.[19] Long-time theologian Vello Salo has also published on the Catholic Church in Estonia.[20]

Several research questions inform and motivate this study. First, what impact did Western religious culture—Lutheran as well as Catholic—have on Soviet religious policy? To be sure, the Bolsheviks did confront Western churches after seizing power in 1917. But czarist Russia was overwhelmingly Orthodox and these non-Orthodox churches represented a small minority, particularly in central Russia. As such, early Soviet policy toward them was relatively tolerant, motivated primarily by its desire to curtail the hegemony of the Orthodox Church in the 1920s. In that effort, enhancing privileges for Lutherans in particular and fostering schism among the Orthodox were instrumental in the state's strategy. In the Stalinist effort to destroy institutional religion, all denominations were equally repressed. But in seeking to save Mother Russia from the Nazis, Stalin could only turn to the national church, the ROC, for support. Indeed, suspect nationalities, such as the Volga Germans, largely Lutheran or Catholic, were deported to Central Asia and western Siberia.

With the incorporation of occupied territories after the war, however, the USSR for the first time confronted non-Orthodox national churches. To what extent did Soviet religious policy accommodate these differing traditions? Did such accommodation attenuate with the consolidation of Soviet power in the Baltics, or did Soviet policy itself moderate over time in response to the cultural idiosyncrasies of Western churches? Was this adaptation to culturally Western churches a stable formation, or merely tactical and transitional? To what extent were the churches reflecting nationalist consciousness, even indirectly? In explaining the outcome of perestroika, was cultural Protestantism a basis for dissent and opposition against the Communist system, or for accommodation to it?

Second, how did the institutional interests of churches affect their negotiating power vis-à-vis the regime? The Lutheran and Catholic churches—in contrast to the sects—are institutional churches characterized by hierarchical structures, supporting bureaucratic organizations and full-time clergy credentialed with higher education. Moreover, they are ritual based, with sacraments and holy days calling for universal and public observance by members. Canon law and standard procedures guide decision-making, in the case of the Lutherans including lay participation. In all these respects they contrast with cultic churches and noninstitutionalized religious movements. The churches seek to protect their institutional interests: conduct of rites and religious instruction, recruitment and training of clergy, maintenance of church infrastructure, protection of internal autonomy in decision-making, and contact with co-confessionals internationally, to name some key concerns.

The institutional basis of the churches gives them a substantial role in civil society, antithetical to the regime's desire to eliminate such intermediary organizations. By the same token, these institutional interests leave the churches vulnerable to co-optation as they seek to defend these interests, even as they are penetrated by security forces. In the GDR case, both phenomena were evident, but the churches' social presence ultimately provided a space for dissent and proved to be a permissive factor in the 1989 revolution. To what extent did the regime curtail the institutional practices of the churches, and were the churches able to reassert their interests over time? To what extent did the institutional role of the Latvian and Estonian churches facilitate social space for dissent, as in the case of the GDR, as opposed to leaving the churches dependent on the regime?

Third, what impact did the churches as transnational actors have on Soviet choices and preferences? Were these international ties a bonus or ballast? As worldwide denominations, both the Lutheran and Catholic churches had enjoyed ties to co-confessional organizations and ecumenical organizations before the Soviet takeover. In particular, for Lutherans, the ties to German Lutherans were deep and longstanding, albeit freighted with national and historical ambivalence. The USSR was highly isolationist in its foreign policy, suspicious of economic imperialism and manipulation of unofficial contacts by the West. The Baltic churches were initially left isolated from their international partners and later these relations were limited in terms of substance.

Yet Soviet foreign policy opened up, beginning under Khrushchev's thaw. Particularly in its détente phase, Soviet policy under Brezhnev entailed increased ties with West Germany. How did the churches' international ties change over time, as a function of these changes in Soviet foreign policy and the strategies of Western church organizations? To what extent did the international ties strengthen the negotiating position of the churches domestically and sow fissures between church leaders and the members on the grassroots?

Fourth, to what extent was policy consistent both among bureaucratic organs in Moscow and between the Moscow authorities and the subnational governmental levels? As large, complex organizations, modern political systems are characterized by bureaucratic politics in policy formulation and implementation. In a federal system one would expect such divergences between national and subnational governments, perhaps even viewing them as indicators of decentralization or subsidiarity that is stabilizing for the political system. Communist systems, however, enthroned the leading role of the Communist party in all policy making and mandated that the principle of democratic centralism guide all decisions, including religious policy. Thus, the party organs—the Politburo, Central

Committee (CC), and Secretariat—were to set policy and hold governmental authorities at all levels accountable for its implementation.

Yet many entities were involved in making religious policy. In addition to the Central Committee apparat and ideology secretary, state organs were created in 1944 to interact with the registered churches: the Council for the Affairs of the Russian Orthodox Church (CROC) and the Council for the Affairs of Religious Cults (CARC) to deal with non-Orthodox churches, later merged into the Council for Religious Affairs (CRA).[21] The security organs (KGB) and the Ministry of Foreign Affairs (MFA) also weighed in at certain points. At the republic or oblast level, Communist party and state authorities were coordinating with commissioners named by the Councils. Meanwhile, at the local level, state and party officials were implementing policy at the grassroots, supposedly in sync with central directives.

Given this plethora of official actors, to what extent did policy preferences vary, both between the party and state officials at the center, as well as between central and republic as well as local officials? To what extent was there uniform implementation of policy, again among central, republic, and local levels? How much leeway did republic and local officials have in implementing policy? To what extent did any differences in preference and implementation change over time? To the extent divergences are found, how are they to be explained—by bureaucratic interests and frictions, acculturation and careerism, or struggles for political power?

This study is based on extensive investigation of official central and republic-level archives of the former USSR. Primary document collections used in Moscow include the State Archive of the Russian Federation (GARF), with its records of the CARC and CRA, as well as the Russian State Archive of Socio-Political History (RGASPI, formerly the Central Party Archive) and the Russian State Archive of Contemporary History (RGANI, formerly the Current Archive of the CPSU Central Committee). Files of republic-level officials were consulted at the Estonian State Archive (ERA) and the Latvian State Archive (LVA), as well as the Lithuanian State Archive (LCVA). In addition, select files of the former Central Committee of the Communist Party of Estonia (ERAF) were utilized. The author did not analyze church documents. Nor was access to KGB records available, although some correspondence between the KGB and state or party bodies was found in state archives. In some cases the author was able to supplement the archival analysis with interviews with the principals.

Given the research base available to the author and the scope of the present study, it will concentrate mostly on Estonia and Latvia. The analysis leaves out the Lithuanian case due to its extraordinary distinctiveness. Predominantly Catholic, Lithuania was slow to sovietize its religious policy in the 1940s and continued to evidence considerable religious-based political dissent throughout the Soviet period. Illegal activity was incomparably greater than in the other republics.[22] The sustained samizdat activity of the Catholic *Chronicle of Current Events* and the Sąjūdis mass movement played a major role in the end of the USSR. The baseline for perestroika in Lithuania was simply qualitatively of a different order of magnitude. By 1988 Cardinal Sladkevicius was holding summits with the Lithuanian Communist leadership and actively consulting with Sąjūdis; illegal priests were being reregistered; property was being returned to the Church; and Catholic dissenters were openly criticizing co-opted Catholic churchmen.[23] Lithuania remained sui generis, and a full treatment of all three Baltic cases is thus beyond the scope of this book. I will limit myself to Latvia and Estonia, focusing primarily on the Lutheran national churches.

Notes

1. World Factbook, www.cia.gov (accessed January 2018).
2. Remmel and Uibu, "Outside Conventional Forms," 5–20. Gallup and Eurobarometer polls indicate only 16 percent of Estonians believe in God, the lowest percentage in Europe. See also Remmel, "Ambiguous Atheism," 244–46.
3. Martin, *Affirmative Action Empire*.
4. For historical background, see Viise, "Estonian Evangelical-Lutheran Church," 9–83 and Aunver, "Estlands Christliche Kirche der Gegenwart," 75–82.
5. Pospielovsky, *Russian Church*.
6. Fletcher, *Religion and Soviet Foreign Policy*; Hebly, "The State, the Church."
7. Freeze, "Counter-Reformation," 305–39; Roslof, *Red Priests*.
8. Husband, *Godless Communists*; Peris, *Storming the Heavens*.
9. Young, *Power and the Sacred*.
10. Shkarovski, "Russian Orthodox Church versus the State," 365–84.
11. Luukkanen, *Religious Policy*.
12. Pospielovsky, *History of Marxist-Leninist Atheism*.
13. Anderson, *Religion, State, and Politics*.
14. Chumachenko, *Church and State*; Shkarovski, "Russian Orthodox Church in 1958–1964," 71–95.
15. Vardys, *Catholic Church*.
16. Veinbergs, "Lutheranism and other Denominations"; Duin, *Lutheranism under the Tsars*.
17. Talonen, *Church under the Pressure*; Altnurme, "Die Estnishe Evangelisch-Lutherische Kirche," 233–46; Remmel, "(Anti)-Religious Aspects," 359–92.
18. Ketola, *Nationality Question* and "Some Aspects,"239f.
19. Pilli, "Union of Evangelical Christians," 31–50; Ritsbek, "Methodism in Estonia."
20. Salo, "Catholic Church in Estonia," 281–92.
21. Luchterhandt, "Council on Religious Affairs." Loeber, "Administration of Culture," 135. Writing in 1968, Dietrich Loeber mistakenly concludes that religious policy was outside the competence of the LSSR Council of Ministers; this study will find that republic-level state authorities also influenced policy.

22. ERA.R-1989.1.134, l. 24–27. CRA Chair Kuroedov, in "On Contemporary Condition of Religion and Tasks to Strengthen the Control of Observance of Law on Religious Cults," described the Lithuanian Catholic clergy as disloyal, agents of the Vatican, and violators of Soviet law on parish governance, among other allegations. In 1987, the Lithuanian Commissioner found fifty-two legal violations, compared with the Latvian Commissioner, who found only two. LVA.1419.3.266, l. 1–6. The 1987 informational report of the Lithuanian commissioner is replete with references to the "complicated religious situation in the republic." See LCVA.181.3.128, l. 1–26. It is not surprising that a Western study of protest demonstrations in the Baltics in the 1960s and 1970s found only 5.3 percent were Estonian and Latvian national protests; Baltic Jews at 35.1 percent and Lithuanian national and Catholic protests at 53.2 percent predominated. See Kowalewski, "Dissent in the Baltic Republics," 309–19.

23. LCVA.181.3.135, l. 2–24.

1 The Early Stalinization Process: 1944–1949

THE PROCESS OF bringing the churches under Soviet control had hardly begun, much less been completed, in the short period of the first Soviet occupation in 1940–41.[1] To be sure, the harsh Soviet legislation of 1929—nationalization of church property, denial of juridical status to churches, prohibition of religious instruction of youth, elimination of religious holidays, limitation to cultic functions, and onerous taxation on clergy and church property—was introduced, though not fully implemented. Monasteries and church schools were targeted for closure. The theological faculties in Riga and Tartu were eliminated, substantial deportations and executions of clergy and bishops took place, and many of the German pastors still active in the Baltics fled to Germany. Clergymen lost their homes in the nationalization process and cells of the League of Militant Godless launched a propaganda campaign against religion. The People's Commissariat for Internal Affairs (NKVD) was tasked with "reorganization or liquidation" of the churches in February 1941.[2] Deportation of remaining clergy was being planned in June 1941. But the organizational capacity of the Communists was inadequate and their priorities were eliminating political opposition and introducing collectivization and nationalization into the economy. After cutting short the Soviets' plan by its invasion of the USSR in June 1941, Germany did not restore independence to the Baltic states, but instead subjected them to direct rule under the German Reichskommissariat Ost. Most of the Soviet strictures on religion and the churches were rescinded, although the theological faculties were not reinstated. Many church leaders and clergy—some under German orders—were evacuated ahead of the advancing Red Army and, along with large numbers of other civilians, founded Lutheran exile churches in the West. Latvians from traditionally Catholic Latgāle fled to Lutheran areas, depopulating Latgāle and leaving other areas more mixed confessionally.[3]

Tentative Early Steps

With the return of Soviet rule in 1944 the Baltics fell victim to more sustained efforts to control the churches. Initially, however, the devastation and collapse of the infrastructure in the wake of war limited the state's capabilities, as did the paucity of cadres. Even while hostilities with the Germans continued in some areas, the Soviets named CARC (Council for the Affairs of Religious Cults) commissioners in each republic, in August 1944 in Latvia, in September 1944 in Lithuania, and later in 1944 in Estonia. But they often lacked clear directives from Moscow for implementing policies and were given more leeway in their work than their counterparts in the Russian Soviet Federative Socialist Republic (RSFSR).[4] For a considerable period after the German retreat, the regime faced armed opposition from rural guerrillas known as "forest brothers."[5] In the early years, commissioners were often delegated to conduct "party work" in the provinces, especially in the struggle against these guerrillas, and were thus unavailable to oversee religious policy. Commissioners faced logistical difficulties and were overstretched, resulting in delayed submission of reports and supporting materials to Moscow. Voldemars Šeškens, the Latvian commissioner, complained in mid-1945 that he had no translator or typist and, for these services, was forced to rely on "directive organs," which sought speedy action based on their own motives.[6] The Soviet desire to avoid antagonizing the Western Allies also argued for a moderate approach to economic and political transformation throughout the newly conquered areas in this period.

Behind this tentativeness lay divisions among CPSU ideological officials regarding the correct approach to religion in 1944–45. A September 1944 analysis by the Red Army political command concluded that the Baltic population "was not yet accustomed to our Soviet ways." In straightforward terms, the military conveyed the fears of the population—"would churches be permitted, where would they find pastors, will there be russification in the Baltics, is it not true that in Russia they oppress and even shoot believers"—but made no specific recommendations.[7] On the other hand, Communist Party Agitprop officials in Moscow were alarmed by increasing religiosity during the war and pressed chief ideologue Andrei Zhdanov to crack down and end disputes over the religious question.[8]

For their part, the churches were also left dramatically weakened at the war's end. One-half of the Lutheran pastors, many German, had fled to the West. Eight of the eleven district deans (middle-level administrators, in German *Probst*) in Latvia were exiled, shot, or had died. Flight among Catholic clergy was significantly less than among Lutherans: Archbishop Antonijs Springovičs ordered them to stay, but nonetheless three bishops and 19 percent of the clergy fled.[9] Large numbers of church buildings had been laid to waste as a result of the war, many occupied by Red Army units or itinerant groups of people. The church leadership was also left in limbo.[10] In Estonia, the emigration of Bishop Johan Kõpp to Sweden in 1944 left the church leadership in the hands of Anton Eilert, who went into hiding after KGB intimidation. Eventually, on the basis of a provisional church council, August Pähn was chosen as bishop in January 1945, although his apostolic succession could not be conveyed by foreign bishops.¹¹ A similar situation existed in the Latvian Lutheran Church, where Bishop Teodors Grīnbergs named Dean Kārlis Irbe as acting bishop. The financial base of the churches had naturally been greatly weakened by the destruction and dislocations of war; foreign ties that had flourished in the interwar period were now abruptly ruptured.

In the context of this mutual weakness and uncertainty regarding the state's strategy regarding the churches, the early postwar period was characterized by a relatively conciliatory policy, particularly on the part of the central authorities in Moscow.¹² On the key contentious issue in the Stalin period, the registration and opening of parishes, the regime sought to follow Soviet practice established in 1918, but was quite liberal in implementing it initially and gave considerable leeway to republic officials. In 1945, CARC ordered that automatic registration be granted to all Baltic parishes with religious headquarters in Moscow, namely the ROC, Baptists, Jews, and Adventists; the regime hoped in particular that these confessions would thereby be more supportive of their new status subordinate to their respective central headquarters in Moscow. Those functioning parishes lacking such centers, such as Lutherans and Catholics, would require CARC approval but would be given careful consideration for registration.¹³ In this initial registration process, to be completed in six months, CARC was more interested in compiling an inventory of property and clergy, deferring its later insistence on signed agreements nationalizing church property. CARC called for forthcomingness in allocating permanent buildings to parishes. When the Estonian commissioner invoked a lack of canonical qualifications in denying registration to certain clergymen, he was reprimanded by the CARC in Moscow.¹⁴ Similarly, the Estonian government forbade the closing of churches by local authorities except in exceptional cases and with the approval of CARC and the commissioner. In some cases churches were able to continue using church buildings officially listed as nonworking churches, due to the immobilization of the local authorities on this question.¹⁵ In principle, construction of new churches and materials for repair of damaged churches were permitted. In one Latvian case, a future hard-line Communist leader, Otto Lātsis, offered assistance to a future church dissenter, Leons Taivans, for the restoration of his heavily damaged church!¹⁶ The churches were granted limited rights as juridical entities, entitling them to acquire means of transportation, produce items for religious activities, and rent or purchase buildings in addition to their prayer houses.¹⁷ Many local authorities wished to quickly close the parishes that now lacked clergy, but central authorities restrained them, mandating a one-year waiting period before declaring them to be nonworking churches.¹⁸

On religious practice as well the state showed greater tolerance than it would later. State officials were cautious about the churches' rites of confirmation and first communion, fearing a rise as had occurred in 1940–41. In January 1946, the Estonian commissioner argued that "on the question of confirmation, while adhering as much as possible to the general limits on religious instruction along Soviet lines, I consider it correct to deal with the possibility of confirmation flexibly, in order to avoid the outward appearance of pressure. Outwardly it is necessary to leave the impression with the believer that church and faith is his private matter and his participation in it is free. By itself this feeling will regulate his religious activity."[19] In May 1945 the Latvian Lutherans proposed confirmation at age 15, based on 52 hours of instruction, with no indication of state disapproval.[20] Even Irbe's successor, Gustav Turs, known for his pro-Soviet stance, requested in March 1946 that "the beloved tradition of the people" be continued.[21]

Regarding church institutional interests, the pattern of moderation was also evident. Authorities were relatively generous in approving publication of religious literature. Christmas was even declared an official holiday in Estonia in 1946.[22] In Soviet legal practice, cemeteries were state property, but, responding to the commissioner's concern, CARC opted to study Latvian conditions and delayed forcing the churches to transfer their cemeteries to the government.[23] On theological education, which was to become a constant source of church-state friction in the years to come, the commissioners showed some tentative support, even as they feared it might result in a revival of religion.[24] In 1945, the main focus seemed to be on the Catholic seminary at Aglona and a Catholic request to also open a seminary in Riga. By late 1945, the Latvian commissioner came to support such a seminary; the Kremlin and CARC concurred on the grounds that theology was not taught at the universities.

For their part, the churches also exercised restraint initially. In the context of armed opposition in 1945, the Lutheran churches appealed to members to "maintain order in the kingdom of God, as well as the kingdom on earth, in accordance with the Holy Scriptures."[25] It urged members to cease protest against "the current socio-economic formation" and instead work for restoration of the economy and culture by means of good honest work. The Estonian church leadership urged members to vote in elections and to see the will of God in all things. Meeting with the Estonian commissioner in early 1946, Bishop Pähn excused the failure of the church to shower Stalin with gifts and praise, like the Russian Orthodox Church, since "it would not be credible that they suddenly become Soviet patriots."[26] Nor did the Estonian Lutheran Church issue a declaration on the occasion of the October Revolution in 1946, although serious consideration was given to the idea. In contrast with the Lithuanian Catholic Church, the Catholic Church in Latvia was relatively supportive, discouraging desertion and armed resistance and supporting electoral participation. But, in what would become a pattern, Archbishop Antonijs Springovičs signaled subtle distance from the regime by referring to desertion rather than the Soviet term "banditism," and by authorizing his subordinate, Stanislavs Vaikuls, to issue such pronouncements; many priests in fact sympathized with the armed resistance.[27]

The Regime's Evaluation of the Churches

The state's internal evaluation of the religious situation belied this relatively conciliatory policy. Its views of the Baltic churches, as toward all religion and churches, were certainly filtered through the lens of Marxist materialism and Leninist antireligious policy: religion was a reactionary belief system, destined along with the churches to die out with the construction of socialism.[28] But the early view of the churches' role was also informed by the regime's interpretation of the interwar period and Nazi occupation. In 1942–1943 Agitprop proposals for propaganda actions to undermine support for the German occupation, there is no mention of German repression of religion (except in the case of the Orthodox churches and to a limited extent Lithuanian Catholics) or of potential religious leaders who might be used in such appeals, reflecting the milder religious policy of the Germans.[29] As a result, the Lutherans in Estonia and Latvia were largely viewed by both Moscow and republic officials as linked to interwar authoritarian movements and compromised by the German occupation. In Estonia, the state saw the Lutheran churches as frustrated by the secular-liberal orientation of the interwar government and more comfortable with the authoritarian regime of Konstantin Päts, who became president after a coup in 1938.[30] In this view, the Päts regime pursued a restorationist policy, promoting the Lutheran Church as a state church.[31] Referring to the Free Estonian movement that resisted German occupation and sought to restore an independent Estonia, Estonian commissioner Johannes Kivi attacked the Lutheran Church, charging that "the major portion of the pastors attached themselves to the Vabist movement and turned their churches into tribunes for the propaganda of Vabism." In fact the Baltic Lutherans had long been dominated by Germans and in the interwar period sought to establish a separate profile.[32] But, in a view shared by some modern scholars, to Kivi "an Estonian church, as such, never existed in the full sense of the word. It was merely a German church, with German views and thoughts, just in the Estonian language."[33]

Given this historical analysis it is not surprising that the state viewed the Lutheran churches as essentially a reactionary force. Kivi concluded that "the Lutheran church never sought cooperation with social and politically progressive movements, but tied itself with all its capabilities to the reactionary forces and elements."[34] Only six Estonian pastors had fought in the Red Army, an important yardstick of political loyalty to the regime; few had engaged in "antifascist activity"; 50 percent of Estonian clergy and 40 percent of Latvian clergy had fled with the Germans and no more than five spoke out against the armed guerrillas.[35] Estonian officials were nuanced enough to discern that historically the Lutheran Church had hardly been monolithic, and that it included confessional, conservative, and liberal wings.[36] However, such differences were now overshadowed, it was argued, by the Church's generalized antipathy toward communism.

The regime's view of the Latvian Lutheran legacy varied little from its view of the Estonian churches. Despite ordering compliance with the Soviet laws on registration of parishes, acting Bishop Irbe was tarred with the German legacy, his interwar parliamentary activity, and association with the authoritarian leader, President Kārlis Ulmanis.[37] The Latvian Lutheran clergy was seen as overwhelmingly oppositional, and the archival records suggest that Irbe was hardly given a chance to demonstrate otherwise: he was viewed as strongly anticommunist already in 1944–1945. Irbe refused to write pro-Soviet statements for journalists or hold special services on Soviet holidays. Irbe's ambiguity regarding the forest brother guerillas—his 1945 Advent appeal regretted that "many brothers of our people still are not in a position to return to their means of existence and productive work"—reinforced the regime's antipathy to him.[38]

The Latvian Lutheran leadership suffered from comparison with the large Latvian Catholic Church, which the state viewed more positively, largely due to its perception of Archbishop Antonijs Springovičs and the negative stance of his Lithuanian co-confessionals. The Latvian commissioner emphasized his progressive views: his refusal to heed the German order of evacuation, his missives to clergy proclaiming that "Soviet power does not think of repressing religion and the church" and calling for an end to armed resistance to Soviet rule, his criticism of Pope Pius for pro-fascist leanings, and his support of land reform in Latvia. Though he had experienced Soviet repression in 1940–1941, he was seen as a realist. According to the Latvian commissioner, "externally the Catholic clergy formally declare their desire to cooperate with Soviet power. The biggest proponent of this view is Springovičs himself."[39] Characterizing him as "trustworthy and progressive" in October 1945, the Latvian commissioner supported Springovičs' demand for a seminary in Riga and pressed for Moscow's approval.[40] In an important analysis of the churches sent to Molotov in December 1945, CARC concurred: it conceded the "anti-Soviet orientation" of the Catholic clergy in the "complexity of Soviet power returning to the Baltics," but argued that "this is not a uniform external expression," viewing Springovičs more positively than the Lithuanian and Uniate Catholic leaders.[41] To strengthen relations with him, CARC requested gifts be given to Springovičs, while pointedly ignoring the Lutheran bishops.[42] In an effort to profile him as head of the Soviet Catholic Church, CARC offered him a comfortable trip to Moscow in November 1945, but he declined, citing poor health.[43] This relatively favorable view of Springovičs did give him some room to maneuver in the early Stalin period, but the growing Soviet tension with the Vatican and Lutheran accommodation to the regime after 1948 would erode this advantage in the 1950s.

Given the dominance of the Lutheran Church in Estonia, Estonian authorities paid little attention to the other Protestant sects. Though relatively prevalent on the islands of Saarema and Hiiuma as a result of early Swedish missions, there were few Baptists in Estonia. The authorities noted positively the relatively high number of Baptist pastors (seven) who had served in the Red Army.[44] Their apolitical orientation and small numbers made them a low priority for the state in the early postwar period.

On the other hand, Estonian Methodists, also small in number, were viewed as less reactionary than the Lutherans. Official analysis emphasized that they had not engaged in anti-Soviet propaganda in the interwar period; their clergy had not left with the Germans in 1944. The Methodists' ties to American and British Methodists left them vulnerable to criticism during the German occupation. This interpretation and a desire to weaken the dominant Lutheran Church led Estonian authorities to seek to maintain a separate Methodist Church. In contrast, most Latvian Methodists had left with the Germans, and the Latvian authorities moved to merge them with the Lutherans in October 1948.[45]

The Herrnhuters, on the other hand, were viewed quite negatively, to the extent the authorities could make sense of them. Missionizing by the Moravian Brethren brought this pietistic movement to the Baltics in 1729. Although periodically banned by the Russian tsars and rejected as heretics by the Baltic German-dominated Lutherans in the eighteenth century, they played a significant role in the nineteenth-century national awakening movement as a result of their education of and appeal to the peasantry. The Russification of the late imperial period led them to become loosely affiliated with the Lutheran Church. In the more liberal context of the interwar period, the Herrnhuters became increasingly divided into a moderate faction and a more sectarian one.[46] The Soviet Estonian authorities viewed the radical faction, under Eugene Tanner, as a "reactionary clique" under the influence of the "anticommunist" European Christian Movement in London. Like the Lutherans, the Herrnhuters were seen as inordinately subject to the influence of German co-confessionals, delegitimizing them in national terms.[47]

In a comparison of the regime's early stance toward the various churches, the favor shown to the non-national churches over the Lutheran and Catholic churches is striking. In an effort to overcome opposition to the forced merger with the Baptist religious center in Moscow, the regime was quite forthcoming toward the Baptists in the registration process. Likewise, CARC proposed creating religious centers for Old Believers and for Jews in Moscow, of course with the goal of centralizing control of these religions, but granting them an elevated status politically that it was unwilling to cede the Lutherans or Catholics.[48]

The Revival of Church Adherence

The state's priority of crushing political opposition, restoring order, and reintroducing Soviet political institutions meant that a campaign against religion and the churches was hardly expedient in this early period, despite the regime's essentially negative evaluation of the churches, particularly the Catholic and Lutheran churches. In the absence of such a campaign, the churches regained adherents, despite their continuing weakness in institutional terms. It is difficult to describe this as a return to normalcy, since wartime social disruption had artificially caused dramatic declines in participation in religious rites, resulting in high levels of pent-up demand for rites such as confirmation and marriage.

This resurgence in church adherence did not occur immediately, however. Initially the mass population took a wait-and-see attitude, fearing that religion and churches might be eliminated by the Soviets. However, by 1946, participation had increased dramatically. In 1946 the number of confirmands in Estonia increased to 4,800, a 50 percent increase over 1945 levels.[49] Already, in December 1945, Moscow charged that confirmation "is occurring in an organized form and conducted on a widespread basis," with many children receiving religious instruction after school. CARC requested evidence of proscriptive actions taken by its commissioners.[50] Other measures of church adherence likewise increased.

In their early reports to Moscow, commissioners tried to downplay the significance of this resurgence, for obvious reasons. In Estonia, Kivi argued that "if in religious circles, after liberation from the occupiers there was a fear for the future existence of churches and prayer houses, now this fear has disappeared and people are quiet in relation to the question and the situation in all likelihood approximates that which analogously existed until 1940: in other words, they relate to the church as a natural phenomenon, which neither attracts them nor repels them."[51] In the view of the commissioners, the resurgence reflected a return to the historically cool relationship between the Balts and the Lutheran Church.

Yet even officials at the republic level were forced to admit that the interest in religious rites was widespread, noting that even the working class and local government officials actively took part in church rites.[52] One folk custom that retained a strong attraction was the early-summer "cemetery days" tradition, during which people cared for grave sites, held a religious service, and relaxed. The age distribution of confirmands testified to the phenomenon of pent-up demand: in 1945–1947 in Estonia over 60 percent were older than eighteen, suggesting delayed confirmations.[53]

The increased participation in rites also translated into increased financial support for the churches. In Estonia, the number of contributors to the Lutheran Church increased from 117,775 in 1946 to 124,027 in 1947; the total income of the Lutheran Church rose 12% in this single year. Republic officials again sought to put this increase in context, denying that "100% of this growth stemmed from growth in their religiosity."[54] But, in its fixation on the so-called material base of the churches, the Marxist state became alarmed that growth in church adherence was strengthening the churches financially as well. It was a short step to allegations that parishioners were being forced to contribute in order to obtain rites.

Early Church Claims on the Regime

The churches naturally tried to translate this increased church adherence into a stronger institutional position, in order to recover from the losses of war and restore their lost interwar privileges. The church claims were heightened by the widespread opinion that Stalin's 1943–1944 opening to the churches and the creation of CARC and CROC (the Council for the Affairs of the Russian Orthodox Church) had given the churches new official status in the USSR. In numerous cases the churches requested repairs of buildings damaged during the war. The state often countered that the damage was inflicted by the Germans and rejected compensation.[55] The churches also requested that parish houses be returned to them, despite the Soviet practice of limiting church property to the worship building and a shed. The Lutheran churches in particular realized the need to begin training pastors again, given the severe shortage resulting from the wartime emigration. Understanding there was little likelihood of restoring their traditional theological faculties in Tartu and Riga, the churches limited their requests to the approval of independent theological institutes in each republic. Already, in November 1944, the Latvian church leadership submitted this request, also seeking the return of ten theology professors deported in 1941 and the library of the interwar theological faculty.[56] The Latvian Catholics also posed claims on the regime. In October 1944, Catholic leaders asked for theological education to resume at its monastery in Aglona; by November 1944, Springovičs asked to form a theological academy in Riga. Springovičs repeated the request at every opportunity, citing the existence of two seminaries in Lithuania and the 1922 Concordat that had guaranteed seminaries and even a Catholic faculty at the university in Riga after 1938. The churches also sought to secure church lands (especially monastic lands) and the right to teach religious morals in schools. Springovičs also signaled anxiety regarding the nationalization of church property and sought exemption from military service for clergy members.[57]

The state response to these proposals for theological education was characterized by differentiation. The Latvian commissioner, Voldemars Šeškens, supported the Catholic request for a seminary, arguing that "the behavior of Springovičs shows that he can be trusted with a seminary" and pressed for a central decision on the question. In December 1945, the state responded positively to the request, seeking to reward Springovičs but also to dampen popular resentments after the arrest of a number of priests.[58] Regarding the Lutheran requests, however, the regime temporized, requesting a formal curriculum, a study plan, and a list of students for the proposed theological seminary. The Latvian Church responded in 1946 with more detail and concessions, altering the justification and curriculum to include reference to Soviet socialism and reducing the number of students, but to no avail.[59] Estonian officials also opposed a seminary, and

CARC refused to take up the issue. Despite this uncertainty and temporizing, the churches continued to plan for eventual seminaries in Riga and Tallinn. Similarly, officials rebutted property claims, making reference to earlier decrees and laws denying the churches juridical standing. Ultimately, the state delayed concessions to the Lutherans until a more conformist church leadership was in place and political control more secure.

The Shift toward a Harsher Line by the State

Beginning in 1946, the regime began to up the ante in its policy toward the churches, but its conception was still in flux. Šeškens and CARC continued to advocate playing the "Springovičs card," seeing him as more amenable to working with the regime. Indeed, Vaikuls, dean of Līvanī and close advisor of Springovičs, testified in state trials of Nazi collaborators, and Springovičs gave interviews to local media about this.[60] And Springovičs ordered clergy to encourage parishioners to vote in the 1946 Supreme Soviet elections in Latvia, a key test of political loyalty. The state permitted him to consecrate two new bishops, Peteris Strods and Kazimirs Dulbinskis, in 1947. The Latvian commissioner reassured Springovičs, saying that he "should sleep easily" despite the arrests and purge of Lutheran leadership discussed below.[61]

In early 1946, the state's antipathy toward the Latvian Lutheran leadership, noted above, led to a leadership purge that was entirely orchestrated by the regime. In February 1945, Šeškens had already proposed a plan to depose Acting Bishop Irbe, but continued fighting in the province of Courland and difficulty finding a replacement made such a plan unrealistic. He broached even more draconian ideas, such as merging the Lutherans with the ROC or renaming them as the Evangelical Christian Church, supposedly "in order to break the influence of the Germans."[62] By January 1946, however, CARC came to support a plan to isolate Irbe using harsh tax pressure on the clergy and NKVD measures to prevent Irbe's communications and travel without commissioner approval.[63] A Christian Democrat in interwar Latvia, Irbe refused to endorse the 1946 elections—"my party will not appear here, you don't give us the possibility to have it"—and attempted contact with exiled Bishop Grīnbergs, sealing his fate. The arrests of Irbe in late February 1946 and General Secretary Pauls Rozenbergs shortly thereafter created a vacuum in the church leadership which the state sought to fill by recruiting more conformist leaders (Albertis Virbulus, Krišjānis Šlosbergs, and Gustavs Turs). In a three-day marathon of meetings in his office, Commissioner Šeškens rejected the initial choice of Virbulus as acting archbishop and persuaded Turs to take the position, with Virbulus as his deputy and Šlosbergs as general secretary.[64]

Born in 1890, Turs was an unmarried provincial pastor who had attended gymnasium in St. Petersburg, but was apparently a poor student and did not finish his theology studies at Tartu in 1914. Politically a bourgeois Latvian nationalist, active in the Christian Party, Turs had been elected to the church leadership during the interwar period, which provided the fig leaf for his assumption of the position of bishop. Described by Šeškens in positive terms as "imposing, with gray hair, musical," there was none of the criticism of his personal habits that would later be alleged when he was ousted in 1968.[65] He maintained a close friendship with Virbulus, his classmate from Tartu, and with Šlosbergs, a colonel and official in the Foreign Ministry of interwar Latvia.

The commissioner reveled in his victory and hailed the outcome as "a turning point in the future activity of the church," claiming that he secured "full understanding on all principle questions." In particular, he obtained agreement from the new church leaders that "not one question could be decided without my preliminary sanction" and insisted that the "anti-Soviet line in the church cultivated by Irbe be liquidated." The state set about to enhance Turs's credibility, profiling his charitable appeals in the media, tolerating pre-confirmation instruction for youth, and approving song sheets and calendars for the churches. Officials cynically calculated that most Lutheran clergy would follow Turs for careerist reasons, despite the obvious coercion involved in his elevation from pastor to archbishop. Turs signaled the new line with his April 1946 Appeal to the Latvian People, praising the Red Army for freeing Latvia from "German terror and rapists."[66] With support from Šeškens, Turs rapidly consolidated his control of the church administration with new appointments.[67] In myriad ways he assumed positions supportive of the regime: holding special Soviet jubilee services, urging return of exiles to Latvia, articulating a deference to the state based on Romans 13, and voting in elections.[68]

Springovičs had good reason to ignore the advice to sleep easily in 1946, since a harsher policy against the Latvian Catholic Church and the commissioner's "Springovičs card" was brewing in Moscow. Already in June 1946 CARC officials expressed internal criticism of Šeškens's reporting and policy. Their handwritten commentary on his reports derisively rejected his use of formulations such as "the process of sovietization is finished," "cooperation in civil matters of church and clergy with the government power," and "goodwill with Springovičs."[69] By January 1947, CARC was openly attacking Šeškens's actions toward the Catholic Church as focusing too much on quid pro quos struck with the church leaders and ignoring the anti-Soviet, Jesuit-influenced clergy. CARC indicated that "the task of finally liquidating reactionary clergy is incomplete, a task that has been completed in most other churches of the USSR at one stage or another." It concluded, "the true face of Springovičs remains to be seen. The face of Springovičs will be completely evident when the Catholic Church must adapt totally to the norms of Soviet law."[70]

Central party officials were also shifting to a harsh line in general religious policy by early 1947, as reflected in criticism of CARC's moderate stance and concomitant bureaucratic politics. In a contentious January 1947 meeting with J. Sadovski, the Deputy Chair of CARC, Klement Voroshilov, Deputy Chair of the

Council of Ministers (CM) of the USSR, criticized CARC's "indirect approach," expressed extremely negative views of Baptists, and advocated "quickly arresting Catholic clergy and ... cleaning them out of our country."[71] Sadovski countered that "attempts to influence the clergy using only force will not have the necessary results and may produce even more difficulties." Sadovski added his expectation of "continued decline in religiosity in the near future, along with a faster tempo proportional to the success of socialist construction." Voroshilov conceded that the role of CARC was not to eliminate religion, but "guide religious movement in order to decrease its hostility." Voroshilov's harsher view doubtless reflected the lobbying and criticism by the Agitprop Department of the Central Committee, which argued that religion was growing and that CARC "had transformed itself from an organ to observe and control the church to one of help and connivance with religious adherents."[72] Agitprop attacked CARC's "distorted characterization of religious propaganda" and the do-nothingness of its chair, Ivan Polyanski. Compounding this was CARC's apparent weakness of ties with the party leadership, especially with Zhdanov, which might have defended CARC and its moderate position toward the churches.

The Issue of Confirmation

Most important in the increasing tension was the issue of confirmation, a key sacrament for the national churches in the Baltics. As noted above, Moscow was concerned by the issue already in 1945, but had temporized, awaiting general political stabilization in the Baltic republics. Evoking the counterproductive experience of 1940–1941 policy, the Estonian commissioner urged "a flexible approach to confirmation, to avoid the impression of external pressure," seeing Estonians as having little contact with religion after confirmation.[73] CARC also feared antagonizing in particular the Catholic Church and initially mandated a liberal treatment of religious instruction for both Protestants and Catholics. Even as late as July 1947, CARC took a soft line on confirmation.[74] But the steep rise in number of confirmands in 1946–1947 noted above caused the state to reframe the issue from one of a traditional cool relationship between Balts and their religion to one of increased financial strength of the churches. CARC began to insist on differentiating between the Catholic and Lutheran churches on this issue, taking a harsher line toward the more malleable Lutherans.

Three aspects of confirmation served to divide the Lutherans and the state.[75] First, they disputed the proper age for confirmation. Historically, Lutherans had been confirmed at the age of 16. But preparation that normally preceded confirmation violated the Stalin legislation of 1929 proscribing organized religious instruction of those under age 18. The state thus insisted on confirmation no earlier than age 18. Second, they diverged on the appropriate time of year for confirmation ceremonies. Historically the Lutheran confirmations had been held at certain days on the church calendar, such as Good Friday and Ascension Day. But in the postwar disarray and fear of a Communist crackdown, parishes were holding confirmation on many different occasions throughout the year. Finally, they differed over the scope of pre-confirmation instruction. The Church favored a more extended instruction period, whereas the state wanted a very limited one, if any.

The soft line on confirmation noted earlier gave way to a tightening up in 1947. Estonian authorities sought to limit instruction to three weeks, with confirmation ceremonies in June.[76] Although the church leadership agreed to the proposed limitations, the move backfired on the regime, as confirmations increased by 30 percent over 1946 levels. To be sure, the dramatic increase stemmed in part from immigration of Balts and Finns from other republics, as well as the pent-up demand from veterans and deportees returning after the war.[77] But clearly many new confirmands were motivated by fear that the Soviet regime might forbid confirmation completely.

The bigger issue, the age of confirmation, remained a source of contention. In deliberations with the state, the Estonian Lutheran Church proposed confirmation at age 15, justifying this on the basis of church tradition and by the fact that youth often began full-time work after this age. Commissioner Kivi countered with the proposal of age 18, arguing that Soviet law required this and that other sects, like the Baptists, conducted analogous rites at age 18.[78] As indicated earlier, in Latvia the state took a more flexible line initially, permitting confirmation instruction in 1946 in an effort to "pacify them on this issue," in the context of its purge of church leadership and co-optation of Turs as acting bishop. In 1947, however, it tightened the confirmation process by limiting it to 18 year olds, although no governmental decree was employed in the process.[79]

The dissensus remained unresolved until 1948, when the state moved to forbid confirmation of those under 18 and limit the dates of confirmation to two weeks in June. CARC issued a formal decree limiting confirmation in April 1949, followed by analogous republic-level decrees.[80] Clergy were required to inform the church headquarters of the names of the confirmands, the number of hours of religious instruction, and the date of the ceremony; the churches then informed the state. All clergy were also required to affirm that none of their confirmands was younger than 18. As a result, the number of confirmands under 18 dropped significantly.[81] These strictures, along with the heightened campaign of antireligious propaganda and outright discrimination against confirmands, led to a decline in confirmands that was to continue unabated until Stalin's death.[82]

But the directive of CARC opened new fissures within the state apparatus, since, while cracking down on the Lutheran Church, it continued to deal with the Catholic Church liberally on the issue.[83] Given the weakened position of the Lutheran churches by 1948—arrests of pastors and ousting of church leaders, the nationalization of the churches, etc.—it was hardly in a position to fight the regime on the confirmation issue. Turs attempted to argue that confirmation blunted the influence of sects, but retreated to accepting self-study and exams in place of the now-forbidden confirmation preparation.[84]

The Nationalization of Church Property

The process of registration of churches and clergy in 1945 left incomplete the application of Leninist legislation on religion, in particular the nationalization of church property. As noted earlier, this process had hardly begun in 1941 when the German invasion halted it, and during the 1944–1946 period the state refrained from pressing the matter, "due to various general political motives." By 1947 the matter had become more urgent, since believers began to complain of the lack of a legal basis for the continued occupation of many churches by the Red Army and other Soviet organizations.[85] Moreover, the state was in a stronger position politically and hard-liners in the CPSU were attacking CARC's moderate stance on this issue. Despite the alleged goal of uniform legal treatment after wartime upheaval, Moscow began to privilege certain denominations for registration: in 1947 Voroshilov and the USSR Council of Ministers urged registration for Moslems "as needed," but Lutherans and Catholics only "as exceptions," in the case of those deported earlier to Siberia and Central Asia.[86] By 1948, CARC fell in line with this shift against Western denominations, rejecting or "deferring" registration requests of most places of worship except those that were Armenian, Moslem, or Buddhist.[87]

For the Baltics this meant legal nationalization of church property, under pressure if necessary. As the Estonian commissioner put it, "the first period of work has been completed [the registration of religious communities] and it is now necessary to proceed to the second period ... in order to liquidate the last remnant of bourgeois-organized order which remains in the churches and religious communities."[88] The process entailed first soliciting declarations from the individual parishes of their intent to sign an agreement. Later the agreements were to be formulated and signed by parish and state representatives; then an inventory of property covered by the agreement was to be taken. The agreements would confirm the state's ownership of the property, but confer its use "without charge and without time limit" to the twenty persons (*dvatsatka*) in the parish who agreed to assume responsibility for the property.

But in the republics disagreement over legal issues delayed this process. The Estonian commissioner disputed whether a public decree was needed for the nationalization of churches.[89] He saw such a decree as unnecessary, arguing that Lenin's decree nationalizing churches in January 1918 preceded Estonia's declaration of independence from Russia in February 1918, thus making the current nationalization only a formalization of the 1918 decree. Moreover, he maintained that the 1945 decree of the Estonian Soviet Socialist Republic (ESSR) government had denied legal personality to the churches, including property rights. In 1947, on the other hand, the Estonian Council of Ministers requested a draft decree, seeing it as necessary to give a public legal justification for the action.[90] As a result of this disagreement the Estonian governmental decree mandating the nationalization process was not issued until September 1947, with its distribution "for official use only."[91] The Latvian Council of Ministers issued an analogous decree only one year later, in September 1948.[92] Also producing confusion on the property issue was earlier Soviet legislation. Decree No. 614 (1945) of the Estonian Council of Ministers had eliminated the churches' right to juridical status in Estonia, but Decree No. 232–101 (1946) of the USSR Council of Ministers allowed a limited, union-wide right of juridical status, giving them the right to acquire property after its effective date of January 28, 1946.[93] Also, some churches claimed that the state had issued certifications indicating their properties were in fact not nationalized in 1941.

Complicating matters still further were the peculiarities of church property in the Lutheran tradition, which normally included a parish house (used as an apartment, instruction room, and chancellery for the parish) as well as the church building itself.[94] Yet the Soviet law was tailored for the ROC, with a provision for the guardhouse typical of the ROC but not for the multifunctional parish house used by Lutherans. Considerable bureaucratic energies were necessary to sort out this issue, often pitting the more restrained commissioners against the more aggressive, often venal local authorities bent on confiscating attractive apartments in these parish houses.

The state was initially uncertain about its tactics in pursuing this nationalization. Some argued for crushing the hard-core opposition first; others argued for starting with those churches least opposed to the process. Eventually it opted to strike the easiest agreements first in order to gain a hoped-for demonstration effect on more reluctant churches. Similarly, the Estonian commissioner planned to sign property agreements with several Lutheran parishes, which would then be used to prod the church leadership to accelerate the process.[95] After being forced to join the central Baptist organization in Moscow, the All-Union Council of Evangelical Christians-Baptists (AUCECB), Estonian Baptists entered into the property agreements relatively easily, responding to an order from this body. Methodists and Old Believers initially delayed, but eventually signed. The pace of property agreements in Estonia proceeded according to plan until mid-1947, when it slowed as the Lutherans demonstrated more reluctance.[96] The Lutheran churches were critical of the absence of formal legislation nationalizing the churches, which differed from the treatment of land and commercial buildings. Raising the issue of parish houses, they demanded that the property agreements include church buildings in general, not merely prayer houses.[97] The state refused to budge, however, insisting that only property necessary for the "conduct of the cult" should be included; pastors' housing and other service buildings were to be kept as communal property and rented to the churches if necessary. In order to "avoid protests of believers," the Estonian commissioner forbade evicting pastors from their current domiciles, but the thrust of state policy was clearly to separate the pastor from parish property, making him more vulnerable to state actions and simultaneously less subject to church control.[98]

Local officials often seemed to have other priorities that also delayed the conclusion of agreements with the parishes. This delay naturally allowed the growing antireligious propaganda to take a toll on those in the dvatsatka. When local officials did conclude agreements, they sometimes took a lackadaisical attitude toward them, leaving it to the parish officials to complete the forms and itemize the inventory, resulting in mistakes.[99] Under pressure from Moscow to conclude the process, the Estonian commissioner unsuccessfully sought an internal directive from the Estonian government to the local officials under its authority; the government brusquely suggested that he issue the directive himself.

Commissioner Kivi had more success exerting pressure on the Lutheran church leadership. In June 1947 he threatened to circumvent the leadership and appeal directly to parishes to conclude agreements.[100] Under such pressure, in mid-1947 and again in January 1948 Bishop Pähn ordered all parishes not to hinder the process of nationalization.[101]

Although the pace of agreements then increased, problems arose with the grassroots. The increased use of arrests and terror in general led to rumors among Lutherans that a crackdown against the churches was imminent. Many who had originally signed on as members of the dvatsatka for registration now got cold feet and withheld their names from the property agreements, fearing arrest and deportation.[102] The state sought to counter these rumors, but could not rid the atmosphere of fear. Most property agreements were concluded by mid-1948 in Estonia.[103] The Latvian Lutheran experience is less clear. In a document from early 1949, the commissioner indicated the process was "completed," but his later reports describe the process as "unsatisfactory" and only 65 percent complete by October 1949.[104]

In the case of the Latvian Catholics opposition to nationalization was widespread and intense, as foreshadowed by its opposition to the nationalization of land in 1940. Springovičs insisted the state issue an official written order requiring a dvatsatka, claiming that such a structure was alien to the Catholic Church and its canon law, which forbids lay control of parish governance. Then, pleading that his authority in the church was eroding, he asked for a delay.[105] Recognizing the opposition and currying favor with Springovičs, Moscow decided not to press the matter in September 1945.[106] But by early 1947 Moscow rejected the Catholic stance, insisting that the Lenin decree sufficed to legitimize the nationalization. CARC even began to question the commissioner's strategy toward Springovičs, commenting that "it is completely clear that Comrade Šeškens confirmed his helplessness in relations with Springovičs."[107] Springovičs continued to refuse to order registration into 1948; as late as January 1948 Latvian officials were loath to issue an ultimatum, fearing it would destroy the relationship. Despite his opposition, a considerable number of Catholic parishes registered: by April 1948, 87 of 201 parishes had started registration, far more than in neighboring Lithuania. State officials advocated working with local clergy instead.[108] Despite this progress, CARC pressed Šeškens to take a harder line, even to the point of closing churches and deregistering clergy. By June 1948, Springovičs conceded to the pressure for registration, most parishes followed suit, and the state claimed a "big moral political victory."[109]

Theological Education

The shift toward a hard-line policy on religion was also evidenced on the issue of theological education. As indicated above, this issue was more acute for the national churches, with their professional, ordained clergy, than for the sects, which relied primarily on lay pastors. The large number of exiled and deported clergy exacerbated the problem. In Latvia, approximately three hundred parishes were served by only 98 pastors in 1949, down from 114 in 1947.[110]

In the case of Estonia, the Lutheran Church organized a committee to manage the issue in early 1946. The committee submitted bylaws of the proposed institute to the state. In summer 1947, the committee converted itself into a council, whose secretary, Evald Saag, became the dean of the theological institute. As justification for the institute, the Church maintained that Estonian émigrés in Germany were planning to train pastors with the intention of sending them back to Estonia. Saag argued that "it is necessary to worry that this will be used as propaganda against us, as if here there is no corresponding educational institution or that there are impediments for the Estonian Evangelical Lutheran Church."[111]

The momentum of the Church on this issue was a function of the indecisiveness of the state. As noted earlier, neither Latvian nor Estonian officials rejected the Lutheran proposals for theological seminaries out of hand, but instead delayed with requests for more detailed justifications. To be sure, Latvian officials never seriously entertained the idea as long as Irbe was acting bishop and quickly solicited a new more politically acceptable proposal from Turs after he replaced Irbe in March 1946. The Estonian commissioner rejected the initial church proposal, and the republic authorities consciously delayed taking a stance. By 1947, the increasingly impatient church leadership decided to appeal directly to CARC in Moscow. The Lutheran Church submitted revised draft bylaws to the commissioner in May 1947.[112] CARC was initially inclined to support the proposal and allowed a Lutheran delegation to make its case directly in June, but still did not formally approve the institute.[113] Instead CARC sought the consensus of the party and state organs at the republic level.

Only when the Estonian Church moved to implement its proposal in September 1947 did the central authorities become alarmed, accusing Kivi of a lack of vigilance.[114] The indecisiveness of the central authorities led him to misperceive the importance of the issue. But by November 1947 CARC had tacked in the other direction, sending the proposal to the USSR Council of Ministers with a favorable recommendation.[115] However, the new hard-line approach took its toll on this important dimension of the Church's institutional interests. The wave of arrests and purges in early 1948 undercut the proposal: many of the proposed faculty, including Saag himself, were arrested. The Estonian Communist leadership, which had wavered earlier on the issue, in 1946–1947, now came out strongly against the institute, and it was rejected.[116]

In Latvia, the issue was complicated by the existence of the Catholic Church. As a concession to Springovičs for his relatively moderate stance toward Soviet power since 1944, the state agreed quite early (in December 1945, in fact) to open a seminary for the Catholic Church, with Peter Strods as rector. The rationale of the commissioner, to raise the prestige of the leadership and dampen discontent over the simultaneous arrests of priests, confirms the cynical motives of the state.[117] Nonetheless, the Catholic seminary was in operation by 1947 and enrolling increasing numbers of students. By 1948, however, it was threatened by the plan of Kārlis Pugo (in charge of Catholic and Lutheran affairs in CARC from 1944–1947 and now party secretary of Riga University) to move the female monastery onto the seminary premises as part of a plan to enlarge the university.[118]

For the Latvian Lutherans, the early concession to the Catholics created a wedge. CARC gave its tentative approval during Turs's first meeting in Moscow, in 1947, contingent upon approval of the central Soviet authorities. As late as June 1948, Commissioner Šeškens concluded that "with the beginning of the Catholic seminary in Riga, the absence of a spiritual institute for the Lutherans would of course create an undesirable mood," arguing that negative effects would be minimal due to lack of career appeal and qualified staff.[119] The process dragged out as Latvian officials called for more study of the issue. Even in January 1949, archival evidence suggests it was still supported by officials; Turs lobbied CARC into the summer of 1949. However, the hard-line Soviet religious policy made it untenable, and the Latvian government nixed the proposal officially in September 1949.[120] Both Lutheran churches would have to wait for the post-Stalin thaw for theological training centers.

Internal Church Structure

Despite the Lenin decree alleging the separation of church and state, Stalinization also entailed massive state interference in internal church structures, as we have already seen in the case of the removal of Bishop Irbe in

Latvia. The Lutherans wished to elect new leadership, given the fact that their existing leadership had been chosen before the war and had been decimated by emigration, leaving only acting bishops in place. But before the Soviet authorities would agree to a church synod for this purpose, they insisted that the churches revise their pre-Soviet constitutions to reflect the conditions of "Soviet construction."

In the Estonian case, the Church responded by proposing a draft constitution in December 1946, but the Estonian authorities rejected this draft as indistinguishable from the pre-Soviet constitution.[121] In particular, Commissioner Kivi objected to the provision for an annual church meeting composed of as many as 450 electors. The state preferred synods to be called only when necessary, with the election of the bishop by a smaller, less transparent group of electors, along the lines of the ROC constitution. Later Kivi sought to include a provision acknowledging the nationalization of church property in the constitution. He criticized the inclusion of language that was "too lay-oriented" and promoted evangelization by the churches, as well as the requirement that electors of the bishop be regular contributors to the church.[122]

This criticism demonstrates the state's goal of limiting the democratic dimension intrinsic to the Lutheran Church in order to dampen any potential for criticism and control leadership selection. Moreover, it sought to avoid conferring on the bishop any popular legitimacy, however implicit, as a national leader. Instead the regime sought to apply the narrow hierarchical model of the ROC to the Lutheran Church. In this process Moscow sought to exert control over the republic commissioners. CARC forbade the Estonian commissioner from assisting with rewriting of the draft constitution.

In Latvia, a new Church Order was promulgated in the context of the 1948 synod, which formally elected Turs as bishop, in a process largely steered by the commissioner.[123] The new order centralized power in the archbishop and consistory, particularly over the district deans, and reduced the role of laity and clergy. The General Synod was much smaller than the previous 1932 synod and its members were drawn from local synods held in 1947 without secret ballots, as required by the previous Church Order. Thus the state, using Turs, exerted control over the synod.

Interesting inter-republic coordination occurred in this process as well. The Latvian Lutheran Church sent a fact finder to Estonia prior to the first Latvian synod in 1948 in order to replicate Estonian church structures in Latvia.[124] The recently promulgated Latvian church constitution was in turn used by the regime to pressure the Estonian Church.[125] Responding to this pressure, the Estonian Church amended its constitution to curtail the democratic dimensions which offended the state. Moscow thus sought to keep control over the republic-level authorities as well as promote uniformity in official policy.

Atheistic Propaganda

The hardening stance of the regime was also reflected in an increased antireligious campaign, in order to weaken the churches and the population's attachment to religion. After the absence of significant efforts in 1945–1946, the state began an aggressive campaign in late 1947. The Estonian Minister of Education, Arnold Raud, signaled the new line with a biting speech attacking the clergy, describing them as "black crows" and "mystifiers of the people."[126] Individuals were increasingly warned not to take church rites or risk their educational and career advancement. In 1947 Estonia reversed its 1946 decision to allow Christmas as an official holiday. The pattern in Latvia was similar.[127]

Interestingly, the state was not of one mind regarding the new campaign. Although supporting the Raud attack in principle, the Estonian commissioner criticized it as "raw" and indeed counterproductive. "Religiosity is still deep in Estonia so that any open mention of antireligious propaganda produces the known reaction, which hinders this propaganda. Sometimes the reaction is stronger than our propaganda in the given circumstances." Rather than the blunt assault of Raud, he urged using educators and intellectuals to wean people from the church.[128] Thus different officials at the republic level advocated different policy means, while maintaining the same goals.

Despite Kivi's objection, the Raud attack on religion was a harbinger of a wider campaign. The press began to regularly publish articles attacking religion and exhorting for a more intense campaign against religion. The Estonian Komsomol devoted its Third Congress in 1948 to the issue.[129] This early campaign also attempted to play upon antipathy to the German-dominated church and allegedly anti-religious elements of the Baltic folkloric national narrative.[130]

Along with this propaganda, there was growing pressure on party members to formally withdraw from the church. As Kivi colorfully wrote in July 1948, "In three years of Soviet power we still have only six more atheists [than the 73 registered as such in 1937—author]. In the ESSR thousands have joined the party, thousands of youth are in the Komsomol organizations, but based on old traditions they are still on the lists of some religious parish." He argued that "those who enter into a Marxist world view should publicly and demonstratively strike themselves from the church lists."[131]

Salami-Slicing by the State

In addition to weakening the popular base of the church via antireligious propaganda, the new crackdown also entailed efforts to erode the dominance of the national churches, Lutheran in the case of Estonia, Lutheran and Catholic in Latvia.

Remarkably, in contrast to other Soviet bloc settings, the Baltic republics did not see the formation of organizations of pro-regime priests. These groups, such as the Living Church in 1920s Russia, the Patriotic Priests in Czechoslovakia, and the Pax group in Poland, served to attack and weaken the church from within. This is not to say that the regime did not consider such a strategy. In 1944–1945, a "Committee for the Salvation of the Evangelical-Lutheran Church" issued a call for a "socialist Latvian Lutheran church," free of historical German domination and supportive of Soviet power in Latvia. The initiators never went public, much less became viable politically, and soon dropped illusions of creating an alternative church.[132] In the case of Estonia there was no indication of any such movement, although Bishop Kiivit and Evald Saag broached the idea of a merger with the ROC.[133]

The regime did, of course, recruit pro-regime pastors, particularly after the onset of renewed Stalinization in late 1947. Dissatisfied with its commissioners' focus on the church leadership, CARC ordered the recruitment of "radical pastors," especially those who had served in the Red Army, with the goal of "first carrying to the end the process of rectifying the leadership of the church, and second, a detailed plan of measures directed at creating a group of more radical clergy, whose basic leadership can influence the clergy, using them in the form of an official opposition, to influence the entire life of the church in the desired direction."[134]

In addition, CARC pressed republic authorities to support the role of laity in the parish administrative organs, at the expense of the clergy's influence, and to recruit more loyal laity to these positions. Moscow argued that "you should keep in mind that the political self-consciousness of believers, in comparison with the past, has changed fundamentally.... He now lives in the conditions of Soviet Estonia, all this together should enable the general rectification of the Lutheran church."[135]

In the case of Estonia, another dimension of this salami-slicing strategy turned on the handling of the Herrnhuters.[136] The Herrnhuters had an uneasy relationship with the Lutheran Church and the state in the interwar period. Initially their leaders sought to assert their independence of both the German Herrnhuters and the Baltic Lutheran churches. But the Baltic Lutherans, fearing the loss, reached a compromise by which the Herrnhuters agreed to remain as branches of the Lutheran Church. In exchange, the Lutheran bishop agreed to ordain several Herrnhuters as pastors.

This arrangement began to unravel as a result of divisions within the Herrnhuter group itself.[137] The Herrnhuter leader, Juri Leidtorf, was increasingly challenged by an extreme faction under the leadership of Erik Tanner. Tanner enjoyed Western support from the European Christian Mission in London, which eventually extended to financial control over the Herrnhuter magazine. He began to popularize again the notion of a church independent of the Lutherans, but was expelled by the Herrnhuter synod in 1939. Tanner then organized his own Union of Evangelical Brethren with 15 to 20 percent of the Estonian Herrnhuter members. The Lutheran Church opposed Tanner's movement; the state refused to register his faction as a religious organization, forcing him to register under the voluntary associations law instead.

The Herrnhuter question, including this internal schism, posed both a challenge and an opportunity for the Communist regime. The main dilemma was whether to register Herrnhuters (who comprised 57 groups in Latvia and 54 in Estonia), and if so, in what form. Tanner's adherents initially rejected registration as Lutheran parishes in 1945, seeking independent status as in the pre-Soviet period.

CARC initially tended to see the opportunity, hoping to build up the Herrnhuters in order to weaken the dominant position of the Lutheran Church. In 1946, CARC, joined by the security organs, urged merging the Herrnhuters with the ROC and delayed registering them as independent parishes.[138]

Commissioner Kivi, on the other hand, saw the issue more as a challenge. He painted a picture of a power-hungry Tanner pursuing a very anti-Communist agenda.[139] Alarmed by the traditional Herrnhuter emphasis on evangelization among Lutherans, he argued that "taking into account their religious activity, the organizational capabilities of Tanner, and their relations to Lutheran pastors, they may produce enough unpleasantness for the Lutheran church."[140] He viewed those Lutheran pastors who came from a Herrnhuter tradition as particularly dangerous.[141]

Politically, Kivi discounted the opportunity of using the Herrnhuters against the Lutheran Church. He argued that, with only 3,000 members, they could hardly be used as a fulcrum against a Lutheran Church with 350,000 members. Moreover, he projected that the skewed age structure of the Herrnhuters would soon lead to their extinction. In his view an independent registration of Herrnhuters could not be expected to draw adherents from the Lutheran Church: "If we ask how much influence would change the situation of the Lutheran church, then it is necessary to note, that the hopes of a mass exodus from the Lutheran church are in vain, since most Lutherans are not deep believers, but linked only by long-term traditions of the church, where the desired forms of rites are sober and understandable, but for whom the religious tension which reigns in the Brethren parishes is not desirable." His policy prescription entailed liquidation of the Herrnhuters, placing the main emphasis on winning the support of the Lutheran Church.[142]

As a result of these differing approaches of Moscow and the republics, state policy on this issue wavered. In Estonia, CARC deferred registration of Herrnhuter parishes, seeking more information on the situation, even while it registered other churches in 1945–1946. In August 1947, Kivi complained that the state's temporizing, leaving Herrnhuters active but not registered, was "exerting a demoralizing effect on those parishes which were registered.¹⁴³ He urged their registration as Lutheran parishes, arguing that the Herrnhuters were closest to the Lutheran Church since they received rites in the Lutheran Church, considered themselves subjectively to be Lutherans, and were widely represented in the dvatsatka of many Lutheran parishes. Registration as branches of Lutheran parishes appeared to violate the legal provision of one prayer house per registered parish, in his view creating a double standard.

Eventually, in January 1948, with concurrence of the USSR Council of Ministers, CARC moved to register the Estonian Herrnhuter parishes as branches and negotiate property agreements with them. Under these agreements the neighboring Lutheran parish agreed to take responsibility for the property of the respective Herrnhuter branch. CARC urged the commissioners to be tactful and generous with Herrnhuters in this process, avoiding closure and conversion of prayer houses unless the groups completely refused to cooperate with registration.¹⁴⁴

Despite this approach, the process did not go smoothly. By beginning with the pro-Lutheran Leidtorf faction, the state sought to create momentum before forcing the more independent-minded Tanner faction to register. By August 1948 most parishes from the Leidtorf faction had registered.¹⁴⁵ But in a truly Kafkaesque situation, given the state's refusal to register any Herrnhuters in 1945, attempts by several Herrnhuter groups to register were rejected by the commissioner on the grounds that they had not sought to register in 1945.¹⁴⁶ Some parishes refused to register, waiting to learn the outcome of Tanner's efforts to secure autonomy. During summer 1948, Tanner sought to counter the state's decision by appealing directly to CARC, and then took up talks with the central Baptist authorities in Moscow about registering under their umbrella.¹⁴⁷ The commissioner was able to blunt this move and force the Tanner group to register as branches of Lutheran parishes. Those that refused were closed. By playing this game with Tanner, the state hoped to undercut his credibility with local Herrnhuters and weaken this conservative wing of the Lutheran Church. As will be discussed below, when arrests of Lutheran leaders occurred in 1948, the high proportion of those with Herrnhuter backgrounds was striking.

The process was tumultuous in Latvia as well, revealing slippage between Riga and Moscow and the fact that the Estonian case drove the decision.¹⁴⁸ Commissioner Šeškens initially followed the trend in Estonia of merging the Herrnhuters with the Lutherans. But, in summer 1948, the Latvian Herrnhuters, like Tanner, pressed to join the Baptists instead. Initially the Baptist headquarters in Moscow supported this alternative. Even though the final decision opting for the Lutheran variant had been made by the authorities in Moscow in January 1948, Šeškens went along with the Baptist variant. Then the Baptist headquarters suddenly reversed itself in September 1948, and merging with the Lutherans remained the only option. The Estonian commissioner mistakenly believed that in Latvia the Herrnhuters were being merged with the ROC, further demonstrating the confusion on this issue in both the republics and Moscow.[149]

The state also sought to weaken the Lutheran Church by promoting the Methodist Church as a competitor. To be sure, the Methodists suffered from certain disadvantages: ties to the US and Britain, a pietistic orientation, democratic governance, and small size. But, after a brief consideration of abolishing them, the state decided to retain the Methodist churches in Estonia. They were accorded favorable treatment in the state's analysis and policy, growing in numbers for several decades at the expense of the declining Herrnhuters.[150]

The Use of Terror against the Church

The Stalin regime did not shirk from applying terror to the churches, particularly its leadership. In the period from 1944 to 1947 in Estonia, eleven Lutheran pastors were arrested: nine were charged with anti-Soviet activity during the war, and two for such activity after the war. The pattern was similar in Latvia.[151] In early 1948 a new wave of arrests hit the churches, particularly important Tallinn parishes and the Consistory. Some victims did not require arrest, merely intimidation.[152] In Latvia, the regime had already, in early 1945, recruited informants in the churches and used them, along with other compliant church leaders, to fabricate the legal case against Bishop Irbe.[153] The regime aimed to use the terror to pressure Lutheran leaders to greater political conformity and reduce religious activity. The commissioner's justification in the case of one victim is insightful: he was a "braking influence with large spiritual authority as a member of the Consistory and pastor of one of the most active religious parishes in Tallinn, now he is removed from the center."

The arrests targeted certain groups more than others. In relative terms it affected the Lutheran Church more than other denominations.[154] Given the described antipathy toward the Herrnhuters, it was not surprising that the state targeted pietistic pastors, such as Adolph Horn and Harri Hammer. The state feared their efforts to enliven religion, such as holding multiple worship services each week. Secret police had attempted to recruit Horn and Hammer as informants to manipulate the Brethren away from the Lutheran Church, but they were charged with anti-Soviet activity when this effort failed.[155] The arrests also fell disproportionately on pastors on the islands of Saarema and Hiiuma, reflecting the greater influence of pietism there.

In most cases the arrests were carried out by the KGB and reported perfunctorily by the commissioner, with no indication of the influence of the commissioner on the decisions. In some cases the commissioner sought to justify arrest of certain pastors by invoking the KGB's negative evaluation. In one case CARC rejected a request to remove a pastor, indicating that the commissioner should defer to the authority of the KGB.[156] In another 1949 case the commissioner expressed surprise at the arrest of a mid-level church official by the KGB, but submissively accepted it.[157]

Yet it stretches credulity that these KGB arrests were taken independently of the commissioners. In fact the Estonian commissioner, Johannes Kivi, was an officer in the KGB: he entered its service in 1940, was delegated by it in January 1945 to serve as commissioner, and remained on active reserve thereafter. The same can be said for the Latvian commissioner.[158] The arrests of church leaders clearly had the fingerprints of the commissioners on them.

The underlying goal of the state in these salami-slicing actions and the use of terror was to intimidate and control the Estonian church leadership, along the lines of the 1946 Latvian experience. On issues of substance in this period (for example, confirmation and nationalization) the church leadership had often balked or temporized. In Estonia, the arrests of key leaders, such as Horn and Tanner in 1948–1949, can be traced to the state's antipathy toward their pietistic orientation. The commissioner clearly saw a purge of the Consistory as a means of packing it with those opposed to Herrnhuter pietism and more pliable toward state policy.[159]

Deputy Bishop Pähn was the source of great qualms for the state. The commissioner described him in 1947 as "forthcoming on administrative matters, but hard to characterize as positive on political matters, which goes for the entire Consistory."[160] Although he eventually conceded to state demands regarding confirmation and nationalization, he initially opposed the regime on these issues. He proved willing to issue election appeals, but the state found their content objectionable.

As the state removed and pressured church leaders, it also recruited more manageable successors. In Estonia, Pähn was arrested and sentenced to eight years' imprisonment in 1949; Jaan Kiivit found early favor with the state authorities and was promoted rapidly to assume leadership. In his reports as dean in Virumaa, Kiivit tended to avoid expressions of alarm at the decline in church adherence and moral decay in the population that earned other deans the scorn of the state officials. Instead, in 1947, he gave thanks for the good harvest and the end of armed resistance, distinguishing himself in the eyes of officials.[161] His move to the prestigious Jaani parish in Tallinn marked him as the favorite to replace Pähn as bishop in 1949.

Thus by 1948 the state had achieved its early policy objectives in Latvia and Estonia with regard to the Lutheran and other Protestant churches; to a much less extent this can be said of the Catholic Church as well. The early post-war flexibility in the context of state weakness—due to war damage, armed resistance, and lack of state capacity—had given way to a harsher line in response to resurgent church adherence, church claims on institutional interests, and growing East-West tension. On major issues of conflict, including registration and nationalization, confirmation, theological education, and internal church governance, the regime pressed the churches to adapt to Soviet practice. By suborning and co-opting the church leaderships, first in Latvia and later in Estonia, the regime was in a position to intensify Stalinization. By subverting the intrinsic democratic features in the synodal structure, the regime guaranteed that Lutheran Church leaders would derive very limited legitimacy from synods; the traditional Lutheran deference to political authority reinforced this subordination. The Estonian commissioner summarized well the regime's strategic perspective on the eve of the period of high Stalinism:

> Increasingly I have the intention to apply analogous method to antireligious activity, taking into consideration the situation of religious life in Estonian SSR. Not to distance the active existence of the church from social life, but incorporate it into it, link it with it and work on it persistently, day-by-day. It is clear that such a road is dangerous and demands special attention in relation to these people, demands tense educational work. But if there is patience and sense to use all the possibilities, then the consequences should be evident. And it is not necessary to wait long for them.[162]

This early Stalin period offers some insights into the theoretical questions posed in this study. Not surprisingly, this period confirms the role of terror and coercion in Soviet policy, key features of totalitarianism: Gleichschaltung of the churches by arresting and replacing leaders, as well as clergy and lay leaders; salami-slicing tactics by playing off Catholics against Lutherans in Latvia and Herrnhuters and Methodists against Lutherans in Estonia. Yet, in this early period, the Soviet encounter with Western religions and the non-Orthodox context occasioned a tactical pragmatism in Soviet religious policy, at least until political control was secure. Both Moscow and republic-level officials recognized the need to move cautiously and adapt Soviet norms to these churches' idiosyncrasies, such as confirmation, religious instruction, and church governance structures. Yet this adaption was significantly affected by confession, as evidenced by the slower pace of registration and nationalization and the more intense dispute over confirmation and first communion in the case of the Catholic Church, compared with Lutherans and particularly the Baptists and Methodists. This chapter also shows the importance of institutional interests, such as theological education, building repairs and ownership issues, and governance structure such as synods: less ecclesiastical churches, such as the Baptists, had less at stake and could accommodate the Soviet legal norms more easily than the Catholic and Lutheran churches. In the case of the Lutherans, their institutional interests led to considerable conflict with the state (e.g., rejections of parish and clergy registration, limited publications and access to theological education, deferred and/or tightly controlled synods), deriving from the regime's control of resources and its policy that religion should be relegated to the private sphere. But at the same time institutional interests offered the basis for bargaining with the churches, as part of a co-optation strategy or one of salami-slicing, Springovičs's role in gaining the approval of the Catholic seminary in Riga being the best example. In the process of this bargaining and co-optation, legal and bureaucratic tensions in implementation of religious policy are well-documented: arbitrary actions by local authorities to seize churches; commissioners cross-pressured between CARC and hard-line republic and CPSU officials; and KGB unilateralism. Central control and policy coordination are clear, but cracks in implementation and even different priorities are evident upon closer inspection. In this early period, the two-track strategy of the state becomes apparent: atheistic propaganda to demoralize the faithful and erode church adherence, paired with the veneer of legal status for religion. But given the rise of church adherence, it cannot be said to have been successful, at least not yet. In this period, the closure attendant to Soviet Cold War foreign policy permitted the churches virtually no international contacts; transnational influence was thus nonexistent.

Notes

1. Regarding the first Soviet occupation, 1940–1941, see Altnurme, "Estnische Evangelische-Lutherische Kirche," 235–37; Altnurme, *History of Estonian Ecumenism*, 109–12; Viise, *Estonian Evangelical-Lutheran Church*, 89–105; Talonen, *Church under the Pressure*, 10–16; Bilmanis, *Latvia between Anvil and Hammer*; National Committee, *Religious Persecution*; *Report of the Sufferings*, 1–15; Vahter, "Aspects of Life," 44–45; Perlitz, "Fate of Religion"; Weiss, "Die Baltische Staaten," 35–40; Aunver, "Estlands Christliche Kirche," 82–85. Official Soviet versions are found in Zagaris, *Socialist Transformations*, and Raud, *Developments in Estonia*, 98–101, 124–25, 129. On the theology faculty at Tartu, see Voobus, *Department of Theology*. On atheistic propaganda, see Remmel, "Ambiguous Atheism," 240. For a Catholic perspective confirming that, at the parish level, religious life changed little, see Trups-Trops, "Die Römisch-Katholische Kirche," Teil 1, 80–91, esp. 83.

2. ERA.R-1989.2.5, l. 82, reviewing the Soviet policy in Estonia in 1940–1941.

3. Aunver, "Estlands Christliche Kirche," 86–88. Regarding the Estonian exile church, see Melton and Bauman, *Religions of the World*, 1001–1002. Regarding Catholics in Latvia, see Trups-Trops, "Römisch-Katholische Kirche," Teil 1, 93.

4. GARF.6991.3.3, l. 32; GARF.6991.3.3, l. 31; GARF.6991.3.3, l. 48; and GARF.6991.3.4, l. 52, in which no deadline was mandated, unlike in Polyansky's memo of 25 Sept. 1944 to RSFSR commissioners (GARF.6991.3.4, l. 31).

5. Laar, *War in the Woods*; Anusauskas, *Anti-Soviet Resistance*; Talonen, *Church under the Pressure*, 18–21.

6. GARF.6991.3.22, l. 16–17. Already one can see the linguistic challenge of some imported cadres, who lacked fluency in Latvian or Estonian. Šeškens also complained that

he serviced 90 percent of Latvia's population, whereas the CROC commissioner served only 9 percent, with the same staffing. Apparently Commissioner Šeškens was forced to type all documents himself if confidentiality was involved. Eventually CARC approved a deputy commissioner and extra budget for all Baltic commissioners, but bureaucratic infighting regarding whether this was a Latvian or union responsibility held up the staffing increase. See also Talonen, *Church under the Pressure*, 24–26.

7. RGASPI.17.125.235, l. 137–42.

8. RGASPI.17.117.449, l. 53–55, 60–62.

9. GARF.6991.3.5, l. 19–24; Strods, "Roman Catholic Church," 175; regarding the Latvian Lutherans, Talonen, *Church under the Pressure*, 27–42.

10. Viise, "Estonian Evangelical-Lutheran Church," 112–20.

11. Apostolic succession entails the belief that bishops, consecrated by laying on of hands by a current bishop, represent the continuous line from the original twelve apostles. The Catholic Church contests the claim of Anglicans and many Lutherans that their bishops enjoy this authority. Among Lutherans there are also different positions: Scandinavian Lutheran churches claim apostolic succession, but German Lutheran churches (many formed from Prussian-mandated unions with Reformed churches which reject this belief) do not affirm this element of doctrine. The Latvian and Estonian Lutheran churches had exchanged mutual recognition of this succession with the Anglican Church before WWII. They should be considered among the Scandinavian group rather than the German group, explaining the theological motivation for consecration by a sitting bishop (Melton, *Encyclopedia*, 91).

12. For treatment of this period, see Altnurme, *History*, 113–17; Viise, "Estonian Evangelical-Lutheran Church," 121–28.

13. GARF.6991.3.11, l. 1; GARF.6991.3.11, l. 5.

14. ERA.R-1989. 2.1, 1.4.

15. ERA.R-1989.2.3, l. 83.

16. LVA.1448. 1.188, l. 1 and l. 6.

17. ERA.R-1989. 2. 1, l. 25–26; Altnurme, "Lutherische Kirche," 123–24.

18. ERA.R-1989. 2. 1, l. 79. Chumachenko found this tension in the 1940s between hard-line local officials and Moscow in her study of the ROC (*Church and State*, 190–92).

19. ERA.R-1989. 2. 4, l. 3. According to the commissioner, confirmations averaged between 5,000 and 6,000 per year in 1940, but in the fall of 1940 alone 4,000 were confirmed, as people feared Sovietization would lead to a closure of churches and sent children as young as twelve and thirteen for confirmation.

20. LVA.1448. 1.189, l. 18.

21. LVA.1448.1. 49, l. 56.

22. ERA.R-1989.2.3, l. 83, 89. In 1946, 12,000 song sheets were printed for confirmation ceremonies in Estonia, generous compared with later years.

23. GARF.6991.3.5, l. 32.

24. LVA.1448.1.238, l. 1, indicating Sovnarkom Deputy Chair Molotov approved the seminary on 14 December 1945.

25. See "Appeal of the Church Assembly of the EELK to Members of the EELK," (ERA.R-1989.1.2, l. 31).

26. ERA.R-1989.2.3, l. 47. On the declaration commemorating the October Revolution, see ERA.R-1989.2.3, l. 43.

27. LVA.1448.1.239, l. 7 and l. 25. Vaikuls's article apparently fell short of state expectations, useful only for local press, not foreign consumption; Springovičs also rejected repeated public appeals as compromising his authority. Strods sees strong priest support for the armed resistance and overstates that "the Catholic role was in no way smaller than in Lithuania in the resistance movement," but the Lithuanian churches refused to issue an appeal to end armed opposition ("Roman Catholic Church," 175–78); Trups-Trops, "Die Römisch-Katholische Kirche," Teil 3, 89–92.

28. Staffa, "Religion im Historischen Materialismus," 9–44, 80–120.

29. RGASPI.17.125.93; RGASPI.17.125.106, l. 109–10; RGASPI.17.125.136, l. 146–49; RGASPI.17.125.136, l. 153–56. Reflecting Stalin's opening to the ROC, the three Moscow-based Baltic first secretaries proposed in November 1943 to use the newly rehabilitated Patriarch Sergei in a propaganda attack on the Estonian Orthodox leader, Aleksandr, but were able to cite no Lutherans and only two Catholics who might be useful in such propaganda, based on having been repressed by the Germans.

30. ERA.R-1989. 2. 4, l. 53–54. In a survey of the Lutheran churches in interwar Estonia, Commissioner Kivi argued that "during the period of democratic bourgeois regime, the church in general did not achieve its goals as a result of the restraint of the state organs. This appears to explain why a relatively large number of pastors and leaders of parishes allied with the fascist movement during the development, hoping to achieve the goals of their movement. See also Altnurme, "Form of Piety," 159–61.

31. The Communists placed particular emphasis on the refusal of the Päts government to grant separate registration to the schismatic Tanner movement among pietistic Herrnhuters, attributing this to pressure from the dominant Lutheran Church.

32. Major church buildings and parishes in Latvia, such as the Cathedral, St. Mary's, and St. Peter's in Riga, were contested legally between resident Germans and Latvians. Though only 5 to 6 percent of the population, Germans remained influential until their emigration to Germany in 1939–1940. See Bilmanis, *Baltic Essays*, 106–7.

33. Interestingly, Moscow feared that the article, "The Estonian Church and the German Fascist Occupation of Estonia, 1941–1944," would alienate Lutheran believers who fought against the Nazis and worsen relations with the Lutheran Church, rejecting its publication as "inexpedient" (ERA.R-1989.2. 4, l. 71–74 and l. 75). In fact, Germans dominated the clergy in 1919, but by 1939 76 percent were Estonian, according to Jakob Aunver ("Religious Life," 71). Merilin Kiviorg sees the long shadow of the German colonial legacy: the Estonian Lutheran Church was "on the verge of becoming a truly national church when the Second World War and Soviet occupation put a definite stop" (*Religion and Law*, 80–81).

34. ERA.R-1989.2.4, l. 72.

35. ERA.R-1989.1.4. l. 4–5 lists future bishop Alfred Tooming and pastors Johannes Paesalu, Edgar Hark, Elmar Kuum, Gustav Maar, and Erik Soomire as veterans of the Red Army; GARF.6991.3.5, l. 40.

36. Altnurme ("Form of Piety"), analyzes these theological groups in the Estonian Lutheran Church and their political implications.

37. GARF.6991.3.10, l. 98; LVA.1448.1.239, l. 51–52; Talonen, *Church under the Pressure*, 42–43. The commissioner claimed only 2 percent were loyal to Soviet power and faulted Irbe for evangelizing too much.

38. LVA.1448.1.189, l. 65–66; Talonen, *Church under the Pressure*, 76–77, 85, 88, 156–57.

39. LVA.1448.1.239, l. 50. The commissioner earlier quotes Springovičs: "Communists work for the benefit of people and we work for the benefit of our people, our homeland, thus we support, work together." See LVA.1448,1.239, l. 27–28; Trups-Trops, "Römisch-Katholische Kirche," Teil 2, 80 and 82–83, quoting his circular to clergy of 22 December 1944 and 20 March 1945.
40. LVA.1448.2.239, l. 38–39.
41. GARF.6991.3.10, l. 95.
42. GARF.6991.3.10, l. 123–24.
43. LVA.1448.1.239, l. 44.
44. ERA.R-1989.1.4, l. 7. By contrast, among Lutheran pastors only three had served in the Red Army, a relatively small portion of the 156 pastors.
45. ERA.R-1989.2.4, l. 47–51. S.T. Kimbrough, "Rise and Fall of Methodism in Lithuania and Latvia," in Kimbrough, ed., 123; Pajasoo, *Heroes of the Cross*, 58–108, profiles Methodist leaders, many from Saarema, who were deported or executed; Talonen, *Church under the Pressure*, 234–38.
46. Talonen, "Herrnhut and the Baltic countries," 98–109; Simons and Westerlund, *Religion, Politics and Nation-Building*, 144–45. The pietism of the Herrnhuters clashed with the emotional quietism of the traditional Lutherans, yet the Herrnhuters advocated infant baptism and confirmation, rites normally associated with the Lutherans, not the sects. A move to assert independence from the Lutherans in 1922 was headed off in a compromise brokered by the German Herrnhuter leader, Bishop Jensson, and the Estonian Lutheran Bishop, Kukk. The Lutheran Church agreed to ordain several Herrnhuter preachers as pastors and in return the Herrnhuters agreed to forego "spiritual sessions" during the worship service and take sacraments in the Lutheran churches. In the late 1930s the compromise frayed under the influence of Tanner, who began ordaining pastors independently and holding spiritual sessions during normal worship services. Eventually Tanner was expelled by the Herrnhuter synod under pressure from the Lutherans. He formed his own group, the Union of Evangelical Brethren, taking 20 percent of the Herrnhuters with him.
47. ERA.R-1989.2.4, l. 39–42.
48. GARF.6991.3.10, l. 99–105; Durasoff, *Russian Protestants*, 124–25. This conflicts with Remmel's ("Believers, Human Rights") conclusion that smaller religious organizations were more affected by rejected registrations in this period.
49. ERA.R-1989.2.3, l. 72–73.
50. ERA.R-1989.2.2, l. 47.
51. ERA.R-1989.2.3, l. 46.
52. Ibid.
53. ERA.R-1989.2.5, l. 47.
54. ERA.R-1989.2.7, l. 195.
55. LVA.1448.1.239, l. 42. Irbe protested this finding, to no avail. Talonen (*Church under the Pressure*, 150–52) indicates that 43 percent of Latvian churches were either destroyed or seriously damaged.
56. GARF.6991.3.5, l. 37–38; GARF.6991.3.10, l. 99. The commissioner refused to assist with the deported status of Drs. Edgar Rumba and Ludwig Adamovich. The library request is found in LVA.1448.1.188, l. 2.
57. LVA.1448.1.237, l. 1–5; GARF.6991.3.5, l. 34–35r, l. 41. The draft exemption of clergy was granted in February 1945 by the Sovnarkom, according to GARF.6991.3.10, l. 5–7.

58. LVA.1448.1.239, l. 38–39, 57. The political motivation to enhance Springovičs' prestige and dampen criticism of religious repression is evident.
59. LVA.1448.1.183, l. 24–25.
60. GARF.6991.3.471, l. 30–31. Moscow vetoed central media usage of the church testimony.
61. GARF.6991.3.471, l. 32; Trups-Trops, "Römisch-Katholische Kirche," Teil 2, 89–92.
62. GARF.6991.3.17, l. 1–2; GARF.6991.3.17, l. 4. CARC responded by suggesting more study and asked for potential candidates for archbishop. See also Talonen, *Church under the Pressure*, 26, 84–85.
63. LVA.1448.1.239, l. 55; LVA.1.239, l. 58; Talonen, *Church under the Pressure*, 89–91.
64. GARF.6991.3.471, l. 4–6, including *Spravka* on Turs (March 7, 1946), l. 12 and "Autobiography of Šlosbergs", l. 13. This is a key document, detailing step-by-step the tactics used in the ouster of Irbe and installation of Turs, as well as the motives and expectations. In addition to his pietistic inclination, Rozenbergs refused to vote in the elections. The new leadership used the elections of Turs and Virbulus to the Higher Church Administration during the interwar period and the fact that the fleeing predecessor, Grīnbergs, had transferred his power to Irbe without a synodal decision to legitimize the new leaders. Ironically Virbulis was to die less than a month after this March 1946 purge. See also Talonen (*Church under the Pressure*, 56–57, 108–15) on the trials and legal basis used by the regime.
65. GARF.6991.3.471, l. 4–6; Talonen, *Church under the Pressure*, 99–104.
66. GARF.6991.3.10, l. 154–57. Talonen (*Church under the Pressure*, 105–7, 136–47) documents that Turs urged Latvians to buy Soviet bonds and wore red vestments instead of black, and sees the state getting the best of the bargain regarding church publications, since authors were politically reliable and many were designated for foreign export.
67. Talonen, *Church under the Pressure*, 145–48. Kaulins, Kleperis, Saurums, and Šlosbergs filled deanships and spots on the Consistory.
68. Talonen, 163–68. Talonen sees Turs not as a red bishop, but "playing a role in political theater with the communists."
69. GARF.6991.3.471, l. 158–71.
70. GARF.6991.3.471, l. 207–8.
71. GARF.6991.3.8, l. 98–108.
72. RGASPI.17.125.407, l. 134–35.
73. ERA.R-1989.2.4, l. 1–2.
74. RGASPI.17.125.506, l. 122, for CARC's support of confirmation at age sixteen and four weeks of instruction.
75. Commissioner Kivi summarized the main issues in ERA.R-1989.2.5, l. 42–44.
76. ERA.R-1989.2.5, l. 42–44; ERA.R-1989.2.7, l. 57. The Estonian commissioner argued that this was a response to requests from local authorities, as well as an experiment offering "a special grounds and exploratory step in terms of seeing how they react and what effects the action yields."
77. ERA.R-1989.2.7, l. 59. High percentages of confirmands in the early postwar years were found in the over-twenty cohort: 23.8 percent in 1946 and 29.4 percent in 1947. Confirmation of those over twenty was particularly high on the islands of Saarema and Hiiuma, perhaps reflecting the relatively strong influence of the Baptists there. The number of confirmands increased from 8,039 in 1946 to 10, 428 in 1947, roughly reaching 1937 levels. ERA.R-1989.2.7, l. 79. Ironically, CARC blamed the commissioner for curtailing the confirmation period.

78. ERA.R-1989.2.5, l. 45–48. The commissioner cynically argued that the churches sought to activate young cohorts who had no definitive worldview yet, operating on the principle that "it is more useful for the pocketbook if people come to God earlier rather than later."

79. GARF.6991.3.471, l. 33; GARF.6991.3.471, l. 249. Polyansky indicated a tougher line was needed in Latvia now. Even in October 1947, there was no CM LSSR legislation, with a preference for vagueness over a legal basis for confirmation, which might require catechism books and encourage churches to confirm. LVA.1448.1.242, l. 12; Talonen, *Church under the Pressure*, 177.

80. LVA.1448.1.246, l. 96–97 refers to these actions, as well as the CARC directive to Turs in advance of his meeting to explain the new policy to the deans in Latvia.

81. Ten pastors were cited by the Estonian commissioner for violations of confirming underage youth, according to ERA.R-1989.2.7, l. 187–89.

82. Ibid., l. 189, regarding widespread charges of discrimination in university admissions in Estonia.

83. The Catholic Church was permitted to hold religious instruction throughout the entire summer and to offer first communion at age twelve. The Estonian commissioner protested the new lack of uniformity on the confirmation question as discriminatory, but CARC rebutted that no unified policy was possible, since different republics had peculiarities (ERA.R-1989.2.8, l. 45; ERA.R-1989.2.8. l. 46).

84. LVA.1448.1.1, l. 66–69.

85. ERA.R-1989.2.5, l. 67.

86. RGASPI.17.125.506, l. 183.

87. GARF.6991.3.8, l. 153.

88. ERA.R-1989.2.5, l. 79, 85.

89. ERA.R-1989.2.5, l. 62–64.

90. Ibid. l. 60–62. The draft decree of the commissioner emphasized his control over the process, requiring that property agreements be made only with parishes that had been registered by him previously. His draft instructions also called for the parish executive organ to be elected by the parish, but subject to his approval. The commissioner was thus asserting his power vis-à-vis the local authorities as well as the churches (ERA.R-1989.2.5, l. 72–78).

91. ERA.R-1989.2.7, l. 85.

92. Decree n. 925 (4 Sept. 1948) LSSR Council of Ministers, referenced in LVA.1448.1.244, l. 40.

93. ERA.R-1989.2.5, l. 64 and l. 83; ERA.R-1989.2.5, l. 9–10.

94. ERA.R-1989.2.5, l. 68–69; Talonen, *Church under the Pressure*, 157–59.

95. ERA.R-1989.2.7, l. 29.

96. ERA.R-1989.2.8, l. 18–19. Kivi criticizes foot-dragging by local authorities, rather than the churches, and asks for help from the Estonian republic officials. Regarding the forced merger of Baptists, see Pilli, *Dance or Die*, 20–25.

97. ERA.R-1989.2.5, l. 119.

98. ERA.R-1989.2.7, l. 113–15 reflects the rigid stance on parish houses in Kivi's instructions to local authorities. In mid-1948, CARC indicated that pastors who left the churches could not be deprived of garden land tilled by them, widening opportunities for insubordination in the churches and collaboration with the regime. (ERA.R-1989.2.8, l. 50, 50r).

99. Moscow's response to the Estonian commissioner's last 1947 report complains of slowing of the process, urging him to mobilize Estonian government pressure on local officials (ERA.R-1989.2.7, l. 120–120r).

100. ERA.R-1989.2.5, l. 108. Kivi gave Bishop Pähn the choice: "If the Consistory does not consider it possible through its means to convey my order in the matter, then I ask them to tell me now, so that I can direct my request to every parish, which I consider necessary. No slow down or delay in this matter can be considered possible."

101. ERA.R-1989.2.7, l. 173.

102. According to the Estonian commissioner in March 1948, "one of the most important means of agitation against concluding property agreements is fear. Rumors of deportation to Siberia and special economic and financial responsibilities on those who sign the agreements are spreading." See ERA.R-1989.2.8, l. 66. Failure to maintain a dvatsatka was often used as grounds to eliminate a parish from registration.

103. ERA.R-1989.2.7, l. 122–24. Controversy did not cease, however, as CARC attacked the allocation to the parishes of land tilled by the respective pastor, arguing that Estonian law permitting this violated Leninist norms. See ERA.R-1989.2.8, l. 50r.

104. LVA.1448.1.244, l. 47; LVA.1448.1.246, l. 38 and l. 91.

105. In his interpretation of the 1940–1941 occupation, Soviet scholar Zagaris highlights that "the Catholic Church was especially active making use of its influence among certain layers of the peasantry …" (*Socialist Transformations*, 125–26). Springovičs' objections are documented in GARF.6991.3.471, l. 243, 244. CARC's rejection is in GARF.6991.3.471, l. 264.

106. LVA.1448.1.242, l. 4–6.

107. GARF.6991.3.471, l. 248, quoting the handwritten comment of Sadovski.

108. LVA.1448.1.244, l. 6–11.

109. GARF.6991.3.472, l. 121–121r; GARF.6991.3.472, l. 124–25.

110. Talonen, *Church under the Pressure*, 245–47.

111. ERA.R-1989.2.6, l. 112.

112. ERA.R-1989.2.5, l. 91–94.

113. ERA.R-1989.2.5, l. 86–89 and l. 95.

114. ERA.R-1989.2.6, l. 110–11; ERA.R-1989.2.6, l. 112.

115. ERA.R-1989.2.6, l. 113.

116. ERA.R-1989.2.8, l. 30. In March 1948 Commissioner Kivi informed CARC that the theological institute had been rejected in meetings with Lutheran leaders.

117. LVA.1448.1.239, l. 57. Trups-Trops, "Römisch-Katholische Kirche," Teil 2, 88–89. The fact that Foreign Minister Molotov gave formal approval for the seminary indicates how the decision was framed by the Soviet leadership.

118. LVA.1448.1.244, l. 27. The commissioner objected to this plan, but his objections were overridden by the Latvian republic officials.

119. Ibid., l. 29; LVA.1448.1.244, l. 38; GARF.6991.3.471, l. 233; Talonen, *Church under the Pressure*, 119–25.

120. LVA.1448.1.244, l. 57–58; Talonen, *Church under the Pressure*, 245–49. Turs countered with the proposal for a Baltic-wide theological institute, which was rejected.

121. ERA.R-1989.1.4, l. 6; ERA.R-1989.2.8, l. 98.

122. ERA.R-1989.2.8, l. 97–101.

123. Talonen, *Church under the Pressure*, 180–207. Talonen interprets Turs as seeking to protect church interests. But in so doing he subverted church autonomy and ecclesiastical processes. Sacrificed in the process of obtaining state approval to hold the synod were two church leaders who opposed Turs's undermining of church governance. Hugo Grivans and Alberts Freijs were arrested in the months before the synod.

124. LVA.1448.1.185, l. 22–24.
125. LVA.1448.1.244, l. 14–19, esp. l. 17.
126. ERA.R-1989.2.6, l. 126–29. The speech was excerpted in the daily press and published in full in *Soviet Teacher*, which few read. As a result, the full weight of the attack was lost on most clergy and laity. Only after several months did the Estonian Consistory protest Raud's insults in a letter to the Council of Ministers; the Baptist leader, Johannes Lipstok, was "uncomfortable" about the address, but did not formally protest.
127. Talonen, *Church under the Pressure*, 96–97.
128. ERA.R-1989.2.6, l. 128. Kivi: "Of what use is a talk on attending church for schoolchildren if they go to church with their parents? How can one demand antireligious attitudes from a student, if his professor is religious?"
129. ERA.R-1989.2.7, l. 192.
130. Remmel, "Ambiguous Atheism," 242.
131. ERA.R-1989.2.7, l. 196.
132. LVA.1448.1.189, l. 33–38. The confidential proposal to Šeškens was associated with Pastor V. J. Vaskis. Talonen (*Church under the Pressure*, 86–87) finds the commissioner interested in promoting it. Overall opposition to Irbe was weak, hindering this strategy.
133. Altnurme, *History*, 150, 154. The motive for this radical idea was to conduct theological education jointly, but both churches' clergy opposed it, as did the state.
134. ERA.R-1989.2.5, l. 9.
135. Ibid., l. 9–10.
136. The Herrnhuters were founded by Graf von Zinzendorf in eighteenth-century Germany, based on a pietistic Bohemian movement from the fifteenth century (and so also known as Bohemian Brethren). As a result of German missionary work, they came to Estonia in 1729 and even to Russia. The Bohemian Brethren maintained a loose relationship with the provincial Lutheran churches in Germany.
137. ERA.R-1989.2.6, l. 59–69 gives Kivi's overview of the history of Herrnhuters in interwar Estonia, emphasizing German influence and anti-Soviet orientation.
138. ERA.R-1989.2.4, l. 27. Though listed as agent Fevralski in KGB documents, Tanner rejected the Orthodox merger, suggesting his unreliability to the regime. Altnurme, "Herrnhuter," 14–23.
139. ERA.R-1989.2.4, l. 42. Referring to the pre-Soviet period, he concluded that "around Tanner was organized a reactionary clique, which under the pretense of a religious movement fought against the progressive ideas in the political, social as well as religious life." The commissioner saw Tanner as particularly tied to conservative Western religious agencies, an increasingly telling argument as the Cold War escalated.
140. ERA.R-1989.2.4, l. 10.
141. ERA.R-1989.2.7, l. 24 and l. 197. The Herrnhuter practice of holding Bible hours particularly bothered the commissioner. Lutheran pastors who also held such Bible hours, like Adolf Horn, an assessor in the Estonian Consistory, were sharply criticized by him: Bible hours are practiced only on an exceptional basis by Lutherans, when the cult servant belongs to the conservatives. CARC's decision to forbid such Bible hours would hit primarily the sects and Herrnhuters, and "would effectively mean the end of all their activities." From 1937 to 1947 church services declined by one-half, but Bible hours only by one-third, which the commissioner attributed to the influence of the Herrnhuter pastors in the Lutheran Church.

142. ERA.R-1989.2.4, l. 11–12. "Finally if we place the emphasis of our future activity on the Lutheran church, in the hope of its deterioration in view of Soviet construction, then the naturally correct decision in relation to both Herrnhuter factions is their liquidation."

143. ERA.R-1989.2.6, l. 45.

144. ERA.R-1989.2.8, l. 65, 65r.

145. ERA.R-1989.2.8, l. 141–42 and l. 149–50. Of forty-two parishes in the Leidtorf group, thirty-two had requested registration by August 1948. Of these, twenty-four were accepted, five were given to the Lutherans as confirmation houses since they were located too close to a Lutheran church to be a prayer house, and three were rejected as branches by the respective Lutheran church. In some cases members of the Lutheran parish dvatsatka refused to assume responsibility for the property of the Herrnhuter filial. Ten did not apply for registration at all.

146. ERA.R-1989.2.7, l. 182. The commissioner blamed local officials for permitting the continued functioning of these Herrnhuters, despite the fact they used "non-working churches."

147. The central Baptist authorities in Moscow appeared to give Tanner liberal conditions of autonomy, if he would forego proselytization for infant baptism and opposition to baptism by immersion. This dismayed the local Baltic Baptists, who saw Tanner's followers as refusing to adhere to these conditions. The Estonian commissioner also strenuously opposed their registration as Baptists, fearing this would hurt relations with the more conformist Lutheran Church and end in schism of the Baptists in any case. See ERA.R-1989.2.8, l. 150–53.

148. LVA.1448.1.244, l. 31–32 and l. 39–40. Interestingly, Harald Kalnins, later to gain profile working with Soviet German Lutherans, sought to woo the Herrnhuters for the Lutheran option. GARF.6991.3.472, l. 1 indicates the January 1948 decision, ordering Latvia to adopt the Estonian position. Talonen, *Church under the Pressure*, 238–41.

149. ERA.R-1989.2.6, l. 52.

150. Elliott, "Methodism," 151–52.

151. ERA.R-1989.1.4, l. 4. Pastor Hugo Parno was arrested and sentenced to incarceration for five years for hiding a group of forest brother guerrillas. Viise ("Estonian Evangelical-Lutheran Church," 132) indicates twenty-two arrests in 1944–1953; Altnurme ("Lutherische Kirche," 127) cites twenty-three arrests in 1944–1949; Talonen (*Church under the Pressure*, 126–36) lists Latvian clergy deported.

152. ERA.R-1989.2.7, l. 191–92; ERA.R-1989.2.7, l. 171–171r. Arrested in February 1948: Adolf Horn, pastor of Peeteli Parish in Tallinn and member of the Consistory; Dean Jan Laane of Maryama (Läänemaa province); Harri Hammer of Paulus Parish, Tartu; Elmar Paldra, pastor of Toom-Nikuliste in Tallinn. Ferdinand Jürgenson, Pastor of Jaani Parish, Tallinn, left "voluntarily" and was sent far away to Virumaa province; Archbishop Pähn replaced him with Jaan Kiivit, future archbishop.

153. Talonen, *Church under the Pressure*, 51–55, 108–15 describes and documents the informant status of Šlosbergs and Arnold Kondrats, along with the testimony of Gustavs Saurums and Arvids Perlbachs in Irbe's trial. It should be noted that others in the church leadership, such as Pauls Rozenbergs, refused to confess or testify against Irbe and were convicted. Silke was blackmailed to inform for the NKVD, but the conspiracy ended when he told Irbe of this recruitment. Šlosbergs informed against Silke. Irbe received a sentence of ten years, Rozenbergs and Silke eight years each. Interestingly, Altnurme ("Lutherische Kirche"), 127 sees the NKVD as having difficulty recruiting agents in the Estonian leadership until 1949.

154. ERA.R-1989.2.7, l. 191–92; ERA.R-1989.2.7, l. 171–171r. Fifteen pastors were removed in the first three months of 1948, including eleven Lutherans, one Methodist, two Baptists, and one Old Believer. Four pastors were removed on Saarema, one on Hiiuma.

155. Altnurme, "Form of Piety," 161–65. Horn and Tanner were recorded as agents Pravdin and Fevralski, respectively. Hammer was not recorded as an informant. Charges did not mention pietism, but rather engagement in anti-Soviet activities. Altnurme discounts the liberal versus pietistic orientation as a factor, citing the arrest of liberals and variations in adaptability to explain collaboration. But pietists were more likely than liberals to enliven religious practice.

156. ERA.R-1989.2.8, l. 167 and l. 168, 168r. Kivi sought the ouster of the pietist, Pastor Voldemar Koppel, member of the Consistory and pastor of the largest church in Estonia, Kaarli Parish, as well as Pastor Bernhard Leib, associate pastor of Jaani Church, now the main parish of the regime's favorite Jaan Kiivit. He argued that the KGB wished to eliminate them. But CARC indicated that this was only possible in the case of pastors who had limited passports due to a criminal conviction, which did not apply in these cases. Referring to the KGB, CARC admonished that "the question of removal from this or that place of a cult servant, in case of the rejection of the renewal of the residence permit, is not in your competence and belongs to the activity of the responsible organs."

157. ERA.R-1989.2.12, l. 57. Kivi admits his positive view of Dean Henn Unt, arrested in early 1949, despite Agitprop support. In Orwellian language, he concludes "it is necessary to conclude that his anti-Soviet activity was masked by an external loyalty, which was expressed by participation in social life."

158. ERA.R-1989.2.5, l. 118. The Estonian commissioner was often ordered away from Tallinn on business, implying special KGB security assignments. Moreover, in a 1947 communication to the Ministry of State Security, USSR, he requested the special financial subsidy given to active officers in the KGB. In Latvia, both Voldemars Šeškens and Julijans Restbergs had worked for the NKVD or border police of the USSR before being named commissioner. Based on personnel records, see Krumina-Konkova, "Collaboration," 150, 176. Trups-Trops, "Römisch-Katholische Kirche," Teil 2, 80.

159. ERA.R-1989.2.7, l. 153. In early 1948, Kivi supported Dean Jaan Konsin of Tartu as new member of the Consistory, after the 1948 purge of the Estonian church leadership, due to his opposition to the Herrnhuters.

160. ERA.R-1989.1.4, l. 5. Kivi concluded: "The Consistory gives declarations in patriotic tones, but does this with great care and preparation. For many it is necessary to direct and advise. It is obvious that the hardest word for them is 'Soviet power,' they always write only 'power' or 'government.'" This suggests that Pähn was trying to use traditional Lutheran deference to authority in order to justify issuing a supportive election appeal, without endorsing the Sovietization process. The state refused to print Pähn's election appeal. Pähn's fate is noted in "Martyrdom of the Churches," 299.

161. ERA.R-1989.2.7, l. 104–5.

162. ERA.R-1989.2.12, l. 61.

2 The Period of High Stalinism: 1949–1953

By early 1949 the regime had achieved its goal of Gleichschaltung, exerting control over the church leaderships and introducing most Soviet legal norms for religious activity in the Baltics. The initial tasks of crushing armed resistance and building of Soviet institutions were complete, compelling the churches to abandon illusions of liberation and accept the Soviet reality. But in terms of its longer-range goals of eroding religious belief and eliminating the churches' social role, the policy still fell far short. Church adherence remained high, the churches' social footprint was considerable, and even implementation of the Soviet legal forms remained incomplete. Penetrated by the secret police, the church leaderships were nominally loyal, but their professions of loyalty were suspected of being merely opportunistic. Bishop Turs was seen as externally loyal, but not reconciled to Soviet power; worse yet, key Catholic leaders were seen as anti-Soviet. Particularly worrisome was the Catholic Church, which had enjoyed a type of honeymoon with the regime after World War II, but represented an international, hierarchically organized institution with extensive social presence and deep popular attachment in Latvia.

Compounding the regime's challenge were the policy tasks associated with Stalinization in the acquired territories: collectivization of agriculture, state-driven industrialization, increased immigration from other republics, heightened military presence, rupture of ties with the West, and cult of personality. Now high on the political agenda, these tasks would pose dilemmas for the churches, occasioning dissent in some cases and accommodation in others. Increasingly the co-opted church leaderships would be pressured to dampen dissent in their ranks under threat of losing their already limited space for religious activity, in turn risking their credibility with their own flocks. New rounds of terror and deportation would raise the stakes for the churches. Even CARC and its representatives, having established a certain modus vivendi with the churches, would be caught in the crossfire as the CPSU shifted toward a hard-line pursuit of long-term goals related to religion and church-state relations.

International issues attendant to the onset of the Cold War intruded on this already fraught church-state relationship. The nuclear arms race engendered a Soviet disarmament campaign. The Korean War raised world tensions that the Soviets attempted to blunt with peace propaganda. International church organizations, such as the World Council of Churches (WCC) and the Lutheran World Federation (LWF), sought to reorganize after World War II, raising questions of participation by Soviet churches. Pope Pius XII excommunicated members of the Communist Party in 1949, adding to the issues dividing Catholics from the regime. Lastly, the implications of the formal division of Germany complicated life, especially for the Baltic Lutheran churches.

Registration and Closure of Churches

Most indicative of the new harsh line was the restriction on the number of parishes. As noted in the previous chapter, most existing parishes had been registered during the relatively liberal period from 1944 to 1948. Many of these parishes now lost their registration and were effectively closed. Already in mid-1948 the Soviet leadership was pressing CARC to determine if religion was growing or dying out; the priority was no longer on simply organizing churches into state legal structures.[1] This crackdown, engineered by CARC, was by no means limited to the Baltics.[2] But by targeting mainly Western-based churches and sparing Moslem, Armenian, and Old Believer parishes, it affected the Baltics disproportionately. The rationale for rejecting applications to open new churches was simple: fear of a domino effect leading other groups of believers to also seek registration. Protests by church leaders, such as Bishop Turs, were to no avail in most cases.[3]

In this period of intense Stalinism, the initiative sometimes came from zealous local officials who sought to aggrandize their power at the expense of the churches and proposed closure of churches in order to convert them to alternative uses (e.g., libraries, cultural centers, sport halls). In some cases the republic and/or central officials would deny such requests.[4] The Estonian commissioner also frequently sought to reprimand local officials who violated the law by arbitrarily seizing churches and converting them for alternative uses.

In other cases, republic officials themselves were the main instigators. They were not always successful, as in the case of the large Jesus Parish in Riga, coveted by Riga Communist officials for use as a cultural building. But the church had been placed under architectural protection by the Latvian Architectural Administration and Commissioner Šeškens was sympathetic to Turs's objections to closure. Despite the lobbying of the Latvian republic leadership, CARC rejected the local Communist request.[5] However, such reversals of local decisions were rare until after Stalin's death.

Other times the priest would be arrested as part of a maneuver by local authorities to seize a church. For example, local authorities sought to close the Lutheran parish in Ilukste, Latgāle, in early 1949 and convert it into a "house of culture."[6] But Šeškens found that the parish, though small, met the legal requirements for registration. Since it was in a Catholic region, he urged that the local government provide alternate premises should the church be converted. Archbishop Turs also opposed the closing of the parish. But, after the KGB arrested the parish pastor for alleged anti-Soviet activity in September 1949, republic officials and CARC sustained the decision to close the parish.

In the context of the wave of clergy arrests in 1949, it would have been logical to expect closure of their parishes for lack of a priest. But commissioners did not necessarily advocate this. Instead, the Estonian commissioner argued for a slow death of religion: if priests served more than one parish, they would perform fewer services in each parish, leading to a decline of religious practice among parishioners.[7]

In certain cases, hard-line Moscow officials with a vested stake in Baltic issues pressed for closures to aggrandize state and personal power. For example, after returning to become party secretary at Riga University in 1948, hard-liner Latvian Communist Kārlis Pugo, former vice-chair of CARC, targeted churches for claims by the university, namely the Catholic curia building for use as a dormitory and an Adventist church for use as a polyclinic.[8]

Of course, the state offered pretexts, often of the flimsiest nature, to justify rejection of applications. Registration requests were rejected, for example, on the grounds that members of the dvatsatka were of the wrong nationality, lived outside the territory of the proposed parish, or were already listed as members of the dvatsatka of another parish.

Still another tactic was to close a parish for financial reasons, such as failure to pay taxes.[9] Of eleven Lutheran parishes closed in 1950, the justification in nine cases was alleged financial insolvency. The Finance Ministry added additional taxes on the churches and clergy, presuming that all church income—including hidden income—accrued to the pastor, as in the ROC.[10] Even though the Latvian commissioner seemed to advocate for fair taxes on churches and clergy, CARC used taxes to crush unregistered parishes in this period.[11]

Alleged violation of legal separation of church and school was sometimes used to close a church. For example, the local, republic, and central officials reached a consensus to close the Latvian Lutheran parish in Baltin, which met on the second floor of a school.[12]

In order to "avoid offense to parishes" the state would sometimes merge two or more parishes into one larger parish rather than closing them entirely, for example reducing three Baptist parishes in Riga to one and five to three in Liepāja.[13] Pressured by both the commissioner and local parishes, church leaders often accepted such mergers as the lesser evil, despite the apparent discredit they brought. Local officials on the island of Hiiuma, Estonia, sought to merge Lutheran and Baptist parishes, but met with the opposition of the commissioner, who feared that the pietistic Baptists would "infect" the more formal Lutherans.[14]

But he was not opposed to merging parishes of the same denomination in order to weaken the churches. A prime example of this was the large Oleviste Church in Tallinn, which in 1949 was taken from the Lutherans and given to the Baptists, who were then forced to merge seven separate parishes into one.[15] The state's motives included not only limiting Lutheran influence and Baptist evangelization in Tallinn, but also sowing dissension among the rather independent-minded Baptists.

Posing another dilemma for the regime in terms of its twin goals (legal registration and yet closing parishes) were the sects, especially the Herrnhuters and the Methodists. As noted in the previous chapter, the state had delayed a decision on registering these parishes, nervous about their zealous activity but not wanting them to go underground. Registering them as branches of the Lutherans raised red flags as well, both increasing the number of parishes and perhaps activating the Lutherans. In 1949, judging that the Lutherans had adjusted to the Soviet system, that the dogmatic differences between Herrnhuters and Lutherans had disappeared, and that "the Lutherans would absorb the Herrnhuters and gradually eliminate their peculiarities," CARC resolved the issue by registering the Herrnhuters under the Lutherans in the Baltics.[16] The Latvian Methodists were likewise registered under the Lutherans; in Estonia, however, Methodists were permitted to retain an independent identity.[17] This outcome did not resolve the tension between goals: in this period of crackdown, the increased number of Lutheran churches reflected badly on the CARC commissioner, who would seek to merge and close the branch parishes.

The Catholic-Lutheran angle also informed the state's deliberations, in particular the regime's rising conflict with the Catholic Church. Closing Lutheran churches was easier for local officials in Catholic-dominated areas, such as Latgāle. The commissioner noted, "in recent times we observe the appearance that in local districts where Catholicism is dominant over other confessions, Soviet organs promote petitions to liquidate Lutheran churches, in essence Lutheran parishes of believers. These measures at this time would not be desirable in such a wide measure."[18]

In addition to these aspects of high politics, the process of closing churches was often characterized by horse trading and venal interests, producing considerable arbitrariness despite the alleged legal norms. The case of a Methodist church in Tallinn is illustrative. In 1949 Commissioner Kivi struck a deal with the Ministry of Communications, agreeing to close this church, whose building was desired by the Ministry, in exchange for the prompt installation of a telephone in his office. Kivi also essentially looted a piano for his own personal use from the Kaarli parish.[19] Despite the repeated claims to attempt to prevent such illegal actions on the local level, the republic authorities undermined their case by their own behavior.

Repression of the Catholic Church

A major change of this period was the heightened focus and crackdown on the Catholic Church, reversing the earlier, more cooperative relationship with the anti-German Archbishop Antonijs Springovičs. In a 1950 review of party work in Latvia, the Agitprop Department of the CPSU decried the weak anti-religious propaganda and singled out the Catholic Church and sects for their opposition to collectivization, anti-Soviet stance, and agitation against the regime.[20] Latvian Communist leaders and KGB officials joined the Moscow chorus targeting the Catholic Church, proposing repressive measures and reinforcing scientific-atheistic work among the population.[21] Pope Pius XII was a lightning rod for the regime, particularly his decree excommunicating Communists and his declaration of 1950 as a Holy Year. Along with the now-illegal practice of religious instruction, these were the main criticisms of CARC officials in meetings with Springovičs in July 1949 and April 1950. CARC officials attacked the Catholic Church as the only Soviet denomination subordinate to a foreign power and demanded separation of papal authority from politics. Concretely, they alleged that Archbishop Springovičs's missive on the Holy Year had not been vetted with the commissioner and constituted an "unfriendly act of political content" ordered by the Vatican. CARC accused Springovičs of adding his voice to "the papal chorus" of Pius who "uses the holy year as protection, a curtain of fog, to hide from the simple people his support for the Anglo-American imperialists in spreading a new world war."[22] Certain party officials, especially in Lithuania, had pressured priests to sign a petition opposing the papal decree, but only 103 priests had signed it. CARC opposed the petition initiative as counterproductive.[23] Perhaps hoping to avoid further deterioration in relations with the Catholic churches under its jurisdiction, CARC initially interpreted the decree as not binding on Soviet Catholics and not being implemented.[24]

Though earlier vested in the relationship with Springovičs, by 1950 CARC faulted him for his disloyalty: his opposition to registration of parishes and demand for a special directive beyond the Lenin separation decrees, his opposition to property agreements with laity as inconsistent with Catholic tradition, and his ties to the Vatican. Not surprisingly, CARC replaced Commissioner Šeškens in Riga with a new one, who distanced himself from Springovičs, reflecting the new line.[25] Summarizing this shift, the new commissioner wrote that Springovičs "has not changed and does not think of changing, and continues his Jesuit line of deceiving Soviet organs. He appears to be loyal and attentive, but in reality he permits all manner of not only disloyal but also hostile betrayals."[26] Giving substance to the new line, in July 1949 CARC ordered a ban on activity outside the republic (especially in Belorussia and Ukraine), curtailment of pilgrimages, elimination of para-church organizations, and the halving of theological seminary enrollments, pending complete elimination of them by 1951.[27]

Unlike with the Lutheran churches, Catholic resistance to registration had not yet been overcome. Large numbers of Catholic parishes remained unregistered as a result. CARC ordered commissioners to act quickly and uniformly to implement this requirement; the LSSR (Latvian Soviet Socialist Republic) government enjoined implementation in two weeks.[28] This opposition now served as a justification for closing parishes and rejecting Catholic efforts to open new parishes.[29] Sixty-five percent of parishes remained unregistered at the beginning of 1949, mostly Catholic; by the end of the year, most had acquiesced to registration.[30]

The new favor enjoyed by Lutherans over Catholics in this period was reflected in CARC policy directives to open Catholic churches "in eastern regions, only if expedient" while, regarding Lutherans, it counseled "not to hinder opening churches in eastern regions."[31] This line continued through the period: for example, in 1952, in Latvia, fourteen Catholic registration requests were rejected and only two approved.[32] Unlike for Lutheran closures, financial collapse was hardly ever the reason for closing Catholic churches.[33]

This shift was also demonstrated in the skewed statistics of clergy decertified or arrested. CARC ordered commissioners not simply to close a parish, but to refuse certification to a priest if "politically compromised."[34] During 1949, in Latvia, twenty-one Catholic, five Baptist, and four Adventist clergy were decertified due to arrest or death, yet only six Lutheran clergy were removed.[35] Moreover, the assault on the Catholic Church was not limited to the Baltics: in the USSR, in 1951, eighty-three Catholic priests were decertified, compared to only three Lutheran pastors.[36]

In this new context, the five Latvian monasteries came into the crosshairs of the regime. Of course, ideologically, the regime had long seen monastic orders as a drain on the labor force, but hesitated to ban them. Now officials sought to close or merge them, converting them for use as a dormitories and polyclinics.[37] In May 1949 the Latvian government acted to merge three of them and move the nunnery from central Riga to rural Aglona, a center of pilgrimage.[38] After the KGB arrested its monks, the Capuchin monastery at Skaistkalne was liquidated in 1949, despite the fact that local officials had no ideas for an alternative use![39]

Integrally connected with the monastery issue was the popular Catholic practice of pilgrimages, also seen by the regime as a sapping economic productivity. Pilgrimages, especially to Aglona, remained extremely popular and involved large numbers of priests, despite all the state's administrative measures to curtail them.[40] The declaration of a Holy Year in 1950 produced even more pilgrimages. Yet the state's own interest on this issue was ambiguous; some local governments even raised monies by charging pilgrims!⁴¹ Alarmed by this trend, in June 1949 CARC ordered pilgrimages to be curtailed and officials pressured Catholic leaders to limit them.⁴² New measures were implemented to curtail pilgrimages to Aglona, both carrots (such as a song competition, circus artists, and sporting events) as well as sticks (such as militia checks on highways and mobilization of party activists). Reports suggest some success in this campaign by 1950: services were shorter, and fewer priests and no nuns participated.⁴³

Probably the clearest blow in the assault on the Catholic Church in this period was the closing of the Catholic theological seminary. Opened in 1946 during the "Springovičs honeymoon," the seminary symbolized the state's tilt toward the Catholics in the early postwar period. Initially officials had sought to use indirect means—Komsomol pressures to dissuade potential students, denial of draft exemptions for students, demands for teaching the USSR Constitution—with the goal of cutting the enrollment in half by 1949 and closing it by 1951.⁴⁴ In late 1949 the new Latvian commissioner also sought to reduce the number of students by requiring prospective students to first obtain authorization from their local government in order to receive a residence permit for Riga. These measures had limited effect, however; ten new students brought the enrollment to forty in 1950.⁴⁵ By late 1949, Moscow moved more decisively to close the seminary. The official pretext for the LSSR Council of Minister's decision in December 1950 was alleged deficiencies revealed in a sanitary inspection of the seminary. But the political motivation is clear from the documentary record citing the seminary's "training of reactionary elements hostile to Soviet power."⁴⁶ The decision was accompanied by press attacks on the seminary director, Strods, and various students of the seminary.⁴⁷

When his protests were fruitless, Strods sought permission to continue theological education by correspondence course, like the Lutherans. CARC approved this in March 1952, but hoped to limit the number of students by eliminating draft deferments for theology students.⁴⁸ The correspondence courses enrolled only sixteen to twenty-four students for biannual eight-week sessions, a far cry from the forty students in residence at the seminary previously.⁴⁹

As director of the seminary, Strods sought to delay its closing and, when unsuccessful, to register the students as assistant priests, which was also rejected by state officials.⁵⁰ Springovičs unsuccessfully requested the reopening of the seminary in 1952. State officials in Riga and Moscow rejected this, maintaining that the Catholic seminary in Kaunas could accommodate the need for theological education.⁵¹ Yet despite its official closing, it apparently continued on an illegal basis to train priests, and parishes proved resilient in supporting seminarians; in the wake of Stalin's passing, it would be reopened.⁵²

Another hot-button issue for the regime regarding Catholics proved to be religious instruction. The Latvian Council of Ministers forbade it on

July 29, 1949.⁵³ The "Springovičs honeymoon" bought Latvian Catholics some time—religious instruction had already been banned in Lithuania and Belorussia in 1948—but ultimately, in April 1949, they and the Lutherans were forbidden from giving organized instruction to youth by Latvian state decree.⁵⁴

In the near term, state policy sought to use Lutheran churches to offset Catholic opposition in Latvia.⁵⁵ Thus, CARC and Latvian officials moved cautiously on the local requests to close Lutheran churches in Latgāle, arguing that the Catholics would see this as a victory and lead to growing Catholic influence.⁵⁶ The Lutheran clergy shortage was producing a growing number of conversions to Catholicism, also "an undesirable trend."⁵⁷ The Latvian commissioner even went so far as to suggest a reorganization of the Catholic Church along more collegial, Lutheran lines!⁵⁸ Arrests of clergy also spiked: in Latvia seven Catholic priests were arrested in 1950, compared to only two Lutheran pastors, with theological professors particularly targeted.⁵⁹

The regime increasingly blocked church administrative appointments of those considered oppositional, as reflected in the commissioner's evaluations (called *characteristika* in the files).⁶⁰ Dulbinskis, chancellor of the Curia and auxiliary bishop, was arrested in May 1949 and sentenced to ten years in a labor camp, leaving the Curia without leadership.⁶¹ As his replacement, the regime opposed Michael Dukalski ("fanatic," "reactionary oriented against Soviet power"), and also Stanislavs Vaikuls ("high profile," "reactionary oriented against Soviet power"), who was arrested in 1950.⁶² Seen by the regime as more accommodating, Strods ("no evidence against Soviet power," "activity directed in loyal relations with Soviet power to maintain cadre of priests") and Valerian Zondaks ("devoted," "closed, no evidence of activity") were forced to assume most of the responsibilities at the Curia and Liepāja Diocese.⁶³ Yet, by 1953, Zondaks would be arrested as well, apparently for his internal criticism of Strods's political activity supporting the regime.⁶⁴

In contrast, the Lutheran churches developed a modus vivendi with the regime. Bishop Turs cooperated with Commissioner Restbergs to avoid political tension and consolidate his control over church decisions. After several delays and meetings with CARC officials, the Latvian Church was permitted to hold a synod again in 1951. Turs consulted closely with CARC officials in Moscow regarding the theme (peace and antifascism) and timing of the synod, moving it to December to accommodate the state regarding outstanding personnel issues and the agenda.⁶⁵ At the synod, the Latvian Church moved to revise its church law to increase the role of the Higher Church Administration (HCA) in naming of pastors, eroding the power of parish governance.⁶⁶ After state criticism, Turs dropped his proposals for a vicar bishop and a bishop's council. With CARC consent, the synod consolidated Turs's authority by selecting "conservative cronies" of Turs to the HCA.⁶⁷

The Political Subservience of the Churches

The Lutheran churches exhibited greater political subservience to the regime than the Catholics. "The sharp stage of political differentiation among clergy is completed," stated CARC Chair Polyansky in his 1949 report, referring to the Lutheran churches.[68] The purges and Gleichschaltung of church leaderships had proceeded faster in Latvia than Estonia, but even in the latter case Moscow felt confident enough to approve a synod ratifying Archbishop Pähn's replacement by Jaan Kiivit. The regime's 1952 characteristika in Kiivit's personnel file describes him as "loyal, thoroughly evaluating the situation.... In connection with the behavior of Kiivit, his transfer to Tallinn was organized and then his promotion to the high post of archbishop."[69] Encouraged by the state, in 1949 Kiivit consulted with Turs regarding the experience of the 1948 Latvian synod that ratified Turs as archbishop.[70]

Fostering this subservience were particular Lutheran vulnerabilities. They continued to be attacked by the state for their alleged complicity with the interwar and Nazi regimes.[71] Moreover, the extensive penetration of the church leadership by KGB informants crippled any resistance to the Stalinist campaign after 1949.[72] In both Latvian and Estonian churches, key positions in the leadership were held by informants of the KGB. Archived Estonian KGB files document that leaders, including bishops Pähn ("Homo"), Kiivit ("Juri I"), Hark ("Ego"), and Pajula ("Rein"), along with other leading officials such as the General Secretary August Leepin ("Parn"), were compromised as informants with the KGB to some extent.[73] This does not mean that they were complete instruments of the KGB—the arbitrary arrests and deportations understandably terrorized all church officials—but it does suggest that autonomous decision-making by the churches was crippled.

Pursuing a long-term strategy, the regime used coercion and manipulation of certain clergy to position them for eventual leadership roles in the churches. For example, Estonian pastor and future archbishop Edgar Hark was blocked from a secular career and directed into church work after his demobilization from the Red Army in this period of high Stalinism.[74] Another future Estonian archbishop, Alfred Tooming, had been arrested in August 1945 by the NKVD and charged with membership in a fascist organization and actions against the Red Army; he spent 1946–1957 in a camp and special exile.[75] Among Latvian Catholics, Julijans Vaivods, future archbishop, remained in Liepāja after Bishop Antonijs Urbšs was evacuated by the German military, and was already being touted for promotion ("authoritative," "progressive-minded," and "loyal to Soviet power").[76]

The political sycophancy and propaganda of the churches reached new heights during this period. For example, all churches, including the Catholics, sent greetings to Stalin on his seventieth birthday in 1949.[77] Both Estonian and Latvian churches continued to endorse participation in the 1950 Soviet elections. However, the Lutheran leaders in both republics did so more publicly and demonstratively. For his part, Springovičs did so via a lower-profile circular letter.[78] Overall, electoral participation was much higher than in the first elections in 1946, although some Baptists and Pentecostals refused to participate.[79]

Sects were increasingly targeted by the regime for monitoring and control, but the regime had an added advantage with the Baptists and Seventh-Day Adventists that it did not have with the Lutherans and Catholics, namely the existence of religious centers that these denominations had in Moscow. The regime was able to use pressure from these co-opted church leaders to discipline their new Baltic outposts. For example, Yakov Zhidkov and Nikolai Levindanto, from the AUCECB in Moscow, were sent to Riga to help promote the regime's preferred candidate for the position of senior presbyter in 1949.[80]

The churches were particularly challenged in this period by the introduction of Stalinist economic policies, particularly collectivization. The Estonian church leadership officially urged the population to support the state's campaign. Under the influence of Bishop Kiivit, the Consistory officially supported collectivization; some pastors even sought to join the new kolkhozes. Even before Pähn's arrest and replacement by Kiivit, the Consistory issued a circular on March 1, 1949, mandating that clergy give rites only to members of their parishes, pay taxes as obliged, and conduct church burials only for those who made such a request while yet alive (even if their relatives desired a religious funeral for the deceased). The Consistory urged pastors to strengthen the believers in their daily civic duty, especially now that Estonia "is subject to foreign propaganda opposed to the USSR."[81]

Turs and the Latvian Lutheran leadership also supported collectivization, even arguing that early Christians also practiced communal ownership of property. To a meeting of the Latvian deans, Turs maintained that "in the economics of the current period we should keep in mind that the early Christian parishes.... stood closer to their God and Savior and are an example and ideal for us."[82] But numerous grassroots clergy opposed the process, and some were arrested. Catholic opposition was more widespread, with clergy having "a negative influence on the less conscious mass of peasants."[83] Turs's accommodation to the new Soviet context was so complete that he apparently even considered converting to the ROC at one point.[84]

Despite these "progressive" positions of the Lutheran leaderships, the regime still did not trust them. Most Latvian church leaders under Turs (e.g., Gustavs Shaurums, Alberts Vitols, Krišjānis Šlosbergs, and Oskars Blumbergs) were described in their characteristika as "bourgeois nationalists" and "fanatics" who had been "members of one or another fascist military organization, such as

Aizsargov [Latvian Home Guard]" during the interwar period.[85] Commissioner Restberg was suspicious of Turs's peace activities, viewing him as envious of the authority of Kiivit, seeking to consolidate his power base, and enlivening religious activity at the parish level by mounting festive services under the pretext of peace and parish jubilees.[86] Moreover, the Latvian authorities were alarmed by Turs's fascination with the ROC and opposed the nascent but growing Lutheran contacts with ROC Bishop Filaret.[87]

Church Institutional Interests and Limiting to Cultic Functions

Having succeeded in registering most parishes and closing significant numbers of them, the regime now pressed to align the churches' activities with Soviet legal practice, namely limiting them to cultic functions and reducing their social role. For example, the status of cemeteries became an issue of dispute: the Baltic tradition of ownership and oversight by the individual parishes proved inconsistent with Soviet law, according to which they were nationalized and under local authority. Latvian government officials proposed an exception to this norm, to permit continued responsibility by the churches, presumably since local governments were reluctant to take on yet another financial obligation. Vetoing this Latvian initiative and rebuffing church objections, the Soviet norm was implemented in the Baltics in 1950.[88] State authorities cited anti-Soviet inscriptions on tombstones as a justification for closing cemeteries.[89] Yet vandalism of cemeteries in Riga and elsewhere increased dramatically after the nationalization.

Activities outside the parish were increasingly limited. In a pattern that would extend to the Lutherans in the future, visitation by Baptist choirs to other parishes incurred the ire of the state officials.[90] Bible hours given by Lutheran pastors did "not constitute normal church service of this cult" and were banned by state order.[91] All charity work by churches, which was traditional for these Western churches, was an anathema to the regime.[92]

Church efforts at pastoral care outside Estonia and Latvia were usually opposed by the state. Lutheran clergy were forbidden from providing pastoral care to Lutherans in the Pskov oblast.[93] Catholic efforts to send a priest to western Ukraine and Rostov-on-Don were similarly rebuffed.[94] Turs's efforts to visit the small Lithuanian Lutheran and Reformed churches were approved by Commissioner Restberg as part of the peace campaign, but provoked objection by the Lithuanian officials.[95]

Certainly a key issue of church institutional interest was the restoration of training of clergy and other church service personnel. As noted in the previous chapter, the churches had unsuccessfully requested approval for theological seminaries, after the closing of their university faculties of theology in 1940. In Latvia, as part of a process to restore the theological institute, Turs requested permission to do a lecture cycle in 1949.[96] Though generally more inclined toward the Lutherans as part of the pivot away from the Catholic Church during this period, the Latvian authorities nonetheless opposed opening a Lutheran seminary at the same time they were closing the Catholic one. The regime also opposed training auxiliary service personnel, such as organists and wardens, as "unnecessary and harmful, since this 'cadre' will be composed of other strata of the population and non-working groups." By 1950, Turs had given up hope for a theological institute, but still hoped for approval of the lecture cycle, with students from Lithuania as well as Latvia. The central authorities in Moscow sought to delay a decision by requesting more information on curriculum, size, and students.

Church requests for publications, such as Lutheran calendars and the Baptist *Bratskii Vestnik*, were now routinely rejected by central authorities, after they had approved them before 1949.[97] CARC Chair Polyansky continued to advocate for them as part of the heightened peace campaign in 1950, but the Ministry of Culture under Voroshilov rejected the request, another indication of the bureaucratic tensions produced by the shift toward hard-line governance.

Also striking in the documentary record is the increased number of cases of vandalism against church buildings and cemeteries reported in this period. It became open season against church property, with little policing by authorities in the context of the new hard-line policy.[98] Most of these crimes, of course, went unsolved.

Impact of the Antireligious Campaign on Clergy and Individuals

The state's campaign sought to undermine the authority of all clergy by attacking individual clergy. In particular, the state sought to use cases of compromised clergy to weaken the relationship between parishioners and the churches. For example, the state sometimes prosecuted pastors for homosexuality, illegal under Soviet law, with the side-effect of sowing dissension among parishioners, some of whom sided with the state and sought to have their rites repeated by unsullied pastors.[99] In another case the state threatened to close a church unless it rejected a temporary pastor sent by the Consistory, but apparently living out of wedlock and alleged to be a drunkard by local officials.

Coercion of clergy continued to be applied: the arrest and imprisonment of clergy grew in this period, particularly affecting Catholic, Baptist, and Adventist clergy.[100] But even among Lutherans, clergy with distinguished records as scholars of theology or religious studies, such as Roberts Feldmanis and Alberts Freijs, were arrested.[101] In some cases the commissioner targeted pastors for arrest by the KGB.[102] Sometimes the KGB arrested pastors despite the support of the commissioner, as in the case of Dean Henn Unt in Vilyandi, Estonia.[103] In some cases, sermons were monitored.

Persistent harassment was applied to many clergy, particularly those who were energetic in carrying out their role as pastors. A particularly brazen case of harassment targeted Pastor Ewald Saag of Rapla.[104] Long known for his activist style, Saag had conducted well-attended cemetery day services. Initially the harassment was mild: disrupting Good Friday services by cutting trees down near his church or delivering a new stove on Christmas Eve. Later, however, he was beaten on the road by thugs dressed in Red Army uniforms.

In some cases, the commissioner argued that he had sought to limit such intimidation of clergy, either due to its illegality or its negative effect on believers. Conflicts between local authorities and the commissioners occurred repeatedly. In Latvia, for example, the commissioner rejected demands by local officials for veto power over the content of worship services and for lists of clergy and parish members.[105] In Estonia, local officials coveted the apartments of prominent church officials, Lembit Tedder and Peter Ilves, and sought their arrest and deportation as kulaks, but they were spared after Kivi intervened.[106]

The state also intensified its antireligious campaign to wean individuals from religion, particularly by using rather crude methods of intimidation and administrative pressure.[107] Local officials widely used administrative actions to reduce participation in the annual cemetery days, a Baltic tradition to commemorate the dead.[108] They sought to forbid the churches from holding these services entirely, despite the standing order from the Estonian commissioner since 1948 to allow one service per year. In some cases local authorities would approve the cemetery day service, but for a different date than requested, giving the churches inadequate time to inform parishioners of the change. Such administrative chicanery was clearly directed at disrupting popular participation in this traditional Estonian custom, under the guise of legal-administrative requirements for official approval of outdoor church services. Joint cemetery days with the ROC were likewise blocked.[109]

Children were a particular target of the antireligious policy. School directors urged pupils not to attend Christmas services.[110] Officials insisted on Adventist children attending school on Saturday, maintaining that "since they were not yet members of the church, the rights of the cult did not apply to children."[111] The "non-organized population," presumably grandparents and nonworking adults, were blamed for the religiosity of children.[112]

Local authorities and the Komsomol sought to pressure youth not to take confirmation.[113] Officials sometimes manipulated work schedules to interfere with confirmation classes. The Komsomol in some cases disrupted confirmation services and demanded lists of confirmands. Not surprisingly, active church members were discriminated against in their careers, especially in the education sphere.[114]

The state's policy toward the churches can hardly be viewed as uniform, even in this period of high Stalinism. With local officials responsible to the republic governmental and party apparatus, but also accountable to the commissioner and CARC, the conflicting lines of authority created built-in opportunities for policy disputes. But divergence from the overriding line was quite limited among officials at various levels and the ideologically charged repression of high Stalinism militated for a hard-line approach by all state officials.

Religious Rites and Church Adherence

Consistent with the antireligious campaign against clergy and individuals was a targeted attempt to constrict church rites per se. As seen earlier, in 1944–1948 the regime had sought to restrict the age of confirmation and dates of confirmation. But it had not sought to eliminate the instruction itself, even though such instruction violated the legal ban on religious teaching of minors. Beginning in 1949, however, the regime sought to prevent such confirmation preparation entirely. It argued that confirmation preparation did not require clergy, but could be conducted by laypersons, and that confirmands at the new legal age of 18 already knew the prayers and Bible texts for confirmation. CARC thus issued a directive in April 1949 to ban such preparation.[115] The republics followed suit with legal directives in June and July 1949. Moscow authorities reckoned cynically that the popular preference for confirmation would collapse in the face of these strictures.[116] Although Kiivit countered that the politically less-reliable sects would benefit at the expense of the Lutherans from the new rule, the Latvian and Estonian churches largely fell into step behind the new policy.

Related actions by the regime sought to reduce participation in church rites.[117] Not surprisingly the authorities refused to publish a catechism for Lutherans and for Catholics. They demanded that Catholics cease use of underage altar boys. Seeking to reduce church weddings, the regime forced churches to surrender their marriage records to ZAGS, the state body in charge of civil marriages.

The arrest of clergy, legal restrictions, and general antireligious campaign took its toll during this period. With the exception of burials, all measures of church adherence dropped precipitously. For example, in Latvia, Lutheran communicants dropped by 26 percent and confirmations by 30 percent between 1948 and 1949.[118] In particular, confirmations declined dramatically in 1949. The decline was greater among Lutherans than Catholics.

Despite this decline in specific religious rites and the administrative measures discussed above, participation in the folk tradition of cemetery days showed remarkable resilience. Notwithstanding the state's limit of one annual celebration per parish, 122,000 participated in Estonia in the peak year of Stalinism, 1952, according to church statistics.[119] CARC became alarmed by this development, but the commissioner sought to dismiss cemetery days as social occasions at which no more than 50 percent of the people listened to the sermon and participated in the church service. Still, officials at all levels began to consider means of curtailing this religious element of popular tradition.

Nor do statistics capture the entire reality. For example, a not inconsiderable number of people began to baptize and confirm their children outside their home parish in order to avoid the repercussions from local authorities. Church leaders even began to urge pastors not to record confirmations in church books to protect the privacy of confirmands.[120] And more youth began to be confirmed in large cities, such as Riga and Tallinn, rather than their hometowns. Articles in the official press and internal state reports indicate that a certain number of members of Communist organizations, particularly the Komsomol, continued to participate in church rites such as confirmation or marriage.[121]

The Estonian Lutheran Church also sought to blunt the state's campaign by linking church rites to active membership in the Church. Under a decree of the Consistory ("On the Ordinary Church Rites of the Evangelical Lutheran Church"), to take effect January 1, 1952, rites were to be administered only to those who regularly attended and contributed to the Church. The Church hoped to stanch the decline in church rites, appealing to the population's traditional religious attachment that was being shaken by the state's atheistic campaign. The Church informally introduced such a requirement in spring 1951, without the approval of the state.[122] The state did not react until late 1951, but then forced the Church to rescind the decree in April 1952, arguing that it violated the Church's new constitution of 1949.[123] Thus the Church failed in its efforts to link performance of religious rites to sustained support for the parish.

An interesting side effect of this loss of church adherence was the defensive tactic of Baltic Lutheran leaders to accentuate the danger of sects. Like the ROC, they hoped to ease state pressure against them by highlighting the allegedly greater political threat from sects. This argument would gain increasing cogency over time with growing immigration to the Baltics, but at this early period was largely ineffective.[124]

The measures to reduce church adherence impelled the state to consider offering alternative rites to the populace. The state realized that some rites, especially the burial service, retained importance for many individuals as well as their surviving family and friends, however secularized they might be. It is worth quoting extensively from a policy statement to the Estonian party leadership by Kivi, arguing for greater attention to the psychological needs of individuals:

> In the battle with religion in this sense great importance is attached to the battle with religious rites, since they are an external sign from which the cult servants draw the conclusion regarding the condition of religiosity among the population. The fight with religious rites may succeed only if more take part

and if there is a deepening among the population of the secular rites instead of the religious rites. This will happen only when all social organizations, in their general work also include this question, but the basic organization which should serve this role is the labor union.... We cannot forget the events in the personal lives of people, as if they are only getting married, the baptism of children and death. Organizations should not omit, but remember that members, their comrades, are very happy if their fellow comrades in organizations note the special occasions in their personal life somehow. Small gifts from organizations or comrades on the occasion of marriage, baptism, make the interested party closer to the organization and to society. Expressions of sympathy on the death in the family and help, this strengthens the unseen ties of people to organizations, to society, but simultaneously weakens the ties to religious habits. If they know over time that the social organizations give attention to their lives, then they will not use the services of the cult servant in this question. Especially important I think is the interference in the matter of burial. If from the speech of the pastor we can make the conclusion that all burials are by church rites, then that is only because in this question until this time there has been insufficient attention. Of course we cannot in a short period destroy church burials, but we can push aside the cult servants. For a certain time we must live with the situation in which church burials as well as secular rites coexist, but we must organize so as to eclipse the church rites so that even the cult servant feels superfluous. Among the population it is necessary to create the understanding that in the case of death each will have a celebratory funeral, which his comrades at work and in organizations will organize for him. Then he will think less about the church and cult servants. Only various church rites tie the large portion of the people to church organizations, with the religious organizations of the Lutheran church, but they may be taken from the church only when they are guaranteed the knowledge that they may get around without the church. The leadership of the church in the form of the decree undertakes measures for the strengthening of its organizational position. This may give it some results in increasing the number of contributors (material basis), but if from our side we take the measures which I discussed above, then this result will not be achieved, but rather they will continue the road to elimination.[125]

The Peace Issue and the Churches' International Ties

The heightened tensions of the Cold War led the regime to seek to mobilize world public opinion for peace, in effect to neutralize Western positions. With their status outside the party-state, the churches would in theory enjoy greater credibility in the West. They would be pressured to participate in ad hoc peace conferences and to make propagandistic contributions to media.

As might be expected, given its role in WWII, the ROC and its Patriarch Aleksei were given pride of place in such actions. The ROC role in USSR peace propaganda began soon after the war and is well documented. Archival records from 1949 indicate its part in spearheading criticism of Western policy by autocephalous Orthodox churches ("instead of the voice of peace and Christian love, from the fortress of Catholicism—the Vatican—and the nest of Protestantism—America—we hear praise for a new war and praising hymns for atomic bombs and weapons dedicated to the destruction of life").[126] In 1949, the ROC, with CROC support, promoted an appeal for a world congress of supporters of peace, the so-called Stockholm Appeal. Sensing itself somewhat sidelined by this CROC-initiated action, CARC sought to include the Armenian Church in the campaign but was overruled by the Central Committee.

After the outbreak of the Korean War, however, other churches were recruited to broaden the base of this peace movement. The August 1950 appeal by the three Orthodox patriarchs (Russian, Georgian, and Armenian) inveighed against nuclear weapons and the "American aggression" against the "undefended people in Korea."[127] The Latvian and Estonian Lutheran churches joined in the peace propaganda. Both endorsed the Stockholm Appeal and the Orthodox Declaration, using statements officially issued by the synods rather than by the respective bishop or church executive body.[128] The Lutheran statements were publicized by the regime using media throughout the Baltic region. Turs sought to limit the damage to his credibility by joining the ROC appeal rather than issuing an independent appeal. In contrast, the Estonian pronouncement was politically blunter, rejecting use of nuclear weapons and attacking "American aggression" against the "defenseless people" of Korea. However, unlike the Latvian appeal that was very deferentially addressed directly to Patriarch Aleksei, the Estonian appeal was addressed to "all Christians of the world," an attempt at political nuance from the ROC.[129] Both Turs and Kiivit participated in the Second Union Peace Conference of Peace Supporters in October 1950, though only Turs was permitted to make an address.[130] Church peace statements were to be distributed in Scandinavia, but not domestically in the USSR.[131]

The Estonian Church also promoted the peace campaign internally. Shortly after taking over as the new bishop in early 1949, Kiivit sent a circular supporting the regime and proposed a special peace service. The commissioner demurred, seeking to "avoid the impression among believers that this contradicts the normal routine of the church."[132] Representatives of the Estonian Church participated in various Moscow conferences devoted to the issue of peace, convening local meetings later to disseminate the results of these propagandistic demonstrations. For example, a special synod called by Kiivit in 1951 "called for all parishes to stand vigilant in defense of peace and pray continuously that God permits the work of the whole world and does not permit the enemies of peace to turn our suffering homeland into a victim of some kind of cruel aggressor."[133] In 1952, at the ROC headquarters at Zagorsk, Kiivit went so far as to attack "Anglo-American imperialism which exploits Christianity for subjecting other peoples and seizing foreign territory."[134]

In Latvia, the peace issue gave Turs a concrete vehicle to pursue his strategy of accommodation. The regime supported this since Turs crafted his public statements in close consultation with the authorities and it hoped to sway opinion in largely Lutheran Scandinavia.[135] He became a regular on the radio and at Moscow conferences. In costly travels around Latvia, Turs celebrated more than eighty services for peace in local churches during 1951; the reports to local synods underscored the churches' overly effusive support for Soviet peace policy.[136] In the early 1950s, Turs, rather than Kiivit, was the primary contact with the German Lutherans.[137] Turs also encouraged pastors to participate in republic-level peace meetings. In planning republic-level conferences on peace, Turs sought preeminent standing for the Lutheran Church. Using peace as the vehicle, Turs was even able to develop contacts with Lutheran parishes in Lithuania.[138]

The Estonian Church also facilitated radio propaganda on behalf of the Soviet position on peace. For example, Consistory member Lembit Tedder gave a radio address in October 1950 criticizing the US "aggression" in Korea and development of the atomic bomb. To be sure, Tedder also cited Bible verses and spoke of "the peace of the Lord" as well as the Estonian Lutheran Church. But Tedder composed the text "politically correctly" using "appropriate instructions" from the state.[139]

For its part, the regime remained ambivalent about the churches' new peace profile. The state did use the issue to evaluate clergy, based on the quality of their participation in various church forums. Some were praised for emphasizing the "true political moment in the international arena, peace movements and the leading role of the USSR." Others were viewed less positively for mixing religious aspects with their political perspectives. Even more questionable were those who emphasized only the religious aspect in peace, "without reference to real life." Most negative in the state's view were those who demonstratively avoided participation in such peace meetings.[140] The state remained suspicious of the authenticity of even the "progressive" clergy. Particularly the republic party leadership held a more hard-line position on the role of the churches in the peace movement. The state would increasingly discount the churches as opportunistic on the peace issue, but nonetheless saw the expediency of indulging the churches' activity.

Archival records suggest that Turs sought to gain leverage with the state from this peace activity. For example, his importance in the peace campaign was sufficient for CARC to veto the Latvian government's request to close the Jesus Parish in Riga.[141] Turs proposed peace declarations in increased print runs of church calendars, with German editions designated for export; the commissioner supported his request but CARC reduced the print runs and rejected a German edition.[142] The Latvian commissioner, Restberg, cynically saw Turs's peace publicity as an effort to use Moscow's emphasis on peace to increase his leverage in Latvia, at the expense of the commissioner's power. He complained of Turs's direct contacts with local governments and Latvian party officials, as well as his overtures to the local ROC bishop. He set as his goal preventing "the spread of wide religious propaganda under the guise of defense of peace."[143] This anxiety that the churches' international role might impinge on achievement of the other goals of the regime would be even more pronounced under Khrushchev.

Catholic pronouncements on peace remained rare and wanting, from the state's viewpoint. Unlike the Lutherans, the Catholic Church refused to sign the appeal of the three Orthodox patriarchs. It did issue a lukewarm statement in support of the Stockholm Appeal, but only after state officials rejected the first version of the communiqué.[144] Seeking to retain his credibility among the faithful, Springovičs continued his pattern of deferring to his subordinates on these issues. More vulnerable, as director of the Catholic seminary, Strods was the only Catholic leader to issue peace pronouncements, but often his drafts were rejected by the regime. His speech at the 1950 Moscow World Peace Conference was seen as "more red" but his proposed radio message for foreign consumption was seen as too religious.[145] His 1951 statement was more laudatory of Stalin.[146] The Catholic Church refused to distribute documents from the World Congress of Peace in Zagorsk, and its statements were more politically perfunctory and religious than Lutheran ones.[147] As in 1950, Springovičs opposed participation in the Zagorsk peace conferences, but agreed to send Strods and Vaivods in 1951 and Strods, Vaivods, and Zondaks the following year.[148] Although the state began to see Strods's role more positively by 1952, its overall evaluation of the Catholic Church remained negative: "It is clear from all recent activities that the higher Catholic clergy has gone the road of non-interference in matters of spreading the idea of peace, if that activity affects Catholics living outside the territory of the LSSR.... Their decisions are guided by directives received from outside.... In this question all goals aim to realize the politics of the Vatican and fulfill its conditions."[149]

In the early Stalin period there were virtually no external Baltic church relations except with the ROC and limited contact between the Estonian and Latvian churches.[150] In this period of high Stalinism, the initial overtures for international church contacts were fruitless. For example, Swedish Baptists tried twice in 1949 to develop an exchange with Soviet Baptists, to no avail; Baptist participation in the World Congress of Baptists was supported by CARC, but vetoed by the CPSU.[151] Voroshilov, Minister of Culture, was vehemently anti-Baptist, commenting that "Baptists (Truman, too) are generally the most hostile and vile sect of all vile sects."[152] The Baltic Lutheran churches sought apostolic legitimization by foreign churches of Turs and Kiivit as archbishops, but the Finnish Church refused the request. As an alternative, the Estonians favored seeking a Lutheran bishop from Eastern Europe, whereas Turs hoped to make arrangements with the Swedish Church. None of these initiatives came to fruition, however.[153] Unsurprisingly, Moscow vetoed offers from the Lutheran Church in America to construct new churches in the USSR, as well as contacts with leftist Catholic delegations, such as German and Czech Catholics.[154]

But the regime's interest in foreign ties started to change in 1952. On June 21, 1952, CARC issued a directive to commissioners to recruit church representatives for foreign travel.[155] CARC commissioners tended to be very cautious: for example, Restberg recommended Turs and Strods only for trips to socialist Eastern Europe.[156] Also indicative of a nascent shift on international ties was Stalin's approval of CARC's request for three new senior personnel to handle these issues in 1951.[157]

The regime's newfound interest was occasioned by the issue of divided Germany. In an early indication in April 1948, CARC had proposed recruiting appropriate Baltic Lutheran church representatives to visit the Soviet Zone in Germany to "acquaint society with religious conditions in the USSR," but this proved a still-born initiative in the context of the Berlin crisis and the Gleichschaltung process in the churches.[158] A more successful engagement with the German churches was the January 1952 visit of German church leader Martin Niemöller to Moscow at the invitation of the ROC, and later that of Bishop Dibelius of Berlin at the invitation of the Baltic Lutheran churches. Although CARC tried to prevent his meeting with Baltic Lutheran leaders, the Germans predicated their trip on such a meeting, citing domestic criticism of the trip.[159] The German church leaders wished to raise primarily issues of German POWs and the widening division of Germany; the Soviets wished to discourage rearmament and NATO membership by West Germany. The German churches invited Turs and Kiivit to their Kirchentag in Hanover in 1952, but the East German Communists and the Soviet Control Commission objected.[160] Intriguing for the future development of Soviet church ties with Germany, however, were the exaggerated statistics about Lutherans provided by CARC to Niemöller and CARC's evasiveness regarding Niemöller's inquiries regarding German POWs.[161]

Bureaucratic Politics

Largely responsible for the new hard-line religious policy was the Agitprop Department of the CPSU Central Committee apparatus, but, even in this period of high Stalinism, policy preferences and implementation were less than uniform. Differences between Moscow and the regions, as well as among bureaucratic actors in Moscow, can be discerned.

Particularly caught in the cross fire during this policy shift were the councils in Moscow, CARC and CROC. Both had invested a certain amount of credibility in cooperation with the church leaderships, and would logically be on the defensive during a repressive period. The CPSU apparatus criticized CROC and its chair, Georgii Karpov, as being too liberal toward the ROC.[162] CARC pressed for more inspectors, fearing weakness of state control in the western regions, with their large non-Orthodox population.[163] In a major dispute in 1952, CARC Chair Polyansky was attacked by both CROC and the Agitprop Department of the CPSU for "poor cadre policy" and policy mistakes, such as approving the Catholic correspondence courses in Latvia and sending the Baptist delegation to an international conference in Denmark. The Agitprop Department accused Polyansky of "being more interested in strengthening religion than the believers themselves."[164] The archival record suggests the key role of Voroshilov (USSR Council of Ministers) in the shift to a hard-line position: his existing antipathy toward the Catholics and to sects was augmented by his advocacy of an almost total ban on opening churches and on formation of central religious bodies by Old Believers, Adventists, and Moslems.[165] Also clear is the absence of informal ties between CARC under Polyansky and the Central Committee apparatus under Zhdanov.[166]

The shift to a hard-line position in Moscow resulted in cross-pressures on the CARC commissioners.[167] The Latvian commissioner, for example, supported Easter song sheets for the Lutherans in 1949, but was sharply criticized by CARC for supporting this request. Estonian party leaders objected to the religious content in peace pronouncements by Bishop Kiivit, whereas the commissioner saw them as necessary for their credibility among believers.[168] As seen in the previous chapter, CARC commissioners often countermanded lenient local decisions to give buildings to parishes that were not registered by the commissioner.

Personnel changes also marked the shift toward a hard-line policy. In October 1948, CARC replaced its Latvian commissioner, Šeškens, seen as too identified with cooperation with Springovičs and Catholics after 1944 and not complying with CARC policy.[169] His replacement, Restberg, wasted no time distancing himself from the policy of Šeškens.

Tensions between republics, as well as between CARC and the KGB, were also evident in this period. For example, the Latvian and Lithuanian commissioners engaged in recriminations regarding the role of Lithuanian Old Believers in Latvia.[170] As noted above, they also quarreled about any overture by Latvian Lutherans to Lithuanian Lutherans. CARC and the KGB disagreed over the number of parishes permitted per clergy. Seeing the issue legalistically, CARC insisted on a maximum of one parish per registered clergy. The KGB, concerned that parishes without clergy would continue underground even if deregistered, argued for permitting more than one parish per clergy.[171]

Still another major bureaucratic fissure that would widen further in the late 1950s was that between CARC and CROC. Chair Karpov began to agitate in 1951 for a single council, arguing that CARC was too lenient on the churches, failed to consult, and diverged on foreign policy. Karpov claimed that his council had succeeded in co-opting the ROC. A single council, he argued, would also be more effective in using the churches for Soviet foreign policy. At this point, the CPSU leadership was unwilling to concede Karpov's position, which presumed cooperation with the church leaderships.[172]

Another bureaucratic disagreement developed between the Ministry of Foreign Affairs (MFA) and CARC, a relationship that would become more complex after 1958. However, even in this late Stalin period, differences can be discerned.[173] For example, MFA wished to promote contacts between the independent Protestant churches in Eastern Europe (e.g., Reformed Church in Hungary) and those in the USSR. But CARC argued that these Protestant churches were too weak in the USSR to be useful as role models for the East Europeans. On the other hand, CARC endorsed a positive response by Turs to Niemöller's overtures as a means of hindering German remilitarization; MFA opposed such contacts.

Thus tentative international ties of the churches, virtually absent in the 1944–1948 period, were now possible, but only in the context of the peace imperative in this period of extreme East-West tension, enticing church accommodation to the regime. During the period of high Stalinism, the rewards for such cooperation with the state were meager indeed. More traditional international contacts were largely impossible, until the German question partially opened a window.

Summary and Conclusion

By the end of this period, state officials were claiming major success in their religious policy, as evidenced by declining church adherence, attributing this to the broader socioeconomic development (collectivization, financial collapse of the churches, and better mass-political work).[174] The state also achieved success by bringing the churches largely into conformity with Soviet law regarding registration of parishes. Related issues, such as how to deal with minor Protestant groups like the Herrnhuters and Methodists, were resolved. The regime had put the churches on the defensive in terms of their institutional interests as well, especially as indicated by closure of many parish churches, new limits on theological education, and reduction of religious publications, particularly those related to religious instruction (confirmation).

The heightened antireligious campaign sought to undermine the authority of the clergy and in particular woo the youth away from religious beliefs and church adherence. As a result, confirmation levels plummeted, although certain national traditions (e.g., cemetery days) and particular rites (e.g., church burial services) remained popular.

The Lutheran leadership was largely *gleichschaltet*: the bishops surrounded themselves with reliable church officials, supported the peace campaign of the state, and were unable to protect their clergy, who were subject to increasing intimidation and arrest. The Catholic Church retained more autonomy than the Lutheran, but the relatively favorable policy toward Archbishop Springovičs in Latvia was a major casualty of the new hard-line approach. The Catholic Church refused to accommodate the peace policy of the regime and was subjected to the regime's attack on the Vatican. Despite the dramatic decline in Lutheran rites, as to closure of actual parishes and decline in clergy, the state's hard-line policy during late Stalinism hurt the Catholics and Baptists, along with the ROC, more than Lutherans.[175] In 1951, in the USSR, the Catholics lost eighty-three clergy, the Lutherans only three. High-level official contacts with the Catholic leadership practically came to a standstill.

International ties of the churches were initially almost impossible in this early stage of the Cold War, but, as a result of Soviet efforts to promote West German neutrality, tentative contacts between Baltic and German Lutherans became possible. Though the harsh policy of high Stalinism left little room for major bureaucratic disputes among state officials—indeed, Moscow orchestrated significant personnel changes at the level of the republic commissioners—the archival record reveals cross-pressures between CARC and the CPSU, as well as between Moscow and the republic level, concomitant with the policy shift. Such differences would become more pronounced over time, as Soviet foreign policy and Baltic distinctiveness would increasingly affect religious policy.

Explaining the religious policy during this period of high Stalinism is in many respects easier than for other periods: the totalitarian impulse to subordinate any social organization to the control of the party, and the ideological dictate to inculcate scientific atheism, clearly determined most of the policy measures in the Baltic cases under study. The two tracks of state policy were aligned in this period: on the one hand, atheistic propaganda to abandon religion and the pressure to join mobilization organizations such as Komsomol; on the other hand, curtailing the institutional interests of the churches (closure of churches, theological education, religious instruction, and confirmation). There was little basis for compromise between church and state other than political sycophancy, which the suborned church leaderships provided. In this context of repression, however, confession still mattered: the Catholic Church proved a more challenging opponent to the regime, less penetrated by informants and retaining a more coherent position due to its hierarchical organization. The stance of the Catholic Church on issues of peace was also less conformist than that of the Lutherans. Yet, as revealed in the case of the closed theological institute and the measures against monasteries and pilgrimages, the Catholic Church also lost more ground institutionally than the Lutherans in this period.

Making the political and ideological explanation less compelling, however, is the evidence of political differences in the apparat, reflecting bureaucratic priorities and interests: the KGB and CARC sparred over the registration process of clergy and parishes; the MFA and CARC did not see eye to eye on contacts with German churches; and divergences between CARC and CROC widened. Even during high Stalinism, the party was not monolithic, despite the apparent shared goal of marginalizing the churches. Transnational ties, another explanatory factor considered in this study, provided little leverage for the Lutheran churches and, in the case of the Catholic Church and the Vatican, actually worsened an already fraught relationship with the state. The dramatic decline in church adherence during this period suggests a growing disconnect between nation and religion in Soviet Estonia and Latvia, but the continued popular observance of certain quasi-religious practices, such as cemetery days, was a harbinger that cultural Christianity retained a national appeal.

Notes

1. GARF.6991.3.8, l. 154–55. Voroshilov of the CM USSR ordered CARC to get a handle on the growth or dying out of religion as "the main task of the Council."

2. GARF.6991.3.68, l. 171. In 1950 it rejected all 461 applications to open parishes.

3. LVA.1448.1.3, l. 5–6. Turs appeals directly to Moscow to prevent the merger of two parishes in Saldus. LVA 1448.1.3, l. 6. The commissioner supports closure, arguing that Turs will accept the merger. Earlier the commissioner had taken his procedural objections to the Komsomol laying claim to the Saldus church directly to the Latvian government, but cynically indicated delaying closure until after the upcoming elections. See LVA 1448.1.3, l. 5.

4. LVA.1448.1.3, l. 31, 34. In 1950, the local officials proposed closing or converting Catholic churches in Preili (grain storage) and Rezekne (movie theater), but CARC balked at this. LVA.1448.1.3, l. 46, indicating CARC's skepticism of the proposal. Only later, in September 1951, did the Latvian CM fall in line behind Moscow and rejected the requests as "inexpedient," according to LVA 1448.1.3, l. 73–74. Similarly, the Latvian Agricultural Academy sought unsuccessfully to pressure an Adventist parish to share a Lutheran one, so that it might seize the Adventist church building; this was vetoed by Restberg. See LVA.1448.1.249, l. 10–11.

5. LVA.1448.1.3, l. 26, l. 17, 66–67. The commissioner made the case that the Jesus Church was well attended, meeting its tax obligations, and that the nearby Jaani Church could not physically accommodate both parishes. Countering this, Latvian leaders Lācis and Kalnberzin argued that no major reconstruction was needed and that thirteen Lutheran churches sufficed for Riga, in LVA.1448.1.249, l. 78.

6. LVA.1448.1.1, l. 18, 19, 21. LVA.1448.1.246, l. 101–2, indicated that, by November, the arrest of the pastor and the actions of the local governments had created a fait accompli for the commissioner, who supported closing the church.

7. ERAF.1.14a.37, l. 162–64.

8. LVA.1448.1.244, l. 48; LVA.1448.1.1, l. 16, approving the seizure of the monastery.

9. LVA.1448.1.246, l. 111. In the last quarter of 1949, four Lutheran churches were closed based on the inability to pay taxes and their pastors.

10. LVA.1448.1.250, l. 14–15. Describing the Finance Ministry stance as contentious, the commissioner submitted some pastors' complaints to Moscow for correction.
11. GARF.6991.3.76, l. 83.
12. LVA.1448.1.1, l. 10 and l. 30. CARC concurred rapidly with the CM Latvia proposal of April 1949.
13. LVA.1448.1.246, l. 85–86.
14. ERAF.1.72.26, l. 206. Opposing the Hiiuma CP leadership for closing churches, Commissioner Kivi argued that "in Hiiuma raion, where Baptists are strong and active, you cannot put Baptists and Lutherans in one building.... In that case you create a kitchen, where the conservative sects and relatively progressive Lutheran are located together, in which case the Lutherans will come under attack as less active and more sober."
15. The move was planned by the commissioner, Kivi, in late 1949. According to him, the action would achieve the goals of reducing the number of Baptist churches from ten to three in Tallinn, the number of Baptist deacons from seventy to twenty-one, and the number of services by six, thereby effecting a decline in believers. The Council of Ministers and Central Committee of the CP ESSR found the action "desirable." ERAF.1.14a.37, l. 200–202. The commissioner proudly proclaimed the decline of baptisms at Oleviste following the merger. ERAF.1.72.26, l. 260. The goal to "curtail direct religious propaganda" by sects was confirmed by him in ERA.R-1989.2.9, l. 34. On Baptist church closures and the Oleviste case, see also Pilli, *Dance or Die*, 38–41.
16. RGASPI.17.132.111, l. 55.
17. LVA.1448.1.1, l. 2.
18. LVA.270.2.5716, l. 27. Restberg indicates support for reversing these actions in several districts in Latgāle. Talonen, *Church under the Pressure*, 225–29.
19. ERAF.1.72.26, l. 192; ERA.R-1989.2.19, l. 53–54. Pastor Saar, returning from prison, made claim on the widow of the deceased Commissioner Kivi for the piano in 1957.
20. RGASPI.17.132.285, l. 1–3.
21. GARF.6991.3.473, l. 268–69. Lācis, Kalnbērziņš, and Pelše all supported liquidating the Catholic seminary, reducing the Curia, and curtailing pilgrimages. CARC representative Karpov reported that Secretary Pelše was spearheading the new ideological campaign. The three Latvian leaders "were less negative toward the Lutherans than the Catholics and sects."
22. LVA.1448.1.246, l. 64–66; quotation from GARF.6991.3.473, l. 274–77.
23. In January 1950 Chair Polyansky argued that the petition was an untimely response to the July 1949 papal decree and not advisable unless part of a general campaign against the Vatican. RGASPI.17.132.285, l. 5–6 and l. 15–17 (text of petition and signatures).
24. GARF.6991.3.68, l. 15–20. CARC relied particularly on Bishop Strods, citing him as indicating no order had been given by the Vatican to implement the decree. CARC saw the papal decree as focused primarily on the East European peoples' democracies.
25. The replacement of Šeškens by Restberg in October 1949 is noted in LVA.1448.1.244, l. 46. Restberg delayed an introductory meeting with Springovičs.
26. GARF.6991.3.473, l. 282.
27. GARF.6991.3.473, l. 67–68.
28. GARF.6991.3.473, l. 48.
29. GARF.6991.3.61, l. 59, in which CARC seeks "by means of closing, in stages, in the first instance, those violating the demands of Soviet law, especially Catholic and Baptist churches." Forty-eight parishes remained unregistered by late 1951; the commissioner

rejected registration since "they are not considered parishes, lacking premises, property or other signs indicative of a cult." LVA.1448.2.249, l. 89.

30. LVA.1448.1.246, l. 91; LVA.1448.1.247, l. 18 and 20. "Guided by the strict orders of the CARC we did not register a single religious congregation," Commissioner Restberg reported in 1950.

31. GARF.6991.3.53, l. 42–45. Others who were relatively favored for opening churches were Moslems, Armenians, and Old Believers; Baptist and Adventist requests to register churches were to be refused.

32. LVA.1448.1.250, l. 88–89.

33. LVA.1448.1.247, l. 67.

34. GARF.6991.3.473, l. 67–68.

35. LVA.1448.1.246, l. 115. Net losses of clergy were somewhat lower due to newly certified clergy, but the losses of the Catholic Church were still disproportionate to those of the Lutherans.

36. GARF.6991.3.76, l. 33–36.

37. GARF.6991.3.61, l. 80; LVA.1448.1.244, l. 64–65 regarding the decision to eliminate the Capuchin Monastery in Riga. Trups-Trops, "Römisch-Katholische Kirche," Teil 3, 62–64.

38. LVA.1448.1.246, l. 50–51; Trups-Trops, "Römisch-Katholische Kirche," Teil 2, 92.

39. LVA.1448.1.247, l. 57.

40. Active measures taken by the state to deter participation included refusing food and use of cars or horses by the pilgrims, according to LVA.1448.1.246, l. 74–75.

41. LVA.1448.1.247, l. 45–46. Citing the case of Preili, in 1950 the commissioner requested that CARC order a limitation of commerce during pilgrimages. The KGB intervened to stop this.

42. LVA.1448.1.246, l. 96, citing the June 1949 CARC decisions. LVA.1448.1.246, l. 49; Trups-Trops, "Römisch-Katholische Kirche," Teil 3, 67–68.

43. LVA.1448.1.1, l. 43–47; LVA.1448.1.249, l. 72; LVA.1448.1.247, l. 50–53.

44. GARF.6991.3.61, l. 59–60; GARF.6991.3.473, l. 59–60.

45. LVA.1448.1.247, l. 53–54. Frustrating the plan to squeeze the seminary, the church made repairs to meet code and local authorities gave documentation for residency permits in Riga for students.

46. CARC concurrence with the decision of the Latvian authorities is found in GARF.6991.3.66, l. 80–81. The rationale for closure included that the seminar was planned for eighty students, but had normally enrolled only forty-five, and that the Latvian Catholic Church met its reduced needs with existing priests. LVA.1448.1.247, l. 74–75. The commissioner suggested that Riga seminarians might continue instead at Kaunas seminary in Lithuania, enter the workforce, or change to state higher education institutions. Trups-Trops, "Römisch-Katholische Kirche," Teil 2, 117–19.

47. LVA.1448.1.247, l. 5–7, discussing the allegations that the premises did not meet code, as well as the attack by a former seminarian against priests and the seminary, printed in *Soviet Youth* (15 March 1950). An entire archival file (LVA.1448.1.248) is devoted to the Latvian decision to close the seminary.

48. An entire archival file (LVA.1448.1.251) is devoted to the decision to open the correspondence courses. Earlier the military was opposed to taking Catholic seminarians into the Red Army, but now became amenable to it as they were to be placed in construction battalions, similar to those created later in the GDR. LVA.1448.1.250, l. 3. In 1952, the

Church requested sixteen deferments, but even the six that CARC endorsed were rejected by the Soviet military. GARF.6991.3.476, l. 42–43, 56. CARC requested the exemptions, and the military rejected them. CARC initially appealed the rejected deferments, but by October 1952 fell in line behind the military and rejected the deferments, according to LVA.1448.1.251, l. 3.
  49. LVA.1448.1.250, l. 36–37.
  50. LVA.1448.1.249, l. 3–6.
  51. GARF.6991.3.476, l. 109–110; GARF.6991.3.476, l. 115–16 (CARC's rejection).
  52. LVA.1448.1.249, l. 14–15. After several years, the regime reversed its decision to close the seminary. GARF.6991.3.476, l. 187. Restberg was urged to study reopening the seminary in 1953.
  53. LVA.1448.1.246, l. 79. This action occurred shortly after Vice-Chair Sadovsky's visit to Latvia, indicating the role of CARC in this crackdown.
  54. GARF.6991.3.68, l. 168.
  55. LVA.270.2.5716, l. 27. The commissioner argued: "In the conditions known to you, these measures at this time would not be desirable" and urged the Latvian Council of Ministers to reverse local decisions to close Lutheran churches in Karsava and Ludzens.
  56. GARF.6991.3.473, l. 96. CARC Chair Polyansky indicates the differing line in Catholic regions: "in Latgāle, where there are many Catholics, measures intended for small Lutheran parishes, may appear as a positive moment for Catholics, who without doubt would use it to attract Lutherans into the orbit of their influence." But the commissioner realized the limits of Lutheran potential in this Catholic area, due to lack of funds and members to restore damaged churches.
  57. LVA.1448.1.244, l. 52–53.
  58. LVA.1448.1.249, l. 66.
  59. LVA.1448.1.247, l. 75–81. As head of the seminary, Strods attempted to negotiate with the KGB for their release; LVA.1448.1.244, l. 50. LVA.1448.1.246, l. 25–26, discussing cases of priests accused of "not doing useful work" or being kulaks.
  60. LVA.1448.1.1, l. 31, regarding the arrest of Dulbinskis. The commissioner's handwritten characteristika are found on the reverse side of the papers and autobiographies filed by all Catholic priests with his office, in GARF.6991.3.473, l. 97–153.
  61. Trups-Trops ("Römisch-Katholische Kirche," Teil 2, 97–99) indicates he refused to denounce the Church or become an informant, whereupon he was accused of collaborating with the German military.
  62. LVA.1448.1.247, l. 57.
  63. LVA.1448.1.246, l. 47–48.
  64. LVA.1448.1.252, l. 33. Trups-Trops, "Römisch-Katholische Kirche," Teil 2, 99–106.
  65. Internal church deliberations and communications with CARC are found in LVA.1448.1.187, l. 28–30 and l. 31–33. LVA.1448.1.3, l. 83–84 details the meeting with CARC Chair Polyansky at which Turs vetted issues for approval.
  66. LVA.1448.1.187, l. 28–29.
  67. LVA.1448.1.249, l. 21; LVA.1448.1.187, l. 75–99, for the protocol on the synod, particularly election results on l. 96.
  68. GARF.6991.3.61, l. 112.
  69. ERA.R-1989, no opis, Personnel Files of CARC Commissioner, ESSR, accessed 1993.
  70. LVA.1448.1.246, l. 51.

71. In 1953, songbooks from the Nazi period with nationalistic songs were discovered in St. Paul's Church, Riga, confiscated by the state, and used to admonish Archbishop Turs. LVA.1448.1.252, l. 39.

72. LVA.1448.1.247, l. 77. Šlosbergs, general secretary of the HCA of the Latvian Church, was a regular informant to the Latvian commissioner and likely a KGB collaborator as well.

73. Jürjo, *Pagulus*, 154–74. Jürjo indicates that the KGB claimed thirteen agents by 1947. According to Altnurme (*History*, 115) six of seven new members of the Estonian consistory in 1949 were agents. Altnurme ("Estnische Evangelisch-Lutherische Kirche," 233–43) reviews Jürjo's evidence (e.g., reports by church informants after international trips) and the controversy over complicity.

74. ERA.R-1989.2.12, l. 59–60. Commissioner Kivi was ambivalent about the effects of blocking Hark's preferred career, "I consider it incorrect that in relation to Hark, conditions were created which forced him to enter church service, so that he could later be useful to fit another work and later still a propagandist against the church."

75. ERAF.129SM.1.25217, regarding the indictment, trial, and conviction of Tooming by the secret police in Sverdlovsk.

76. GARF.6991.3.473, l. 131; Trups-Trops, "Römisch-Katholische Kirche," Teil 1, 97.

77. LVA.1448.1.246, l. 110. Unlike the Catholics, the Lutheran churches consulted with the commissioner regarding the greetings.

78. LVA.1448.1.247, l. 4–5, 8.

79. LVA.1448.1.247, l. 72–73; LVA.1448.1.246, l. 23. Strods mustered the seminary students to vote, despite the fact that it was being closed.

80. LVA.1448.1.246, l. 31.

81. Estonian Lutheran Circular no. 1/119 (March 1, 1949), cited in ERA.R-1989.2.12, l. 63–64.

82. LVA.1448.1.1, l. 66–71. The agenda for the meeting included the item "On the Idea of Socialization and Public Property in the early Christian Period and the Realization of this Idea in our Time."

83. GARF.6991.3.68, l. 176; LVA.1448.1.246, l. 46.

84. LVA.1448.1.250, l. 6–7. Talonen (*Church under the Pressure*, 276–83) argues that in this Turs "deserted the entire political territory previously occupied by the church."

85. GARF.6991.3.473, l. 155–93 for the characteristika of all Lutheran leaders. LVA.1448.1.250, l. 137–39. Major leaders recruited by Turs, such as deans Alfons Vetsmanis, Peteris Kleperis, and Wilhelm Migla, were implicated by the regime.

86. LVA.1448.1.250, l. 72, 75; LVA.1448.1.250, l. 130–33. Turs increasingly lobbied directly with local and republic officials when the commissioner sought to discourage these efforts to use peace as a vehicle for parish mobilization. Turs sought to purchase a gold cross, such as Kiivit wore. The commissioner began to object to some of Turs's appointments as well.

87. LVA.1448.1.250, l. 15.

88. LVA.1448.1.2, l. 7, 27–34, referencing the CARC decision and Latvian decree. Turs's futile objection is recorded in LVA.1448.1.247, l. 37. Talonen, *Church under the Pressure*, 230.

89. The commissioners of CARC and CROC both objected to the exception for church cemeteries, claiming this violated the Soviet decree of 7 Dec. 1918, "On Cemeteries and Burials," according to LVA.1448.1.2, l. 22 and LVA.1448.1.3, l. 54–63. The Riga Executive Committee decree of 11 July 1951 called for "greater controls" due to vandalism.

90. LVA.1448.1.247, l. 37. The regime used the Moscow Baptist leadership as leverage to implement this action over Baltic churches.
91. LVA.1448.1.246, l. 97.
92. LVA.1448.1.2, l. 14. Even assistance for the disabled and orphans was taboo.
93. GARF.6991.3.58, l. 118. Turs informed Pskov officials of the naming of Leons Taiwans as pastor in Pokrov Parish, Pskov Oblast. GARF.6991.3.58, l. 117. Pskov officials decried this "arbitrary behavior" of Turs as well as Kiivit regarding an unregistered parish and asked CARC for clarification. Polyansky (8 June 1949) directed the two commissioners to warn of this "impermissible activity" by Lutheran leaders. That did not resolve matters, since the parish appealed directly to CARC to accept Taiwans, according to LVA.1448.1.2, l. 41. Taiwans was evaluated negatively by state officials based on his religious views on peace.
94. LVA.1448.1.1, l. 15, on rejecting a priest to Rostov-on-Don; LVA.1448.1.250, l. 45 and LVA.1448.1.247, l. 55–56, on rejecting priests to two parishes in Ukraine.
95. GARF.6991.3.476, l. 33.
96. LVA.1448.1.1, l. 4, l. 50–51; LVA.1448.1.2, l. 25; LVA.1448.1.247, l. 12.
97. RGASPI.17.132.285, l. 188–89; RGASPI.17.132.285, l. 190; Trups-Trops, "Römisch-Katholische Kirche," Teil 3, 91–92.
98. LVA.1448.1.247, l. 60 documents vandalism by youth in several Latvian churches. In 1952, the commissioner reported that the police had solved only two of five reported cases of vandalism. See LVA.1448.1.250, l. 50.
99. ERA.R-1989.2.9, l. 93–94.
100. LVA.1448.1.247, l. 5, 11, 14, and 17 document the arrests across all denominations in early 1950. Trups-Trops ("Römisch-Katholische Kirche," Teil 2, 106–11) indicates eighty-one of one hundred forty priests in Latvia were arrested.
101. Feldmanis and Freijs were arrested by the KGB and charged with anti-Soviet activity in connection with foreign ties, according to LVA.1448.1.247, l. 37 and l. 80. Remmel (2013) cites statistics in Estonia during the1941–1953 period.
102. ERAF.1.72.26, l. 196. The commissioner provided evidence to the KGB of the distribution of brochures with Bible verses by an Adventist, Willi Noemmik, after the head of the Adventists in Estonia implicated Noemmik. Talonen (*Church under the Pressure*, 273–75) notes that Feldmanis was accused of criticizing Komsomol membership.
103. ERA.R-1989.2.12, l. 57. Kivi cited the local Communist Agitprop officials' positive view of Unt regarding collectivization, but concluded cravenly "Unt's anti-Soviet activity was masked by an external loyalty."
104. ERA.R-1989.2.9, l. 83–84. The predations against Saag produced sympathy for him and a doubling of attendance at cemetery days in 1953.
105. LVA.1448.1.246, l. 32.
106. ERA.R-1989.2.12, l. 58.
107. Remmel ("Believers, Human Rights") cites ninety-eight articles of atheistic propaganda in the Estonian press between 1945 and 1953.
108. LVA.1448.1.247, l. 36.
109. LVA.1448.1.250, l. 48.
110. LVA.1448.1.244, l. 54. "Directors of some schools limited themselves to only warning on eve of the holiday that students should not go to church."
111. LVA.1448.1.250, l. 54–55.
112. LVA.1448.1.250, l. 137–38.

113. LVA.1448.1.247, l. 59–60, documenting actions by local and Komsomol officials. ERAF.1.72.26, l. 167, documenting the 1951 Komsomol attack in Turi.

114. See the Riga Agitprop official's stance in LVA.1448.1.53, l. 19.

115. RGASPI.17.132.111, l. 54–55; LVA.1448.1.1, l. 52 and l. 65–71; ERAF.1.14a.37, l. 122–124.

116. GARF.6991.3.61, l. 133–37. CARC's cynical view of confirmation is insightful: it remains a "powerful weapon of propaganda in the hands of Lutheran pastors, but should not be considered a sign of deep religious feelings. Most youth go to confirmation according to the wishes of parents."

117. GARF.6991.3.476, l. 194–95 and GARF.6991.3.476, l. 269, rejecting the Catholic catechism. LVA.1448.1.247, l. 9, indicating rejection of the Lutheran catechism. CARC criticism of implementation of the ban on underage youth in services, in LVA.1448.1.249, l. 70. Latvian KGB officials requested support of the commissioner in securing church compliance with turning over birth and marriage records, in LVA.1448.1.3, l. 38, with the commissioner's note warning Turs.

118. Talonen, *Church under the Pressure*, 245–47; LVA.1448.1.246, l. 37, 90; ERA.R-1989.2.9, l. 19–23. In Estonia, baptisms dropped 48 percent from 1947 to 1952, constituting less than 25 percent of the newborn cohort. Church marriages dropped 55 percent in the same period. To be sure, some individual parishes managed to hold their own, such as the Jaani and Kaarli parishes in Tallinn and the Vastselina, Rapina, and Rapla parishes in rural Estonia.

119. ERA.R-1989.2.9, l. 23–27. Later the state would introduce a secular equivalent of cemetery days.

120. RGASPI.17.132.497, l. 45–46 (CARC reporting to Mikhail Suslov in the Central Committee); LVA.1448.1.250, l. 49. To stanch the decline in confirmations, Turs discontinued registering them in church books and transferred records to individuals' homes. He also discontinued recording communicants.

121. ERA.R-1989.2.9, l. 18. The commissioner railed against "hidden participation of some Komsomol members in confirmation, which shows the weakness and superficiality of the ideological-political work of the Komsomol organizations, demonstrates that they inadequately indoctrinate their young members and do not study with them."

122. ERAF.1.72. 26, 1. 236. Pastor Stillverk of the Holy Ghost parish in Tallinn was apparently an informant, since he told the state that Kiivit had given an informal order to link rites with active membership already in April 1951. The number of contributors in his parish increased from 1,191 in 1950 to 2,621 in 1951, apparently as a result of this new policy of the Church.

123. ERAF.1.72.26, l. 231–35. The incident caused considerable consternation in Moscow and criticism of the commissioner by both CARC and the Estonian party. Commissioner Kivi rebutted the attacks on him by CARC, maintaining that CARC had not given him guidance and that Bishop Kiivit had secretly given the directive without his knowledge. ERAF.1.72.26, l. 239. Communist party secretary Leonid Lentsman noted that Commissioner Kivi "made a big mistake allowing the decree to be approved without informing the CC or CARC."

124. RGASPI.17.132.111, l. 146–48; LVA.1448.1.1, l. 68. An ROC mission center for priests to fight sects was rejected, with concurrence by Voroshilov and Malenkov.

125. ERAF.1.72.26, l. 221–22.

126. RGASPI.17.132.109, l. 51–54; RGASPI.17.132.109, l. 57–58, 66. With its leading role among Armenians globally, the Armenian Church was eventually to become more prominent in Soviet foreign policy, but in 1949 Agitprop rejected a special publication of its appeal.

127. GARF.6991.3.68, l. 202–3.
128. LVA.1448.1.247, l. 33–34; GARF.6991.3.68, l. 54–67, indicating all churches joining the Stockholm Appeal. GARF.6991.3.71, l. 25–28, includes copies of all non-Orthodox responses to the Orthodox Appeal.
129. GARF.6991.3.68, l. 204–6.
130. GARF.6991.3.68, l. 262–65. Unlike Turs, however, Kiivit did not give a speech at this conference, reflecting the preferential position accorded Turs in this period. LVA.1448.1.247, l. 77–79, discussing Turs's speech and its resonance.
131. GARF.6991.3.68, l. 137. A handwritten note in the archival record indicates that the CC staff approved Scandinavian distribution but objected to publication of the Latvian Lutheran peace appeal in the Soviet press.
132. ERAF.1.14a.37, l. 136–37. Reports from clergy informants to the state indicated that parishioners were upset by the Kiivit circular, walking out of services during its reading and suggesting Kiivit take up Agitprop work.
133. ERAF.1.72.26, l. 246.
134. ERA.R-1989.2.17, l. 146. See also *Conference in Defence of Peace*.
135. LVA.1448.1.249, l. 113. CARC Chair Polyansky supported Turs's activity for peace "despite the fact that the propaganda intertwines with his church work and does not have the typical form of propaganda of the fight for peace conduct by Soviet and social organs."
136. LVA.1448.1.3, l. 51–54; in Cēsis and Riga Region in LVA.1448.1.186, l. 19, 40.
137. Voroshilov met with Polyansky on 21 February 1951, as noted in GARF.6991.3.8, l. 229–30. Niemöller's overture to Kiivit was rejected by both CARC and the Soviet government, in favor of Turs. This was to change by the early 1960s.
138. LVA.1448.1.249, l. 90–91, l. 93–96; LVA.1448.1.3, l. 18. Seeking to check Turs's ambitions on the peace issue, the Latvian government rebuffed his bold request for a large Lutheran delegation to the republic-level conference and did not select him for the Third All-Union Peace Conference in 1952. LCVA.181.3.29, l. 136. The Lithuanian commissioner approved this, unusual given the bureaucratic caution between republics, but criticized Lithuanian Lutheran participation at the December 1951 Latvian synod, just as the Latvian commissioner had vetoed Old Believer contacts in Lithuania.
139. ERAF.1.72.26, l. 16–21. Although the Soviet Radio Committee had originally requested Archbishop Kiivit for the propaganda address, he was "sick outside of Tallinn," perhaps a small signal of independence from him.
140. LVA.1448.1.250, l. 17. In Latvia, Kalnins, Taiwans, and Augstkalns were seen as avowing that the "fight for peace must be led by believers, since if led by atheists it will not be successful." ERAF.1.72.26, l. 247–50. Differentiating based on similar criteria, the Estonian commissioner viewed Varik, Tooming, and Stillverk as most positive; mixing religion with the political were Hark, Vatter, and Roosvalt; downplaying the political were Põld, Terasmas, and Kannukene; most negative were Soosar, Sild, and Pohlamets, who made no mention of "real life."
141. GARF.6991.3.76, l. 123–24. CARC argued that closing the parish was not "politically expedient, since ... Archbishop Turs is a member of the Soviet Committee for the Defense of Peace and has a loyal position toward the Soviet government."
142. GARF.6991.3.474, l. 342; LVA.1448.1.249, l. 1–2.
143. LVA.1448.1.250, l 72—73, 75, 81; LVA.1448.1.249, l. 93–94.
144. GARF.6991.3.473, l. 292–95. The first draft emphasized praying for peace; the second more directly supported the Stockholm Appeal. Springovičs utilized a communiqué instead

of a more authoritative episcopal letter to the parishes. LVA.1448.1.247, l. 56, on the Catholic refusal to join the Orthodox Appeal.

145. LVA.1448.1.249, l. 120–21.

146. LVA.1448.1.3, l. 95–100; Trups-Trops, "Römisch-Katholische Kirche," Teil 3, 52–54.

147. GARF.6991.3.475, l. 61–62; GARF.6991.3.475, l. 64–65. LVA.1448.1.2, l. 62, cites the perfunctory Catholic telegram to the 1950 Peace Conference: "We greet the Congress of Peace for the world, wish you success in the prevention of war and pray for peace in the whole world." LVA.1448.1.4, l. 63–64, notes that Strods offers no recipients for the 1952 Zagorsk brochure.

148. LVA.1448.1.250, l. 11; LVA.1448.1.4, l. 5–7. This was the beginning of the increased profile of Vaivods in relations with the regime, a harbinger of his future as a progressive, pro-regime Catholic leader and eventual successor to Archbishop Springovičs.

149. LVA.1448.1.247, l. 73–74.

150. Talonen, *Church under the Pressure*, 160–63.

151. GARF.6991.3.61, l. 14 and GARF.6991.3.61, l. 90–92 indicate the repeated rejection of the invitation to the World Baptist Youth Congress in Sweden. GARF.6991.3.68, l. 219–20.

152. GARF.6991.3.68, l. 7–8, for note by Voroshilov.

153. LVA.1448.1.247, l. 35.

154. In communications with the MFA, CARC rebuffed such requests. GARF.6991.3.88, l. 182, rejecting American aid since "in the USSR there are 492 working Lutheran churches and these completely meet the religious needs of believers"; GARF.6991.3.88, 50, 50r, and 51, rejecting German Catholics seeking to visit the USSR; GARF.6991.3.71, l. 16–17, opposing a visit from Czech Catholics, maintaining that "a trip to the Baltics is impossible, since there is no guarantee that their visit will go smoothly."

155. LVA.1448.1.250, l. 57.

156. GARF.6991.1.476, l. 143–44.

157. GARF.6991.1.76, l. 171–74. The proposal called for one new position each for Moslems, for Catholics/Lutherans/Armenians, and for sects/Old Believers, to know more about "progressive clergy abroad" as part of the "fight for peace." GARF.6991.3.76, l. 176, for order signed by Stalin.

158. ERA.R-1989.2.8, n. 166c (9 Apr. 1948), Polyanski—Kivi, l. 71. CARC Chair Polyanski asked Estonian Commissioner Kivi to propose "several Lutheran clergy, with necessary education, theological preparation, knowing well the history of the Lutheran church and able to appear with sermons and lectures in the Soviet Occupation Zone of Germany." They should "not raise any doubts from a political point of view and be able to completely fulfill this mission." Despite repeated inquiries from Moscow, there is no indication of Kivi responding to this request in the archival records. Nonetheless it suggests CARC's early openness to using the Lutheran church for Soviet foreign policy on the German question, despite the general closure regarding international church ties under Stalin.

159. CARC's evaluation of Niemöller is found in RGASPI.17.132.509, l. 2–10; RGASPI.17.132.509, l. 187–88, documents Karpov's support for Bishop Dibelius of Berlin to visit the USSR, including Lutherans in Latvia; RGASPI.17.132.509, l. 213, regarding the LWF meeting in Hanover, seen as dominated by American Lutherans "who are motivated to use the congress for reactionary statements versus the state of the camp of peace and democracy."

160. LVA.1448.1.250, l. 60–61. Turs astutely indicated he would rather visit the GDR anyway. Internal analysis of the LWF congress in Hanover was very negative. The MFA evaluated the LWF Hanover congress very negatively in GARF.6991.3.80, l. 96–98.

161. GARF.6991.3.8, l. 265–68. Polyansky claimed over two hundred Estonian and three hundred Latvian Lutheran churches, a substantial overestimate. Polyansky purported to have no knowledge of the religious needs of German POWs, since it was not in his competence.

162. RGASPI.17.132.110, l. 28, 30–31, 35–36. The resolution blames CROC Chair Karpov for being too permissive toward and taking bribes from the ROC. The memo to Stalin proposes a new basis for the CROC, reducing its authority particularly over local governments and clearly stating the supremacy of the CM USSR for application of law.

163. GARF.6991.3.61, l. 61.

164. RGASPI.17.132.509, l. 214–18; RGASPI.17.132.509, l. 219–23.

165. GARF.6991.3.8, l. 175–77. The differing political positions on central religious organizations is intriguing. Voroshilov felt it was necessary to build a curtain against this question of centers, since until now none existed for them. In case they were created they would have to find work for themselves. The result would be an enlivening of religion in the land. Polyansky disagreed with this, arguing that it would be easier for CARC to deal with one religious center than three hundred separate Old Believer parishes.

166. GARF.6991.3.8, l. 105–6. The CARC representative admitted to Voroshilov that he did not know who handled church and religious issues in Zhdanov's bureau of the CPSU Secretariat.

167. LVA.1448.1.1, l. 13. He was criticized for not consulting with Latvian party and state officials.

168. ERAF.1.72.26, l. 253–54. Estonian Central Committee Secretary Lentsman contended with Kivi.

169. LVA.1448.1.244, l. 46; GARF.6991.3.473, l. 282–84. According to Restberg, persuasion—that which Commissioner Šeškens did—did not work on Springovičs; it was necessary to demand that he fulfill Soviet laws. See also Talonen, *Church under the Pressure*, 97–98, 215–16.

170. LVA.1448.1.250, l. 53–54. Restberg complains of Old Believer directives from the Higher Old Believer Council in Vilnius and of Lithuanian Commissioner Pusinis's rejection of his interference. Rejecting their request for a religious center, Restberg claimed the Old Believers were drunk, chaotic, and uncultured.

171. LCVA.181.3.19, l. 26.

172. RGASPI.17.132.497, l. 113–19. In a rare case, Karpov appeals directly to Stalin.

173. GARF.6991.3.66, l. 46–50; GARF.6991.3.66, l. 51. This would parallel the efforts in the late 1950s to wean the Baltic churches from the EKD by promoting ties with the GDR Lutherans. The MFA disagreement with CARC is reported by Polyansky in GARF.6991.3.68, l. 269–70, particularly the handwritten note from MFA: "Given the hostile position of Niemöller in relation to the USSR, MFA considers it inexpedient to send a telegram by Latvian Archbishop Turs."

174. LVA.1448.1.247, l. 66–67.

175. RGASPI.17.132.509, l. 88–94. During the 1948–1952 period in the USSR, Baptists lost 574 churches, Catholics 190. GARF.6991.3.76, l. 31–36. Even allowing for the many Catholic churches in Ukraine, it still indicates that the brunt of repression fell on the Catholic Church.

3   The Post-Stalin Thaw: 1953–1957

At the death of Stalin in March 1953, the churches and their adherents found themselves embattled. As the previous two chapters explored, the churches had been subjected to attacks on their institutional interests, their clergy and members assailed by antireligious propaganda and recruited by mobilization organizations. The leaderships of the Lutheran churches had been co-opted by the regime, and that of the Catholic Church was on the defensive. Other than at highly choreographed venues of the regime's peace campaign, international ties were virtually nonexistent in this intense Cold War atmosphere. Unsurprisingly, given this assault, church adherence had dropped precipitously, with the exception of certain national traditions.

In a party dictatorship, particularly the one-man rule of Stalin, it might be expected that a change in party leader would bring a shift in various policies. Stalin's death and the ensuing contest for power did in fact lead to a relaxation of religious policy under Khrushchev. The main features of religious policy would remain unchanged, namely, political control of the churches and propagation of atheistic ideology. But the early Khrushchev period would see a noticeable moderation, particularly regarding institutional interests of churches and their Western ties. However, in the case of religion, the de-Stalinization process did not lead to a more sustained thaw in church-state relations, but rather served as a prelude to renewed repression in the later Khrushchev period.[1]

The Dawn of a New Era

Though Stalin was soon to pass from the scene in early 1953, his repression continued unabated in the Baltics. A wave of arrests swept major Catholic leaders into prisons, including Valerians Zondaks, the chancellor of the Curia in Riga. Major churches, such as the Catholic church in Daugavpils, were closed after searches allegedly yielded "gold coins, anti-Soviet literature, pictures of fascists."[2] Unregistered groups were broken up by the state and requests to register were rejected. The Latvian leadership launched anti-Semitic attacks in the press, in sync with the charges of a Jewish doctors' plot in Moscow.[3]

The Baltic churches responded in varying manners to the death of Stalin. While he was sick the Latvian Lutherans prayed for him; along with most other churches, they rang bells and conducted special services upon his death. The Catholics remained the exception, demonstratively retaining Lenten violet rather than black for mourning.[4]

Soon after his death, religious policy began to shift. To be sure, internecine conflict inside the apparat abounded and the liberalization was hardly uniform. Moreover, it proved rather short-lived. However, the Khrushchev antireligious campaign launched after 1958 would be played out against a backdrop, particularly in terms of the churches' international ties, that had been partially altered by this transitional period of relative liberalization.

The shift in policy was most evident in the legal standing of parishes regarding registration. As noted earlier, most parishes and clergy—Lutherans earlier than Catholics—had submitted to registration by 1949. Unlike in other republics, there were thus few unregistered, "underground" groups in the Baltics. To be sure, increasing migration to the Baltics brought a growing number of unregistered groups, especially the Baptists and Pentecostals, which benefited from the new policy to register these groups. Preliminary investigation by the Latvian commissioner indicated twenty-four unregistered groups as of July 1955, with plans to register nine of them. Yet twelve of the groups were long-standing Old Believers and closer investigation in October 1955 revealed that only thirteen of the twenty-four groups possessed church buildings and were eligible for registration, two of which were Lutheran and three Catholic.[5]

More beneficial to the mainline churches was a slowing of the process of church closures and mergers. In numerous cases, efforts by local governments to close and convert churches were now reversed by Moscow. For example, following a fire at its "house of culture," the Hiiuma raiispolkom sought to seize the Kardli Lutheran church and convert it into a cinema. In the past such a request would likely have been approved, but in 1954 CARC and the Estonian commissioner rejected it, reacting to the discontent of the members of the parish and fearing damage to the state's relationship with Archbishop Kiivit. The Estonian Communist leadership and the KGB were outflanked in this intriguing case.[6] Similar cases occurred in Latvia as well.[7]

In Estonia, the focus of the regime was previously to close some of the Herrnhuter parishes that had been registered as branches of Lutheran parishes.[8] The state objected to the spontaneous involvement of parishioners typical of Herrnhuter services and pressured the Lutherans to "reeducate them in the spirit of the Lutheran church" to adhere to the liturgy.[9] The Estonian authorities continued to seek to undermine these branch parishes, for example, by pressuring the Consistory to move pietistic Lutheran pastors to parishes without Herrnhuters and demanding that certain Herrnhuter preachers and branches be deregistered.[10] But now they sought to shift the onus onto Kiivit and the Consistory to assume responsibility for such actions, framing the issue as dealing with violations of the Lutherans' own church regulations, rather than direct state action.

More significant to the churches was a new flexibility regarding the dvatsatka required for a group to register as a parish. During the Stalin years, pressure on individual members of the dvatsatka resulted in vacancies that the regime sometimes used as a pretext to close the affected parish. Now, however, the state eased the conditions for filling vacancies in the dvatsatka, stabilizing their status.[11]

Initially this more liberal policy toward registration of churches moved ahead rather informally. But it became more systematic in February 1955, when the USSR authorities revised the 1944 regulations for opening churches, allotting a larger role to individual parishes to initiate the registration process and fostering new efforts to register parishes already in possession of buildings.[12] CARC and CROC joined to request this liberalization, arguing that it would dampen dissent in the churches and faulting the previous leadership for the reversal of a more liberal policy in 1948.[13]

Another indication of change was increased support for church repairs or even construction of new churches. In a significant case in Tartu, the center of Estonia's rich intellectual culture, St. Paul's Lutheran parish was permitted to reconstruct its church building in 1954. The building had been heavily damaged during the war, but the state had repeatedly refused to permit its reconstruction during the postwar years.[14] Now such a symbolically important project became possible.

The regime's more liberal stance on the legal status of parishes soon produced a more assertive response by the churches themselves. Parishes increasingly demanded the return of parish houses earlier nationalized by the regime.[15] Parishioners no longer passively accepted the closure of churches. An early example occurred in the aforementioned case of the Catholic church in Daugavpils, Latvia, closed in January but reopened by July 1953 as a result of parishioner petitions demanding that higher authorities overturn the closure.[16] In one Latvian case, the local government sold a Lutheran church to a kolkhoz, provoking protests all the way to the Supreme Soviet of the USSR. The Latvian leadership overturned the sale, but deferred ultimate disposition of the church.[17] In some cases the parishioners opposed their own church leadership. For instance, the regime closed the Lutheran church in Balduri, Latvia, with the agreement of the Lutheran leadership, maintaining that "it had been registered by mistake in 1948." However, parishioners protested to the Latvian government and reversed the decision.[18] In another case the local government in Liepāja, Latvia, sought to seize the Lutheran church for conversion to an art museum in 1956, arguing that the repairs were beyond the capability of the church. The Latvian leadership overturned this action as well.[19]

Not surprisingly, the requests to open churches increased dramatically in this period. By CARC's own statistics there were 50 to 100 percent more requests in 1957 than in 1954.[20] The national churches, particularly the Lutherans in Estonia, used the rising threat of sects to justify the requests to open churches, thereby taking a page from the playbook of the Orthodox Church.[21] In early 1953 CARC ordered all commissioners to pay more attention to and keep better records of petitions and complaints from believers.[22] At the same time, the number of such complaints from parishes dropped significantly, suggesting that the liberalization of policy regarding the legal status of parishes dampened grassroots sources of religious dissent.[23]

The Resurgence of Church Adherence

Periods of liberalization are often accompanied by renewed interest in religion and in church rites in the broader society. As the risk of identifying with religion declines, individual calculus shifts in favor of churches. Although renewed identification with religion may yield new denominational patterns, for the most part liberalization usually benefits traditional churches. In the case of the Baltics, the churches identified with the nations, that is, the Lutheran and Catholic churches, experienced the largest rebound.

Certainly the churches had considerable lost ground to make up after the repression of Stalinism. As the Estonian commissioner summarized in early 1953, "in the ESSR one can talk about religion as a relic of capitalist development that is now attached to the church, which is based on the remaining religious authority of the church and religious tradition, expressed by 100,000 members, the large majority of whom support the church materially and … go to church once or twice a year during the major holidays."[24] The same official noted that increasingly those seeking to avoid detection were taking church rites away from their home parish.[25]

By 1954, however, state officials began to paint a very different picture. Statistical reports of rites showed dramatic increases, particularly for baptism and confirmation, which had fallen so precipitously in the late 1940s. This resurgence was initially more obvious in the Lutheran and Baptist churches than in the Catholic Church, which had in any case seen less remarkable decline in church adherence; but increased activity was noted among Jews in the Baltics as well.[26] Estonian officials regretted that demobilized Red Army veterans contributed to the increase.[27] Lutheran adherence rose not only as measured by participation in rites, but also in terms of other measures. Financial contributions to the Church surged 30 percent in Estonia from 1955 to 1956, along with the number of contributors.[28] Attendance at major holidays such as Christmas and Easter, long monitored closely by the state, increased dramatically in 1956 after years of decline.[29] Participation in cemetery days, likewise, spiked 25 percent in 1956. By 1957, confirmations in Estonia had returned to 1937 levels.[30]

The regime's interpretation of this trend shows its underlying orientation: that religious life was unnatural in the Soviet context. Commissioner Restberg in Latvia highlighted the efforts by Archbishop Turs to drum up interest. Taking a page from the Baptists, Turs initiated a choir which would tour with him to parishes; republic officials accused the choir of singing secular songs. He also increased such visitations by celebrating jubilees of individual parishes. Moscow ordered Restberg to limit these visits with the choir. Archival records of Turs's meetings with him reveal a constant negotiation regarding such "enlivening" activity.[31] Later in 1957, Turs promoted Easter vigils and brass music from church towers in order to activate Lutheran participation.[32]

More threatening to the state were Turs's efforts to give a nationalist accent to the church services. Songs from the Ulmanis period and cemetery services honoring the dead from the same period rang alarm bells in official circles. To attract tourists, Turs also initiated tours of the Riga Cathedral in summer 1957, including brief organ concerts, in order to raise money and the profile of the church.[33] By 1958, the state accused him of resurrecting national traditions, such as wreaths and candles for the dead, in order to raise money and reinvigorate Lutheranism in Latvia.[34] The state may have sought to discredit him with charges of nationalism at a time when Moscow was attempting to purge nationalist deviations in the Communist leadership in Riga.

Another cause cited often by officials was the impact of clergy returning from the gulag. They were blamed for enlivening parishes, though many were dispatched to remote rural parishes by bishops worried about destabilizing the churches' relationship with the regime. But even when they did not agitate in an anti-Soviet fashion, the sheer numbers of returning clergy represented a significant social presence: in the Latvian case, the fifty returning Catholic priests, not including the five returning monks, represented 30 percent of all priests. In the Latvian Lutheran case, twenty-three pastors returned, representing 25 percent of clergy.[35]

Despite these explanations or rationalizations of this trend toward greater church adherence, state officials were not overly concerned about it in the initial period after 1953, sometimes citing contrary evidence.[36] For example, official reports on participation at pilgrimage sites in Latvia during this period tended to underscore the relative consistency, even decline, of such activity.[37]

By the beginning of 1956, however, the regime was becoming alarmed at the increase in religious life, particularly among Catholics.[38] Latvian officials decried the rise of illegal religious instruction of groups by Catholic clergy, particularly in the eastern region of Latgāle. The Catholic Church began to send priests to parishioners' homes to take an annual census of members, a measure banned by Soviet law. Officials charged that the Church was exploiting the less restrictive course of the Central Committee resolution of November 1954. Particularly alarming to the regime were new demands for priests from Catholic groups in Belorussia and Ukraine, signaling a failure of the regime's efforts to blunt Catholic influence in these republics by fostering Orthodoxy. Joining the CARC criticism of Latvian policy, the KGB increasingly weighed in against this enlivening, blaming it on the leadership of Springovičs, Strods, and Dulbinskis.[39] Additionally, hard-liners in the republic-level Communist leadership joined in striving to reverse the liberalization. Although the trend toward increased church adherence affected all confessions, the Catholic resurgence would be more consequential in the coming crackdown.

Increasing Assertiveness Regarding Institutional Interests

The liberalization was marked by increasing church efforts to advance their institutional interests, which had been severely eroded by the Stalinist repression. Certainly one of the most crucial interests of the national churches was the training of clergy. As noted in previous chapters, the state had closed the Catholic seminary in Riga in 1950 and refused to approve Lutheran seminaries in Tallinn and Riga, severely limiting the recruitment of new clergy. The Lutherans were forced to use examination commissions to test self-taught students, resulting in few new pastors.[40] The Catholics had retained a form of correspondence courses to train priests, but the number trained dropped dramatically between 1950 and 1953. One of the first issues raised by the Latvian Catholic leadership was the reopening of the seminary. In his frequent meetings with the commissioner, Bishop Strods pressed this issue; he formally requested it of Polyansky, Chair of CARC, and Prime Minister Malenkov in 1954.[41] The regime was in fact prepared to do so in 1953, but the arrest of Zondaks, chancellor of the Curia and former dean of the seminary, delayed it.[42] In 1954, CARC reversed its earlier decision, finding in the Catholic Church "a positive and more loyal relationship, participating in the fight for peace" and criticizing the closure as an "administrative measure."[43] To be sure, points of conflict still remained, such as the state's denial of the Church's request for military deferments for theology students.[44]

The Lutheran churches also petitioned CARC for seminaries, but faced more resistance than the Catholics. In 1954, and again in 1955, Archbishop Turs proposed a theological institute with a four-year curriculum for thirty to forty students.[45] But Latvian officials delayed a decision, seeking to discern Moscow's position on the issue.[46] With the opening of communication and eventual exchanges with Western churches, the Baltic Lutherans gained greater leverage on this issue. Invitations to send students to foreign universities ensued with renewed international contact. The Martin Luther University at Halle, GDR, invited both the Latvian and Estonian Lutheran churches to delegate students for training, as did the Church of England.[47] The regime vetoed such study abroad for the moment: even the GDR was apparently not reliably socialist for the Soviets. But the offers were utilized by church leaders arguing for a local seminary to train clergy.[48] Eventually, in 1957, the churches were permitted to open correspondence courses in both republics, serving a limited number of students.[49]

Since 1950, the Baptists had requested seminaries to train pastors, in vain. The regime rejected these requests, maintaining that the Baptists had no shortage of pastors and were in any case less educated than Catholic or Lutheran clergy. The increasing anxiety about the growth of the sects also likely motivated the state's rejection of a Baptist seminary.[50] But Baptist evening courses were permitted in 1956, and registration continued to grow.

The churches also became more assertive regarding the rights of clergy. The Ministry of Finance had levied high levels of taxation on clergy as a disincentive. Now clergy and church leaderships began to protest such treatment. Believers began to demonstrate their support for the embattled clergy, seeing them as martyrs.[51] In an early indicator of liberalization, the commissioners began to respond to such protests in late 1953, pressing the financial authorities successfully to roll back this overtaxation.

Another indication of liberalization was the regime's handling of church events held outside traditional cultic functions. Under the Stalin legislation, such activity was extremely restricted as the regime sought to limit the churches' social presence. In the case of the Lutherans, the popular tradition of cemetery days to honor the dead challenged this policy. Chicanery and administrative prohibitions had been used by local officials, but now such measures were strictly forbidden by CARC officials. In this new, more permissive context, participation in the cemetery days—earlier in decline—stabilized, and even grew.[52] State officials did not abandon their fundamental skepticism of the cemetery days, seeing them as an effort by the churches to counter declining attendance by embracing a "cult of remembrance" and as interfering with production in rural areas.[53] Indeed, to curtail these events, commissioners proposed reducing the number of cemeteries and placing rural cemeteries under local government authority. Petitions by parishes to return individual cemeteries to the provenance of the parish were rebuffed.[54] But rather than use coercion to fight cemetery days, which "demonstrated to the clergy that it feared their influence," the regime chose to compete with more effective atheistic propaganda and "cultural-enlightening mass events."[55]

Catholic pilgrimages remained a contentious issue for the state, particularly in Latvia. But state officials recognized that measures to discourage pilgrims to major sites, such as Aglona and Kraslava, had boomeranged.[56] Whereas the regime had earlier pressured the churches to limit the number of priests who would celebrate mass on such occasions, it now countenanced the gathering of large numbers of priests, along with several bishops, including the recently amnestied Dulbinskis. Ironically, the state reports suggest that despite this lifting of strictures, the number of pilgrims did not significantly increase.[57] As with the Lutheran cemetery days, republic officials remained skeptical and refused to facilitate the pilgrimages.[58]

Certainly church interests also entailed publication of literature in order to communicate with members and conduct services. The regime had permitted publication of church calendars and song sheets for the Lutheran churches, but the Central Committee apparatus had typically cut the already much-reduced print runs approved by CARC. Now the print runs were increased substantially.[59] The Estonian Lutheran Church asked for a journal similar to the *Journal of the Moscow Patriarchate*, with Kiivit maintaining that such a periodical would increase the Church's influence among Estonian émigrés; the commissioner supported the request on this basis. However, the Estonian leadership rejected this argument and granted only an almanac instead; the CARC representative was left to console himself that this compromise would dampen Church criticism without giving it a "Bible history textbook which would be harmful for the youth."[60] In a major breakthrough, the Latvian Church was also permitted to publish 1,500 New Testaments in 1957, after indicating that the British Bible Society proposed to donate Latvian Bibles.[61] It should however be noted that fully one-third of the new publications were targeted for export, thus reducing the impact and benefit for the local Soviet churches.[62]

The locus for government vetting of publication requests also changed: previously, song sheets had required approval in Moscow, but, in a harbinger of future flexibility in the Baltics, the regime now decentralized this decision in the case of Lutherans to the republic level.[63] Interestingly, Baltic Baptist publications still required approval in Moscow unless they were in the language of the republic, thus demonstrating the ambiguity of belonging to a confession with headquarters in Moscow.

The limits to this new forthcomingness—and the dilemmas facing the regime—can also be seen in the decision regarding new songbooks for the churches. The commissioner hoped to eliminate "anti-Soviet" songs from the churches by replacing the songbooks with new ones sanitized of such songs. But this was vetoed by CARC, to avoid both the appearance of interfering in internal church matters and any concession that might increase religious activity.[64]

The Catholic Church also requested increased publications. In February 1956, an emboldened Catholic hierarchy systematized its demands on the regime, including request for a wide variety of publications, such as 50,000 catechisms and 20,000 prayer books. This still paled compared to the extensive request of the Lithuanian Catholics.[65] In support of its request, the Church argued that some publications were already available underground at high prices, that none had been published since 1940, and that the publications would be good publicity with foreign delegations.

Although this institutional interest in publication was common to both the Lutheran and Catholic Churches, concessions to the Catholics were more contentious within the Soviet leadership, due to differing perspectives on dealing with the Catholic Church and the Vatican, particularly in the context of 1956 upheavals in Catholic Poland and Hungary. In spring 1956, CARC supported granting the requests, arguing that "this would sharply improve our mutual relations with the Catholic Church and put it on the same basis as that with existing churches."[66] CARC saw the Catholic clergy, including its leaders, as loyal to Soviet power, although "the trust in the Catholic Church is slow to change and it is still in a different position than churches like ROC, Moslems, Baptists and Armenians." The Latvian and Lithuanian Central Committee apparatus, however, saw things differently and opposed the concessions. By September, the Agitprop Department of the CPSU Central Committee weighed in by supporting the publication requests from Lithuania only.[67]

The churches also sought to widen their access to youth by means of religious instruction. Forbidden under Soviet law, the Baltic churches had reluctantly ceased such instruction by 1949, with the exception of the Lithuanian churches, which continued to do so covertly. But in the context of liberalization, the churches sought to reverse this proscription.[68] Lutherans were emboldened regarding this issue by their increasing foreign contacts: Archbishop Kiivit raised the question after his trip to the United States; Archbishop Turs posed it after his trip to Czechoslovakia in 1958. The Catholic Church added it to its list of demands in February 1956. Needless to say, the regime did not give serious consideration to these requests. But CARC did order republic authorities to refrain from cracking down on Catholic violations of religious instruction in 1956.[69]

A basic institutional interest of the churches was autonomy in their internal affairs, which had been severely compromised by the Stalinist repression and penetration of the churches. This penetration continued, although the state officials became a bit more careful when interfering in local parish affairs. Still, among Protestants particularly, factions in the local parishes continued to seek support from the commissioner in their internal disputes, thereby perverting internal church democracy and reducing the authority of the church leadership.[70] But, by 1956, CARC was becoming more reluctant to do so, instead calling upon the KGB to increase its monitoring of religious activity.[71] Though the commissioners did not intervene as overtly as in the previous period, parish autonomy remained a fiction.

State Relations with Church Leaders

Of course the ability of the churches to take advantage of the relaxation was mediated by their leaderships. The Lutheran leaderships in Estonia and Latvia had been essentially gleichschaltet in the Stalinist period, thus reducing their ability to take advantage of the regime's liberalization. Nonetheless, they were hardly powerless. As we have seen, parish protests and Western contacts strengthened their hand in dealing with the regime, particularly with CARC. Archbishop Kiivit, in particular, was courted by CARC and its representatives. For example, the commissioner in Tallinn sometimes opposed the closing of churches, fearing that this might endanger the good relationship with Kiivit. In this stance, he met with opposition from the Estonian Communist leadership and the KGB; however, Moscow trumped this republic opposition.[72] Kiivit would remain a favorite son with the regime until his abrupt ouster in 1967.

By contrast, during this period, the state's relationship with Archbishop Turs became rockier. Commissioner Restberg was constantly troubled by Turs's image problem, rooted in his alleged dependence on alcohol, cronyism, cult of personality in the Church, and tactlessness with foreign visitors, the same issues it would use to justify ousting him in 1967. The state sought material with which to blackmail Turs, developing a network of informants among other leading church officials. In his reports, Restberg alleged that, despite being a lifelong bachelor, Turs led a "Rasputin-like life earlier," during which he was implicated in the suicide of a female paramour, leading him to surround himself with a similar "clique of bad reputations" at the expense of his authority.[73] Turs sought to extend his control over Lithuanian and Estonian Lutherans, used ploys like choirs and jubilees to enliven the churches, and selected immoral pastors for parishes, in this official view. Turs's dealings with foreign visitors also occasioned internal criticism by the local authorities. For example, in 1955, the state regretted his tactless reference to visiting Danish church leaders as "noble descendants of Vikings" and excoriated him for not rebutting anti-Soviet comments by the Archbishop of Canterbury.[74] Turs's vanity did seem evident in his leadership style.[75] For example, he had a white shroud knitted for himself for ceremonial purposes, leading some to call him Father Frost! He also complained about his tight housing circumstances, pressing state officials to arrange a larger apartment.

Despite these problems, Turs was remarkably obedient to the state. The archival record documents his almost weekly meetings with the commissioner, covering a wide variety of internal church affairs. All his correspondence with foreign churches was vetted by the commissioner and CARC. He dutifully implemented orders to discipline pastors who engaged in activities objectionable to the regime and sought to defuse the problem of pastors returning from prison by avoiding placement in their previous parish. Moreover, the Latvian Lutheran leadership as a whole suffered from weakness of character, reducing its popular credibility but leaving it politically pliable. As an example, Arvids Kaulins, a member of the church leadership, was allegedly a philanderer, creating discontent in St. John's parish. Peteris Kleperis was a regular informant of the KGB and state authorities, implicating his fellow clergy for legal violations and tipping off the state about their political views and negotiating positions.[76]

Turs's loyal stance and the weakness of church leadership explains in part the regime's continued toleration of Turs's leadership, despite his personal peccadilloes and heightened assertion of church interests during this period. But this continued support for him also stemmed from differing perceptions of him in Riga and Moscow. CARC officials found Turs quite loyal, whereas Restberg and the Latvian leadership viewed him as a liability, enjoying little authority among other confessions, his own clergy, and international contacts.[77] With the regime's international strategy giving greater priority to blocking Vatican influence by means of a Soviet opening to international religious organizations, Turs enjoyed a de facto elevation in status.

In the case of the Catholic leadership in Latvia, the issue of succession remained acute. The key leader, Springovičs, was now eighty-two years old and increasingly enfeebled. Whereas in the 1940s he had used his infirmity selectively to heighten his influence with the state, it now had become a detriment: the renewed arrest of potential heirs left the succession increasingly in question. Dulbinskis, arrested and imprisoned in 1949, was rearrested in 1957. Although he was released in 1958, he was banned from Latvia and viewed as "an active enemy of Soviet power and powerful bourgeois nationalist" by the state.[78] The Vatican's favored candidate for archbishop, Zondaks, was arrested again in 1958, charged with organizing a secret trip to the Vatican by priest Henrik Trops in 1950 and passing of libelous information to the Vatican in 1952.[79] Vaivods was likewise arrested again in 1958. However, in the case of Vaivods, the regime had clearly tapped him as its desired candidate for the succession and the arrest likely served to immunize him from criticism by the Vatican and church conservatives that he was too close to the state.[80] Strods, the progressive head of the Riga seminary, was initially vetoed not by Rome, but, ironically, by Latvian Communist leaders. Ousted in 1959 by Moscow as a nationalist and resurrected in the context of perestroika, Eduards Berklavs, CPL leader and Deputy Chair of the Council of Ministers, rejected Strods as a successor, despite Strods's critical stance regarding the Vatican. Berklavs's hard-line position was also manifested in his rejection of Strods's requests regarding registration of new parishes, new church publications, and reregistration of priests, among other issues.[81]

Springovičs died in October 1958, at the onset of Khrushchev's repression of religion. His funeral was kept limited by the Catholic hierarchy—non-Catholic representatives were not invited—but 1,500 attended the service, including 160 clergy, and 3,500 were present at the graveside. Only his prewar role was addressed in the eulogies. After earlier praising him for his antifascism, the state now dismissed him in its final internal characteriska as "a servant of the Pope and reactionary" and refused an obituary in the party paper, *Cina*, permitting only a modest death notice in the city paper *Rigas Balss*.[82] Strods managed the funeral and was eventually accepted by the regime after making concessions to the demands of Berklavs and CARC, which refused to recognize him as apostolic administrator unless he proved loyal, actively engaged for peace, and limited priest participation in pilgrimages to Aglona. The long-awaited and halting succession to Springovičs was soon caught up in the new crackdown on religion unfolding under Khrushchev.[83]

Political Dissent by Churches

Although the church leaderships were largely conformist as a result of the Stalin repression, the post-Stalin period did pose new dilemmas for the regime related to the dissent in the Baltic churches. The imprisonment of clergy under Stalin provided the concrete issue: whether they should be amnestied, and, if so, how to reintegrate them into the churches. The numbers affected were significant: 24 of 125 Estonian Lutheran pastors had been imprisoned; in Latvia 46 Catholic priests (30 percent of all priests) and 5 monks returned from imprisonment.[84] If they remained open at all, the churches had replaced the imprisoned clerics with unordained preachers or cantors. The potential for grassroots protest was evident in Juru, Estonia, where a petition by parishioners in 1955 demanded the release of several imprisoned pastors.[85] Even if they were not politically oppositional before incarceration, those amnestied would likely become so as a result of it. The state also feared that they would enliven parish life, counter to its goal of gradual erosion of church adherence. To minimize these risks, state officials sought to prevent them from being assigned to their previous parish and to assign them to poor, rural parishes that had limited contact with other clergy.

Of course, if the previous parish remained a functioning church, returning clergy would threaten to displace their replacements, making for intrigues. For example, the pastor in Riga's large New Gertrude Church fought bitterly to retain his position in the face of claims of returning pastors, even appealing to state officials.[86] In the case of the Peetri parish in Tartu, 1,000 parishioners signed a petition supporting the reinstallation of the amnestied pastor, but the church leadership opposed this change.[87] However, in the case of Robert Feldmanis, later a prominent theology professor in Riga, the state did not take such a laissez-faire stance. Turs sought to assign Feldmanis to his former Riga parish. However, charging Turs with "bowing to fascists," Restberg refused and granted him the required certificate only for the region outside Riga.[88] In general, Bishop Kiivit was less inclined to challenge the regime on this issue and sent the returning clergy to rural parishes.[89]

Even among those who had not been imprisoned, dissent increased. Prominent Latvian theology professor Leons Taiwans was criticized for the fundamentalist character of his sermons, his attacks on science, and "anti-state" lectures at the theological seminary; he was vetoed by Moscow when nominated as pastor to Leningrad. Harald Kalnins, later to lead the Soviet German Lutherans, was charged with giving religious instruction to youth and disciplined by Bishop Turs.[90] Baptists and Seventh-Day Adventists, in particular, increasingly complained of discrimination at school and work.[91]

Still greater dissent was found among Catholics. Unlike the Lutherans, Bishop Strods of Latvia insisted on assigning returning priests to their former parishes.[92] Dulbinskis, recently released from prison, immediately shared the spotlight with Bishop Strods during pilgrimage ceremonies in Aglona in 1956. Claiming that "there was no freedom of religion in the USSR," Strods sought to expand Catholic influence in neighboring areas, such as Belorussia and Leningrad, in the face of opposition from Belorussian officials but with support from CARC.[93] This dissent was by no means limited to the clerical leadership. In 1957, for example, 31,629 persons signed a petition to the Latvian government demanding transport to pilgrimage sites, religious literature, and an end to press articles hurtful to believers.[94]

In order to limit dissent among the clergy, the state heightened its surveillance of them. Local officials were especially ordered to report on the activity of clergy returning from prison. After earlier closing churches and decertifying clergy, the security officials now promoted the legalization of underground clergy and parishes, making them easier to monitor. This affected the Baptist and Pentecostal groups more than others, given the greater institutional inclination of Lutherans and Catholics to register. Although they usually possessed their own KGB connections, commissioners now increasingly included the KGB in the formal paper trail during policy deliberations.[95] KGB penetration of the ranks of clergy clearly increased during this period. As described above, key leaders, such as Kleperis in Latvia and Leepins in Estonia, were likely informants. Eventually this surveillance, taken together with resurgent church adherence, particularly among Catholics and sects, and increasing demands from the churches, would produce a new policy of repression after 1957.

Antireligious Propaganda

A hallmark of regime policy toward the churches was its effort at scientific atheistic propaganda against religion. Although state officials often positioned propaganda and administrative measures as alternative approaches, in periods of repression and transition the two were indistinguishable. In the early post-Stalin period, the regime itself was unclear on the direction of its religious policy. In an early indicator, *Pravda* sharply attacked religion in July 1954, followed by a widespread press campaign against religion. In numerous articles in the republic press, individual clergy were maligned. Also taking the cue, the Ministry of Culture in Latvia ordered a "militant approach" against religion in all facets of culture, going beyond more lectures on atheism to call for eliminating theater and philharmonic works too favorable toward religion and promoting antireligious films.[96] In Estonia the Komsomol targeted highly religious areas, such as southern Estonia, in its political work.[97] Perhaps a side effect of this intense propaganda, vandalism against churches by "hooligans" increased dramatically, with prosecutors often unwilling to pursue the cases.[98] Some state officials saw this "cultural-educational competition" with the churches as politically preferable to the "administrative-political measures" used by many local officials.[99]

The churches, nonetheless, became alarmed by this new antireligious campaign. They protested it in their meetings with the commissioners and in circulars to the parishes, particularly in Latvia.[100] In discussions with the state, Turs proposed holding a meeting of deans in order to warn them against attacking antireligious propaganda in sermons, an idea that CARC scotched as portending heightened criticism of the antireligious campaign.[101] Catholic protests, for instance, by Bishop Strods, were also lodged against the campaign, reaching the Central Committee in Moscow.

Based on the documentary record, it is untenable to claim that this campaign was entirely waged by ideologues in the party organization and press, without any sanction by CARC officials. Indeed the commissioners were actively involved in vetting the articles that appeared.[102] This was not a case of bureaucratic politics at the local level.

Officials did however register the criticism of the churches and helped shift policy on the republic level. Commissioner Restberg informed the Latvian party leadership of the churches' protests, and the Latvian party curtailed antireligious articles in the republic press even before the shift occurred in Moscow.[103] This feedback from the republics may have played a role in eventually shifting the course in Moscow, as reflected in the Central Committee resolution of November 10, 1954, that ended the crude campaign.[104] In March 1954, the Agitprop Department of the CC Secretariat had sounded the alarm regarding weak scientific-atheistic work, especially in Latvia, in a memo to party leader Khrushchev, a significant foreshadowing of the *Pravda* attack in July.[105] But CARC, joined by CROC, clearly weighed in opposing the *Pravda* article and supporting the November resolution. Their argument for moderating the campaign relied heavily on the dissatisfaction of the religious population and damage to Soviet foreign policy.[106] The churches all responded positively to this resolution, expressing satisfaction that it might serve as a check on atheistic propaganda.[107] Thus, the post-Stalin period initially brought a heightened antireligious campaign—couched as a liberal alternative to coercive administrative measures—that was quickly reversed as a result of negative feedback from churches and pressure from state officials in religious affairs. Renewed press attacks in 1958 would signal a new period of repression, reflecting rising alarm in the regime regarding Catholics and sects.

Increased Foreign Relations

A striking feature of the post-Stalin period was the shift in the state's position on the international relations of the churches. Stalin had put them in the deep freeze as a result of his fear of Western church criticism of Soviet religious policy. As discussed in the previous chapter, this meant rejection of bilateral church ties and refusal to join the World Council of Churches (WCC). Relations with the Catholic Church were especially icy during this period. The Soviet churches were forced to issue pronouncements on peace and disarmament that lacked all credibility.

After Stalin the more flexible foreign policy pursued by the Soviet leadership facilitated renewed international contacts by the churches. Eventually these would produce formal ties with international church organizations, but in this early stage they were limited to tentative contacts, typically bilateral. Unexpectedly, leading the way were not the Orthodox, Catholic, or Lutheran churches, but the Baptists and Methodists in Britain and Scandinavia. Active in the early postwar setting, these groups renewed their efforts to establish contacts with their Soviet coreligionists, without needing to contend with rival émigré churches as the Lutherans did. British Methodists visited Estonia as early as 1954.[108]

A key figure in these bilateral contacts was the German church leader, Martin Niemöller, the Lutheran church president of Hesse, noted for his critical stance on Adenauer's German reunification and Western rearmament policy. In an effort to raise the issue of German POWs in the USSR, he made overtures to the AUCECB organization in Moscow in 1953.[109] Niemöller was permitted to publish an article in the Baptist journal, *Bratskii Vestnik*, which represented a breakthrough of sorts. Exploiting this opening, Niemöller initiated correspondence in 1954 with Estonian Bishop Kiivit, who was given the green light to engage in discreet contacts with him. At the same time, facilitated by Swedish neutrality, correspondence between Kiivit and the Swedish Lutheran Church began.[110] By 1955, Niemöller led the first high-level visit by the umbrella body of the Evangelical-Lutheran churches in Germany (EKD) to the USSR at the invitation of the ROC, during which he met Latvian and Estonian church leaders in Moscow.[111] Also in 1955, the first of numerous foreign trips was permitted Kiivit and Turs, in this case to Britain at the invitation of the Archbishop of Canterbury and the British Council of Churches.[112] Eventually, in 1956, Turs and Kiivit traveled to the United States at the invitation of the National Council of Churches.[113] Much attention focused on their return visit to West Germany at the invitation of the EKD.[114]

The basis for these contacts with the German, British, and, eventually, American churches was of course the peace issue, in line with the regime's new effort at peaceful coexistence with the West and opposition to NATO armament of Germany. Kiivit issued declarations on peace, some of which were published in *Izvestia*. Clearly the regime steered these efforts. Kiivit's speeches regarding peace and his correspondence with foreign partners were subjected to prior censorship by the Estonian officials.[115] Although still informed by opportunism, the peace issue represented a broadening of ties that under Stalin had been limited to a rather narrow search for ecclesiastical legitimacy from Scandinavia for the Soviet-dictated bishops.

State officials at the republic level tended to be more skeptical of these new international ties. The commissioner in Estonia opposed the high profile of Niemöller with the ROC and the Baptists, fearing that this international contact would enhance the footprint of the Lutheran Church.[116] Compromises with the churches would have to be made in order to facilitate these contacts, compromises which would threaten to reverse the gains made against religion and the churches. The state approved church publications, such as prayer books and calendars, in part to demonstrate the vitality of religious life. Even though one-third of them were designated for export, the remainder constituted an improvement of churches' institutional position domestically. The republic officials found it necessary to devote more time to hosting foreign visitors, an increase in workload that they did not hesitate to note in reports to Moscow. The reports themselves revealed state officials scrambling to familiarize themselves with religious and political factors introduced by the cosmopolitan visitors to the republics. Usually it was Moscow, not local officials, whose foreign policy interests tipped the scales in favor of these new international contacts.

The Catholic Church did not enjoy the benefits of this international diplomatic opening, reflecting bureaucratic differences and uncertainty in the Kremlin. In 1955 and 1956, the regime did explore relations using covert contacts in Austria. Catholic Professor Marcel Reding visited Moscow in 1955, was granted a meeting with Supreme Soviet Chair Anastas Mikoyan, and promised to "open the eyes of the Pope" regarding the opportunities for Catholics in the USSR.[117] Although Khrushchev did not deign to meet with him, the high-level reception of a mere professor suggests that some in the Kremlin supported an overture to the Vatican at this time. The fact that the regime permitted the Vatican to name two new bishops in Lithuania in 1955 reinforces this interpretation of a partial opening to the Catholic Church.[118] The papal nuncio in Vienna reported to the Vatican on this positive shift in Soviet policy in Lithuania, although confidential KGB sources highlighted the Vatican's doubts about the sincerity of this policy change.[119] The MFA urged wooing the Vatican to develop a deeper constituency for peace, but hesitated to endorse diplomatic relations that would entail a concordat. CARC pressed for an opening to the Catholic Church, arguing in early 1956 for the need "to improve relations sharply" with the Catholic Church in order to "help the peace camp" and "place the Catholics equal to other churches."[120] For its part, the KGB saw the Vatican as simultaneously fearful of national churches becoming domesticated in the new post-Stalin setting, yet hoping to take advantage of this liberalization in the bloc and extend its influence.[121] Both saw the Vatican as pursuing a strategy of geopolitical competition against communism, even seeking alliance with Islam in this effort.

The Catholic stance on peace—the issue that served as the vehicle for the increased visibility of the churches internationally after Stalin—also impeded the churches' international ties. As in the Stalin period, the few Catholic statements on peace tended to be very general, unlike the Lutheran statements that specifically condemned atomic weapons and Western rearmament. The succession to Springovičs hampered the Latvian Catholic position, too. Bishop Strods of Latvia refused to host foreign delegations unless they were sent by the Vatican and was viewed by CARC as "a slave of the Pope," leaving the Catholics awkwardly apart from the Baptist, Lutheran, and Orthodox churches.[122] The authorities noted an increased assertiveness by the Catholic hierarchy regarding direct communication with the Vatican.

By late 1956, as a result of the resurgence of Catholic clout domestically and the waning potential for using the Vatican in Soviet foreign policy, the political tide had shifted against the Catholic Church. The Latvian party leadership opposed any concessions and won support from the KGB and central party apparatus.[123] Particularly after the uprisings in Catholic Poland and Hungary, the more liberal position of CARC toward the Catholic Church, including contacts with the Vatican, left it on the defensive politically. The liberalization of the post-Stalin period had produced increased church adherence among Catholics, especially as revealed in pilgrimages and rites, and emboldened the Catholic leadership to escalate its demands on the regime. Sealing this was the death in 1956 of CARC Chair Polyansky, the key figure supporting the opening to the Vatican, discussed below. The regime increasingly looked to Protestant-based international organizations to serve as a bulwark against Vatican influence in the world.

In this way, this period saw the eventual shift toward formalizing ties of Soviet churches with religious international organizations. The MFA and CARC began to endorse ROC membership in the WCC and the Conference of European Churches (CEC).[124] CARC was particularly supportive of ties to the CEC, the new organization of European churches, since it offered an East-West venue without the prominent American role found in the WCC.[125] The KGB, likewise, endorsed cooperation with the CEC, viewing it as a blow against the Vatican.[126]

The regime also fostered bilateral confessional contacts. For example, Hungarian Lutherans were hosted particularly warmly by the state in Estonia when they criticized the reform leadership of the Hungarian Church that had been deposed in the wake of the failed 1956 revolution.[127] However, Estonian Methodists were forbidden to take up contacts with Swedish Methodists: lacking headquarters in Moscow, the Methodists were subject to the dictates of the Estonian authorities, whose goal at this point was to limit their international access.[128]

More problematic from the regime's perspective was the natural partner for the Baltic Lutherans, the Lutheran World Federation (LWF), due to the émigré churches that were already members of the LWF. In an effort to address the needs of Lutherans in Eastern Europe, the LWF implemented a program for minority Lutheran churches in Europe. LWF representatives initiated contacts with the Baltic churches during their visits to Britain, the United States, and Germany in 1955–1956, culminating in an invitation to send observers to the LWF General Assembly in Minneapolis in 1957. But the state saw the program for minority Lutheran churches as an anti-communist action by the émigré churches.[129] In July 1957, CARC supported participation in Minneapolis, arguing that it would "eliminate the slander against the USSR" and permit exploiting "the fear of the émigré churches of a loss of prestige in international church circles."[130] But fearing that the émigré churches would use the assembly as a platform to criticize and embarrass the Soviet Lutheran representatives, particularly after the Hungarian revolution in 1956, the Moscow leadership reversed course and pressured the Estonian and Latvian Lutherans to decline the official invitations of the LWF.[131]

After the earlier prohibition of contacts with the émigré churches, a subtle shift on the issue can be detected. As early as 1951, Moscow called for increased propaganda efforts to encourage émigrés in Sweden to return.[132] In this post-Stalin period such contacts were now quietly encouraged, but only under controlled, bilateral circumstances. The state hoped to blunt these groups' antagonism toward the Soviet Union. Kiivit and Turs both acquiesced in this initiative with public statements and private diplomacy. However, the Catholic Church refused to make such appeals, deferring to the Vatican.[133]

Finally, it should be noted that the Soviet authorities tightly controlled the composition of delegations. The churches recommended members of the delegations, which the commissioners altered before seeking guidance from Moscow. CARC then exercised the prerogative to further alter the composition. By 1957, CARC favored Kiivit in its international strategy, leaving Turs on the sidelines in some cases. Church dissenters were removed from proposed church delegations, as happened in the case of Leons Taiwans. Criticized by the state for his allegedly anti-Soviet lectures and for advocacy of a Lutheran presence in Leningrad, Taiwans became persona non grata for the state. His fellow delegates showed little solidarity with Taiwans and traveled to the EKD in West Germany without him.[134]

The Bureaucratic Politics of Religious Policy

The liberalization of policy following Stalin opened fissures in the state and party apparatus that only became evident upon the opening of official records in 1991. Local governments increasingly found themselves out of sync with policy at the republic and union levels. In response to local conditions, some local governments were more liberal. Often, however, the local authorities were called up short for lagging behind Moscow's new liberalization. In Liepnins, Latvia, the local government authorized purchase of a church by the kolkhoz, which tore down the bell tower before Riga intervened to halt and reverse the sale. Schemes of local governments in Latvia to seize and sell bells of inactive churches or to seize the land of a nunnery in Aglona were criticized and overturned by republic officials in 1955.[135] The Estonian commissioner reported legal violations involving attempts to delay cemetery day ceremonies, to pressure clergy to subscribe for state loans, to cancel pensions of clergy, and to harass believers with rude songs.¹³⁶

CARC commissioners sought to counter such local deviations by demonstrating a unified republic policy and commitment to legality, an effort that was often hobbled by internecine struggles among republic bureaucracies. The Finance Ministry was reluctant to revise the tax burden on pastors and churches, despite the increasing responsiveness of CARC to complaints from the churches during this period.¹³⁷ These differences were also revealed in state policy toward cemeteries: Latvian state officials attempted to remove them from church jurisdiction using legal maneuvers; for the CARC commissioner provenance of cemeteries was a second-order issue of a dying institution. The Latvian commissioner sought to reinforce local discipline by including heretofore secret republic resolutions in official documents of the Latvian Ministry of Justice, ensuring greater dissemination of laws governing local governments' policies toward churches.¹³⁸

The relative bureaucratic clout of CARC officials and the military also shifted somewhat during this period. As the previous chapters suggest, the Red Army held the upper hand in the closing days of the war: witness the use of churches for storage and bivouac facilities and the drafting of theology students in 1944–1945. Now, however, the state officials were more likely to challenge the military on behalf of the more liberal policy. A prominent example of this in Estonia was the response to the harassment and beating of Pastor Ewald Saag of Rapla by military recruits in 1953. The commissioner lobbied for punishment of those involved, arguing that church adherence was increasing in the Red Army and that the military's harassment merely increased Saag's popularity in this militarily significant town.¹³⁹

At the same time, there is evidence of greater formal coordination between state religious officials and the security forces. Of course, in the Stalinist period, there is strong evidence that CARC officials and commissioners were largely drawn from the KGB. Upon CARC Chair Polyansky's death in 1956, correspondence from the cadre department indicates that he was also a KGB officer.¹⁴⁰ But in this period of liberalization, CARC officials and commissioners also began to formally and regularly copy the KGB when communicating with republic and Moscow authorities. This might be interpreted as closer governmental coordination with the KGB; alternatively, it might suggest that newer commissioners were less likely to be KGB officers themselves and felt the need for political coverage.¹⁴¹ The rise in sect activity prompted state officials to ask the KGB to monitor sects more closely. This paradox—increasing forthcomingness toward religious groups, yet greater monitoring by and heightened coordination with the KGB—is not uncommon in a period of liberalization and increased international exposure, as the GDR case suggests.¹⁴²

Republic officials also asserted their interests by blocking church relations across republic borders, which churches were tempted to promote in a period of liberalization, especially along confessional lines. The issues of Latvian Lutheran ties with Soviet Germans and Latvian Catholic ties with Belarussian and Ukrainian Catholics have been discussed earlier. In another example, Bishop Turs sought to establish links with the Lithuanian Reformed and Lutheran churches, which included in their number several Latvian-speaking parishes. The Lithuanian Lutherans were split over this relationship: it was seen as offering benefits, such as publications and pastors for a small group of parishes on the verge of extinction; on the other hand, reliance on Latvian patrimony threatened their own identity as Lithuanian churches. In the end, however, Latvian and CARC officials refused to approve any requests by Turs for material assistance to the Lithuanians and viewed skeptically his efforts to establish such a beachhead.[143] In the case of the Old Believers, the roles were reversed. The Higher Council of Old Believers of Lithuania had been given jurisdiction over Old Believers in all three Baltic republics. In this period of liberalization, the Higher Council began to make requests for publications for Old Believers outside the Baltic republics. In this case, CARC supported creation of a religious center in Moscow for them, arguing that it would not activate believers, but the Central Committee apparatus vetoed the proposal.[144]

Fissures between the republics and Moscow also rose during this period. Republic officials, viewing religious policy through the prism of their parochial interests, often took hard-line stances. A good example of this was Eduards Berklavs, deputy chair of the Latvian Council of Ministers, who was later purged for alleged nationalist deviations by Moscow. Berklavs railed against CARC as too liberal, especially toward sects. Tangling with CARC directly, Berklavs advocated ending the activity of unregistered groups, rather than studying them and trying to register them; he also objected to placing clergy returning from prison in parishes.[145] Republic efforts to eliminate prewar songbooks on the grounds of "anti-Soviet content" or to block the transfer of clergy were rebuffed by CARC as "hurting our relations with the churches."[146]

These intramural bureaucratic battles occurred against the backdrop of a struggle over power and policy in Moscow itself. In particular, CROC and CARC became locked in a struggle for turf during this period. Lobbying directly to CPSU General Secretary Khrushchev, CROC Chair Karpov proposed merging the two councils in 1953, justifying it on the basis of the growing international relations of the churches and the potential to cut central and commissioner staff costs. CARC Chair Polyansky rebutted the proposal forcefully. The Central Committee rejected the idea in 1953 as provoking "unnecessary talk of unification of all religions under the power of Patriarch Aleksei," but Karpov broached it anew in 1954 and 1955, again unsuccessfully.[147]

The two councils also crossed swords over substantive issues, some of which affected the Baltics. For example, CARC warned its commissioners not to register Pentecostal groups and criticized CROC for laxness in similarly limiting the activity of unregistered ROC parishes, per the mandate of the Central Committee after 1955.[148] For its part, the Latvian CROC commissioner took issue with the Lutheran use of lay preachers and cantors, seeing this as violating the law on registration of clergy and the ban on visitation to other parishes, and blaming CARC for this breach.[149] Efforts by CARC to demonstrate its more liberal religious policy and the growth of non-Orthodox groups to an international audience by publishing a brochure in 1957 were vetoed by CROC, which was quite critical of sects.[150]

Summary and Conclusion

The period following Stalin's death brought liberalization in Soviet relations with the churches and religion. It began haltingly as a result of shifts by the Central Committee, a heightened antireligious propaganda in 1953–1954, and reluctance of republic and local officials. But, after 1954, general policy shifted to benefit the churches' institutional interests, particularly as measured by registration of parishes, parish governance, construction and renovation of churches, church publications, and theological education. As might be expected, church adherence and activity level increased as a result, particularly in the Lutheran and Catholic churches. Imprisoned clergy were released and largely reintegrated into parish work, albeit not always in their original parishes: the regime sought to isolate them and limit the risk of political opposition. New arrests were limited largely to Catholic leaders. After being cut off from international churches since 1945, the Protestant churches were allowed selectively to develop foreign contacts, particularly on a bilateral basis with German, British, and US churches, under the tutelage of the Russian Orthodox Church; Catholic ties with the Vatican remained very strained. CARC sought to establish greater uniformity of local policy, but became engaged in increasing bureaucratic struggles with CROC and other ministries as a result.

Already in 1956, there were signals of backlash to the liberalization by the regime, particularly against the Catholic Church. Officials in Estonia sounded alarms about the weak atheistic work and resurgence of religious activity, opining "what use is atheistic upbringing ... if among 73 confirmands on Hiiuma, 11 percent were in Komsomol, including one child of an official in the raiispolkom."[151] In Latvia, officials cracked down on canvasing of parishioners by Catholic clergy in 1957 and employed various forms of transportation chicanery in an effort to discourage pilgrimages. As noted, recently released Catholic leaders, such as Dulbinskis and Zondaks, were rearrested in late 1957.[152] Major changes of leading personnel in CARC and CROC (the death of Polyansky and ouster of Karpov) also signaled a harder line against the churches. In terms of religious policy,

Khrushchev was to be remembered not for the post-Stalin thaw of 1953–1957, but for the renewed repression of the 1958–1964 period, the focus of the following chapter.

How can the explanatory factors be used to interpret these changes in religious policy in the post-Stalin period? At the most fundamental level, the broader political process of de-Stalinization did not leave the religious policy in Estonia and Latvia unaffected. But in this period of general liberalization, the institutional interests of the Lutheran and Catholic churches positioned them better than the sects to make legal claims on the state (e.g., registration and construction of churches, taxes on clergy, theological education, logistical support for publications and pilgrimages). Even on more politically contentious issues, such as return and assignment of amnestied clergy, the institutional churches could press their cases more successfully. The liberalization benefited these national churches more than others: their increase in church adherence was disproportionate, their criticism of antireligious propaganda was taken more seriously by the regime, and implicit appeals to Latvian and Estonian nationalism appeared in some of their services.

Confession continued to differentiate Lutherans, Catholics, and the sects: the Catholic Church was less penetrated by the KGB and was more assertive regarding returning clergy; the Lutheran Church, though more co-opted by the regime internally, enjoyed more international ties than the Catholic Church, whose ties to the Vatican and other Catholics in the USSR were increasingly suspect after the upheavals of 1956 in Poland and Hungary.

This period of liberalization strengthens further the argument for bureaucratic interests, as shown by the lag among local and republic authorities in shifting course after 1953. The other major shift in this period, the opening of international contacts, also demonstrated the conflict of interest between republics, with their priority of control of religion, and Moscow, with its new interest in utilizing churches in Soviet foreign policy. The disputes between CARC and CROC regarding registration and primacy over foreign ties also undermined the coherence of the regime. To be sure, the early international contacts by Methodists and Baptists do seemingly undercut the argument that national churches reaped the most benefits from liberalization; but the German, CEC, and LWF overtures foreshadow the acceleration of international contacts and preeminence of Lutherans in the 1960s.

Notes

1. On this period, see Viise, "Estonian Evangelical-Lutheran Church," 144–58.
2. LVA.1448.1.252, l. 34.

3. The commissioner rejected twelve requests for registration in early 1953. Catholic migrants coming from eastern Latvia to non-Catholic areas were refused registration. LVA.1448.1.252, l. 36 and l. 21–25, referring to the March 1953 anti-Semitic article in *Pravda* by Arvīds Pelše, First Secretary of the CP LSSR.

4. LVA.1448.1.252, l. 32–33.

5. LVA.1448.2.254, l. 76. The regime viewed the Old Believers as a group destined for demographic extinction, thus less likely to merit registration. The Latvian commissioner concluded that only thirteen unregistered groups had church buildings: eight of them Old Believers, three Catholic, and only two Lutheran, according to LVA.1448.1.7, l. 93–98. By 1957, the commissioner could claim that no unregistered groups remained, other than several small Old Believer groups (LVA.1448.2.256, l. 193).

6. ERA.R-1989.2.11, l. 10–11, l. 217–20; ERA.R-1989.2.14, l. 42. The Hiiumaa local leader, supported by the local KGB head, requested seizure of the church for a movie theater, claiming few parishioners, and put pressure on hard-liner Johannes Käbin. The commissioner concluded that 200 to 250 parishioners would be affected, that the fire occurred after a drunken party by Communist cultural officials, and that local Lutherans were agitated that the church would be given to drunkards. Ultimately CARC followed the recommendation of the commissioner, who came down on the side opposing seizure due to relations with Archbishop Kiivit: "in my view internally he and many others will not be satisfied. Not to consider this is incorrect in my view."

7. LVA.1448.1.252, l. 115, in the case of the Karsava Catholic church.

8. Commissioner Kivi's 1954 report on the remaining Herrnhuters, in ERA.R-1989.2.11, l. 130–34.

9. ERA.R-1989.2.9, l. 29–30. The commissioner pressed Kiivit and the Consistory to make the worship service more Lutheran, which provoked resistance. But the Lutheran leaders acquiesced. Commissioner Kivi: "the Herrnhuters do not have the right to participate: listen, pray and leave."

10. ERA.R-1989.2.10, l. 67–69, l. 185. In one case, in July 1953, an anniversary celebration of the rural Herrnhuter branch parish in Kivi-Vigala, Pärnu raion, involved multiple speakers from other branch parishes, as well as choirs, setting off alarms based on the official proscription against visiting preachers. The commissioner, with CARC approval, moved to deregister the responsible Herrnhuter preacher and the Lutheran pastor whose parish was partnered with the Herrnhuter branch. The state wanted to shift the responsibility for elimination of the branch parish to the Consistory, as a violation of its order of service.

11. ERA.R-1989.2.11, l. 104–5. The Narva parish saw nine members of its dvatsatka resign in a dispute over the pastor, but the state did not move to deregister the parish, suggesting a greater flexibility than in the past. In 1957, the Estonian commissioner proposed formally reducing the minimum for registration, but CARC rejected this, in ERA.R-1989.2.18, l. 36–37.

12. LVA.1448.1.7, l. 17–18. The CM USSR Regulation N. 259 of 17 Feb. 1955 eliminated the 1944 Sovnarkom regulation according to which registration of parishes was initiated by CARC, with approval of the CM USSR, substituting instead a petition of parish believers with approval of the CM of the respective union republic and CARC, thereby decentralizing the process somewhat from Moscow to the republic level.

13. GARF.6991.3.113, l. 110–11. In this memo, Polyansky indicated that 1,237 churches had been closed between 1948 and 1954 and none opened, despite numerous requests. Alone from 1953 through 1955, CARC rejected 1,013 requests to open churches. Polyansky concluded:

"CARC considers that although currently there should not be a massive opening of prayer houses, it is expedient to open them in such locations where it is reasonably necessary, since systematic rejection of all requests without exception creates an unhealthy mood among some portion of the citizens of the USSR."

14. ERA.R-1989.2.11, l. 135–36.
15. LVA.1448.1.255, l. 44–45.
16. LVA.1448.1.252, l. 59.
17. LVA.1448.1.252, l. 97–98; LVA.1448.1.4, l. 38–39. A proper agreement had been signed in 1948, but a formal registration of the parish was not completed. The commissioner earlier ordered the services there be halted in January 1953, but a petition drive by the pastor, Freimanis, produced 216 signatures demanding registration. Chair of the CM, Vilas Lācis, ordered a review and in November 1953 overturned the commissioner's decision to reject registration. Ironically, before this reversal the kolkhoz had torn down the church's tower. Failure to implement the CM decision led to a protest to the Supreme Soviet in Moscow, according to LVA.1448.1.6, l. 36–37.
18. LVA.1448.1.4, l. 59.
19. LVA.1448.1.255, l. 43–44. Local officials based their claim on the extensive war damage suffered by the church. After the seizure was reversed, Bishop Turs requested funds for its reconstruction, which the commissioner supported. LVA.1448.1.10, l.33, 33r, l. 30–31.
20. GARF.6991.3.146, l. 102–3.
21. ERA.R-1989.2.14, l. 102–3, supporting opening a parish in Vastselina and arguing that sects are gaining ground in the absence of a Lutheran church. In 1954, the Holy Synod of the Russian Orthodox Church described the sects as a major threat: "distinguished by high activity, conducting agitation to convert Orthodox to their sect, hostile to ROC." See GARF.6991.3.106, l. 13–20.
22. LVA.1448.1.4, l. 30–31.
23. ERA.R-1989.2.11, l. 58. In his March 1954 analysis, Commissioner Kivi indicated that Bishop Kiivit was pleased that complaints from believers and clergy had fallen substantially, as compared to 1951.
24. ERA.R-1989.2.9, l. 61.
25. ERA.R-1989.2.10, l. 246.
26. GARF.6991.3.147, l. 90–91. CARC noted increased church attendance, especially by Catholics, and increased confirmations. Increased Jewish activity in Latvia was noted in LVA.1448.1.253, l. 35–36. GARF.6991.3.102, l. 65–69. The Catholic Church showed increased clergy from 1950 to 1953 and stable numbers of activists; the Lutheran churches showed stable numbers in Latvia, but in Estonia there was a secular decline in churches and clergy despite an increase in activists after 1950.
27. ERA.R-1989.2.11, l. 169–77.
28. ERA.R-1989.2.19, l. 27–32. The number of services increased as well.
29. ERA.R-1989.2.19, l. 7–10. In Estonia, Christmas attendance rose 20 percent from 1955 to 1956.
30. ERA.R-1989.2.20, l. 67–71. The commissioner confirmed the increase to 10,530 confirmands in 1957, in part due to pent-up demand from the period 1946 to 1952.
31. CARC instructions in GARF.6991.3.114, l. 59–62; negotiations with Turs in LVA.1448.1.257, l. 101–2.
32. LVA.1448.2.256, l. 67.

33. LVA.1448.1.256, l. 179–80.

34. LVA.1448.1.257, l. 100–1. The commissioner dismissed these "superstitious and ignorant relics of the past," used by the church to "strengthen its influence and by clergy for their enrichment."

35. LVA.1448.1.255, l. 135; LVA.1448.1.256, l. 111.

36. GARF.6991.3.129, l. 27–29. CARC noted the relative stability of church attendance at Christmas during the post-Stalin period.

37. LVA.1448.1.255, l. 35–38 and GARF.6991.3.130, l. 51–52, indicating pilgrimage participation to Kraslava and Aglona, major pilgrimage centers for Baltic Catholics, was lower in 1956 than in 1955, despite more clergy involvement.

38. LVA.1448.1.255, l. 134–46. This CARC report, with on-site participation of an inspector from Moscow, constituted a broadside against all manner of alleged Catholic activism and illegality. The clergy involved in the census were deregistered, but criminal proceedings were dropped against them.

39. RGANI.5.33.23, l. 62–63, charged that they showed fealty to the Vatican, as well as organized visitation to parishes and religious instruction of minors.

40. LVA.1448.1.7, l. 6.

41. LVA.1448.1.253, l. 90–92. In justifying the request, Strods argued that five years of full-time study were necessary (not correspondence courses) for celibate students and that of 200 priests in Latvia, only 100 were fully capable. He pointedly indicated the need to train priests for Ukraine as well.

42. LVA.1448.1.252, l. 33–35, l. 79–81. The correspondence courses after 1950 nonetheless involved lengthy stays in Riga, resembling a regular seminary.

43. GARF.6991.3.102, l. 326–27. Polyansky noted on the document that Pokroskii of the CC had called on Nov. 30 and indicated a positive stance by the Secretariat.

44. LVA.1448.1.253, l. 93. CARC Chair Polyansky: "Military obligation is the legal obligation of all citizens of the USSR and students at the spiritual seminary may not back out of this honored obligation."

45. Turs proposed the theological seminary at his meeting with CARC Chair Polyansky in May 1955, according to LVA.1448.1.7, l. 64–65. LVA.1448.1.8, l. 111–17. The Latvian Church had requested 120 students in 1944 and 90 in 1946, thus indicating the effect of Stalinization on church expectations. By confirming instruction in the Latvian language, Turs was also hoping to alleviate any anxiety of the state regarding a broader mandate for the seminary.

46. LVA.1448.1.254, l. 157–58; RGANI.5.16.755, l. 6–7. The Latvian Communists sought direction from the CC-CPSU on the question, but the CC referred it to CARC for disposition.

47. ERA.R-1989.2.17, l. 182–83; LVA.1448.1.7, l. 76–77.

48. LVA.1448.1.253, l. 162.

49. LVA.1448.2.256, l. 108–9.

50. LVA.1448.2.256, l. 176. Pilli ("Union," 46–47) indicates that the courses ended in 1960, however.

51. LVA.1448.1.252, l. 47. The commissioner indicated that the Ministry of Finance was often unwilling to rectify its "overreaching" regarding taxation of clergy income. LVA.1448.1.252, l. 118: cases of local finance authorities placing onerous land taxes on parishes, with the commissioner seeking revision.

52. RGANI.5.33.55, l. 38–51. Participation in cemetery days in Estonia increased from 180,000 in 1955 to 200,000 in 1956.

53. LVA.1448.1.253, l. 116–17. Commissioner Restberg: "Clergy, knowing the decrease in attendance of believers of church services in summer, have begun to raise their activity in open air in cemeteries."

54. LVA.1448.1.256, l. 46–48. Latvian Lutheran Pastor Tsimdin, Smildens parish, obtained 1,400 signatures supporting the return of a cemetery to the parish, but the request was denied and the commissioner eliminated his registration as a pastor.

55. ERA.R-1989.2.11, l. 145–46.

56. GARF.6991.3.93, l. 175: Conclusion by CARC regarding the pilgrimage to Kraslava, Latvia, on St. Donat's Day, 1953.

57. LVA.1448.1.255, l. 60, l. 65. Though trips from kolkhozes were organized for the first time, total participation declined.

58. LVA.1448.1.253, l. 60–61. Bishop Strods requested that the authorities cease work on an electrical plant during services at Aglona in 1954, but Latvian CP First Secretary Pelše rejected the request.

59. LVA.1448.1.253, l. 29–30. The increased print runs (7,000 calendars and 5,000 songbooks) still were woefully inadequate for the number of communicants in the Latvian Church.

60. ERA.R-1989.2.11, l. 50, l. 158: the commissioner indicated the journal was not "desirable for domestic reasons" but supported it for foreign policy interests; l. 202: Estonian Communist and government opposition to the journal. The journal was nixed by Lentsman, as indicated by his handwritten comment, "this kind of journal is not necessary," in ERAF.1.143.25, l. 160. ERA.R-1989.2.14, l. 175–76: church request for an almanac; l. 14: official support by CARC.

61. LVA.1448.1.255, l. 42; LVA.1448.1.256, l. 178–79.

62. ERA.R-1989.2.19, l. 71–72.

63. ERA.R-1989.2.14, l. 122, l. 123–25. Seeking to enhance his own power, the commissioner indicated to the Baptists that publication decisions were still made in Moscow, but to the Estonian party and state officials he indicated CARC deferred to republic directive organs.

64. GARF.6991.3.480, l. 96, l. 112–13.

65. GARF.6991.3.129, l. 43–46, l. 87–91. CARC informed Anastas Mikoyan, the Chair of the CM USSR. Lithuanian requests included 50,000 catechisms, 60,000 prayer books, 30 imported theology books in multiple copies for seminaries, a monthly Catholic journal (1,000 copies), a monthly journal for believing Catholics, 1,000 brochures, and 1,000 calendars for priests.

66. GARF.6991.3.129, l. 40–44.

67. RGANI.5.33.23, l. 19–20. Responsibility for the decision was shared by future CPSU leader, Konstantin Chernenko. But motivating this forthcomingness on publications was the regime's desire to split the Catholic leadership. The relatively pro-regime bishop, Stankevicius, was given the lion's share of the 50,000 prayer books, thus engendering friction with his fellow bishops in Lithuania and the Vatican. LCVA.181.3.44, l. 39; LCVA.181.3.46, l. 42–43.

68. ERA.R-1989.2.17, l. 171; GARF.6991.3.129, l. 87–89; LVA.1448.1.257, l. 34. The commissioner commented: "Since Turs faces again several trips abroad, it is not to be excluded that he will bring something new back."

69. LCVA.181.3.46, l. 27.

70. LVA.1448.1.254, l. 152: "Often questions are posed to the commissioner that go beyond his competence and should be decided by church leaders, but the interested parties prefer to turn to the commissioner as the first resort." ERA.R-1989.2.11, l. 279.

71. GARF.6991.3.1389, l. 153, l. 162–81.

72. ERA.R-1989.2.11, l. 217.

73. LVA.1448.1.252, l. 124–25. A certain agent, "Kristofor," informed the commissioner about Turs's alcohol habits. Peteris Kleperis was a regular informant of the KGB and commissioner. LVA.1448 1.6, l. 85–91: Commissioner Restberg provides an extensive critique of Turs's leadership. GARF.6991.3.135, l. 68–71.

74. LVA.1448.1.254, l. 133–36, l. 155–56. The commissioner summarized: "Turs prepares for meetings with delegations poorly and there is much work ahead with him, in order to adequately prepare him for receiving foreign delegations."

75. LVA.1448.1.254, l. 123; LVA.1448.1.6, l. 3–4.

76. The communications of the commissioner with CARC are replete with reports based on meetings with Kleperis. See GARF.6991.3.482–86. Talonen indicated that the question of Kleperis's KGB role remains open, but at a minimum he was clearly an informant of internal church matters to the commissioner.

77. A CARC official's visit to Riga was reported in GARF.6991.3.479, l. 127–29. Hearing the commissioner's negative views of Turs, the CARC emissary, Koltsev, was amazed at the gap between them and the CARC view in Moscow.

78. LVA.1448.1.255, l. 146; LVA.1448.1.257, l. 136. Dulbinskis was living in Belorussia because he was prohibited from living in Latvia under the terms of his release from prison.

79. LVA.1448.1.257, l. 47.

80. LVA.1448.1.257, l. 104–6. According to the commissioner, Vaivods indicated that after his second arrest, politics no longer interested him.

81. LVA.1448.1.257, l. 137–38. It is ironic that Berklavs was later identified with a Latvian national deviation against Moscow, particularly regarding immigration and economic policy: on religious policy his hard-line position was close to Khrushchev's. Regarding the ouster of Berklavs as a Latvian nationalist in 1959, see Plakans, *Latvians*, 157–59. For a counterview that argues his ouster resulted from a cabal by Pelše and other opponents of Khrushchev, see "Strange Death," 77–98.

82. LVA.1448.1.257, l. 92–96.

83. LVA.1448.1.258, l. 82–83. Strods allegedly agreed with the conditions and the commissioner reported that relations had since been positive.

84. ERA.R-1989.2.17, l. 128; LVA.1448.1.255, l. 135.

85. ERA.R-1989.2.14, l. 7–9. The Estonian commissioner informed the chair of the KGB.

86. GARF.6991.3.480, l. 6, l. 18.

87. ERA.R-1989.2.20, l. 53. The commissioner demurred, claiming it was "an internal church matter."

88. GARF.6991.3.479, l. 315–16, l. 322–23; GARF.6991.3.480, l. 11.

89. ERA.R-1989.2.19, l. 14–15. The commissioner reported that Kiivit did not yield to the pressure of returning clergy for their urban parishes.

90. Both clergy were implicated by the informant in the HCA, Peteris Kleperis, who seems to have had a particular animus toward Taiwans. Kleperis also reported that Taiwans sought religious literature from the Danish delegation in 1955. LVA.1448.1.256, l. 108–9; GARF.6991.3.483, l. 50–54; GARF.6991.3.484, l. 110, l. 133–39.

91. In this more liberal period, commissioners' reports contained growing sections on complaints from believers. Typical was the case of an Adventist child dismissed from school for

missing Saturdays; the parents' complaint is documented in LVA.1448.1.256, l. 196. Commissioner Restberg told the parents they could not use religion to violate Soviet laws on education.

92. GARF.6991.3.484, l. 30–38. In 1954, CARC overrode objections of Latvian "instanzi" (CPL/KGB) to the commissioner's approval of these transfers, further evidence of bureaucratic differences between Riga and Moscow. See the handwritten note of CARC Chair Polyansky, GARF.6991.3.478, l. 212.

93. He demanded the government approve Catholic priests delegated to Belorussia and asked for a Catholic parish to be opened in Leningrad. The Catholic presence in Belorussia was particularly sensitive to the regime. To derail Strods's efforts, Belorussian authorities blocked the return of priests from prison and, apparently relying on a Catholic informant in Daugavpils, accused Strods of Polish and Jesuit ties; CARC objected to the Catholic footprint in Belorussia. See RGANI.5.16.705, l. 89–91, 94–98; LVA. 1448.1.255, l. 35–38, l. 61–63, l. 65, l. 79–82.

94. GARF.6991.3.486, l. 95–98. KGB sourcing was cited by the commissioner.

95. ERA.R-1989.2.14, l. 50–90. Veiderpass, the commissioner who succeeded Kivi upon his death in Jan. 1955, copied the KGB chair regularly, unlike Kivi who did so irregularly. GARF.6991.3.479, l. 282–83. The commissioner rejected Strods's charge of KGB intimidation of a priest ("the activity of the KGB is not in my function"), but confirmed the account with the KGB nonetheless.

96. LVA.678.1.69, l. 87–95.

97. ERA.R-1989.2.10, l. 247, regarding Komsomol work in Vastselina raion.

98. LVA.1448.1.254, l. 77–81, for multiple cases of church complaints of hooliganism and vandalism. In one case that illustrates the backlash and finger-pointing such thefts could produce, the bells of the closed church in Zalva were stolen shortly before Christmas 1954. The thief hoped to sell them, but was apprehended by local authorities, who sought to use the profit for the song festival, not to return them to the church. This produced enough outrage among local residents that a broad-based group, including kolkhoz leaders, Communists, and Komsomol members, petitioned to reopen the church, thereby escalating the mess to Riga. See LVA.1448.1.254. l. 20–25.

99. ERA.R-1989.2.11, l. 145–46. Commissioner Kivi opined in one case that local officials prohibited a cemetery day by the church in Vyaike, "an open interference in internal affairs of believers" and "demonstrating to the cult servants that it feared their influence.... On the contrary, Soviet cultural-enlightening mass attractions should paralyze all religious remnants of any character." He was relieved that there had not been other reports of this ham-fisted approach.

100. LVA.1448.1.253, l. 157–59; LVA.1448.1.254, l. 1–3. Turs's Christmas circular noted the articles offensive to believers in the press. Strods and the Baptists all expressed criticism of the new campaign in 1954. There is little indication of protest from the Estonian Church in the documentary record.

101. GARF.6991.3.479, l. 136, l. 198 (on Turs) and l. 140 (on Strods). Turs canceled the meeting with superintendents in September 1954, but ordered pastors to collect antireligious articles from the press for use with the state.

102. LVA.1448.1.253, l. 159. Commissioner Vereshagin obliquely confirmed when he reported an end of antireligious articles in the press insulting to believers after the November 10, 1954, CPSU resolution: "simultaneously the earlier visits by representatives of publishers and authors of antireligious articles for 'consultation' also ended."

103. LVA.1448.1.252, l. 97. The CC-CPL criticized a 1953 antireligious, anti-Catholic film that provoked objections from Turs as well as Strods, urging restraint. LVA.1448.1.58, l. 77. The commissioner took issue with the proposal to forbid church bells promoted in the party organ, *Cina*.

104. LVA.1448.1.253, l. 159.

105. RGANI.5.16.650, l. 18–24: "In the Latvian SSR there are 736 churches and prayer houses which daily poison the consciousness of workers with religious narcotic, but at the same time scientific-atheistic work is almost non-existent."

106. RGANI.5.16.669, l. 164–68. The moderate tone and foreign policy basis of the argumentation is worth quoting: "The main thing is to approve and publish the Resolution, since after the correct and restrained publication in *Pravda* of 24 July 1954, with many other papers reprinting it, many lectors shifted to wide, unrestrained anti-church and anticlerical agitation, became hostile in actions using fairy tales, sayings, word games, and caricatures, and stopped just short of reprinting the pornographic booklet of Loginov, 'Funny Stories from Holy Scriptures.' These mistakes affected the movement not only of thousands, but also of millions of the population of our USSR; not understanding and drawing the provocative conclusions from these mistakes are individual church leaders in the states of the people's democracies; put in a difficult position were the leaders of religious cults in the USSR who daily take part in visits of foreign delegations to the USSR, and including those church figures who in their church or social capacities periodically visit abroad."

107. LVA.1448.1.253, l. 138–39.

108. ERA.R-1989.2.11, l. 77–78. In order to smooth relations with the Methodists in the context of this visit, CARC approved their use of deacons to replace pastors, overriding the opposition of the republic officials. Regarding early Baptist contacts, see Pilli, *Dance or Die*, 71–73.

109. GARF.6991.3.97, l. 23–24: reported by CARC to the KGB.

110. ERA.R-1989.2.11, l. 286, with notes from Commissioner Kivi's notebook indicating Kiivit's receipt of a letter from Niemöller seeking closer ties; ERA.R-1989.2.11, l. 152, indicating communications with the Swedish Lutheran Church.

111. LVA.1448.1.254, l. 111–16. The regime evaluated the trip very positively, particularly the stance of Heinz-Joachim Held, head of the EKD Foreign Office.

112. ERA.R-1989.2.14, l. 31–41. Commissioner Veiderpass supported the trip. GARF.6991.3.113, l. 131–33: justification of "putting the question before Christians of England and Scotland of their part in the struggle for peace, for ending atomic and hydrogen weapons," and approval by the CM USSR.

113. ERA.R-1989.2.17, l. 116–18.

114. ERA.R-1989.2.17, l. 185–87.

115. ERA.R-1989.2.14, l. 49. The Communist Party chief for ideology, Lentsman, vetted Kiivit's 1955 peace speeches in Moscow and Helsinki. ERA.R-1989.2.14, l. 256. Kiivit's draft letters to the NCC-USA and the WCC were vetted and revised by the commissioner, "in the spirit of the recommendations of the CARC from 17 November, n. 10–81c."

116. ERA.R-1989.2.9, l. 134; ERA.R-1989.2.17, l. 122–25. The scramble to deal with increased foreign contacts is reflected in the work plans of the commissioners, such as that of Veiderpass for the first half of 1956 in ERA.R-1989.2.14, l. 249–51.

117. The memorandum of conversation is found in GARF.6991.3.115, l. 78–83.

118. GARF.6991.3.117, l. 151–56. The Pope named Mazhelis and Stepanovicius, rejecting Stankevicius as too pro-regime.

119. GARF.6991.3.143, l. 22–25; l. 42–43.
120. GARF.6991.3.129, l. 40–45. Polyansky urged meeting the demands of the Catholic Church for large numbers of publications, release of Lithuanian bishops, return of closed churches, and construction of new churches.
121. GARF.6991.3.197, l. 34–47; GARF.6991.3.143, l. 16.
122. LVA.1448.1.254, l. 160; LVA.1448.1.255, l. 52.
123. RGANI.5.33.22, l. 64–68: criticism of increased religious activity, especially in Latgāle and in the Catholic Church, and blame for the commissioner, ordering him to "increase control of the church activists and end their illegal activities." The KGB also targeted Latvian Catholic Church leaders for criticism (religious instruction of youth, subordination to Rome, recruiting contacts in other republics), per RGANI.5.33.22, l. 62–63.
124. GARF.6991.3.189, l. 172–73; GARF.6991.3.190, l. 75.
125. ERA.R-1989.2.21, l. 2.
126. GARF.6991.3.163, l. 52. The KGB's analysis: "This activity of representatives of Protestant churches provoked concern by the Vatican, which sees that this creation of a Protestant organization will pose the issue of interfering with Catholic efforts at a 'unified Europe' with a Catholic character."
127. ERA.R-1989.2.22, l. 112–18.
128. ERA.R-1989.2.18, l. 34, 39, 40. CARC rejected a visit by Swedish Baptists "by directive organs of the republic," and directed the Estonian commissioner to inform the Estonian Methodists that "they are not leaders of an Estonian Methodist church, but merely clergy of a Tallinn religious group and do not have the right to invite in the name of the entire church."
129. GARF.6991.3.135, l. 103–9. The commissioner described the new organizations as "some kind of new organization of émigré Lutheran churches of Estonia, Latvia, Lithuania, and Hungary." CARC asked the MFA for information, in GARF.6991.3.135, l. 110. On the tension between the émigré churches and Baltic churches, as well as the American leadership of the LWF, see Malkavarra, "Dispute," 166–78.
130. GARF.6991.3.146, l. 108–9, l. 110.
131. ERA.R-1989.2.22, l. 26, blamed "the last-minute demand of Washington for fingerprints" for the absence of Baltic Lutheran representatives, but implied the pressure of the émigré churches against formal participation by the Soviet Lutherans was the operative factor. Also, Altnurme (*History*, 134–37) concludes "the West saw Jaan Kiivit as one of the most reliable partners amongst church leaders of the East bloc."
132. RGASPI.17.138.496, l. 4, indicating meetings by officials of the CM USSR with Estonian and Latvian Communist officials.
133. LVA.1448.1.254, l. 162. Strods rejected such appeals to émigrés, stating "such questions do not have a patriotic but rather purely political character." GARF.6991.2.482, l. 12–14: Turs's willingness to make such an appeal, sent to the KGB for placement in the foreign press.
134. GARF.6991.3.135, l. 200–5. Cover to Taiwans' letter to the EKD Kirchentag, in which he argued that Latvian representatives to the Kirchentag "lack the mandate to discuss serious problems of our church. It is almost impossible to completely express that which is shaking the heart and soul of Latvia currently." It should not be a surprise, given the fact that his fellow pastor and church leader, Peteris Kleperis, was a major source of information that the state used against Taiwans. On the Leningrad issue and Kleperis' role as an informant, see GARF.6991.3.482, l. 15–18.
135. LVA.1448.1.252, l. 97–98; LVA.1448.1.254, l. 20.

136. GARF.6991.3.114, l. 73–80.

137. LVA.1448.1.252, l. 47, citing complaints about "overzealous Finance Ministry officials who even if the 'pops' [pejorative for clergy in Russian] are subject to unfair taxation, refuse to curtail the sums of tax."

138. LVA.1448.1.8, l. 47–48.

139. ERA.R-1989.2.9, l. 83–84.

140. GARF.6991.3.143, l. 89: communications between the cadre departments of CARC and the KGB regarding Polyansky's passing, with an attached letter from the NKGB to Polyansky dated 2 June 1945.

141. The first Estonian commissioner, Kivi, was clearly a KGB officer upon taking the position after WWII. But there is no clear evidence regarding his successor, Veiderpass.

142. The Stasi penetration to monitor churches in the GDR increased dramatically after the onset of détente and Ostpolitik in the 1970s.

143. LVA.1448.1.254, l. 72; LVA.1448.1.257, l. 149. Both the Lutheran and Reformed churches in Lithuania were quite small, but geographically concentrated. Based on his informant Kleperis, Commissioner Restberg objected to Turs's merger overture to Reformed Superintendent Shernes in 1954. GARF.6991.3.479, l. 166.

144. RGANI.5.16.705, l. 22–24, rejection by the Central Committee on l. 25.

145. GARF.6991.3.480, l. 54–62; GARF.6991.3.481, l. 115–18.

146. GARF.6991.3.480, l. 112–13.

147. RGANI.5.16.642, l. 140–41, l. 142: 1953 proposal and rejection. RGANI.5.16.669, l. 3–24: 1954 proposal; RGANI.5.16.669, l. 215–18: rejection by the Central Committee apparatus, arguing "it strengthens the position of the church in our society. In current conditions, when religion is increasing in influence on the population rather than declining, measures should be taken to protect the interest of the government." RGANI.5.16.642, l. 120–26: 1955 proposal with memo to the files by V. Khruzhkov.

148. GARF.6991.3.130, l. 78–79.

149. GARF.6991.3.46, l. 154: CROC Latvian Commissioner Sakharov's complaints of the liberal policy of his fellow Latvian CARC Commissioner Restberg. Reflecting its own necessary learning curve after 1945, CARC explained the different role of laity in Protestant traditions to justify this phenomenon.

150. RGANI.5.33.53, l. 16–20. Attacking CARC, Karpov argued that sects were more mystical than the ROC, "a more dangerous form of religion." He argued that the sects received paper imports for publications from CARC, whereas he claimed the ROC had been denied this benefit. Lutherans had 589 churches in the tsarist period; now there are more than 500 in Baltics alone, attesting to the "practical activity of Soviet government in guaranteeing no limitations on freedom of conscience." The CROC critique caused the Central Committee to oppose the publication, which came at the expense of the international publication strategy of CARC (RGANI.5.33.53, l. 22).

151. ERA.R-1989.2.17, l. 169.

152. LVA.1448.1.256, l. 102–3, 113; LVA.1448.1.256, l. 158.

4 Renewed Repression and International Opening Under Khrushchev: 1958–1964

KHRUSHCHEV'S RULE IS often identified with the so-called thaw, and the churches and religion definitely benefited from the de-Stalinization process, as the previous chapter indicated. By 1957, the regime had become more forthcoming on institutional interests of the churches, such as registration and parish viability, financial issues, and even church construction. Those released from prison partially eased the shortage of clergy and theological training was renewed. Church adherence recovered and limited international ties were permitted again.

Yet the later years of the Khrushchev period brought a new wave of repression for the churches, manifested particularly in increased antireligious propaganda and closure of churches. This repression left most Baltic churches severely weakened by the end of the Khrushchev period and challenged the modus vivendi between the regime and the churches that had developed by 1957.[1] The Latvian party paper clearly signaled the new stance:

> In our land the goal-oriented forward development is frequently compromised by remnants from the past, the clearest case of which is religion. Even if they make such efforts to be loyal, the churches and clergy are reactionary forces due to their world-view.[2]

Shift in Policymakers' Analysis

Already in 1957 one could see harbingers of a turn in policy, particularly in the official analyses and treatment of the Catholic Church. As noted earlier, republic officials sounded alarms at the Catholic resurgence, charging that they were exploiting the 1954 decision by the CPSU to liberalize religious policy. Latvian Commissioner Restberg complained to Moscow that "church activists, having many years of practice in the manner of manipulation of citizens in a religious spirit, have had some success in this," citing "demands to register new parishes, return, repair and revival of unfinished and closed church buildings" and "measures to publish church literature, but also to actively spread their influence on the population, especially youth and students."[3] Demographic changes were also increasing the Catholic profile in Riga, as a result of migration since the war from Latgāle and Lithuania.⁴ Reinforcing this increased church adherence was the renewed arrest of Latvian Catholic leaders.⁵ In Moscow, CARC requested help from the KGB in dealing with the Catholic Church.⁶

One might interpret this repression as targeting the Latvian Catholic Church and attempting to split the Catholics along Lithuanian-Latvian lines. As described previously, Springovičs was now viewed as reactionary, after having earlier been considered pragmatic and independent of the Vatican. That his star had waned was demonstrated by the regime's handling of the Catholic priest assigned to the St. Louis parish in Moscow. Since early 1949, the Latvian Church had named this priest, who was jurisdictionally subordinate to the Riga diocese. Joseph Butirovicz, an ethnically Polish priest named in 1949, supplanted the foreign priest in the parish and implemented the Soviet legal restructuring of the parish ordered by CARC. In 1957, Springovičs sought to recall and replace him, but the state refused and pressed for a successor from the Lithuanian Church instead.⁷

The state simultaneously undertook a crackdown against the Lithuanian Church as well. The Lithuanian Communist Party engineered arrests of priests for religious instruction of youth and illegal publications and passed a resolution to heighten antireligious propaganda among its population.⁸ As in Latvia, the Lithuanian officials railed that Catholic leaders viewed the relaxation since 1954 as a "capitulation of Soviet power before religious forces" and had exploited it.⁹

In fact the CARC evaluation of the entire Catholic Church veered sharply negative in 1959. In a major policy memo, dated February 1959 and copied to the KGB as well as the Central Committee (CC), CARC described a hostile relationship to Soviet power, citing the naming of previously incarcerated priests as bishops, underground activity of Uniates in the Ukraine, émigré agitation, and opposition from the Baltic churches. It concluded that "the Catholic Church is the only legal organization in the USSR which exists under the control of a foreign center, the Vatican" and "seeks to strengthen its position in the bloc, activate hostile elements of the clergy, and strangle indications of loyal relations by clergy to socialist states."¹⁰ The proposed countermeasures were quite draconian, ranging from refusing to approve bishops and deregistering disloyal priests to breaking all ties with the Vatican and creating independent churches. Even though the final version of measures approved by the CC was milder—e.g., the proposal to create a Soviet Catholic Church was dropped—the substance of the CARC position and the heightened coordination with the KGB suggest a generalized hardening toward the Catholic Church.¹¹

The regime's concerns about heightened religious activity were not limited to the Catholics. CARC analysis of church adherence alleged an activation of

Lutherans as well.¹² In fact, church rites in Estonia had leveled off by 1958, after recovering from 1953 to 1957, in part due to the missing-generation demographics of World War II.¹³ The rebound in church adherence was more evident in mainstream churches, such as Catholic, Orthodox, and Baltic Lutheran, than among sects, which had managed to better retain adherents during the previous repression. Setting the tone for overall religious policy, a 1958 analysis of the Central Committee apparatus highlighted the increased activity of churches and sects. Although most of its examples were drawn from the ROC, a separate KGB analysis underscored increased interest in religion among intellectuals and the Jesuits' alleged focus on this social group.¹⁴ Sects, especially Seventh-Day Adventists, Jehovah's Witnesses, and Pentecostals, were particularly targeted.¹⁵ Although the crackdown was to affect the Catholics particularly severely, it represented a generalized alarm about a popular resurgence of religion and the churches since Stalin.

In addition to negative reports from the Communist Party officials at the republic level, the crackdown had two other causes. First, unsurprisingly, the brewing bureaucratic battle between CROC and CARC was fought in part over the proper direction of policy. Karpov, chair of CROC, vehemently criticized the content of a new brochure on Soviet religion as too rosy regarding the sects and non-Orthodox churches, arguing that the ROC was in fact less mystical and more Russian than the sects. Bowing to his pressure, the Central Committee canceled the publication, which had been designed for foreign consumption.¹⁶ In this way, CARC's international strategy, which presumed increased foreign ties of the Protestant churches, was called into question. In this context, the death and replacement of Polyansky by hard-liner Aleksei Puzin as chair of CARC not only represented a bureaucratic victory for his rival Karpov, but also signaled that a tougher line with the churches was in order.

Second, the crackdown reflected the strategic thinking of the regime in its foreign policy. The Foreign Ministry viewed the Vatican as an increasing threat, even under the fresh approach of John XXIII.¹⁷ For its part, the KGB evaluation of the Vatican was similarly negative, seeing the Vatican as building a coalition with Protestants in the United States and Moslems in the Near East, directed against communism.¹⁸ The increasing Protestant exchanges between East and West were alarming to the Vatican in this context. The KGB viewed the new pope as more flexible, motivated to keep the Catholic churches in the East bloc under Vatican control by replacing the overtly political stance of Pius XII with a more religious orientation.¹⁹ To counter this threat, the regime would revisit its earlier decision to reject participation in Western church international organizations, such as the WCC and LWF, and would promulgate new organizations, such as the Christian Peace Council (CPC). This approach was designed to outflank the Vatican, particularly after the Pope's 1959 announcement of his intention to convene the Second Vatican Council.[20] This foreign policy would naturally have domestic ramifications, namely a hardening line toward the Soviet Catholic Church, concentrated in the Baltics. The non-Catholic churches would benefit from continued international contact, but would find their credibility at home and abroad tarnished by the new wave of domestic repression.

Institutional Interests: Church Parishes

A clear indication of the harsher line was reflected in the official treatment of church requests to construct or renovate churches. The state's earlier forthcomingness evaporated. High-profile projects already underway were suspended and even reversed, including some which could not escape the attention of Western observers. A prime example, the long-delayed renovation of war-damaged St. Paul's Lutheran Church in Tartu, Estonia, approved by CARC in December 1954, was halted by the state in February 1957.[21] Construction work on low-profile projects likewise became impossible. Latvian Bishop Turs's requests for renovation of war-damaged churches and reopening of unused churches had been approved from 1955 to 1957, but by 1958 the state approved only one such project (Liepaja), and in 1960 all such requests were rejected.[22] In Estonia, all construction requests were denied except for the construction of a house for Bishop Kiivit, a decision clearly tailored to enhance his ability to impress the growing numbers of foreign visitors. State officials rebuffed church construction requests by suggesting that these needs be handled by the "market."[23] Even in cases of arson and fire involving the wooden churches common in Estonia, the Estonian authorities refused to approve insurance compensation to enable rebuilding.[24]

Closure of churches again became the order of the day in this period. A 1962 study by the Latvian commissioner documents the heavy-handed role of the state in this process. Among other measures, local officials sometimes forced the self-liquidation of the dvatsatka.[25] Registration of some Lutheran churches was withdrawn "at the request of parishioners," with state officials citing the "dying character" of the Lutheran churches and the infrequency of services in some churches.[26] Even in Estonia, where the leading Lutheran Church was largely suborned politically in the Stalinist period, decisions to register churches taken in the liberal period from 1953 to 1957 were now reversed.[27]

As before, the confiscated church buildings were turned over to local governments for alternative uses. In one instance, a newly constructed church in Sigulda, Latvia, was seized by the local government for use as a food store.[28] Whether in fact local officials converted most churches to secular uses, or merely left them unused, is debatable. A review of closed churches in Estonia by CARC officials in 1963 caused anxiety among local officials.[29] A Latvian study in 1973 indicated that of the 132 church buildings returned to local authorities in the period from 1950 to 1973, 43 had not in fact been converted, since they were in poor condition. Yet a later study in 1980 indicated that of 142 churches deregistered between 1950 and 1980, only 17 buildings were ruined. The discrepancy suggests that many churches, though deregistered during the Khrushchev era, were neither converted to secular uses nor razed, but in fact kept in limbo.[30]

Local officials sometimes sought to meet their quota of closures by targeting minority faiths. Officials in heavily Catholic Latgāle hit Lutheran churches disproportionately, in order to limit popular resentment of the policy; in more Lutheran regions of Vidzeme and Kurzeme, Catholic mission parishes appear to have been disproportionately closed.[31] Local officials attempted this tactic against ROC churches, but were often overruled by republic-level Latvian officials.[32] This asymmetry was apparent in Estonia as well, with the Herrnhuter and Orthodox churches bearing the brunt of the campaign, to the relative advantage of the dominant Lutheran Church. During the brief period from 1961 to 1963 alone, thirty-four churches were closed, of which fourteen were from the small Orthodox community.[33] The even tinier Herrnhuter movement, registered by the regime in 1948 as branches of the Lutheran churches, saw its registrations cancelled, constituting over 20 percent of all closures in Estonia.[34] The republic officials viewed the Herrnhuters as a dying movement that could be better controlled under the umbrella of the weak Methodist Church, simultaneously reinforcing the uneasy relationship between the pietistic Herrnhuter movement and the Lutheran Church.[35]

In the case of certain high-profile parishes, the policy of closing churches became very contentious, leading to conflict with the churches. In Tallinn, the local government proposed closing the large Peeteli Lutheran parish and converting it into a theater for Estonian television.[36] It claimed that any parishioners who would be inconvenienced by the closure could be accommodated by the other churches in Tallinn. Despite protests by Bishop Kiivit, the church was closed.

In Riga, the Latvian Lutheran Church faced even more contentious battles over two prominent churches that the regime sought to close. With its central location and superb acoustics, the magnificent Riga Cathedral became a lightning rod in the Church's relationship with the state in the late 1950s. Despite its imposing edifice, the number of parishioners had plummeted even as the costs of maintenance had risen. In an effort to develop more support for the cathedral, Bishop Turs had taken advantage of the earlier liberalization to begin public organ concerts, along with outreach activities and tours for visitors. Several times state officials warned him to curtail these activities.[37] During the new crackdown, the state turned up the pressure. Charging that the church was unable to maintain the building, the local authorities in Riga decided to abrogate the registration agreement with the parish.[38] Intimidated by the authorities, the church organist issued a formal statement attesting to the state of disrepair of the organ; students, musicians, and artists signed a petition calling for state control of the church.[39] An expert analysis concluded that the church was unable to pay for the maintenance of the church.[40] The commissioner in Riga supported the planned seizure.

Under fire within the Church for being too passive, Turs sought to counter the state's pressure. He threatened his resignation and made direct appeals to members and clergy republic-wide for contributions to demonstrate the church's ability to maintain the structure.[41] Speculating that Moscow's interest might be different than the local Latvian position, Turs appealed to the Soviet Peace Committee, arguing that the annual services held in the cathedral to commemorate the victory of the Red Army on May 9 could no longer be held.[42] In a measure of the church's new possibilities, Bishop Turs also appealed to foreign churches for political support in deterring the state's efforts to close the cathedral. Turs requested support from the LWF and German Lutheran churches, hoping that the regime's new-found interest in ties with the Western Protestant churches would translate into clout for the Church.[43] The LWF responded by inquiring with Soviet authorities. Delegations to Riga also lobbied the regime discreetly on behalf of retaining Church authority over the cathedral. But despite its high profile, this case demonstrates the limits of international clout and the peace issue during the Khrushchev repression: Turs's efforts to trump the local and Latvian authorities via Moscow proved unsuccessful, and the cathedral was deregistered and seized by the regime on March 25, 1959. It was to serve as a state concert hall for the next thirty years.

In another high-profile case in Latvia, the government sought to seize Riga's large New Gertrude parish. Rumors that the state would merge it with a Baptist parish gave way to a proposal in 1961 for a merger with the Old Gertrude parish.[44] Turs sought to deflect this plan by offering the Riga Reformed parish to the state instead, but this alternative was rejected by the authorities.[45] The Latvian officials' machinations included the tactic of offering Turs an increase in church publications and a meeting with republic leaders in exchange for his acquiescence to the "request" to close New Gertrude. According to the plan, "Turs will consider such a reception as a great honor and trust, as exclusive attention of the government to his person ... and then in the form of a wish, the state will raise the question of transferring New Gertrude to the Gosarchiv (state archive), for which the Reformed church is inappropriate."[46] With this tactic, the state was using the same strategy used with the Russian Orthodox Church by CROC, namely placing the onus for closing churches and monasteries on the church leadership itself.[47]

Finally, the case of the Catholic church in Daugavpils demonstrates the high political stakes involved in the issue of church closures. Located in Latgāle, largely Catholic but with a significant Orthodox population as well, Daugavpils proved a test case of state policy. Local authorities sought to close the Catholic church there in 1961, but Commissioner Pizāns overturned this decision after the visit of the deputy head of CARC to Latvia. But this decision to leave the church open was countered by Arvid Pelše, head of the Latvian Communist party, who apparently possessed sufficient clout with the party leadership in Moscow to reverse the decision. Moreover, Pelše managed to oust the commissioner over the dispute.[48] The case of Daugavpils is indicative not only of the particular antagonism toward the Catholic Church, but also the clout of ambitious republic officials in pursuing the hard-line campaign.

The campaign to close churches clearly targeted some denominations more than others: Catholics, Jews, Old Believers, and Moslems were more affected than Lutherans and other Protestants. By contrast, the Baptists became more vulnerable to indirect pressure from the regime to close churches. With fewer members than the established churches, many Baptist parishes often met in rented premises. However, during this period of repression, the private owners of these premises began to cancel the rental agreements, leaving the Baptists without a place of worship.[49] The archival records are replete with requests to register new parishes that were rejected by the state officials; indeed, in this period, it was rare that a request was approved by the state. For example, repeated Lutheran attempts to register a parish in a new residential suburb of Riga, Salaspils, were rejected, despite a supporting petition with 475 signatories.[50] Catholic Bishop Strods's requests for registration and for construction projects, were repeatedly rejected by Latvian authorities.[51]

The drive to close churches suggests yet another reversal in regime strategy concerning political control. After massive closures during the late Stalin period, the regime had tilted from 1954 to 1957 toward registration of previously unregistered groups in order to better manage them. Now, still alarmed by the activity of these underground groups but averse to registering them, CARC sought to rely instead on mobilizing the KGB to monitor their activity. To be sure, Baltic authorities claimed that few such unregistered groups existed in their republics, but the problem would soon grow.[52]

The state also moved to reclaim large houses and land that had been included in the original registration agreements with parishes. Citing Soviet decrees from 1919 and claiming that these had been included by mistake, the state now seized them. In a high-profile case, the Catholic Church was forced to forfeit its Curia building in Riga, as well as land in Bauska. Protests of Lutheran and Catholic churches were to no avail.[53] Though the Latvian commissioner initially opposed these seizures, fearing criticism by church leaders, by 1959 he fell in line with the property crackdown.

Institutional Interests: Legal and Financial Issues

As noted in the discussion of closures, the regime often used financial pressure as a tactic to justify closing parishes. It also used tax policy to heighten pressure on churches more generally in this period. In Latvia, the Finance Ministry hiked the tax on all church lands, including parsonages and parcels with church buildings. Commissioner Restberg annulled this move, but monasteries remained subject to the higher tax and tax hikes continued to be used against parishes and clergy.[54] Local officials were ordered to clamp down on collection of any money outside church premises or for charitable purposes. In Estonia, the churches were charged rent for use of the parsonages.[55]

An important thrust of the Khrushchev repression was also legal restriction on parish governance. Clerics had dominated the church councils in both Catholic and Protestant churches in the Baltics. Church councils were now limited to three members, and the cleric registered for the parish was prohibited from sitting on that parish council or having any influence over the financial accounting in the parish.[56] In practice, however, Catholic priests continued to dominate parish councils.[57] CARC ruled in 1961 that the constitutions of the Lutheran churches in the Baltics were in violation of this new law and in need of revision.[58] Though the Latvian Church modified its constitution in 1968 to comport with the law, the Estonian Church never adopted the changes, and pastors remained more central to parish governance in that republic. The Baptists' constitution was changed by their Moscow headquarters; the Methodists were also forced to alter their constitution in Tallinn.[59]

Institutional Interests: Publications

Unsurprisingly the harsher line also affected church access to publications. Imports of religious literature were subjected to tighter controls. An analysis by the Central Committee apparatus, based on information from the censorship authority, Glavlit, found a dramatic increase in imported religious literature with anti-Soviet content, especially in the western USSR. Émigré organizations were blamed for this trend.[60] Despite its privileged status, the ROC did not escape this crackdown: dismissing CROC's political and practical objections, Glavlit sought successfully to retract the right of the ROC to import literature directly and made CROC solely responsible for such imports.[61] Significant quantities of imported literature were confiscated from the ROC Theological Academy in Zagorsk as well. Nor was literature sent from socialist countries exempt: books and journals sent by the GDR churches were often seized.

Perhaps more significantly, the recently improved possibilities for domestic religious publication in the USSR were now circumscribed. Suggesting that publication of Baltic church calendars had become routine, CARC proposed devolving decision-making power over such publications to the republic level, a proposal that was rejected by the Central Committee, which wanted to retain veto power over each publication in Moscow.[62] Moscow also moved to cut the numbers of church calendars for the Estonian Lutheran Church in 1958, despite the commissioner's objection to the negative impact of this measure on the Lutheran churches there. For all Lutheran churches, the state reduced the annual publications from 22,000 to 12,000.[63]

But the state hesitated to eliminate the publications for Lutherans entirely, since they represented a distinctive part of the Lutheran tradition.[64] Moreover, the churches cleverly sought to blunt these cuts by linking publications to their increased international work. The Latvian Lutherans proposed to link the sales of songbooks to their dues to the CPC, but were rebuffed immediately by the Latvian authorities; the USSR would pay the dues itself for participation in this organization, largely a creature of the Soviet regime in any case. But eventually this linkage with the increased international ties of the churches would be accepted by CARC, which lobbied the republics to approve increased church publications to finance this activity valued by the regime. In 1960, Commissioner Restberg confirmed the linkage: "These ties exist by order of the CC-CPSU.... Participation by the Latvian Lutherans in these ties is evaluated positively ... since it is the only measure where the church gives well-known advantage to the Soviet government."[65] Both Lutheran tradition and rising international exposure helped limit the damage of repression in this area.

The curtailment of publications did have a chilling side effect on inter-republic church relations. Earlier, Turs had been solicitous of improved ties with the small Lithuanian Lutheran Church. But now the Lithuanians' request for Latvian-language Bibles was rejected by the Latvian Church, and later by the Lithuanian authorities as well.[66]

Repression of Religious Practice

A major step of the regime under Khrushchev was the renewed campaign to eliminate monasteries and curtail pilgrimages to so-called holy places. In the mid-1950s popular participation in Catholic pilgrimages had begun to rise again, after having declined under Stalin. Regarding Aglona and Kannepene, Latvian pilgrimage sites, the state grew alarmed, particularly by the number of Catholics from outside Latvia and by the number of priests celebrating.[67]

Moscow used legal changes to curtail such pilgrimages, namely a resolution of the USSR Council of Ministers promulgated in October 1958, which then served as the blueprint for republic laws.[68] Evidence suggests that the main targets were Catholics and Moslems, but this did not deter CARC from hounding the Estonian authorities on this issue, despite their rebuttal that pilgrimages were not a tradition in Lutheranism.[69] Lumping Catholics with Moslems and Armenians, CARC concluded that "it is necessary for administrative organs and procurators to strengthen the battle with parasitic elements which exploit religious feelings of believers for their selfish goals."[70] Latvian authorities sought to pressure the Catholic leadership in 1959, making their recognition of Peter Strods as new apostolic administrator contingent on his guarantee that only local priests would participate in the pilgrimage services at Aglona and that there would be no processions outside church territory.[71]

The legal campaign against pilgrimages initially seemed ineffective, leading the regime to resort to administrative chicanery, such as forbidding the use of kolkhoz trucks to transport pilgrims, scheduling sporting events during the pilgrimage, and forbidding sale of food near the site. By 1959 and 1960 the intensified measures apparently brought the desired results: state officials claimed that "mass-cultural programs" and warnings had sharply reduced participation in Latvian pilgrimages to Aglona.[72]

Latvian authorities eventually sought to completely close the Catholic monasteries and nunneries. The nunnery at Aglona was dismissed as "a center of oppression of women" exerting a "negative influence," particularly on younger women. Along with the monastery at Vilani, it was slated to be closed to find work for the "dropouts from life" who resided there.[73] In 1960, despite protests from the German Embassy, it was liquidated. The Orthodox monastery in Latvia, however, was spared this fate, suggesting the favored treatment for the Orthodox.[74]

In addition to new proscriptions of pilgrimages and monasteries, other forms of religious practice were restricted. The 1945 law permitting religious rites in the home was abrogated.[75] The existing sanctions against youth work and religious instruction were again enforced more strictly. Catholic priests were warned and deregistered, and even arrested and convicted in increasing numbers.[76] Although the conflict over religious instruction had largely ended for Lutherans by the late 1940s, the increased international contacts led some leaders to reopen the issue.[77] After his visit to Czechoslovakia for the formation of the CPC, Turs was intrigued by the existence of religious instruction there, to the chagrin of the commissioner. Turs announced that confirmation would occur at age fifteen instead of eighteen, citing the practice of other socialist countries to confirm at age fourteen. The Catholic leadership was again skewered for permitting the participation of youth in services.[78]

Lacking a monastic tradition, Lutherans avoided conflict with the regime over pilgrimages, but found other aspects of religious practice now impeded. For example, local authorities increasingly prohibited cemetery days commemorating the dead unless preapproved by authorities. Large numbers of complaints led the republic-level commissioners to correct these authorities' illegal actions.[79] Implementing a new Soviet law, local officials increasingly also sought to prohibit the ringing of church bells.[80]

Clergy replacement also became more difficult during this period. Under liberalization clergy released from prison camps had been reintegrated into parish life, but now they found it more difficult to obtain the certification from the commissioner necessary to legally serve a parish.[81]

Theological Education

Hard-hit again by the renewed repression was the churches' ability to train clergy. In Estonia the correspondence courses begun by the Baptists were eliminated in 1961, though the Lutherans were permitted to continue.[82] The regime began to question the political reliability of those admitted to theological training, increasingly expelling them for this reason. In 1960, current students were expelled from the Latvian Lutheran courses, and new admissions were curtailed in draconian fashion.[83] The students protested to the Latvian government and Moscow, to no avail. By 1962, the state suspended the training entirely, not to reopen until 1968.

In one aspect of theological education, namely postgraduate training, there seemed to be a modest breakthrough for the churches. A leading concern of the churches, particularly Lutheran ones, had been the training of professors of theology. With the emigration of pastors, the aging demographic of those remaining, and particularly the closing of the theology departments at the universities in Riga and Tartu, the churches feared that they would be unable to sustain a professorate with advanced degrees in theology in order to prepare the future generation of clergy. As a result of the Lutherans' new international ties, the British churches sought to ameliorate this danger by inviting the Baltic churches to send students to Britain to study for doctorates in theology. CARC approved the churches' request and the commissioners handpicked two candidates, Kaide Rätsep of Estonia and Janis Vejs of Latvia, to attend Oxford in 1958.[84] Various indicators also point to KGB assignments for the two candidates. The initiative was only partially successful: Rätsep returned to Estonia as a pastor but never taught theology; Vejs recanted his faith and became a researcher in scientific atheism. As a result the churches lost their enthusiasm for this option. Later, the son of Bishop Kiivit was rejected by the state for study abroad in Germany, though Kuno Pajula of Estonia was approved to study for two years in Göttingen, Germany, in 1960.[85] Ironically, invitations from the theology faculty of Martin Luther University in Halle to send theology students to the socialist GDR were never approved by the regime.

Atheistic Propaganda

Not surprisingly, the Khrushchev period was characterized by heightened propaganda in the media against religion and the churches, with corresponding resolutions by party and state organizations and an explosion of publications.[86] Party propagandists increasingly monitored sermons, which were seen as "reactionary, anti-scientific, and hostile to Marxism-Leninism" and "interfering with the success of construction of communism."⁸⁷ The antireligious campaign focused particularly on teachers and youth, including harassment at school and pressure to forego participation in church choirs and confirmation. Atheist clubs were started in schools and universities.⁸⁸ Estonian Commissioner Veiderpass exhorted, "we should now fight for every young person who has fallen prisoner to the church and its agents. The closer we move toward communism, the clearer the inconsistency between these relics of the past and the spiritual perspective of the person of the new society."⁸⁹

Often this took very crude forms, such as impugning the morals of clergy. For example, under the title, "Serving Two Masters," *Cīna*, the Latvian party paper, accused Professor Smigal of the Riga seminary of a loose lifestyle with women.⁹⁰ Catholic internal documents from interwar Latvia were used to denigrate priests.⁹¹ Underscoring the state's refusal to accept his succession to Springovičs, the press incorrectly referred to Strods as bishop of Liepāja, not archbishop of the Riga diocese.⁹² In *Komsomolskaya Pravda*, the Latvian head of Komsomol accused Strods of ordering Catholic priests to buy all available copies of the anti-Catholic Czech novel, *The Good Soldier Schweik*.⁹³

The vehicle for the antireligious campaign was the new organization, Znanie (Knowledge), and its publication, *Nauka i Religiia* (Science and Religion). Znanie sought to carve out a larger role for itself in the state apparatus for religious policy, unsuccessfully proposing creation of an inter-ministry council to promote scientific atheism.⁹⁴

In a particularly pernicious tactic, clergy were blackmailed into recanting their faith and ordination and then were showcased in the regime's atheistic propaganda.⁹⁵ For example, Estonian Commissioner Veiderpass facilitated such an exposé of an Estonian Lutheran pastor.⁹⁶ Nor were Catholic priests immune to this tactic. The commissioners in the Baltic republics tended to initially defend the Church against this crude campaign. They upbraided the publishers of the attack against Bishop Strods.⁹⁷ Seeing the propaganda as largely ineffective, even counterproductive to the goal of regulating religion, some state officials opposed a return to it. The Estonian commissioner argued in 1959 that the "shrill and exaggerated perspective" in the newspaper attacks promoted "talk among believers of a 'repression of clergy.'"⁹⁸ Yet CARC in Moscow promoted the campaign, praising the high quality and frequency of the articles in Estonia and Latvia.⁹⁹

An important part of this new promotion of atheistic propaganda was the introduction of secular rites of passage to substitute for the religious ones, particularly confirmation. Pioneered in 1954 in the GDR and based on the coming-of-age (*Jugendweihe*) ceremony of the atheistic movement, they were now imported into the Baltics by the Soviets and modified as "summer days of youth" celebrations. They eventually proved quite successful from the regime's viewpoint. Reflecting "the time of year when nature tells of the change from stormy spring to a time of courageous maturity," they were to be "political, patriotic, and atheistic measures, manifested in emotional, aesthetic and ritual form." Yet in the pledge at the final ceremony, there was to be no mention of God *or* atheism.[100] Their contacts among German church leaders likely informed the Baltic Lutheran pastors of the insidious danger to confirmation participation.

In Estonia, officials employed traditional folk customs in an effort to increase the attractiveness of the secular rites.[101] Ironically, following Khrushchev's lead and using *Nauka i Religiia*, party propagandists attacked similar Latvian folk holidays, such as Ligo Day, as heathen and ideologically reactionary. However, like the Estonians, the Latvian party leadership supported Ligo Day and lobbied against such attacks, fearing the counterproductive effect of banning its celebration. The regime was ambivalent as to whether such folk practices represented a means of eroding religion, or a religious celebration in different form.[102] In the new climate of repression, the Komsomol and local authorities sometimes intimidated confirmands in order to pump up participation in the summer days of youth.[103] The least popular of these rites was burial: state officials called for increased "participation of the workers' collective in the burials of those who worked in the enterprise [which would] not only deliver a decisive blow to the main income of Lutheran pastors, but would contribute to the development of the new traditions."[104]

The response of the church leadership was muted. Bishop Kiivit requested reports of antireligious articles in the press from his subordinates, but the Estonian authorities interdicted the distribution of his letter and Kiivit offered little protest over this usurpation of internal church communication.[105] The loss of youth engagement in the churches due to the secular rites would eventually, in the late 1970s, produce a backlash among younger clergy disappointed with the passivity of church leaders in the face of the atheistic campaign.

International Relations and the Churches

Guiding the international relations of the churches during this period was a heightened effort by Moscow to use the churches in its foreign policy. The regime continued to view most international church organizations ideologically as tools of Western policy, but it began to see some progressive elements and political advantage in them. CARC Chair Puzin maintained that "in contrast to the churches in the USSR, those abroad are politically powerful, capable of influence over public opinion and the official policy of their countries."[106] To be sure, CARC's main thrust was to increase ties with Moslems and Buddhists in Asia, reflecting Khrushchev's interest in bridgeheads in the Third World. But increasing the coherence of the East bloc by consolidating ties among the East Bloc churches and opening a new flank against the Catholic Church was also an essential component of this strategy. The Central Committee of the CPSU took the decision to support this opening to international religious organizations in 1960.[107] Destined to become a lead vehicle for this mobilization of the churches throughout the Soviet period was the CPC. Organized by Josef Hromadka in Czechoslovakia, it was designed to be more effective than the World Peace Council, which had been the Soviets' main propaganda instrument in the early 1950s. Though most Western church leaders were skeptical of it, the CPC did find easy partners in Eastern Europe.[108] CARC and CROC largely controlled CPC planning, with the GDR Communists giving major input.[109]

Another organizational vehicle under the new strategy was the WCC. The documentary evidence is fairly convincing that the opening to this Western ecumenical organization was motivated by the desire to blunt the perceived threat of the Vatican to the Russian Orthodox Church, rather than by the WCC's usefulness for the regime's peace campaign or its need to compete with émigré churches. Moscow's analyses of Pope John XXIII's proposed Vatican Council were suffused with alarm, seeing it as a tactical shift by the Vatican in its efforts to battle communism.[110] The KGB concurred, concluding that Vatican representatives had lobbied hard but unsuccessfully with the WCC, particularly Protestant and Orthodox members, to prevent Soviet membership.[111] In this orientation the regime certainly found encouragement from the ROC, despite rumors of patriarchal interest in participating in the Vatican Council.[112] After state-supported overtures to the WCC by the ROC, the other Soviet churches followed suit.[113] A WCC delegation to the USSR in 1959 explored the issue of membership with the Soviet Lutheran churches. The decision to accept the Soviet Lutheran churches was more fraught in the case of the Estonian Church than the Latvian Church: the Estonian exile church had been a founding member of the WCC in 1948 and lobbied against admitting the Soviet church; the Latvian exile church, on the other hand, joined the WCC only in 1971 and as a non-member was in a weak position to oppose admitting the Soviet church.[114]

The opening to a third international organization, the LWF, was more complicated, due to émigré church opposition and the failed attempt to join in 1957. As host to the LWF Assembly in 1963, the Finnish Church was to play a key role in reversing this outcome.[115] CARC promoted Kiivit's contacts with the Finnish Church as an avenue to explore membership. Despite the close political ties with the USSR, the Finnish churches had earlier been cool to the Soviet Lutherans: contacts had been limited to the bishop of Tampere and focused primarily on their fellow Ingrian Finns in the Leningrad Region, not the Baltic churches. In 1959, however, they expressed an interest in visiting Estonia. By linking their visit with an invitation to the LWF General Secretary, Kiivit managed to obtain state approval for such an invitation.[116] Latvian and Estonian admission to the LWF was crucial to the regime's strategy for the WCC, namely to counter the

Vatican. Eventually, in 1962, the Finns reciprocated with invitations to Kiivit.[117] In preparation for admission to the LWF in 1963, the number of international visits to Estonia and Latvia skyrocketed.[118]

The CEC provided an attractive new venue for the Soviet churches, since, unlike the WCC and the LWF, American churches were not members of the CEC. The regime increasingly encouraged deepening contacts with this organization, and the Baltic Lutheran churches became active members.[119]

In their contacts with all these organizations, the Soviet church leaders engaged in a certain amount of deception. In an effort to increase their attractiveness and clout, the churches vastly exaggerated the numbers of their members.[120] Always instructed by CARC, they whitewashed the problems facing their churches from the regime and painted relations with the ROC in overly rosy terms.[121]

Not surprisingly, given the diplomatic opening between Khrushchev and Adenauer in 1955, this period also saw increasing contacts with churches in Germany. For the Lutherans, Germany represented a kind of mecca, given its many Luther sites and the large Evangelical-Lutheran churches. During this period contacts were initiated and soon became established; however, they were heavily politicized and manipulated by the regime in pursuit of its German policy. In particular, the regime used them in an effort to undermine the position of conservative West German church leaders opposed to a split in the German churches along East-West lines.[122] Kiivit indulged the regime in this regard, emphasizing in his reporting to the state his success in reducing the influence of the United States and conservative German church leaders in international organizations, such as the CEC.[123]

In this context, exchanges with "progressives" in the GDR were particularly encouraged by Moscow. In 1958 and 1960, the East German Christian Democratic Union (CDU), a puppet party of the GDR Communists and a vehicle for their efforts to build legitimacy among GDR Christians and outflank the West German churches, invited the Soviet Lutherans to send a delegation to its congress.[124] The Soviet embassies in East Berlin and Bonn, as well as CARC, strongly supported these ties, considering it not simply "expedient" but "necessary" for Soviet Lutherans to participate in meetings of "progressive" GDR groups, such as the CDU and Weimar Circle; the Central Committee apparatus concurred.[125] Capstone of this GDR-strategy was the visit of Bishop Moritz Mitzenheim and his adjutant Ingo Braecklein to the Baltics in 1962.[126] Thus the Baltic Lutherans came to play an integral role in the Soviets' German policy.

The small but established Lutheran minority churches in Eastern Europe also represented considerable potential for contacts. After early suspicion, the state came to promote activity in the LWF's subgroup, Lutheran Minority Churches in Europe, seeing it as anti-Catholic.[127] Similarly, the state encouraged the Baltic Lutheran leaders to establish contact with the Polish Lutheran Church, again with an eye to offsetting Catholic power in Poland.

Within the overall context of these new international opportunities for the non-Catholic churches in the Baltics, the state increasingly differentiated among its church diplomats. In particular, it grew increasingly dissatisfied with Turs's role. His obsequiousness toward the Orthodox Church hierarchy, particularly in the presence of visiting church delegations such as the EKD, undermined his credibility and reinforced Western preconceptions of ROC preeminence in Soviet foreign policy.[128] After his international meetings he was often upbraided by CARC for attempting to activate religion in Latvia.[129] Turs was particularly interested in ties with the West German *Bruderschaften*, whose leftist stance and influence in the Federal Republic of Germany (FRG) was seen by the Soviet regime as useful.[130] But Turs's request to attend the WCC General Assembly in New Delhi in 1961 was vetoed by CARC.[131]

By contrast, the star of Kiivit continued to rise during this period, with both Western churches and Soviet officials. CARC instructed Estonian officials to widen his contacts with "progressive" church leaders in Europe (especially in Germany and the CEC).[132] Kiivit, rather than Turs, was invited by Ernst Wilm, prominent leader of the Westphalian regional church and EKD, to lecture throughout West Germany in 1958.[133] Again in 1959, the EKD invited only Kiivit, in contrast to 1956 when both Turs and Kiivit were invited.[134] LWF officials also implied that the Turs-led Latvian Church was not a good candidate for admission to the LWF.[135] The GDR Peace Committee in 1960 requested a visit by both Turs and Kiivit, but Edgar Hark substituted for Kiivit; similarly, Kiivit declined to attend the CDU party congress in the GDR. Kiivit's growing credibility with Western church leaders would have been compromised by visits to such Communist-dominated organizations in the GDR, and the Soviets sent lower-level Estonian representatives instead.[136] Turs resented this treatment and sought to convince the state he was a stronger supporter.

Some groups did not benefit from the international opening. Overtures from the Reformed World Alliance to the Reformed churches, including those in Latvia, were rebuffed by the state, due to fear of contacts with oppositional Reformed elements in Transcarpathian Ukraine.[137]

For its part, the Catholic Church continued to be quite problematic from the regime's perspective, particularly on questions of foreign policy. To be sure, the state found Bishop Strods's strong opposition to atomic testing encouraging.[138] But the Church rejected participation in Soviet friendship societies and public positions on foreign policy issues, such as the US intervention in Lebanon in 1958. Indeed, state officials labeled Strods a "true slave of the Pope."[139] Contacts with the Vatican continued to be taboo. CARC rejected a Soviet Catholic delegation to the funeral of Pius XII in 1958 ("none of the higher Catholic clergy are reliable").[140] The state forbade annual reports by the Soviet dioceses to the Vatican, fearing that such reports would increase "anti-Soviet propaganda."[141]

Instead of Catholic leaders, the regime sought to encourage the development of international contacts with "progressive" Catholics. The Latvian Catholic Church was pressured to join the Berlin Conference of European Catholics, a largely lay organization formed in the 1950s by the GDR to advocate for peace, justice, and socialism and critical of the Vatican. Yet requests by Soviet embassies in the West for Catholic delegations were usually rebuffed by Moscow with the categorical statement that "Catholic clergy do not travel."[142] The regime also attempted to promote contacts with East Bloc Catholic leaders deemed acceptable by the state. For example, Hungarian party officials promoted Archbishop Joszef Grösz of Hungary for a visit to the USSR.[143]

The regime was interested only in highly orchestrated support for its peace campaign by the churches. Efforts by the Latvian Lutheran churches to raise voluntary contributions for the Soviet Peace Fund were vetoed by CARC.[144] The regime desired only formal contributions by the church hierarchy, not a popular test of its peace propaganda in the parishes.

Local and republic officials were often less enthralled than Moscow by the increased international exposure. As noted above, the heightened contacts, particularly with churches in the East Bloc, led some church leaders to make increased claims on the state: Lutherans raised anew the issue of religious instruction and broached the confirmation of youth at age fifteen instead of sixteen; the churches sought to leverage the international contacts for increased publications.[145] The German churches sought to use the Baltic Lutherans as intermediaries to establish contact with the isolated Soviet German Lutherans, efforts rebuffed by both church and state officials.[146] Indeed, local officials saw the ties as "useful only for the German friends, since foreign delegations constitute a 'happening' for local believers."[147]

Moreover, the local officials lacked the background to master the nuances of foreign partnerships and were forced to rely on church leaders themselves for information. The commissioner in Estonia, for example, incorrectly equated the German Bruderschaften (anti-Nazi and often leftist in political orientation) with the "fanatical" *Bratsvo* of Herrnhuters in Estonia, leading him to oppose visits by these Germans.[148] At the republic level officials were often disinclined to encourage foreign ties, fearing an activation of religion and churches.

An archival study of the growing communications flow necessary to deal with this increasing international contact illuminates the decision-making process itself, and the bureaucratic interests that developed as a result. International invitations were initially discussed between the commissioner and the responsible church leader in an effort to determine the level of interest of the church leader and the preferences of the commissioner. The commissioner was charged with obtaining the approval of republic authorities. Then he would make a recommendation to CARC, which would inquire with the Foreign Ministry as to the advisability of the travel from the perspective of Soviet foreign policy, usually after consulting with the particular Soviet embassy in question. Only then would CARC submit its recommendation to the CPSU Central Committee apparatus for final approval. The lengthy and involved bureaucratic process certainly complicated international church relations, although they did acquire a certain routinization by the end of this period.

The Soviet intelligence apparatus, particularly in the Eastern Bloc, made these international contacts somewhat risky for the individuals involved. For example, CDU informants in the GDR reported on Estonian delegates attending the CDU convention in 1960. The Estonians' confidential criticism of their fellow Baltic Lutherans was then often reported indirectly back to Moscow.[149]

The state officials responsible for the churches sought to accommodate the increased workload attendant to this growing international activity. The Baltic commissioners now included extensive time for international relations in their work plans and asked for additional staffing to deal with the new responsibilities. Likewise, CARC and CROC requested the creation of deputy director positions to handle international relations. Despite the new demands on the commissioners, the Central Committee rejected their efforts to bargain for more staff by playing the "international card."[150]

The archival record also suggests the growing import of Eastern Bloc allies in the decision process, particularly the GDR officials regarding the German question. At the republic level, officials were rather disinclined to encourage contacts with the Lutheran churches in the GDR, naturally fearing the infection of ideas and demands stemming from the far more liberal policy toward religion in the GDR. But the evidence is clear that GDR officials repeatedly lobbied successfully with the Soviet Embassy, whose endorsement "at the request of the comrades" was usually sufficient to overcome republic level resistance. Hans Seigewasser, in charge of religious affairs in the GDR government, pressed for invitations to the USSR for Bishop Friedrich-Wilhelm Krummacher in order to influence him regarding inter-German church issues.[151] The GDR Communists vetoed the visit of Soviet Lutherans to the July 1961 all-German Kirchentag in Berlin and lobbied against inviting the new head of the EKD, Kurt Scharf, to Moscow, suspecting him of using ecumenical ties to maintain inter-German church unity.[152]

Yet, in other cases, Moscow overrode concerns of the Foreign Ministry, as regarding contacts with the LWF. In 1959, LWF officials had visited Estonia, but the state vetoed a 1962 visit by Kiivit to Bishop Martti Simojoki of Finland, due to his anticommunist orientation, and was ambivalent about contacts with LWF officials. However, Moscow's interest in joining the LWF trumped the objections of the Soviet Embassy in Helsinki and the Foreign Ministry: with the LWF General Assembly scheduled for Helsinki in 1963, Kiivit was permitted to accept Simojoki's invitation.[153]

Church Leadership and Political Dissent

As this discussion of his foreign role suggests, Latvian Bishop Turs continued to leave the regime ambivalent. Without a trace of irony, state officials criticized him for being authoritarian and out of step with the post-Stalin era, citing his failure to schedule a synod since 1951 and reliance on his close clique in the HCA.[154] Yet the regime sought to exploit his weak authority among the grassroots in the churches by increasing his international activities and reveled in his lukewarm resistance to repressive measures by the state. In a clear statement of the regime's strategy, the commissioner wrote, "it is desirable to use Turs even more for various international ties and distract him from the direction of church affairs in the republic. This would enable the future decline of parishes and mass exodus of believers from the church."[155]

With the Latvian Catholic Church, the regime confronted a much more oppositional leadership. A key confrontation with the regime developed over the Latvian Catholic leadership. Despite his earlier role in the Soviet peace propaganda campaign in the 1950s, Bishop Strods was now seen by the state as a nationalist, fanatically committed to the Catholic Church and the Pope. Critical of the lack of religious freedom in the USSR, he had become reluctant to lend public support to Soviet initiatives regarding émigrés and foreign policy.[156] The regime, as earlier described, contested the Vatican's planned succession of Bishop Strods as apostolic administrator of the Riga Diocese and used this uncertainty to gain bargaining advantage over him and the Catholic hierarchy. Strods was forced to concede to some state demands: limiting priests at pilgrimage services, prohibiting activity of priests outside their registered parish, banning processions outside church territory at Aglona, and forbidding reunions of priests.[157] The regime refused to permit Dulbinskis, rearrested in 1957, to return from exile in Belorussia, despite the entreaties of Strods.[158]

Strods's premature death in 1960, only two years after he had assumed the archbishopric following Springovičs's death in 1958, thrust a renewed succession crisis upon the Catholic Church. Because Dulbinskis, his intended successor as apostolic administrator, remained banned from Latvia, Strods had proposed instead Julijans Zachests of arch-Catholic Latgāle. Zachests was duly named by the Vatican, but like Strods before him, the regime conditioned its approval on concessions by the Church regarding issues in dispute. Zachests refused to agree and indeed criticized the Khrushchev repression; CARC then rejected him as apostolic administrator, refused interaction with him for two years, and threatened to close the Curia office in Riga.¹⁵⁹ Applying heavy pressure to Zachests, the Latvian authorities forced him to resign and yield to Julijans Vaivods in 1962. Despite his advanced age (sixty-seven) and his earlier sentence to a labor camp from 1958 to 1960, Vaivods had long been favored to become head of the Latvian Church by the regime.¹⁶⁰ In addition to his deference to the regime, the regime expected Vaivods to dampen what it perceived as the growing attractiveness of the Polish Church under Cardinal Wyszynski among Latvian clergy, embodied particularly by the banned Dulbinskis.¹⁶¹ After having enjoyed milder treatment than the Lithuanian Catholic Church in the early postwar period, the Latvian Church had now become in fact less autonomous than the Lithuanians.

For individual clergy, who were now monitored more closely, expressions of political dissent were punished by loss of certification. In one example, a funeral sermon equating the military's killing of a child during target practice with murder sufficed to cost a Latvian Lutheran pastor his certification.¹⁶² The monitoring was intensified by the formation in 1963 of local commissions to report on the content of sermons, as the state sought "deeper dissolution of religion ideas and superstition in church sermons and strict limitation of their content to the appropriate limits of the law." In particular the Estonian authorities attacked "active propagation of passivity," arguing that "checks by propagandists keep the clergy in line best of all."¹⁶³

Bureaucratic Friction over the New Repression

The shift toward a hard line on religion precipitated some differences between CARC representatives and republic-level officials. In the case of Latvia, for example, the Council of Ministers pressed for a policy toward the churches harsher than that endorsed by Commissioner Restberg. Commenting critically on Restberg's report, the point man at the Council of Ministers, Berklavs, insisted on notification and approval by local authorities for the Lutherans' cemetery days and repairs to churches. Berklavs also masterminded the blanket rejection of registration requests by the Catholic Church and the initial refusal to accept Strods as the successor to Springovičs.¹⁶⁴ Berklavs was at least partly responsible for the ouster of Restberg and his replacement by hard-liner Pizāns in 1960.¹⁶⁵

Tensions in Moscow also occurred over the shift in policy. As noted, following the death of the more liberal Ivan Polyansky, Aleksei Puzin was named chair of CARC. The Central Committee apparatus criticized the "serious mistakes" of CARC in religious policy; Puzin rebutted that these mistakes belonged to his predecessor.¹⁶⁶ This change was followed later by the ouster of Karpov as chair of CROC. Both Councils were blamed for "serving the church."[167] Like the churches, CARC sought to leverage the churches' increased international contacts into greater resources, but was rebuffed by the Agitprop Department of the CPSU.[168] Repeated proposals during this period to merge the two councils, CROC and CARC, on the grounds of the need for greater coordination of foreign ties and consistency in policy, were rejected by the CPSU leadership.[169]

Summary and Conclusion

There is little doubt of the impact on the churches and believers of these various measures of the Khrushchev repression. After rebounding during the earlier liberalization, church adherence now plummeted, particularly among Lutherans.[170] Even attendance on holidays fell off, and many began to take rites in secret. Official estimates in Estonia claimed that only 10 to 15 percent of church members were observing rites. Pilgrimage participation declined also. As measured by participation in church rites, the drop among Catholics was certainly lower than among Protestants and Orthodox. State reductions of students enrolled at the Catholic seminary in Riga hobbled the ability of the Catholic Church to prepare sufficient numbers of replacement priests.

The Khrushchev repression was clearly a response to the union-wide resurgence of religion during the post-Stalin liberalization. Perhaps the antireligious policy was motivated more by ideology and affected Slavic core areas more, but, in the case of the Baltic churches, the implementation naturally carried antinational overtones, given that most churches were national churches, and that even leaders compromised by their rise to power under Stalin, such as Turs and Kiivit, had sought to broaden the churches' base after 1953.[171] The study demonstrates the intriguing cross-currents produced by simultaneous domestic and foreign developments. Commissioners often sought to soften the crackdown, aware of confessional nuances and fearing the impact on their working relationships with church leaders. In this they were more often than not trumped either by hard-line republican officials, such as Pelše and Berklavs in Latvia, or by Moscow's diktat. Just as CARC underwent personnel upheaval at the top, so too its commissioners in the Baltics found themselves replaced as a result of this bureaucratic battle.[172]

This period also suggests the countervailing effects that Soviet foreign policy can have on the implementation of religious policy. Because the Protestant churches became a key part of the regime broadside against the Catholic Church under John XXIII, republic level officials and commissioners were forced to deal with the increased leverage, however limited, that these ties (WCC, LWF, etc.) brought the churches. Inclined to limit such contacts with Germany and Finland, they found themselves trumped by the Soviet leadership's new effort to use the churches as part of a broader policy shift toward the West, in particular on the German issue. Credibility with both Western church interlocutors and their own grass-roots—even as the churches' institutional interests and those of believers were being curtailed—became tricky for church leaders to maintain.

In terms of the explanatory factors being considered in this study, atheistic ideology and political control provide contextual understanding for this period of renewed repression: no churches or religious actors were exempt from it; though outright terror played much less of a role than in the 1944–1953 period, the state used coercion; and virulent antireligious propaganda again assumed a prominent role. The national overtones of the crackdown could not be avoided, as the traditional churches (Lutheran and Catholic) were affected most, losing many of the institutional advantages they had enjoyed during the previous more liberal period: churches were closed, new registrations rejected, construction projects canceled, publications reduced. The spread of secular rites challenged an important national tradition, namely, confirmation and first communion. But in this particular repressive period, even the already less-institutionalized Baptists lost ground, with legal limits on the role of clergy and pressures against rental of church premises. Thus the repression affected all churches, regardless of the size of their institutional footprint.

But this repression was not a copy of the Stalinist period: it is necessary to add secondary factors to provide a more complete explanation of the pattern. First, the confessional factor offers insight into the regime's differentiation strategy. Unlike the 1940s, however, when it worked to the disadvantage of the Lutherans, this time the Catholic Church was hit harder by the crackdown: pilgrimages, monasteries, religious instruction of youth, theological education, church governance and leadership succession—all were subjected to the harsher policy. International and transnational ties explain a large part of the confessional difference: the Lutherans benefited from the opening to international church organizations in the early 1960s, a function particularly of the Soviet Union's German policy, but also of its anti-Vatican stance. This foreign policy factor provided some limited leverage to the Lutherans that the Catholics lacked.

Bureaucratic politics and interests were on display again, even in this period of repression. Republic officials pressed for a harder line against the churches than that advocated by the commissioners and CARC. Ministries differed in their stance on the direction and tempo of contacts with Western churches and organizations. Lacking information and expertise and fearing the cost in terms of their narrower goals (managing churches, religious leaders, and the decline of religiosity) republic officials and commissioners balked at such contacts.

Notes

1. On the general measures of the Khrushchev antireligious campaign, with focus on the ROC, see Chumachenko, *Church and State*, 154–87, and Pospielovsky, *Soviet Antireligious Campaigns*, 98–108; on the campaign particularly in Estonia, see Viise, "*Estonian Evangelical-Lutheran Church*," 159–79, and Remmel, "(Anti-)Religious Aspects," 362–63.
2. *Cina*, 16 August 1959, cited in Rozitis, "Evangelisch-Lutherische Kirche," 112.
3. In GARF.6991.3.166, l. 87–91, CARC Chair Puzin reported to the Central Committee a similar pattern in Lithuania: Catholic confirmands in Lithuania rose from 43,000 in 1954 to 65,000 in 1956, before declining to 42,000 in 1957. CARC also noted increases among Lutherans between 1954 and 1957, particularly related to holidays and cemetery day events. LVA.1448.1.256, l. 158.
4. LVA.1448.1.260, l. 49.
5. LVA.1448.1.256, l. 112–13; LVA.1448.1.255, l. 146. Bishop Kazimir Dulbinskis and seminary instructor Valerian Zondaks, sentenced earlier to long terms in prison but amnestied after 1954, were rearrested by the KGB, allegedly on the basis of previous mistakes in the amnesty process. Dulbinskis was described in internal *characteristika* as an "active enemy of Soviet power and powerful bourgeois nationalist"; Zondaks was accused of arranging for the secret escape of a critical priest to the Vatican in 1950–1952.
6. GARF.6991.3.146, l. 162–81.
7. GARF.6991.3.486, l. 144–48: Springovičs's request to replace him with Kazimir Sosnovsky and the handwritten note of CARC official Rumyantsev rejecting the idea and planning to use a Lithuanian priest instead. Springovičs and Zondaks were apparently unhappy with Butirovicz's links with the KGB. On the Butirovicz episode in Moscow, see also Fortin, *Catholic Chaplaincy*.
8. RGANI.5.33.55, l. 60, for the resolution of the Lithuanian Central Committee ordering a crackdown.
9. LCVA.181.3.49, l. 5. In this 1957 report, the commissioner particularly highlighted weaknesses in the party line permitting group catechism of children.
10. GARF.6991.3.188, l. 28–42, for the proposed countermeasures.
11. GARF.6991.3.188, l. 47–56, for the final version of the countermeasures.
12. RGANI.5.33.90, l. 103–4.
13. ERA.R-1989.2.22, l. 7–11. Analyzing the one-year increase in church adherence (15 percent for baptisms, 23 percent for weddings in 1957) the commissioner attributed much of the increase to "complex rites," namely, clergy insisting that parents marry and even be confirmed in the church before they baptize their children. The pent-up demand was spent by later in 1958, according to ERA.R-1989.2.22, l. 143–45.
14. RGANI.5.33.126, l. 85–87; GARF.6991.3.97, l. 1–2.
15. In 1961, the Central Committee liquidated the Adventists' religious center, affecting Baltic Adventists along with others throughout the USSR. The KGB's role in eliminating the Adventists' religious center and compromising its leaders and preachers and the continuing effort to remove republic leaders in Latvia is documented in RGANI.5.33.215, l. 78–80. Other sources on the liquidation of the Adventists include GARF.6991.3.210, l. 57–61; LVA.1448.1.261, l. 32–33; ERA.R-1989.2.26, l. 131–33.
16. RGANI.5.33.53, l. 16–20. Karpov attacked the brochure as reflecting the soft line of CARC and the alleged discrimination against the ROC in publications for churches.

Agitprop officials Chernenko and Snastin indicated that reviews of the manuscript were negative, in RGANI.5.33.53, l. 22.

17. See the analysis of the MFA in GARF.6991.3.172, l. 97–100, which sees the new pope as continuing Pius XII's anticommunist stance.

18. GARF.6991.3.197, l. 2–3; GARF.6991.3.197, l. 27–29. Even Vatican overtures to the Serbian Orthodox Church were interpreted in this light.

19. See the KGB's 1959 analysis, GARF.6991.3.197, l. 34–47.

20. The joint 1959 appeal by CARC and CROC chairs, documented in GARF.6991.3.188, l. 22–25, confirms the main motive for permitting the Soviet churches to join the WCC was to "explode the influence of the Vatican as an international center."

21. ERA.R-1989.2.19, l. 55–60. The decision occurred after a consultation visit from a member of CARC to Estonia in November 1956. Oddly the consultation included the commissioner for the ROC in Estonia in the decision-making; in February the Estonian Communist Party and CM ESSR acted to reverse their earlier approval.

22. LVA.1448.1.10, l. 30–31, 33–33r; LVA.1448.1.260. l. 8.

23. ERA.R-1989.2.26, l. 27.

24. ERA.R-1989.2.24, l. 173–74.

25. LVA.1448.1.261, l. 11–16, which contains revelations of "administrative overreaching" by local officials, such as their writing of requests to dissolve parishes and pressuring active churchgoers to quit the dvatsatka.

26. LVA.1448.1.262, l. 13. The state claimed that the Latvian church leadership and parishioners supported the closures. LVA.1448.1.155, l. 19–23 and LVA.1448.1.260, l. 2 and 11–12 are among the numerous reports replete with statistics suggesting declining numbers of services at many parishes, especially Lutheran ones, and with allegations that the churches overestimate their members and underestimate their incomes.

27. ERA.R-1989.2.32, l. 10, documents the case of Krudneri, Põlva raion, which had been registered in 1956. The commissioner reveals the supply-side orientation of the state: "This all indicates that it has become necessary to curtail the network of churches and prayer houses to a number reasonably approximating the true needs of believers."

28. LVA.1448.1.259, l. 35–37.

29. GARF.6991.3.1577, l. 4–8.

30. LVA.1419.3.262, l. 170–76. Seventy-four of the one hundred forty-two churches deregistered during the period 1950–1980 were Lutheran, forty-five Russian Orthodox. Anderson (*Religion, State and Politics*, 66) sees local officials as more hard-line. This seems plausible, given their incentive system, but these later investigations suggest a considerable falloff of actual implementation and the limitations of central oversight, thus a softer line in practice.

31. Trups-Trops, "Römisch-Katholische Kirche," Teil 3, 58. In Daugavpils, repeated requests to reverse decisions to close a Lutheran church were rebuffed by the authorities.

32. LVA.1448.1.261, l. 1–5. In Talsi, Latvia, local authorities closed an Orthodox church in 1961 or 1962 and gave it to the Catholic Church; the Latvian government reversed the politically incorrect decision to give the church to "the more reactionary Catholic Church."

33. ERA.R-1989.2.34, l. 14.

34. ERA.R-1989.2.30, l. 8–9. Of the thirty-four Lutheran parishes closed by 1960, fourteen were Herrnhuter parishes.

35. ERA.R-1989.2.30, l. 38–39. The strategy stated, "under the roof of Methodists, this remnant sect from bourgeois times will not conduct illegal meetings in numerous apartments and there is the possibility to limit its activities to the framework of existing laws on cults." On the other hand, the state reckoned that managing the Methodists would be more complicated with the Herrnhuters.

36. ERA.R-1989.2.30, l. 81–83. "Despite the absence of sufficient information regarding the current Lutheran parish there to justify the closing," the state moved to close the church.

37. LVA.1448.1.257, l. 56–57 documents the commissioners' warnings against organ concerts disguised as worship services, and proposes forbidding them and using state cultural offices to perform such concerts. Rozitis, "Evangelisch-Lutherische Kirche," 118.

38. The decision by the Riga City Executive Committee to cancel the property agreement with the cathedral and set up a government commission to manage it is documented in LVA.1448.1.11, l. 92–93.

39. Letters of Cathedral Organist Nikolai Kachalov to Vilas Lācis, CM LSSR (20 Oct. 1958) and to Riga City Executive Committee, alleging phony repairs on the organ by the church (18 Feb. 1959 and 13 Feb. 1959), and the petition for nationalization (10 Jan. 1959) are documented in LVA.1432.6.242, l. 13–16, 30–31, 33–34, 37.

40. LVA.1448.1.257, l. 139–40. The commission of "authoritative specialists" found that the building was in need of repair, that the organ was not kept in necessary order (particularly due to the lack of heat in the building), and that repairs would cost 1.1 million rubles. It concluded that "the Cathedral has more importance as a museum than as a church for the goal of services" and not surprisingly recommended giving the building to the state.

41. The state forbade the distribution of Turs's appeal, on grounds that it was illegal to solicit contributions outside the particular parish. LVA.1448.1.258, l. 73–75. Turs solicited funds and organ parts from the GDR as well. His threat to resign was apparently made during a meeting of the church leadership in May 1959, in response to dissatisfaction with his role in the cathedral issue.

42. LVA.1448.1.258, l. 79–80 documents Turs's appeal to the Soviet Peace Committee to "defend my conduct of the worship service for peace so that the prohibition of the service by the local government may be annulled" and warns of the "foreign anti-Soviet propaganda" that prohibition would cause.

43. LVA.1448.1.11, l. 63–64, 76, 82. Turs recapitulated to officials the Church's activities in support of peace and friendship of peoples since 1946 and attempted to play on his West German ties to reverse the state's decision. The document is found in LVA.1448.1.11, l. 30–35.

44. LVA.1448.1.258, l. 46–53. Rejecting such merger pressure, the commissioner blamed the rise in Baptist activity on such administrative overreaching.

45. LVA.1448.1.260, l. 61–62. The commissioner argued that the Reformed church building was heavily damaged, in a bad location, and less adaptable for state use than New Gertrude Church. A merger between Reformed and Lutheran groups also portended intramural disputes.

46. LVA.1448.1.260, l. 62.

47. RGANI.5.33.126, l. 74–84 for the Patriarch's agreement to close monasteries in Moldavia SSR and to forbid admission to the remaining monasteries to those under age 30. The Agitprop Department of the CPSU criticized CROC's coordination of harsh measures with the Patriarch as making the commissioners de facto part of the church apparatus, in RGANI.5.33.126, l. 146–47.

48. GARF.6991.3.1426, l. 100–2 confirms that the personnel change was precipitated by the approval of church construction in Daugavpils by the previous commissioner, Pizāns, who ran afoul of the Central Committee in April 1961 and was replaced by Liepa as commissioner on January 17, 1962. See also Trups-Trops, "Römisch-Katholische Kirche," Teil 3, 59. RGANI.5.33.190, l. 105–7, l. 108. This case would support the conclusion of Anderson (*Religion, State and Politics*, 27–28) that regional party officials could trump CARC in a power struggle.

49. Anderson (*Religion, State and Politics*, 55–56) goes so far as to conclude that the number of Lutheran churches actually increased during the Khrushchev period, which seems exaggerated, though Lutherans certainly emerged more unscathed than the ROC and Baptists. GARF.6991.3.1434, l. 1–4. CARC favored permitting the Baptists to build churches, rather than pressuring apartment owners to terminate rental contracts.

50. LVA.1448.1.258, l. 77–78; LVA.1448.1.11, l. 46. The commissioner rejected the petition, arguing that Riga churches were only 19 km away and that petitioners had used scare tactics to collect signatures, alleging the plans of a collective farm to seize the church.

51. In the first half of 1959, Strods requested registration for ten parishes and completion of construction on five buildings, all of which were rejected. Often local parishioners sent formal complaints to Riga regarding these issues. LVA.1448.1.258, l. 76, 93–94.

52. LVA.1448.1.257, l. 24.

53. In 1959, the commissioner reversed the confiscation of the Curia. LVA.1448.1.258, l. 76. On Bauska, see LVA.1448.1.257, l. 151–54. Citing 1919 decrees on separation of church and state of the temporary Soviet Latvian government, Latvian officials rebuffed complaints by local Lutherans in Sabile about the house confiscation, according to LVA.1448.1.10, l. 24.

54. LVA.1448.1.257, l. 135; LVA.1448.1.261, l. 61–65; LVA.1448.1.260, l. 2, 5, alleges underreporting of income by pastors and tax hikes on them.

55. ERA.R-1989.2.26, l. 26.

56. Similar to the earlier debate regarding whether Soviet decrees from 1918 were sufficient to legally support nationalization in the newly added Baltic republics after 1945, LVA.938.6.91a, l. 105–8 indicates that J. Fredrickson, Chair of Juridical Commission of CM LSSR, rejected the need for particular Latvian decrees or legislation, maintaining that the new 1961 Union legislation regarding cults provided sufficient legal basis.

57. For Lithuania, see LCVA.181.3.59, l. 50–51, and LCVA.181.3.61, l. 29, regretting that "the priests are removed from the executive organs of the parish, but parishioners are not the real masters."

58. LVA.1448.1.156, l. 15. CARC ruled that the Latvian Lutheran constitution was in violation of the law on cults. ERA.R-1989.2.27, l. 32. CARC ruled that the Estonian Lutheran constitution was also in violation. Confirming this Estonian exception, Lieberg, "Aus der Estnischen," 107; Veem, "Estnische Evangelisch-Lutherische Kirche," 106–7.

59. ERA.R-1989.2.28, l. 41–46.

60. Twenty-five percent of the literature confiscated by customs officials was religious in character, according to *Glavlit*, in RGANI.5.33.88, l. 73–84. *Glavlit* indicted émigré organizations in RGANI.5.33.121, l. 122–30.

61. RGANI.5.33.126, l. 22–24. The CPSU apparat agreed with the *Glavlit* proposal to eliminate the right of the ROC External Affairs Department to import foreign literature directly, overriding CROC's objections.

62. GARF.6991.3.167, l. 8, l. 55–56, with handwritten comment by Comrade Zagorski of CARC that Comrade Alexandrov of Agitprop had indicated the CPSU leadership wanted to retain central control of church publications.

63. ERA.R-1989.2.21, l. 27; ERA.R-1989.2.22, l. 182; GARF.6991.3.188, l. 82–92. In 1959, the state cut the printing of song sheets dramatically for Estonian Lutherans and completely canceled publication of their almanac, according to ERA.R-1989.2.26, l. 28.

64. LVA.1448.1.158, l. 34–35. The commissioner supported the Church's request, justifying it on the importance of their international ties.

65. In 1960, the CPL head, Arvid Pelše, bowed to CARC pressure on this issue, though he cut the print run. The arm-twisting of Pelše regarding even these modest levels of church publications is documented in LVA.1448.1.259, l. 48–49. A total of 1,600 New Testaments were approved for Latvia, although the state ordered Turs to use more for his work abroad. LVA.1448.1.155, l. 7.

66. LCVA.181.3.53, l. 41. Lithuanian Lutheran leader Vilhelmas Burkevicius indicated that the Latvian Church had rejected a request for 400 New Testaments in Latvian and suggested that he contact CARC instead.

67. LVA.1448.1.257, l. 107; LVA.1448.1.257, l. 73–77. Forty priests gathered in Aglona in 1958. Fifty percent of the pilgrims to Kannepene were from Lithuania.

68. LVA.1448.1.258, l. 37–38, citing Decree N. 584, "On Liquidation of Monasteries on the Territory of the LSSR," CM LSSR (15 Nov. 1958), itself based on Resolution N. 1159, "On Monasteries in the USSR," CM USSR (16 Oct. 1958). Based on this resolution, CARC reported plans to close one Catholic monastery and forbid new monks at two others, in anticipation of eventual closure. GARF.6991.3.167, l. 43–47; LVA.1448.1.258, l. 37–38. See also Trups-Trops, "Römisch-Katholische Kirche," Teil 3, 62–64. See also Anderson, *Religion, State and Politics*, 31–32, and Chumachenko, *Church and State*, 168–71, on the similar crackdown on ROC monasteries.

69. ERA.R-1989.2.23, l. 24.

70. In the 1958 CARC report to the Central Committee, GARF.6991.3.167, l. 13–26.

71. In meetings with CM LSSR officials and the commissioner, Strods insisted on the need for seventeen priests to conduct pilgrimage services in Aglona, but the commissioner approved only three or four, arguing that this sufficed for similar services of the ROC in Moscow. Allegedly Strods agreed to abide by this stipulation, and the commissioner reported curtailment of pilgrimages in 1959. LVA.1448.1.258, l. 60–62; LVA.1448.1.258, l. 82–84.

72. The state claimed the number of pilgrims to Aglona dropped by half, from 8,000 in 1959 to between 3,000 and 4,000 in 1960, according to LVA.1448.1.260, l. 3; LVA.1448.1.258, l. 107–9; LVA.1448.1.259, l. 23–25.

73. "Since the absolute majority of the residents of monasteries are dropouts from life in Latvia, the question of creating work for them can be decided positively." The state mobilized support from the nearby school personnel and kolkhoz for closing the nunnery in Aglona, as well as the monastery in Vilyani. LVA.1448.1.258, l. 2–7. Trups-Trops ("Römisch-Katholische Kirche," Teil 3, 64) indicates the library was largely destroyed also.

74. LVA.1448.1.259, l. 19–21.

75. Referencing the new directive, CARC Chair Ryazanov indicated to the Agitprop Department that it reversed earlier Soviet decisions from 1930 and 1945 that permitted religious rites in the home by registered clergy. GARF.6991.3.210, l. 65–66.

76. LVA.1448.1.257, l. 29, l. 137 documented the widening criminal charges against Catholic priests and Strods's futile efforts to reverse their decertification.

77. LVA.1448.1.257, l. 33–34. The commissioner opined that "since Turs faces several trips abroad again, it is not to be excluded that he will bring back something new."

78. LVA.1448.1.258, l. 142. Arguing that the Moscow Patriarch had issued a directive against children participating, the commissioner ordered Strods to likewise instruct his priests: "When children reach the age of maturity, they may themselves choose which path they go."

79. LVA.1448.1.260, l. 10. In Latvia, fifty complaints were generated in 1961, a high number given past experience. However, apparently the violations continued. In 1962 the Chair of the Council of Ministers of LSSR, Krūmiņš, criticized local officials for prohibiting cemetery days: "such administrative prohibition ... is illegal and politically incorrect. It does not serve the interest of atheistic upbringing of workers." LVA.1448.1.268, l. 27–29.

80. The law was promulgated on March 16, 1961. Considering the importance of bells and music in the Baltic tradition, the Latvian commissioner advised warnings, rather than fines, for violations. LVA.1448.1.156, l. 56–57. See also LVA.1448.1.156, l. 38–39. The state threatened to cancel the registration of a church that did not curtail bell-ringing.

81. LVA.1448.1.257, l. 142. Pastor Rozenwalds, freed in 1955, was denied certification in 1958, on grounds that he had served in the Latvian Legion during World War II.

82. ERA.R 1989.2.28, l. 68–70. The commissioner indicated that he opposed the decision to permit such correspondence courses in 1956, but that the "international conditions" required it. In 1960 CARC eliminated the courses.

83. LVA.1448.1.256, l. 116–19. In the 1959–1960 academic year, the state expelled nine and admitted only two of seven new applicants, leaving the Riga seminary with twenty students, as opposed to thirty the previous year; the Latvian officials were responding to the CARC directive "to eliminate those students who are very undesirable for us in the political context." The students protested to Latvian officials and "responsible authorities" in Moscow, according to LVA.1448.1.258, l. 151. See also Hoffmann, et al., "Chronik," 123.

84. Regarding Rätsep, see GARF.6991.3.166, l. 198. CARC approved three years for Vejs in Britain, according to GARF.6991.3.188, l. 134. Rätsep ("Ants") was apparently a KGB informant, according to Jürjo, *Pagulus*, 166.

85. ERA.R-1989.2.26, l. 104–6. Pajula was approved by the Estonian Politburo on 30 Aug. 1960, according to ERAF.1.216.23, l. 13–16.

86. Trups-Trops, "Römisch-Katholische Kirche," Teil 3, 86–89; Cuibe, *Lutheran Church*, 4–7, 9–11; Remmel, "Religioonivastane võitlus." Dubnaitis, "Der totale Kampf gegen Religion," 133–52, places Baltic development in the context of the Soviet-wide ideological campaign against religion.

87. ERA.R-1989.2.28, l. 39–41.

88. Rukis, "Verfolgung der Katholischen Kirche," 101–4.

89. ERA.R-1989.2.28, l. 34–41.

90. LVA.1448.1.257, l. 30. Extensive examples of media slander against religion, churches, and clergy are found in Dubnaitis, "Der totale Kampf gegen Religion," 165–77.

91. Rukis, "Verfolgung der Katholischen Kirche," 104–5; Trups-Trops, "Römisch-Katholische Kirche," Teil 3, 86–87.

92. LVA.1448.1.257, l. 147, referring to a feuilliton, "Strods tells a fairy tale," published in *Soviet Latvia*, 2 Nov. 1958.

93. The *Komsomolskaya Pravda* article was published 18 April 1958. Strods denied such an order; in fact, upon investigation, the commissioner found no evidence of such an order. CARC criticized as "poisonous" such propaganda by Komsomol, in GARF.6991.3.148, l. 76–77.

94. RGANI.5.33.59, l. 27–28, for Znanie's 1958 proposal; the Central Committee officials' rejection is indicated in l. 29.

95. Znanie was the forum for meetings and publicity for two such Latvian Catholic priests in 1958, one of whom later returned to the Church, but was refused recertification as a priest by the state. See LVA.1448.1.257, l. 137. Catholic authorities insisted on a published statement by priests who wished to return to the Church, which state media, of course, refused. See Trups-Trops, "Römisch-Katholische Kirche," Teil 3, 64–67. Trups-Trops attributes the renunciation of vows to the weak theological foundation in the context of a shortage of priests, but other human factors were doubtless at work, exploited by the security forces.

96. ERA.R-1989.2.26, l. 26–27. Commissioner Veiderpass discusses his role in facilitating an article, "Do not go to Confirmation," authored by former Pastor Laubach of Pärnu in *Rahva Hääl* and *Golos Molodezhi*.

97. LVA.1448.1.257, l. 31.

98. ERA.R-1989.2.24, l. 172–73. The press "revelations" regarding alleged economic venality, phony healing services, and moral flaws of pastors provoked numerous complaints to the officials from the churches.

99. GARF.6991.3.209, l. 79.

100. LVA.1448.1.258, l. 82. Quotations from RGASPI.606.4.189, l. 11–12, 33–35. The "new Soviet traditions" detracted from church rites, despite Turs's spin that these were merely religious rites in new form. Viise, 159–60, discusses the advocacy by Estonian Agitprop Secretary Johannes Undusk for introduction of the secular rites in *Eesti Kommunist* in February 1958. See also Salo, "Antireligious Rites," 28–33; Anderson, *Religion, State and Politics*, 46–49; Rukis, "Verfolgung der Katholischen Kirche," 107–9; Staffa, "Religion im Historischen Materialismus," 86–87.

101. As indicated in RGANI.5.16.554, l. 42, Agitprop officials in Moscow hailed the fact that "the social organs of Estonia strive to imbue the old folk holidays, customs and traditions with new content." Altnurme (*History*, 119–20) documents the role of the Komsomol in marginalizing confirmation with the summer days of youth rites.

102. RGANI.5.33.190, l. 71–74. Latvian CP leader Pelše criticized the articles ("they give support to the remaining nationalist elements in the republic ... and directly contradict the policy of the CC CP Latvia in relation to the holiday Ligo"); the CPSU leadership agreed to correct the views.

103. LVA.1448.1.260, l. 47 and LVA.1448.1.258, l. 135 documented that some local officials forbade confirming more than two youth in one service, in order to heighten the success of the secular coming-of-age ceremony.

104. LVA.1448.1.260, l. 46.

105. ERA.R-1989.2.28, l. 34–35.

106. Puzin, quoted in GARF.6991.3.166, l. 78–79, 80–83. On the new foreign policy line for the churches, see Mankusa, "Over the Iron Curtain," 313–35; Staffa, "Religion im Historischen Materialismus," 88–92. On the Third World emphasis, see Fletcher, *Religion and Soviet Foreign Policy*, 53–92.

107. ERA.R-1989.2.26, l. 118; Altnurme, *History*, 131–37.

108. GARF.6991.3.166, l. 111–13. The CARC/CROC report indicated the state's early disappointment with the unrepresentative character of the Western delegates to the 1958 CPC congress. On the Soviets and the CPC, see Fletcher, *Religion and Soviet Foreign Policy*, 39–64.

109. ERA.R-1989.2.27, l. 16–17, documenting CARC's plan for goals and agenda of the upcoming CPC assembly in Prague, in consultation with the GDR.

110. RGANI.5.33.92, l. 76–79. Both CARC and CROC supported ROC membership in the WCC, "which will decrease Vatican influence as an international center." LCVA.181.3.53, l. 35–36. Both Bourdeaux (*Opium*, 223–31) and Fletcher (*Religion and Soviet Foreign Policy*, 119–28) seem to ignore the alarm regarding the Vatican as a motive and even see an interest in rapprochement with the Catholic Church by the Kremlin. Here the archival record serves as a useful corrective.

111. GARF.6991.3.125, l. 5–7. In the KGB analysis, Vatican prelate Johannes Willebrands went to Holland to meet Willem Visser't Hooft of the WCC, arguing that admitting the ROC to the WCC would derail ecumenical efforts by the Vatican, and that the Vatican directed its representatives in Protestant and Orthodox societies to "take action against the new maneuver of the Moscow Patriarchate."

112. RGANI.5.33.126, l. 134. The regime pressed the Patriarch to issue a public denial of such participation amidst Italian publicity regarding an alleged meeting between the ROC and Papal Nuncio in Vienna.

113. The cautious initiatives of the ROC toward the WCC from 1958 to 1960 and the state's analysis and steering of this process are detailed in RGANI.5.33.126, l. 187–91 and RGANI.5.33.126, l. 223–26. See also RGANI.5.33.162, l. 1–4.

114. Rozitis, "Geschichte und Aufbau," 74–75. Rozitis indicates the failure to join was due to uncertainty regarding the Latvian exile churches in the United States and oversight by Archbishop Grīnbergs. In any case, the Estonian exile church strongly opposed admitting its Soviet Estonian counterpart, but was outvoted.

115. Moscow's decision to support membership in the international Lutheran organizations is documented in RGANI.5.33.190, l. 112–16. On the Finnish Church role, see Ketola, "Relations," 138–42. Émigré church opposition is described in Pähn, "Martyrdom," 300, and Cuibe, *Lutheran Church*, 1–31.

116. GARF.6991.3.189, l. 28. Kiivit argued that the ties with the LWF would strengthen the Estonian Church vis-à-vis the émigré churches. See Malkavarra, "Dispute," 179–80.

117. The Finns saw the LWF as providing cover against domestic criticism of such a shift, according to ERA.R-1989.2.24, l. 105.

118. LVA.1448.1.261, 103–5, documents the extensive plans for international visits in 1963.

119. GARF.6991.3.189, l. 53–65.

120. LVA.1448.1.258, l. 126, includes Turs's report of the visit of a WCC delegation to Latvia, during which he estimated Latvian Lutherans at 600,000 to 700,000 members organized in 280 parishes.

121. The regime strategy in 1960 for utilizing the churches internationally is elaborated in RGANI.5.33.162, l. 51–80.

122. RGANI.5.33.91, l. 32–34 indicates that the regime was pleased with the "blow against Berlin Bishop Dibelius" (head of the EKD and vociferous opponent of the GDR) from a West German delegation hosted by the ROC in 1958.

123. ERA.R-1989.2.24, l. 29–30.

124. Future Bishop Edgar Hark of Estonia led the Baltic delegation, along with the ROC Exarch in East Berlin. LVA.1448.1.257, l. 113–21, contains the report of V. Ozolins from the Latvian Lutheran Church.

125. GARF.6991.3.209, l. 46. The Soviet embassy in the GDR concluded that visits by the Soviet Lutheran churches "help the transformation of the clergy of the GDR toward a loyal position toward the government of the GDR, assist in diffusing anti-Soviet libel and strengthening position of opponents of atomic arming of the *Bundeswehr* in the FRG." GARF.6991.3.209, l. 149. Contacts with the Weimar Circle ("organized to counter the reactionary policy of German church leadership of Dibelius") were supported in RGANI.5.33.190, l. 48–51.

126. LVA.1448.1.261, l. 85–95. The state received two separate reports from church officials regarding this visit. The reports suggest that the GDR church leaders were particularly interested in the availability of theological literature and training in Latvia.

127. RGANI.5.33.162, l. 65. The Conference of Lutheran Minority Churches is described as "opposing the influence of the Vatican and Catholic church in states where this church is dominant."

128. LVA.1448.1.257, l. 36.

129. LVA.1448.l.257, l. 139. Turs held special services after his visits abroad, to which the commissioner objected. State officials took satisfaction in Turs's toning down of such efforts thereafter, seeing this as part of the "dying character" of the Lutheran Church.

130. LVA.1448.1.259, l. 41–45.

131. LVA.1448.1.156, l. 68.

132. ERA.R-1989.2.21, l. 2; Altnurme, "Foreign Relations," 159–65.

133. GARF.6991.3.166, l. 127–28.

134. GARF.6991.3.188, l. 93–94.

135. ERA.R-1989.2.24, l. 28.

136. Along with Bishop Turs, the Soviet authorities sent Estonian Consistory member Julius Voolaid to the CDU congress in 1960, according to GARF.6991.3.209, l. 46.

137. GARF.6991.3.171, l. 44–46; LVA.1448.1.258, l. 8.

138. LVA.1448.1.10, l. 141–46, for Strods's text opposing testing of atomic weapons and implying his consent to publication, if in full.

139. LVA.1448.1.257, l. 105, 110.

140. GARF.6991.3.172, l. 7–8.

141. LVA.1448.1.259, l. 3–4.

142. GARF.6991.3.189, l. 108: rejection of a trip to Ireland by Soviet Catholics. Trups-Trops, "Römisch-Katholische Kirche," Teil 3, 54–55. The Latvians joined the Berlin Conference (BC) in 1961, attempting to keep the profile low, but eventually hosted a BC conference in Riga in 1975 and raised the protocol of its participation to the level of Bishop Zondaks in 1982.

143. GARF.6991.3.167, l. 40–42. Both CARC and the Soviet Peace Committee vied for the opportunity to invite Grösz, but the Peace Committee won that battle; the Lithuanian Catholic hierarchy was clearly not involved at all.

144. LVA.1448.1.10, l. 77.

145. LVA.1448.1.259, l. 30.

146. ERA.R-1989.2.24, l. 106–7. Kiivit advised against approval of an invitation to Pastor Eugen Bachmann of Akmolinsk by German churches, since this might "direct the German

bishops' attention to the Germans in the USSR." But Soviet authorities did hesitate to deregister the Bachmann parish, fearing West German reaction. GARF.6991.3.188, l. 190–93.

147. LVA.1448.1.259, l. 30.

148. ERA.R-1989.2.24, l. 107–8.

149. Estonian delegate Julius Voolaid criticized Latvian Bishop Turs to Wolfgang Heyl, CDU leader, who in turn reported this to the Soviet Ambassador Pervukhin, who informed Yuri Andropov and other central party organs, according to RGANI.5.33.162, l. 40–41.

150. GARF.6991.3.166, l. 58–60; RGANI.5.33.162, l. 32–39.

151. GARF.6991.3.1364, l. 7. Seigewasser sought an invitation for Krummacher "to enable him to remove himself from the influence of reactionary all-German church leadership and attract him to loyal cooperation with the state organs of the GDR."

152. GARF.6991.3.1375, l. 8–10. According to the KGB, "the German friends consider that the invitation of Scharf to Moscow may be used by him against the policy of the GDR."

153. GARF.6991.3.1394, l. 73; ERA.R-1989.2.30, l. 103.

154. LVA.1448.1.257, l. 98–99. Restberg describes Turs as having "little authority among believers, among pastors" and labels him as "amoral" and "ambitious" particularly toward the Reformed and Lutheran churches in Lithuania.

155. LVA.1448.1.260, l. 26.

156. LVA.1448.1.255, l. 134–46. In this presentation for the Moscow CARC, the characteristika of Strods was very negative. It emphasized his alleged pressure to expand Catholic influence in Belorussia and among Catholics in Siberia, and his dependence on the Vatican.

157. LVA.1448.1.258, l. 82–83. State authorities did then grant him recognition as apostolic administrator. Trups-Trops, "Römisch-Katholische Kirche," Teil 3, 57–58.

158. LVA.1448.1.258, l. 136.

159. For its part, the Vatican likely feared disruption in church activity with Strods's death, as the state began to register priests without their being named by the Vatican. But the state accused Zachests of refusing to follow the state's recommendations and violating Soviet laws, such as in preparing youth for first communion. He was arrested and convicted in 1964. LVA.1448.1.261, l. 59–60; Trups-Trops, "Römisch-Katholische Kirche," Teil 3, 69–73.

160. LVA.1448.1.262, l. 16–17. After CARC approved the removal of Zachests, he was called to the commissioner's office 25 Sept. 1963 and told to name possible successors. The commissioner approved Vaivods and arranged for him to meet with the Chair Krūmiņš of the Council of Ministers, LSSR. Vaivods indicated he would "do all possible so that the church may live in peace and accord with the organs of Soviet power." Vaivods's letter to the Pope is found in LVA.1448.1.262, l. 32–36. Trups-Trops ("Römisch-Katholische Kirche," Teil 3, 73–74) sees the selection of Vaivods as bishop more felicitously, reflecting the influence of exiled Latvian Catholic bishops rather than regime manipulation.

161. LVA.1419.3.283, l. 26–27.

162. LVA.1448.1.260, l. 18. Allegedly, Pastor Kalks said, "you cannot trust weapons to idiots; then death would not walk the streets and fields."

163. ERA.R-1989.2.28, l. 39–41; Remmel, "Believers, Human Rights."

164. LVA.1448.1.257, l. 138, 143–44. Strods was faulted for political abstinence and not criticizing "reactionary forces" in Lebanon and France: "Thus it is clear that the leadership of the Catholic Church refrains from any kind of participation in the matter of the fight for peace."

165. LVA.1448.1.259, l. 6. Commissioner Pizāns reported directly to the Latvian party leadership, August Voss, suggesting his caution regarding republic authorities.

166. GARF.6991.3.166, l. 110.

167. Chumachenko (*Church and State*, 145–53, 161–63) discusses the CPSU Central Committee battles with Karpov in 1956–1958.

168. Puzin argued that the churches "may become an active channel of Soviet propaganda and counterpropaganda abroad," but his request to create a Department of International Affairs within CARC was rejected in the CPSU Secretariat by Snastin and Chernenko, according to RGANI.5.33.91, l. 161–63.

169. RGANI.5.33.54, l. 11–12.

170. LVA.1448.1.260, l. 25. Latvian Lutheran baptisms dropped precipitously, from 5,305 to 3,423, between 1958 and 1960; first communions by Catholics dropped from 4,454 to 3,657 during the same two years. Weddings and burials showed similar declines. ERA.R-1989.2.28, l. 26; ERA.R-1989.2.28, l. 24–25.

171. Anderson (*Religion, State and Politics*, 112–13) maintains that the nation-religion linkage was not a major factor motivating the campaign, "although it may have affected its implementation in certain areas." I might add that perception of the policy was also viewed through a national lens.

172. This finding conflicts with Anderson (*Religion, State and Politics*, 27–28), who argues that the commissioners followed the Central Committee's harsher line, rather than the more moderate position of CARC/CROC.

5 Détente and Stagnation During the Brezhnev Era: 1964–1985

As the previous chapter indicated, the Khrushchev repression, starting particularly after 1958, brought intensified attacks familiar from the Stalinist era—albeit with less reliance on terror—and added new ones, including financial pressures on churches, curtailment of the role of clergy in parish governance, and closing of monasteries. At the same time, the Khrushchev era saw an opening of international doors for the Lutheran and other Protestant churches as they joined ecumenical and confessional organizations long suspect as Western-dominated. Bureaucratic tensions, with personnel upheaval, also developed between CARC representatives and both party officials in Moscow and hard-line republic authorities, for whom the revival of religious adherence represented the threat of nascent Baltic nationalism. As the USSR sought to blunt global Catholic influence under John XXIII, the Protestant churches and the ROC assumed a more prominent role in the international arena. However, the churches' efforts to leverage this international role to their domestic institutional benefit bore only modest fruit. Meanwhile, religious adherence nosedived again in this period.

After Khrushchev's political demise and his replacement by Brezhnev in 1964, the question of the impact of this leadership upheaval on religious policy naturally arose. Reacting to the turbulence under Khrushchev, the hallmark of the Brezhnev era politically was that of stability of cadres and avoidance of policy experimentation. Thus, one might expect continuity. But in foreign policy the Brezhnev era would eventually see major changes, namely the advent of détente with the West, and in particular with the FRG. The Baltic Lutheran churches were already invested in this relationship as a result of the international opening under Khrushchev, though they and republic officials remained ambivalent about the full implications of these ties. In the case of the Vatican and the Catholic Church, however, it was not clear there was room in détente for them. The Brezhnev period would also see the rise of dissent in various forms, including religious dissent in the ROC, the underground movement among Baptists known as *initsiativniki*, and in the Lithuanian Catholic Church. Add to this the rise of the Helsinki human rights movement and political crackdowns in the Soviet bloc (in Czechoslovakia in 1968 and Poland in 1981), and one had a context that portended political instability. How would the Estonian and Latvian churches be affected by this rising religious and non-religious dissent? Finally, if the Khrushchev repression were lifted, one might expect the churches to recover lost ground in terms of their institutional interests, but in their suborned state would the churches have the clout or vision to reclaim it?

Church Adherence and Institutional Interests

In some respects, these two Baltic republics became models for Soviet officialdom under Brezhnev. Reports of the commissioners during this period suggested dramatic declines in church adherence, greater among Lutherans than Catholics. Participation in church services had sunk to less than 6 percent by 1977.[1] In a 1967 Estonian report, Lutheran clergy were described as demoralized, anticipating the end of religious belief.[2] Increasingly services were being cancelled by pastors due to lack of interest. Participation in Christmas services was considerably higher, but state administrative measures sought to discourage participation in this national tradition. Church rites, a better measure of intensity of church adherence, likewise continued to fall, especially confirmations and weddings.[3] In Latvia the percentage opting for a church wedding dropped from 7.6 to 4.2 percent between 1965 and 1975; religious burials dropped from 31.8 to 23.8 percent in the same time period. Most sermons by pastors tended to be apolitical, focusing on the Bible and man's sinful nature. Whereas earlier some sermons had sought to facilely equate socialism and Christianity, leaving state officials ambivalent, now some pastors sought to adapt to and accept socialism as a function of modern science and reason, with religion still necessary to address spiritual and cultural issues.[4]

Compounding this decline in church adherence was the erosion of institutional interests of the churches. Shortages of pastors became increasingly acute as the state limited admissions to theological courses. By 1968, in Estonia, there were only twenty-five students studying theology, including four above age forty.[5] Four of these twenty-five were already functioning as pastors, as increasingly the Church was forced to rely on unordained pastors to fill vacant positions.

Church closures continued even after the wave of closures under Khrushchev ended. Internal Latvian statistics indicate that 142 churches were closed between 1950 and 1980, 74 of which were Lutheran and 45 ROC; only 6 were Catholic. Of these 74 Lutheran church closures, only 29 occurred before 1965, many of them *after* Khrushchev's ouster in 1963; 45 took place between 1965 and 1980, 40 of them in the period from 1965 to 1973 alone.[6] Even though most of these closures were in rural areas, the Lutheran churches suffered disproportionately compared to other denominations. Without diminishing the repressiveness of the Khrushchev period, these statistics also strongly suggest that, once started, the Khrushchev campaign to close churches continued long after his rule ended. Only late in the Brezhnev period did the closures abate.

Local authorities often took an indifferent attitude to the physical security of church buildings, devising a pretext to close them. Cases of "hooliganism" (vandalism and theft of church properties) went uninvestigated. Local police in Cēsis, Latvia, told church officials to find the culprits themselves and, despite the commissioner's direct request, dismissed them as pranks, with a low priority for investigation.[7] Latvian republic authorities, on the other hand, upbraided local authorities for "allowing cultural monuments to fall into decay" and pressed them to secure "articles of historical and ethnographic value," transferring them to museums upon the closing of churches.[8]

The security problems of the many closed churches suggest that the eventual disposition of these closed churches had been left in limbo.[9] Official investigation in 1967 in Latvia revealed that many of the closed churches, especially in rural areas, had not been converted to the alternative uses proposed when the closure was approved. Local authorities had simply not implemented the planned conversion, causing dissatisfaction among believers and requests to reopen the empty churches.[10] It does raise the question of motive: simple misplaced priorities or a subconscious effort to avoid antagonizing believers and keep options open to eventually reopen the churches? By the mid-1970s, republic officials again studied the failure to implement conversions and urged razing the forty-three closed churches in poor condition. However, the 1980 study found that only seventeen of the churches were actually in poor condition. This suggests that republic officials had become less vigilant regarding the conversion and razing of closed churches, and perhaps less militant.

Many of these parishes were closed as a result of chicanery practiced by officials on the lay members responsible for authorizing registration. In 1965 alone, Latvia closed twenty-one churches, including fifteen Lutheran churches; in the same year, thirty clergy were deregistered, only half due to death.[11] No pastor, no church. The state closed the churches "at the request of the parishioners themselves."[12] As noted in the previous chapter, clergy were forbidden to participate in parish governance under the Khrushchev legislation.

Despite this evidence suggesting the regime's upper hand over the churches and religion, the state sought to press its advantage by controlling not just the extent of church activity but also the content of such activity. As outlined in the previous chapter, in 1963 the USSR set up Commissions to Check Legality, composed of local officials and tasked with monitoring sermons and checking for legal violations. In principle, they were to report violations by either the churches or the local officials. The early Brezhnev years indeed saw efforts by the state to review the legality of some Khrushchev actions and to consider some believer protests.[13] But the content of the legislation clearly intended that the commissions would focus primarily on the churches' activities. In practice, they often exceeded their authority. The republic commissioners sought to broaden the social monitoring of the parish churches beyond Communist functionaries and the KGB.

By the late Brezhnev period, however, it became increasingly difficult to recruit local officials to this mundane and unrewarding task.[14] Local officials wished to abandon the effort, particularly with the decline in Lutheran religious activity and relative quiescence of the clergy in the 1960s. Some local officials claimed there was no legal basis for the commissions.[15] In this context, the Estonian commissioner called for formal republican legislation to strengthen support for and institutionalize the commissions at the local level, which was realized in 1968. Evaluations in the late 1970s suggested that most reporting was being done by full-time party officials tasked with atheistic cultural responsibilities, not by the commissions. Even though one may assume that much of the reporting was pro forma, it doubtless had a chilling effect on many clergy.

Also giving pause to the state was the financial situation of the churches. Khrushchev had turned the financial screws on the churches by increasing taxes and insurance rates. Assessed on the size of the buildings, the increased insurance rates hit the Lutheran and Catholic churches disproportionately due to their relatively spacious churches; with their more modest, utilitarian structures, Baptists and other sects were spared the hardest impact.[16] Many Lutheran parishes made extra appeals to parishioners for contributions to help cover the new costs, and many complaints and petitions were lodged against the hikes. The state forbade church headquarters from offering financial assistance to help parishes meet these new costs. Nonetheless, the commissioners' reports suggest that individual contributions did increase in response to this need. In fact, even as the churches could count on fewer members and adherents, per capita contributions increased.[17] Overall financial resources were growing as a result of improved economic circumstances and greater financial effort by parishioners. The sects demonstrated far higher per capita contributions than the Lutherans.[18] State officials themselves conceded that progress toward some goals of "socialist development," that is, economic growth, in fact came at the expense of achieving other goals, such as eroding the financial base of the churches.

Heavy taxes on clergy continued to dissuade clergy recruitment.[19] Tax rates on clergy far exceeded those imposed on independent workers, not to mention collective farmers. Many clergy were forced to moonlight in secular professions as a result of insufficient income.[20] But the state rewarded clergy active internationally by lowering their tax rates, reinforcing the churches' inclination to participate in the regime's propaganda efforts.

Another Khrushchev initiative, enhancing lay control and reducing the clergy role in parish governance, continued to produce tensions with the churches. Especially the Catholic churches in Latvia resisted this policy. Priests were considered unchallenged authority figures by their parishioners; warnings and decertifications of Catholic priests were not uncommon throughout the Brezhnev period. Bowing to state pressure, the Latvian Curia forbade use of children in services after May 1961, but this was resisted in practice by local clergy and laity.[21] Likewise, priests continued to organize religious instruction in the parishes, despite legal action taken by the regime. Even in Lutheran churches, by tradition more accommodating to lay authority, clergy continued to exert control in parish governance. The Estonian Church pressed the authorities to permit clergy participation in local parish councils and retained this provision in its church constitution throughout the Brezhnev period, despite the Khrushchev regulations.[22]

Theological education, a target of the Communists for some years, remained limited for these churches. Caps were placed on enrollment in the correspondence courses in theology in the Latvian and Estonian Lutheran churches. All prospective students were vetted by the republic commissioners. After a disappointing 1950s experiment in sending postgraduate students to Britain to prepare for teaching theology, the Baltic churches lowered their expectations: henceforth such study in the West was conceived more as a testing ground for future bishops than for renewing the aging professorate in theology.[23] Western churches, such as the Finnish Church, offered opportunities to study, but were blocked by the regime.

State pressures on the character of theological education continued during the period under study. Theology professors were periodically ousted from their positions. In 1970, Professor Harri Hammer was labeled a reactionary and ousted in Estonia.[24] Teaching of the Soviet constitution was added to the curriculum, precipitating new tensions with the faculty and students.

Yet, by the 1970s, unexpected changes had begun in the state's stance on theological education. In 1963 the Catholic seminary in Riga was permitted to admit students from other republics, such as Belorussia and Ukraine, although security officials in both jurisdictions made it very difficult; in the late 1970s even German Catholics from Kazakhstan were able to matriculate. By the fall of the USSR, Latvians represented less than 25 percent of students and Russian became the language of instruction.[25] The Lutheran churches benefited from comparison with the more politically unreliable sects. Perhaps they had become more useful for Soviet propaganda internationally, or had simply paid their dues with political quiescence. Whatever the reason, the regime began to loosen strictures on theological education. Increased numbers of students were admitted to the Lutheran courses. In a remarkable reversal from the days of Stalin, when the state saw a highly educated clergy as a threat and sought to reduce this source of the clergy's authority in the eyes of parishioners, the state now saw it as expedient to increase the education level of the clergy.[26] Clergy with higher education were seen as less likely to be politically oppositional than those, such as most sect clergy, who tended to lack this education. An aging professorate was to remain a problem, even until perestroika. A restoration of theological faculties at the state universities remained unthinkable, and vetting of students and part-time study remained the norm. But as a result of the tacit shift by the state, stabilizing the Lutheran clergy base, rather than helplessly watch it wither away, seemed at least possible by the late Brezhnev era.

Comparisons of church adherence and interests with the Khrushchev period do suggest considerable continuity. There was no religious revival after the Khrushchev repression, unlike in the 1953–1955 period following Stalin. Economic pressures on the churches continued, exacerbated by regime policy but moderated somewhat by economic growth. Theological education stabilized, albeit at the low levels associated with the Khrushchev years.

Secular Rites and Scientific Atheism

Concomitant with the decline in church adherence, the secular rites promoted by the regime to supplant religious ones were increasingly taking hold among the population in Latvia and Estonia. Patterned on those in the GDR, these rites were touted by the commissioners: in 1968 Estonian Commissioner Teder hailed them as "satisfying the aesthetic-emotional needs of the people," growing in appeal commensurate with the dying of religious rites.[27] Even Hungarian Communists consulted with the Baltic specialists in atheism regarding their success with this policy.[28] Council for Religious Affairs (CRA) Chairman Vladimir Kuroedov promoted the Baltics as models for other Soviet republics; the Baltics would remain "the most systematic and successful application" of this strategy.[29]

In an indirect indication of the positive picture from the state's perspective, official reports increasingly opined about the routinization of scientific atheistic propaganda and its limited effectiveness. Commissioners repeatedly called for intensification of efforts at inculcation of atheism in the population. Declining marginal returns from the campaign led officials to shift atheism efforts to focus on preschool children.[30] Increasingly, impact was measured in mind-numbing, Gosplan-like input statistics: in 1975, for example, Estonia reported holding 19 seminars in atheism with 800 participants; in a republic of 1.5 million residents, 2,063,880 reportedly attended the 3,600 atheistic lectures in 1977![31]

Despite the increased efforts to promote the secular rites and inculcate atheistic attitudes, troubling signs were developing. In Estonia, the apparatus to oversee secular rites became more bureaucratized, even byzantine, with a Republic Commission for Secular Rites augmented by a Methodical Council in the Ministry of Culture and a Ministry of Customary Service, along with local staff. Despite these multiple organizational layers, the decline in rite participation was dramatic in the early 1980s: for example, participation in the summer days of youth dropped by 50 percent between 1981 and 1982. By 1983, the commissioner stopped reporting participation levels in the secular rites.[32]

A noteworthy aspect of this shift in emphasis was reflected in the rise of a cadre of scholars who studied the remaining roots of religious belief in the population using quasi-scientific methods of public opinion research as well as analysis of theological developments in the churches. The impulse for this came from the Institute for Scientific Atheism, housed within the Academy of Social Sciences of the CC-CPSU, and reflected a bloc-wide trend to develop scientific atheism as an academic enterprise. But the Baltic specialists carved out a particular profile in this group.[33] Not coincidentally, a leading scholar in this group, Estonian Kuulo Vimmsaare, had earlier analyzed the Lutheran Church from the Communist ideological perspective. Now he sought to explore the psychological explanations for why religion remained, despite the dramatic de-Christianization among Estonians.[34] Vimmsaare headed a group of social scientists mobilized to analyze the various religious movements in Estonia. His publications and conference participation in the 1970s and 1980s, along with those of philosopher Janis Vejs in Latvia, complemented those of researchers in the GDR, such as Olof Klohr, who operated in a similar Lutheran setting.[35] All agreed, of course, that religion was destined to die out, but detected psychological needs and international sources for its continued existence, long after the "construction of socialism" was complete and the alleged class roots of religion eliminated. These atheistic researchers began to recognize that the Lutheran doctrine of personal salvation distinguished it from Catholics and made it harder to judge the decline of religious belief simply by measuring attendance and participation in rituals.[36] They recognized the large role of family traditions in maintaining Lutheran beliefs and urged greater study of Scandinavian Protestant churches for their influence on the Baltic churches.

In their analysis of Lutheran theology and sermons, Vimmsaare and his colleagues saw the Lutheran Church emphasizing moral issues, avowing no contradiction with natural science but remaining hostile to the Marxist view of social relations. The Lutherans sought to claim a special role as "natural bearer of national development of the Baltic states," especially by fostering Baltic literacy, music and culture. Based on analysis of 750 sermons monitored over several decades, they characterized Lutheran theology as "traditionalist" and "neo-orthodox," emphasizing the sinful nature of mankind, pessimistic regarding social change, and reflecting little modernism at the parish level.[37] Almost half of monitored sermons invoked the Apostle Paul, seen as reinforcing the narrative of personal salvation. Ecological problems and the arms race were seen as resulting from the failure of man to submit to God.

The regime was still more concerned about the sects and larger religions, such as Orthodoxy and Islam. Vimmsaare countered that though some saw the Lutheran Church as less dangerous, Lutheran church activists could take advantage of this complacency.[38] Like the GDR, Estonia instituted a chair of scientific atheism, along with a priority research project in eastern Estonia, Kohlta-Järve.[39] Kohlta-Järve was selected because it was an area of mixed population: Russian as well as Estonian; Baptist and Orthodox as well as Lutheran. The fact that Estonia and Latvia produced a regional center of research on scientific atheism, despite their relatively small size, suggests the vanguard role allocated to them by Moscow as a result of the relative success of official atheistic policies in those republics.

Détente and the Germans

The advent of East-West détente, and particularly the Helsinki process, raised the question of religious human rights in the USSR. In response, the well-known Kuroedov memo of 1975 reflected an attempt at greater codification and uniformity of religious policy, updating the 1929 Stalin law on religion. Citing the difficulty of enforcing legality using the secret 1929 legislation, CRA argued for the need to reduce the state's violations of religious rights and to acknowledge exceptional situations, such as in the Baltics.[40] The new legislative basis for religious policy sought to liberalize the registration process, although the tough line of the KGB was reflected in the condition that registration be denied "in case of anti-state activity."[41] Already, during the 1950s, the Baltic Lutherans had taken up contacts with their co-religionists in Germany and membership in international organizations. With the advent of détente in the 1970s, the opportunities for such relations increased greatly. An added fillip for the Lutherans was the question of the Soviet Germans. Deported to Central Asia and western Siberia during the war, they were now granted amnesty by Brezhnev in 1964. In 1974, CRA estimated 580 groups of German believers, only 89 of which were registered parishes.[42] Most could not return to their earlier homes in the Volga region, but increasing numbers chose to migrate to the Baltic republics in hopes of possible repatriation to West Germany. By 1971, 14,000 Germans resided in Estonia, according to CRA.[43]

This situation posed new problems for the republic authorities who had begun to pride themselves on the slow death of religion in their jurisdiction. Many of the German migrants were very pietistic. Most did not join existing churches, but attended them.[44] Many began to hold services in homes, especially Baptists and Mennonites. Some sought registration of new parishes.[45] Officials were forced to report to Moscow that after years of declining church rites, confirmations and weddings were on the increase in the early 1970s, caused by German immigration.[46]

Implementing a June 1974 decision of the Central Committee, CRA ordered its regional officials to register these groups, if they were law-abiding. To be sure, the local officials and the KGB continued to oppose their registration: local officials feared the impression of a resurgence of religion; the KGB managed to monitor the groups by infiltration. Estonian Commissioner Leopold Piip reported in 1976 that the CRA order had been fully implemented. In Estonia most of these new registrations were by German Baptist parishes, rather than Lutherans. Piip clearly saw this as a temporary problem, viewing religious Germans as likely to emigrate to the FRG or return to Central Asia ("the climate in Estonia is not comfortable for them, too dry and cold") and tending to ignore them in his monitoring activities, probably seeing this as a KGB task.[47] But by 1977 CRA Chair Kuroedov could report that 70 groups of Germans had registered since the 1974 decision; as a proportion of the 800 known groups, the 190 registered groups still was quite low.[48]

Ironically, along with the obvious opportunities, this internal migration of Germans also posed problems for the Baltic churches themselves. Many of the Germans were Lutheran, but Catholics, Baptists, and Mennonites were also well-represented among them. Most, however, had no known religious affiliation. Complicating the situation further was the Baltic Lutherans' love-hate relationship with Germans historically: the Baltic Germans represented the *Herrenkirche*, source of the earlier repression of the ethnic Balts, yet also of the cultural-national awakening in the nineteenth century. Ties with Germans became even more fraught as a result of the legacy of WWII. Language problems also arose: most Balts did not speak German, and, as Russophones, the Germans did not easily integrate into Baltic churches.

Thus the Baltic Lutheran churches were quite reluctant to engage in outreach to the German migrants, reinforcing the relative disinclination of the commissioners to integrate them into the republic religious landscape. In Estonia, German-language services began to attract Germans away from Baptist parishes, producing tensions. In Latvia, Pastor Harald Kalnins, having spent the war in a German POW camp, was permitted to conduct services in Riga for German Lutherans.[49] Eventually he was authorized to hold meetings in other parts of Latvia. But initially he was strictly forbidden to pursue any contacts with Germans still residing in Central Asia.[50] Latvian Bishop Janis Matulis only lifted this stricture as a result of growing pressure from churches in the FRG and the LWF.

The 450th anniversary of the Reformation in 1967 offered the opportunity to build on the growing contacts with the GDR churches, begun in the late 1950s and fostered by the GDR regime as a means of outflanking the West German-dominated EKD. High-level visits by Thuringian, Saxon, and Greifswald church leaders demonstrated the pride of place accorded the GDR in Soviet religious policy.[51] In reciprocity the GDR solicited high-profile Baltic participation in its main celebration in October, even as it curtailed West German representation after construction of the Berlin Wall. However, the Baltic authorities were unable to realize the political potential, since the 1967 celebration occurred during the fraught ouster of bishops in Estonia and Latvia; both Kiivit and Turs were excluded from the downgraded delegations.[52] At home, the Baltic churches recognized this anniversary with low-key theological lectures, reflecting the continued political sensitivity of German national culture.[53] Overshadowed politically by the other anniversary, the Estonian Church praised the fruits of the Bolshevik Revolution, attempting awkwardly to draw similarities with Luther's Reformation.

But increasingly these ties with the GDR churches were being augmented by contacts with the LWF, which was interested not only in the Baltic Lutherans, but also the German Lutherans in the USSR. Initiated in 1966 by General Secretary André Appel, a French Lutheran, and expanded later by General Secretary Carl Mau, accompanied both times by Paul Hansen (Danish Lutheran and staffer tasked to the subgroup, Lutheran Minority Churches in Europe), the LWF sought to integrate the Baltic churches into its activities and develop contacts with the unorganized German Lutherans.[54] The KGB viewed the LWF as a stalking horse for Western intelligence services and Baltic émigré churches. In its view, Soviet Germans in the Baltics were spies, as were the church charitable agencies Aktion Suhnezeichen, Gustav-Adolf-Werk, and the Home Mission and Aid Society of the EKD, "aided by the reactionary heads of Soviet Lutherans."[55] It is understandable that Baltic churches were nervous about assuming a greater profile with the German migrants, even with LWF encouragement. Seeking to avoid problems with the regime, Latvian Bishop Turs referred LWF head Appel to Estonian Bishop Kiivit for answers to his queries regarding the Soviet Germans.[56]

Despite the KGB's misgivings, by the 1970s, West German Ostpolitik and the Helsinki process produced increasing interaction between the Soviet churches and the LWF, CEC, and WCC, including covert financial assistance and supplies of badly needed theological literature. In turn, the high profile of the West German churches in these organizations produced greater Soviet willingness to permit contacts with Soviet German religious groups, in an effort to demonstrate human rights progress. With LWF support, CRA designated Kalnins as responsible for the unregistered German Lutheran parishes in Central Asia and Siberia, authorizing his use of a car, literature and funds for this work. The CRA's authorization occurred over the objection of the Latvian commissioner and Latvian republic officials, who continued to fight a rear-guard action against expanding Kalnins's role, especially regarding theological education for Germans.[57] Latvian church officials were likewise reluctant to support Kalnins's activity, which in any case violated the Latvian bureaucratic jurisdictions of both church and state, even if it conformed to Lutheran confessional boundaries.[58] The Latvian Church opposed publications for the Germans, as well as financial authority for Kalnins. In this context of détente, the LWF delegations also focused attention on the

Lithuanian Lutherans, who lacked an ecclesiastical framework and membership in international organizations. In this case, however, in contrast to the German Lutherans, Latvian church leaders sought to advocate on the Lithuanian behalf, despite state objections.[59]

Even while the KGB saw primarily disadvantages in these international ties, the regime also began to see particular advantages in dealing with émigré churches in these forums. The regime opposed any contact with émigré Baltic churchmen during the first two decades after WWII, viewing them as arch-reactionaries who opposed the Baltic church leaders as illegitimate. Operating out of Sweden, West Germany, and North America, these churches had been very anticommunist. By the late 1960s and early 1970s, the regime began to encourage contacts between the Baltic churches and these émigré churches, seeing the international organizations as a vehicle to blunt the clout of the émigrés and their criticism of the USSR. In meetings, such as the 1968 WCC Assembly in Uppsala, and in sermons to Latvians in West Germany, Latvian church officials interacted for the first time with émigré Latvian Lutherans, interaction that was approved by and reported to the state.[60] By the early 1970s, the Estonian authorities were in fact encouraging such visits and publications targeted at Estonian émigrés, with the goal of "paralyzing" the "reactionary church figures," particularly among younger cohorts.[61] By the 1970s, state officials saw the LWF as willing to sacrifice the émigrés' hard-line stance for the sake of developing contacts with Soviet Lutherans.[62]

Of course, church leaders encouraged this shift by the regime through their condemnations of the émigré churches. In internal documents to the state, Latvian Bishop Matulis described the émigré church leaders as "all compromised by their Nazi past," supported by the German government for their revanchism.[63] In an ironic reversal from the situation earlier in the 1960s when the Baltic churches struggled to overcome émigré opposition to their membership in church international organizations, the Latvian Church lobbied successfully against admission of the Latvian émigré church to the WCC in 1968. In the context of detente, the émigré church in fact succeeded in joining in 1971, but the WCC took into account Soviet Latvian opposition by placing conditions on the émigré membership.[64]

The regime had earlier opposed contacts with the Finnish Lutheran churches for the same reason. By the mid-1960s, however, the regime accepted these ties as a means of reinforcing the special Soviet relationship with Finland.[65] In addition, the advent of mass tourism to Estonia in effect made it impossible to block informal contacts with Finnish churches. With their linguistic similarities and good reception of radio broadcasts from Finland, Estonians were exposed to Finnish media influences also. It was incumbent on the regime to somehow gain more systematic control over the contacts, rather than forbid them outright. LWF leader Bishop Mikko Juva of Finland, seen earlier as anti-Soviet, was permitted to visit the Baltic churches regularly.

By the late 1970s, the international ties of the Baltic churches had become almost routine, as a result of mutual political expediency. Participation in the LWF's Vienna-based group, Minority Lutheran Churches in Europe, earlier viewed suspiciously by the regime, was now promoted.[66] After vetoing the proposal in 1972 on grounds that it would enliven the church, in the context of increased East-West tensions and boycotts over Soviet intervention in Afghanistan, the regime eventually permitted this group to hold an international consultation in the Baltics in 1980. Originally the LWF had suggested holding the meeting in Riga, but the Latvian authorities objected, "in connection with the complicating situation in the republic" (namely, disgruntlement with Kalnins's role with the Soviet German Lutherans), and it was held in Tallinn instead.[67] State officials evaluated the conference positively, particularly the LWF officials' support for peace and condemnation of President Carter's policy on the neutron bomb and limited nuclear war. State officials were also pleased with the LWF cooperation on "measures to 'secure' the propaganda of the conference," seeing as "politically useful" the filming for Soviet television and "purely religious events."[68] In turn, the state permitted Hansen and other LWF officials to travel directly to Central Asia to visit the German parishes themselves, without relying on the Baltic churches as intermediaries.[69] The impact of Soviet interest in détente extended even to the Catholic Church: the first foreign bishop, Bishop Gerhard Shaffran of Dresden, GDR, was permitted to visit Riga in 1982.[70]

Another Luther celebration, the 500th anniversary of his birth in 1983, demonstrated the increased effect of relations with West Germany on Soviet policy. Although it was in no way comparable with the GDR's treatment of the event, the Baltic commemoration was a far cry from the low-key affair in 1967, not to mention 1949, when a Luther monument in Kaila, Estonia, was arbitrarily removed and smelted down.[71] In December 1982, CRA opted for a so-called special jubilee meeting in the Baltics, clearly linked to its decision to upgrade Kalnins's role to superintendent. The regime even contemplated designating a union-wide headquarters for German Lutherans. Lacking their own such religious center, the Latvian Lutherans opposed this proposal, as did the Latvian commissioner.[72] Again, however, East-West tensions—this time over Euromissiles—intruded, as the Soviets sought to use the churches to influence public opinion in West Germany. The Estonian commissioner responded to the CRA's gambit with a proposal for a major conference, with 275 participants representing all Estonian parishes and including foreign delegates as well as the émigré Estonian church. CRA rejected the unprecedented émigré participation, but approved the rest of the proposal, including publications with significant print runs. Riga also hosted five foreign delegates for its ceremonies; both Estonia and Latvia sent two to three delegates each not only to the GDR, but also to the FRG.[73]

On international issues, the Baltic churches could be reliably counted on to support Soviet foreign policy. They supported the 1968 Warsaw Pact invasion of Czechoslovakia and opposed the WCC criticism of it.[74] At international forums, the Baltic churches came to the defense of the Soviet bloc regarding human rights. At the 1970 LWF meeting in Evian, Switzerland, devoted to that issue, Latvian Bishop Matulis railed against mission organizations and Richard Wurmbrand (a smuggler of Bibles into Eastern Europe) and rejected allegations of discrimination against Jews or dissident Baptists in the USSR. In his view, capitalism was the source of racism, discrimination, and war; Western society was hopelessly decadent.[75] The Latvian Church was so conformist as to parrot the Soviet condemnation of the Chinese invasion of Vietnam in 1979.[76] Peace efforts by the Estonian Church predominated in Bishop Hark's 1982 booklet, designed in English for foreign consumption.[77]

Church Autonomy and Leadership Issues

Since 1948, the regime had been dealing with the same Lutheran leaders in Latvia (Turs) and Estonia (Kiivit). Both bishops had consolidated control of their respective church leaderships with the assistance of the regime and the elimination of opposition in the churches. At age seventy-seven, Turs was ripe for retirement, but that of the energetic sixty-one-year-old Kiivit was considered premature. But, in 1967–1968, both leaders were unceremoniously and secretively ousted from their positions.

The motives and processes of these removals remain murky. Interviews by the author suggest that Turs's dissolute character, his alcoholism in particular, and Kiivit's considerable popularity with Western church leaders were the state's motives for ousting them.[78] Certainly archival records reveal considerable long-standing dissatisfaction with Turs's style of leadership, indicating his lack of theological credibility and rapport with Western church leaders, his cronyism with the HCA, and his periodic unreliability. Yet, the archive is filled with praise for these very failings of Turs, evaluating them as conducive to the regime goal of eroding the influence of the Church and religion. Documents from the commissioner's office dating from early 1968, shortly before his removal, reveal a mounting attack on his governance of the Church, alleging that Turs acted dictatorially by not holding a synod for seventeen years, relied on reactionary clergy for power, promoted a personality cult, and failed to consult with the commissioner's office.[79] He was charged with "seeking to play first fiddle" in international relations and invoking the Latvian national poet Janis Rainis to claim a national role for the Lutheran Church.[80]

In a succession that was orchestrated by the Latvian authorities but hardly documented in the archives, Turs was ousted as bishop by a hastily called synod in March 1968 and replaced by Peteris Kleperis. Kleperis had been a member of the HCA for many years and was a reliable informant of the KGB, with considerable international experience.[81] However, in April 1968, he died suddenly of a heart attack on the train to a LWF meeting in Budapest.[82] Alberts Freijs headed the Consistory on an interim basis, but lacked state support for succession as bishop and died in November in any case.

Taken by surprise by this turn of events, but not entirely flat-footed, the regime arranged for Janis Matulis to succeed Kleperis. Matulis could not boast of the international experience of Kleperis, deputy Archbishop Viktors Ozolins, or theology instructor Roberts Priede, but had proven himself supportive of the regime in the 1940s and 1950s. He was installed in 1969, with a retired Swedish bishop serving to legitimize the apostolic succession.[83] Although less authoritative than installation by a sitting bishop, it nonetheless demonstrated greater legitimacy than that enjoyed by Turs and Kiivit at their installations in 1948, when no bishop at all had been present. Overriding the HCA, the state engineered the naming of Eriks Mesters as Matulis's successor upon Matulis's death in 1980.[84]

Archbishop Kiivit of Estonia was also ousted in obscure circumstances, in 1967. It would seem that his growing stature in the West and his facilitation of Western contacts with the Soviet German Lutherans were the precipitating factors.[85] In 1966, the CRA was already putting the brakes on Kiivit's international ties, even with the GDR and the CPC. The KGB engineered a case against him in early 1967, alleging that his family had been enemies of the USSR during the war, that he had voted against Soviet interests in international forums, that he was greedy and had a secret bank account in the West, and, not least, that he had compromised himself with a mistress in West Germany, implying ties to Western intelligence agencies. The Estonian commissioner quickly concurred and persuaded Kiivit to resign in September 1967.[86] The visit of a high-level LWF delegation was canceled abruptly in mid-September, but the resignation—justified on grounds of health—was not publicly communicated to international partners until November, after the new bishop was selected.

Kiivit's successor, Alfred Tooming, mild-mannered and pietistic but lacking authority and, at age sixty, hardly younger than Kiivit, was seen by the state as "loyal, realistic," and unlikely to pose a challenge.[87] His appearances in international forums were vetted by the authorities and often consisted of attacks on US foreign policy. Tooming also demonstrated his loyalty by initiating contributions to the Soviet Peace Fund in 1968 and increasing these annually. Tooming's successor in 1978 was Edgar Hark, aged seventy, viewed in the Church as a polished public speaker and more cosmopolitan than Tooming. Hark had been groomed for the role even more than Tooming or Kiivit and was viewed as reliable and patriotic. Having served as a soldier in the Red Army, as a young pastor he was already favored by the regime with trips to the West and other preferential treatment.[88]

By contrast, the Latvian Catholic church leadership enjoyed increasing stability in its relations with the regime, doubtless in part a function of the Vatican's Ostpolitik. In 1972, the state approved the naming of an auxiliary bishop of Riga, Valerian Zondaks, by Pope Paul VI. In 1982, the aged Bishop Vaivods was able to name a successor, Jānis Cakuls, whose status as a wounded combatant in the Red Army in World War II reassured the state. Finally, Vaivods was elevated to cardinal in 1983 by Pope John Paul II, despite a cool reaction by the ROC and Moscow authorities.[89]

One should also not overlook the fact that the Lutheran administrations were penetrated by the KGB with informants. In particular, the general secretaries of both churches were most likely informants. The record of reporting by the head Estonian administrator, August Leepin, is quite extensive in archival records. In Latvia, church informants were likewise widespread, including Kaulins, Kalnins, and Kleperis himself.[90]

In addition, consistent with the Brezhnev stagnation, complacency began to characterize the arrangements between state officials and church leaders. For example, proposals for special medical facilities for bishops were floated. State officials approved construction of private houses and automobiles for some "patriotic" church officials.[91] Tax rates on clergy were lowered.

The evidence suggests that during the Brezhnev era the regime secured ever greater control over leadership recruitment in the churches, particularly the Lutheran Church. In both Latvia and Estonia bishops were removed by fiat or death; there is no indication of a competitive election for successors, as is common in Lutheran churches.

Dissent in the Churches

Political dissent in the Lutheran churches was quite limited during the early Brezhnev period. A CRA analysis of legal violations by churches and clergy in 1969 found that, of 1,300 union-wide violations, Latvia and Estonia reported only 18 and 1, respectively.[92] KGB analyses of religious dissent highlighted the Orthodox, Baptists, Jehovah's Witnesses, Seventh-Day Adventists, and Mennonites, but hardly mentioned Catholics or Lutherans.[93] The work plan of the Latvian commissioner in 1972 is insightful: priorities included schismatic Baptists, Catholics in the distinctive Catholic region of Latgāle, large increases of income by the Russian Orthodox Church, and school boycotts on Saturday by Adventists; no mention was made of Lutherans.[94] The Lutheran Church was repeatedly described in official reports as passive and not representing a political threat. Human rights appeals to the United Nations and international advocacy organizations by Estonian dissident groups seldom mentioned religious violations, but rather focused on Russification and independence.[95]

Not unlike other parts of the USSR, however, the rise of the *initsiativniki*, underground schismatic Baptists, in the 1960s posed a growing threat to Baltic authorities as a result of migration from other republics, especially Russia. Often officials couched the threat in terms of Russian nationalism, a taboo that indirectly reflected Baltic anxieties regarding this trend. Commissioner Teder attacked a Baptist pastor in eastern Estonia: "Among less educated Baptists of Russian nationality, he slyly and cleverly … tries to use the existence of elements of great-Russian chauvinism, since he is a convinced nationalist himself …" and moved him to southern Estonia, the heartland of Estonian nationality.[96] By the late 1970s, the Baptists and Methodists were taking advantage of growing Western contacts to introduce Western musical influences and host prominent visitors, such as an American astronaut.[97] Latvian officials criticized the Baptists' emphasis on "personal peace with God" instead of international peace as "reactionary and nationalistic" and acted to forbid them from meeting in Lutheran churches.[98] Baptists protested against the new Brezhnev constitution and the Kuroedov regulations on religion. Underground Baptists agitated for the renewed right of religious proselytization.

Heightening the state's fear of dissent was its analysis of the sects' contrast with the Lutherans. Compared with the Lutherans, sects such as Methodists, Baptists, and Adventists tended to demonstrate higher levels of education among the laity represented in the organs of parish governance, namely the dvatsatka and ispolorgans of the local parishes. Their financial giving per capita was also more robust than the Lutherans.[99] Moreover, the sects managed, via Finland, to increase their international contact and assistance, another worrying factor for the state, particularly in Estonia. Lutherans were more reliable in international work than Baptists, who were cross-pressured between the underground groups and the regime.[100]

State officials particularly worried about the convergence of the two migrant groups, Germans and Russians, a phenomenon more evident in Latvia than Estonia. Already in 1968 the specialists in atheistic work in Estonia noted the challenge to their work posed by the arrival of unregistered Baptists.[101] Officials advocated integrating them into existing parishes, fearing that the Germans might be attracted to the schismatic Baptists instead of the Lutherans.[102] The Latvian government in fact took steps to limit German migrants to Latvia.[103]

Although the Lutheran churches evidenced little dissent, they sometimes sought leverage with the state as a result of the dissent among the sects. In 1975, Bishop Tooming successfully obtained state approval to use central church funds to repair parish churches, previously forbidden by the state.[104] Lutheran leaders also pressed for permission for clergy to participate in parish governance, contrary to the 1961 Khrushchev legislation.

By the mid-1970s, however, indications of Lutheran dissent did appear, albeit isolated. Evaluating the Estonian Church for its political stance, the Estonian authorities listed four dangers: indifference by officials, bourgeois nationalism, foreign influences, and curiosity among youth.[105] "Foreign elements," especially Pentecostals, youth, and tourists, were seeking to undermine the authority of the official churches, it was claimed.[106] Religiosity among youth was seen to be increasing. The churches' growing use of music, facilitated by the Tallinn Conservatory, was seen as increasing the churches' attractiveness.

The state also began to target individual Lutheran pastors for the content of their religious activities as well as their opposition to the Estonian church leadership. Some pastors were "ignoring traditional content of worship services in the Lutheran church, using sermons for the introduction of sophisticated anti-Soviet propaganda."[107] Other pastors, such as Tiit Salumäe of Haapsalu, were alleged to exhibit "Catholic tendencies," which conjured up discontent with the passive stance of the Lutheran leadership and even visions of links with Catholic dissidents in Lithuania.[108] Joel Luhamets criticized materialist philosophy and disparaged Communist morality in his sermons. Villu Jürjo began to attract growing numbers of youth to religion by organizing summer church camps; his criticism of the new religion law of 1975 and refusal to vote in elections also put pressure on Bishop Hark.[109] Some pastors even verged in the direction of Estonian nationalism: in southern Estonia, Vello Salum preached increasingly that the spirit of the Estonian people was being destroyed. His message was echoed by Harri Mõtsnik, delegated in 1975 by Hark to serve the Estonian Lutheran parish in Leningrad, who decried the secular order's destruction of spiritual values.[110] Joining this group of young Turks were isolated old Turks who attacked the regime's repression of religion, as did Harri Hammer, a theology professor who had earlier been relegated to a parish in southeastern Estonia, far from Tallinn. A young believer, Illar Hallaste, was expelled from law school and proceeded to study theology, becoming an activist dissident in the late 1970s.[111] The archival record of these dissenters in 1977–1978 is the first indication of active dissent in the churches since the 1950s. Commissioner Piip belittled the young pastors as psychologically sick failures and claimed that "the activities of the leaders of the youth religious movement have been paralyzed" by the KGB and local officials, but he was forced to concede that "well-known activities of bourgeois-clerical centers of the West have made inroads, affecting even loyal pastors."[112] More problematic was the case of Mõtsnik: Archbishop Hark attempted to remove him from Leningrad, but the commissioner of the Leningrad region defended Mõtsnik's popularity in the parish and objected to such "interference" by Hark. Eventually he was marginalized to a small parish in Estonia, the tactic used by the state in most other such cases.[113]

Latvia experienced fewer manifestations of dissent than in Estonia. Indications of Latvian national themes in Lutheran sermons did begin to appear in the late 1970s.[114] But the clergy were largely loyal, and the future dissident group, Renewal and Revival, did not hold its first meeting until August 1983, at the cusp of the post-Brezhnev upheaval. This group would eventually produce greater internal church turmoil, toppling Bishop Mesters, unlike Estonia, which did not undergo ecclesiastical upheaval during the perestroika process. But the stronger link between the Estonian nation and Lutheranism produced a cultural swell against Soviet rule, of which Lutheran pastors were early harbingers.

Bureaucratic Politics

Certain aspects in the relationship between the republic-level commissioners and the central authorities in Moscow did not change over time. Neither the Lutheran Church nor the Catholic Church had authorized headquarters in Moscow; throughout the Soviet period they were forced to conduct their international ties through CRA and/or the ROC, and the republic officials were necessarily cross-pressured and supplicants in this process. For allocations of paper for printing, the absence of a Moscow center also left the churches dependent on republic authorities, who would try to shift the responsibility for paper to the CRA, resulting in repeated bureaucratic hurdles.[115] Access to foreign publications by the churches, as well as by the commissioners, remained controlled by Moscow.[116]

In Estonia, Commissioner Piip demonstrated increased assertiveness and self-confidence in relations with both the churches and the central authorities in the later Brezhnev period. In 1976, Piip proposed a Consultative Council of Churches (later renamed the Central Council of Religious Organizations) to "counter the passivity and neutralism of the church against imperialism".[117] The proposed Council was to serve as "an organ of self-rule," a "buffer between religious organizations and the government" to "resolve the tasks of limiting religion." The ROC was to predominate in the proposed council, but Lutheran Bishop Hark was to be given a high profile in it also. Despite the expedient political justification, the proposal did suggest a pragmatic organizational innovation somewhat analogous to ecumenical church forums in the West. The later draft of the proposal narrowed the role for discussion and criticism by the churches, but the KGB and the CPSU nonetheless objected to this ambitious plan and it was eventually vetoed by CRA.[118]

Another indication of innovation on the republic level was the introduction of consultative seminars on policy issues, held by high-level government officials with church leaders of all confessions in Estonia. Piip justified these as part of "prophylactic work" with church leaders "due to their high levels of education," who have "great freedom of action," and "can set the tone for meetings of religious centers and often have contact with foreign leaders." Viewing these meetings with passive Lutheran churches as positive and unthreatening, CRA endorsed this Estonian model of meetings in 1977.[119] Topics included morals, economics, crime, and Chile, among others. Although suspended briefly in 1979 due to KGB opposition, they soon began again, including one on events in Poland in 1981. The parallel to the GDR is striking: similar *Sachgespraeche* began with the Lutheran churches there in 1977. One should be careful not exaggerate the influence of the churches: the consultations were initiated by the state and co-optation of the churches was the goal. But it does reflect a significant change in the role of the institutional church, even if one can hardly call it partnership.

Republic officials also became more solicitous of the preservation of churches for the architectural and historical value they represented. Increasing reports of thefts and vandalism, especially of church organs, led the Latvian commissioner to urge greater protection, even to the point of charging local officials with theft and undervaluing of church inventory.[120] Paradoxically, state officials assumed legal ownership of the churches' property after the nationalization in the 1940s, yet many officials at the local level saw theft and vandalism as either less critical or even a sign of the success of antireligious policy.

Not surprisingly, the Estonian officials also requested more authority from CRA to deal with religious policy. In particular, Piip wanted more control at the republic level over the registration process, church finances, church repairs, and church conferences, to "give CRA more time to handle important strategic issues."[121] Requests for staff increases also became routine in the late Brezhnev era, justified on the grounds that "border republics, like Estonia, are active zones of hostile propaganda." In part this reflects bureaucratization and stagnation, but it also reflects the routinization of the church-state relationship in these republics dominated by traditional, quiescent Lutheran and Catholic churches.

The growing international contacts (a fourfold increase between 1972 and 1977, for example) also stretched the republics' resources.[122] Commissioners requested more information on international organizations, additional manpower to monitor the contacts, and even more trips abroad for themselves in conjunction with the churches' own activities. CRA in Moscow did supply more information, but again denied requests for more personnel and bureaucratic expansion at the republic level.

Summary and Conclusion

A study of religious policy in Latvia and Estonia during the Brezhnev era reveals considerable continuity with the Khrushchev era, with some nuances. The decline of religious adherence continued unabated under Brezhnev. Secular rites of passage continued to marginalize church rites; the Baltics became a model for other socialist states and Soviet republics. Church institutional interests suffered further: the decline in numbers of clergy continued and their role in the parish remained circumscribed. High taxation levels continued to discriminate against clergy. Church closures, the defining feature of the Khrushchev repression, were widespread in the early Brezhnev period, disproportionately affecting the Lutherans compared with other denominations. By the 1980s, closures had tapered off considerably, though few new churches were opened. Theological education began to stabilize in the 1970s also, as the regime shifted course to support higher education for Lutheran and Catholic clergy, now preferring this to the less-educated, more activist clergy characteristic of the sects. Church leaderships were penetrated by KGB informants and lacked autonomy in decision-making; bishops were selected and ousted by administrative fiat of the regime. Antireligious propaganda took on new, more routinized forms, such as monitoring of sermons by activists and academic research on scientific atheism. On the whole, there was no rebound of the churches after Khrushchev, unlike in the early 1953–1956 post-Stalin period.

The détente process brought considerable interaction with Western churches, particularly the ecumenical organizations and the LWF, and changed the trade-offs for church and state. The relations became almost routine. Baltic Lutheran participants were politically reliable from the regime's perspective. The ties with East German churches continued, but were increasingly overshadowed by those with the LWF and West German churches. New relationships also started with churches long considered reactionary by the regime, as with the Finnish and émigré churches.

But the détente process also produced dilemmas and tensions with the state. German migrants to the Baltics disturbed the modus vivendi reached between the church leaders and the state, raising questions of registration, enlivened religious practice, and even the possible privilege of a union-wide headquarters for German Lutherans. Central authorities in Moscow weighed in to permit greater Western contact with Soviet Germans, overriding republic concerns that the Germans were interested in a springboard to the FRG rather than accommodating to the Baltic context. Embedding them in the Lutheran Church was preferred by the state, but many found the Baptist Church more to their liking.

Dissent also began to grow in the Brezhnev period in the Orthodox and Baptist churches. Such dissent was on the increase in the Baltics as well, due in part to the migration pattern indicated above. State officials were primarily worried about the growth of Pentecostal groups, underground Baptists, and growing Orthodox religious adherence. Orthodox and Baptists resisted participation in secular rites more than Lutherans. Dissent in the Lutheran Church remained quite muted, but began to grow in the late 1970s as younger clergy criticized the submissive approach of the church leadership and began to appeal to youth and sound nationalistic themes. But there is little evidence to suggest infection of dissent from the Soviet bloc reform efforts, unlike in the case of Lithuania.

The state authorities dealing with religious affairs were confronted with new challenges, despite the decline in religiosity of Lutherans. They struggled to manage the growing number of international contacts, particularly with tourists from Scandinavia. They sought to monitor policy implementation of local authorities who sometimes failed to convert closed churches or exceeded the bounds of official policy. Greater efforts at legalizing the relationship with the churches were evident under Brezhnev, especially with publication of new regulations in 1975, but there was no wholesale rollback of the legal restrictions introduced by Khrushchev. Seeking to increase their autonomy, republic officials, particularly in Estonia, sought to decentralize decision-making from Moscow to the republic. They proposed a council of churches to give the churches more ability to self-regulate and undertook informational meetings with church leaders to discuss state policy in various policy areas.

By the end of the Brezhnev era, church-state relations in Latvia and Estonia reflected the stagnation characteristic of that period. The churches were largely co-opted, enjoying certain privileges in exchange for political conformity. Local officials lacked the ideological fervor to pursue atheistic indoctrination and primarily wished to avoid developments—in-migrating Germans, schismatic Baptists of any nationality, international pressure to make trade-offs—that threatened to shake the status quo. In many aspects of Soviet life—economic, cultural, and even political—the stage was set for perestroika. But in the religious sphere in Latvia and Estonia it would be hard to detect this. Isolated dissenting Estonian Lutheran clergy, unregistered Russian Baptists, and an increasingly bureaucratic atheistic establishment offered little foreshadowing of the singing revolutions to come.

The Brezhnev-era religious policy described in this chapter can best be described as the routinization of relations with the weakened national churches. Church closures continued, but were more a function of the sustained decline in church adherence (particularly among Lutherans) and the lack of resources (financial and clerical personnel) than of focused state policy. Regarding other institutional interests, such as publications and theological education, status quo was the pattern. The spread of secular rites caused the apparat to lose interest in the churches; atheistic propaganda became rote and ineffective. Institutional weakness and lack of autonomy resulted in leadership changes choreographed by the state. Even relations with the Catholic Church became more routine as the state tacitly accommodated many of the institutional interests of a quiescent actor.

To the extent that changes did occur in this period, they turned on the confessional as well as the international factors. The defining confessional divide was no longer between Lutheran and Catholic, but rather between these national churches and the Baptist and Pentecostal sects, whose numbers rose as a result of often-unregistered migrants from other parts of the USSR. This development provided a focal point for state policy and tacit convergence of the interests of the republic officials and national churches. Relatedly, the international factors associated with the Soviets' foreign policy became even more significant in explaining the Brezhnev period: East-West détente produced increased ties with Western churches; even relations with the Vatican normalized under Pope Paul VI and Cardinal Vaivods. The increased ties with East and West German churches brought some leverage to the Lutherans, but also revived the Baltic cultural ambivalence regarding Germany.

In this changed context, bureaucratic interests began to diverge from Moscow. CRA commissioners began to see the national churches as more benign and sought to stabilize them, as seen by Estonian notions regarding consultations and seminars with the churches, architectural preservation of churches, and the benefits of formal theological education or the Latvian aversion to Soviet German Lutherans. Combined with the heightened attention to Luther and atheistic researchers' new interest in Lutheran national traditions, one can discern the outline and impact of national religious culture, however faintly, at this point.

Notes

1. ERA.R-1989.2.54, l. 121; ERA.R-1989.2.58, l. 138; Benz, "Schwieriger Neubeginn," 130–31.
2. Viise, "Estonian Evangelical-Lutheran Church," 197–98; RGANI.5.63.89, l. 99. Equating the Lutheran Church with the very obscure sect of Molokans, CRA concluded in 1971 that both are "weak and dying out as religious groups."
3. LVA.1419.3.12, l. 76–77. According to an interview (30 Jan. 1991) with Kuulo Vimmsaare, researcher in atheism, the few religious youth in Estonia turned to the Protestant sects in the 1970s, returning to a Lutheran pattern in the 1980s.
4. LVA.1419.3.4, l. 25–26.
5. ERA.R-1989.2.41, l. 83–84.
6. LVA.1419.3.262, l. 177. According to this official survey of the period 1950–1980, 142 churches were closed and deregistered, including 74 Lutheran, 6 Catholic, and 45 Russian Orthodox. More of these occurred during the Khrushchev repression than the Stalinist era, but 40 occurred between 1965 and 1973. See LVA.1419.3.281, l. 59–65; LVA.1419.3.9, l. 71–74.
7. LVA.1419.3.280, l. 30–34. The commissioner called for more work with youth on tolerance of churches and believers, as well as reprimands to the local police.
8. LVA.1448.1.264, l. 1.
9. LVA.1419.3.262, l. 170–76; LVA.1419.3.262, l. 177.
10. LVA.1419.3.281, l. 63–64. The commissioner urged that the "illegal and incorrect activities of local authorities be eliminated."
11. LVA.1419.3.280, l. 6–7. Twenty-two new clergy were added in 1965, for a net decline of 8.
12. LVA.1419.3.7, l. 25–30, documents this process in one such parish in Talsi raion, LSSR.

13. "Secret Instructions," 30–33. LVA.1448.1.264, l. 25–27, evaluating implementation in Latvia of the legislation by the Supreme Soviet USSR (27 Jan. 1965) to review criminal legal actions against religious citizens since 1961. As argued by Commissioner Liepa, however, these legal reviews uncovered few cases of violations in the Baltics. Viise ("Estonian Evangelical-Lutheran Church," 199–200) indicates the Commissions were to attend worship services and parish council meetings and report violations such as unauthorized preachers, services in homes, and political disloyalty. Also see Remmel, "Religioonivastane Võitlus," 2.

14. ERA.R-1989.1.165, l. 187: a 1975 evaluation of Estonia by CRA, highlighting the inadequacy of the Commissions on Legality to report on sermons, clergy, and Bible studies and the reliance on full-time party officials for this function. Viise ("Estonian Evangelical-Lutheran Church," 206–7) documents a 1978 CRA inspector report highlighting high levels of vacancies on Commissions and poor background in theology and church practice. See also Remmel, "Religioonivastane Võitlus," 3 and Remmel, "(Anti-)Religious Aspects," 374–78, on the fuzzy legal mandate and administrative problems of the Commissions.

15. ERA.R-1989.2.38, l. 40–43. Commissioner Tedder reported extensively on sermons and explained the new ESSR CM decision to create local commissions in his 1968 Informational Report, ERA.R-1989.2.41, l. 178–215.

16. ERA.R-1989.2.34, l. 1–2; ERA.R-1989.2.36, l. 33–37. In Estonia in 1963, insurance costs skyrocketed from 6,480 to 41,467 rubles and property taxes from 12,126 to 70,930 rubles. Lutherans represented 67 percent of all these costs. One-third of all Estonian Lutheran parishes protested, leading the commissioner to initially fear a permanent advantage for sects; but all appeals were rejected by the Ministry of Finance and the commissioner eventually viewed the expenses as affordable and protests as mere "religious propaganda."

17. In most reports after the late 1950s, the commissioners noted this discrepancy. See LVA.1419.3.287, l. 42–44: services averaged less than 1 per week and 140 confirmations republic-wide, but income was up 1.1 percent.

18. ERA.R-1989.2.38, l. 24–26. Lutherans averaged 4.2 rubles per member, whereas Baptists and Methodists averaged 14.10 and 11.50 rubles per member, respectively. Adventists gave a remarkable 22.20 rubles per member.

19. LVA.1419.3.1, l. 1; LVA.1419.3.1, l. 39–41. Clergy were taxed 15 rubles per person, compared with independent workers at 7.5 rubles and kolkhozniks at 2 rubles. Latvian church leaders such as Turs, Kleperis, and Kaulins received the tax break after 1966.

20. LVA.1419.3.284, l. 29. Latvian officials indicate in 1969 that one-fourth of Lutheran pastors were forced to work in secular jobs as well.

21. LVA.1419.3.281, l. 93–94.

22. ERA.R-1989. 1.165, l. 189. A 1978 CRA review again highlighted the legal anomaly in Estonia, but the state was reduced to hoping the selection of a new bishop in 1978 might change the situation to conform to the Khrushchev legislation. ERA.R-1989.1.199, l. 121.

23. As chapter 4 indicated, future bishops Kiivit and Hark were selected to study in Germany, but did not assume positions teaching theology when they returned. Finnish National Committee, LWF, 24 Aug. 1967; the archive describes repeated official rejections of Finnish offers of stipends for Estonian students.

24. ERA.R-1989.2.43, l. 114.

25. Benz, "Schwieriger Neubeginn," 112; Trups-Trops, "Die Römisch-Katholische Kirche," Teil 2, 120–24, 127, and Teil 3, 100. During the Communist period, 69 of the 133 graduates of the Riga Seminary were from other republics.

26. ERA.R-1989. 1.188, l. 77f. CRA reports approvingly that 70 percent of Lutheran clergy in 1977 possessed higher education, compared with 60 percent a few years earlier; CRA Chair Kuroedov maintained that it was "better to produce patriotic oriented cult servants from theology schools than have as clergy illiterate and half-literate fanatics and extremists."

27. ERA.R-1989.2.41, l. 222–40, suggests that in Estonia the civil weddings and the summer days of youth had triumphed over their religious counterparts; civil burials were now on par with church burials; name-giving ceremonies still lagged in popularity. Remmel ("(Anti)-Religious Aspects," 382–86) discusses the success of the secular rites, as well as the less successful ones, such as funerals, and the decline of the atheistic component in them over time.

28. RGANI.5.60.24, l. 178–80.

29. Text of Kuroedov speech in ERA.R-1989.1.134, l. 1–40; Binns, "Soviet Secular Ritual," 300; Binns ("Sowjetische Feste," 110–21) found that the secular rites did not eliminate religious needs, but that Soviet society had adopted and adapted them to fulfill social functions.

30. ERA.R-1989.2.36, l. 22–25. The Estonian commissioner saw "children's institutions, especially in cities, as removing the influence of religion on a large portion of children and infusing them with an atheistic worldview. This curtails the upbringing of conservative neighbors and grandmas in the family. Pre-school institutions should be a filter and assistance to schools, helping in their manner to protect children from religious manipulation in families."

31. ERA.R-1989.1.177, l. 18–20; ERA.R-1989.2.58, l. 165; Remmel, "Religioonivastane Võitlus," 4.

32. ERA.R-1989.2.66, l. 121–22; ERA.R-1989.2.67, l. 17–46; Remmel, "Religioonivastane Võitlus," 3; Remmel, "(Anti)-Religious Aspects," 367–75.

33. RGASPI.606.4 has the documents of the Institute for Scientific Atheism of the Academy.

34. ERA.R-1989.2.41, l. 195–96; Vimmsaare, "O religioznoi ideologii," 138–91; Vimmsaare, *Religioon ja kirik Eestis*.

35. Central Committee, *Ideologiia i Praktika*.

36. RGANI.5.62.38, l. 118–20. See the Vimmsaare address found in RGASPI.606.4.16, l. 45–68.

37. Vimmsaare, "Sovremenoe Sostoianie"; Liemets, "Propovednichestkaia Deiatel'nost," 9–11, 33–37; Vimmsaare, *Sovremennoe L'iuteranstvo*.

38. RGASPI.606.4.16, l. 45–68, especially l. 67–68, on the 1964 Baltic seminar of atheist researchers.

39. RGASPI.606.4.189 and RGASPI.606.4.200 hold the record of this project, including an evaluation of the coming-of-age ceremonies in RGASPI.606.4.189, l. 33–35. Studying the Estonian experience of the model project at Kohlta-Järve, the Latvian Council of Atheists, attached to Znanie, decided against giving gifts at the "summer days of youth," the secular rite for confirmation. This contrasted with the GDR practice that encouraged gifts. "Fakten und Zahlen," 196, reported its findings of sustained religiosity among youth.

40. ERA.R-1989.1.165, l. 50–57, which summarizes the Kuroedov speech.

41. ERA.R-1989.1.165, l. 103. In its reaction to the draft decree of the Presidium of the ESSR Supreme Soviet, the KGB also sought to limit traveling choirs.

42. ERA.R-1989.1.155, l. 54.

43. ERA.R-1989.1.165, l. 185. By 1975, 6,000 of these had emigrated.
44. ERA.R-1989.1.155, l. 123–27. Commissioner Piip in ERA.R-1989.2.50, l. 82, reports that Catholics in Estonia, previously a miniscule group in the religious landscape, increased dramatically, from 750 to 2,000, during the 1969–1972 three-year period.
45. ERA.R-1989.2.50, l. 125–27. The commissioner conceded that the Germans did not oppose Soviet power, but described them as "at a low cultural level," refusing along with their children to participate in social life, and critical of daily life. He concedes a silver lining in the growth of German Catholics: "In this case one can choose the lesser of two evils—they may be checked on." On the German migration and the schism among Baptists, see also Pilli, *Dance or Die*, 57–64, 80.
46. ERA.R-1989.2.48, l. 20.
47. ERA.R-1989.1.199, l. 105.
48. ERA.R-1989.1.188, l. 77f includes the speech by Kuroedov, "On Tasks of the Council and its Commissioners in Increasing the Effectiveness and Quality of Control of Monitoring Law on Religious Cults in the Light of Decisions of the 25th Congress of the CPSU."
49. LVA.1419.3.281, l. 157–58. Archival documents indicate that Kalnins was, in fact, an informant for the regime. Kalnins informed the commissioner about the unapproved visit of Professor Hans-Dieter Döppman of the GDR to preach in Riga in 1967.
50. LVA.1419.3.17, l. 142–44. The Latvian Communist leadership opposed designating Kalnins as the specialist in the Latvian Consistory for Germans; the Latvian Church opposed his authority outside Latvia. Hoping to leverage the human rights debate into growing access, Carl Mau and Paul Hansen lobbied for Kalnins to assume a wider role in 1976, including participation in the 1977 LWF Assembly in Dar es Salaam, seeing it important that "at the largest international church conference following [the WCC Assembly in] Nairobi, a specialist on German parishes in the USSR be present."
51. LVA.1448.1.264, l. 30–34 and LVA.1448.1.264, l. 49–68, on the visits of Bishops Krummacher (Greifswald), Jänicke (Saxony-Magdeburg), and Noth (Saxony-Dresden) and Superintendent Jacob (Berlin-Brandenburg). LVA.1419.3.286, l. 64 and LVA.1419.3.287, l. 20 report on visits by Bishop Schönherr (Berlin-Brandenburg) and Bishop Braecklein (Thuringia), respectively.
52. LVA.1419.3.3, l. 52; LVA.1419.3.3, l. 53–54. Originally four delegates were planned from Latvia; Kleperis and Matulis were substituted for them. The Estonians sent newly elected Bishop Tooming and future bishop Pajula. The Estonian Church statements are in ERA.R-1989.2.39, l. 76–81.
53. Regarding the Estonian commemoration, see Hark, *Estonian Evangelical Lutheran Church*, 67; regarding the Latvian commemoration, see Felmy et al., "Chronik," 134.
54. See LVA.1419.3.280, l. 43–55, on the visit by the LWF delegation under Appel and Hansen in 1966, with reports by church informants. On these initiatives of the Swedish and German churches, the LWF, and individuals, such as Johannes Baumann, see Mankusa, "Over the Iron Curtain," 317–21.
55. RGANI.5.33.233, l. 20–30.
56. LVA.1419.3.280, l. 35, with Turs-Appel letter, l. 36.
57. LVA.1419.3.200, l. 24–26. Latvian authorities opposed theological education beyond that provided in the Latvian language. Referring to the regime's perspective in the 1960s, Fletcher (*Religion*, 152) sees the foreign policy benefits of these international church ties outweighing the domestic costs, but this issue of the Germans suggests that certainly by

the 1970s local and republic-level officials weighed the trade-offs more negatively than Moscow.

58. LVA.1419.3.198, l. 145–47. Bishop Matulis, the commissioner, and "directive organs" in Latvia sought to prevent Kalnins from printing missals and song sheets and rejected a bank account. Under CRA pressure, the Latvian synod named Kalnins specialist for German Lutherans in May 1977. LVA.1419.3.291, l. 71–72. V.I. Krūminš, the chair of the Latvian Council of Ministers, strenuously objected in 1978 to any support by Bishop Matulis for work with the German Lutherans, ordering that issues of German Bible literature (from the Bible Society and LWF) and theological education be taken up with CRA. He also objected to the formation of a religious center in the USSR for German Lutherans. LVA.1419.3.292, l. 84. At the same time, the Catholic seminary in Riga received the permission, under pressure from CRA, to educate Ukrainians and Belarussians. But the Latvian authorities feared the precedent of this decision for Lithuanians and Germans.

59. LVA.1419.3.280, l. 36–37 and LVA.1419.3.282, l. 196, with Bishop Turs's letters to the LWF and Lithuanian Lutherans offering to facilitate their contact. See also Mankusa, "Over the Iron Curtain," 329–31.

60. LVA.1419.3.282, l. 222–27, includes the report of Pastor Ozolins on interaction with the émigré Latvian representatives at the WCC Ecumenical Assembly in Uppsala; LVA.1419.3.5, l. 174–79, includes the report of Ozolins on his trip to the FRG at émigré church expense. It certainly helped that the WCC rejected membership for the émigré Latvian Church in 1968 and took strong political positions critical of the US war in Vietnam and supportive of Third World economic demands. Even the KGB evaluation hailed Uppsala as a success for Soviet foreign policy, in RGANI.5.80.24, l. 136–39.

61. ERA.R-1989.2.52, l. 161–62.

62. LVA.1419.3.284, l. 87–102, with attachment of Bishop Matulis's report. Matulis reports that at this major LWF meeting in Evian, Latvian émigré Bishop Arnolds Lūsis was relatively passive, outflanked by LWF officials more interested in the Soviet churches. The utter fealty of Matulis to the ROC is evident in his reliance on Pavel Sokolovski, representative of the ROC, a nonmember of the LWF, for direction regarding whether to be a candidate for the LWF Executive Committee and how to vote on resolutions critical of Soviet restrictions on Jews.

63. LVA.1419.3.284, l. 138–58. Émigré Bishop Lūsis is described as "an open fascist" and the German government is accused of subsidizing the émigré churches for revanchist reasons.

64. Matulis and the Consistory repeatedly protested admission of the émigré church to the WCC, as found in LVA.1419.3.6, l. 241–42. He argued that the WCC "cannot permit that those who left their state twenty-five years ago speak in the name of the Latvian people, for which the Latvian people did not give them the right, the power." In LVA.1419.3.7, l. 37, he argued that "the activity of émigrés has no religious character, but only interferes with church work in the Latvian homeland and generally has demagogic character." LVA.1419.3.7, l. 36. As a condition for its decision to admit the émigré church, the WCC stipulated that it only work outside the Latvia SSR.

65. The opening to Finland did not, however, prevent regional authorities from intervening in the process. Registration of a Lutheran parish in Petrozavodsk in 1967–1969 was approved by CRA, which argued that 10,000 believers were without a church and that Finnish church leaders were pressing the issue. But the Central Committee authorities in Moscow deferred the issue after the proposal was rejected by the Karelian and Leningrad oblast Communist officials, who argued that the Soviet Finns were nationalistic and

maintain illegal ties to Ingrian Finns in Finland. RGANI.5.59.24, l. 147–48; RGANI.5.80.24, l. 173–74; RGANI.5.80.24, l. 175–77.

66. ERA.R-1989.2.17, l. 176–81. The commissioner suspected that the LWF Minority Churches group was a front for the émigré churches in western Europe. By 1960, CARC viewed this group more positively as "opposing the influence of the Vatican," according to RGANI.5.33.162, l. 65.

67. LVA.1419.3.198, l. 86, 98.

68. ERA.R-1989.2.50, l. 131. The CRA's plan to "realize the necessary control of the work of journalists" is found in ERA.R-1989.1.224, l. 27–29. Commissioner Piip's post-mortem on the LWF meeting is in ERA.R-1989.1.224, l. 107–13. Interestingly, the commissioner praised the purely religious events and concerts at the LWF meetings for "creating the proper political atmosphere.... True, if such concerts were conducted frequently, they might lead to a significant activation of the religious movement, but in this case as counterpropaganda measures, they were appropriate and politically useful." But he criticized the apolitical conservatism of Estonian churchmen, by contrast with the highly political action of Western churchmen.

69. "Lutheraner in der Sowjetunion," 255–326. Walter Grassman, "Geschichte der Evangelisch-Lutherischen Rußlanddeutschen," 238–67.

70. Trups-Trops, "Römisch-Katholische Kirche," Teil 3, 78–79.

71. ERAF.1.14a.37, l. 220.

72. LVA.1419.3.196, l. 89–92.

73. LVA 1419.3.196, l. 102–3; ERA.R-1989.1.264, l. 13–14, and CRA plans "On the Conduct of the 500th Anniversary of Luther," l. 12. Unlike the GDR, with dueling biographies (Marxist and Christian) published on the occasion, the USSR published only a Marxist biography, by the Komsomol press, after the event. Solov'ev, *Nepobezhdennyĭ eretik* [An Invincible Heretic].

74. LVA.1419.3.4, l. 133, 163, and RGANI.5.80.24, l. 151–56, refer to the letters sent by both churches objecting to the WCC criticism of the Warsaw Pact invasion and clergy views on the issue.

75. LVA.1419.3.284, l. 88–102 (Matulis Report on V. LWF Assembly); LVA.1419.3.284, l. 113–21(Matulis Report on Sept. 1970 delegation to Hungary and Romania, LWF Minority Churches in Europe).

76. LVA.1419.3.193, l. 11–12.

77. Hark, 49–58.

78. Interview, Jaan Kiivit Jr.

79. LVA.1419.3.280, l. 7. The commissioner raised the question of replacing Turs in 1966, describing him as "deaf," "hostile," tactless with pastors, and tending to violate Soviet law. By 1967, the commissioner evaluated Turs even more negatively: "Over time, after becoming archbishop, he governed the church for a long time, refused to call a General Synod despite the fact that a portion of the Higher Church Administration had died, after he obtained his supporters from a group of reactionary clergy, after he became known in international church circles as a result of the ecumenical ties of the church, his behavior changed radically." Turs created a "personality cult," stopped consulting with church leaders, overturned HCA decisions, and stopped "informing the commissioner in a timely and objective fashion" or taking his recommendations. The main objection to Turs was that his weak authority was impeding the use of the church for international ecumenical activities in the "fight for peace and democracy." See LVA.1419.3.28, l. 32–35.

80. LVA.1419.3.283, l. 37–38. Turs was notably absent from state-approved delegations to international conferences in 1967–1968 and bumped from the 450th celebration of the Reformation in the GDR and CEC in Austria in 1967. LVA.1419.3.3, l. 52; LVA.1419.3.3. l. 53–54; LVA.1419.3.3, l. 26. The state substituted its preferred candidate, Roberts Priede, for Turs's proposed representative, Alberts Freijs, in the delegation to an LWF meeting in 1967.

81. LVA.1419.3.282, l. 78–79. In the context of promoting his selection as bishop, the commissioner's charakteristika describes Kleperis as loyal, with "no undesirable ambiguous expressions in all these years," a supporter of the Red Army, well-traveled, and reporter of violations committed by other clergy.

82. Freijs and Kalnins made a written report of the untimely death of their fellow delegate, in LVA.1419.3.282, l. 136–38; LVA.1419.3.283, l. 30. Curious is the fact that there is no mention of the fate of Bishop Turs in the commissioner's report.

83. LVA.1419.3.283, l. 202–4 and l. 209–13 for reports by Matulis and Ozolins. The sitting archbishop of Sweden, D. Ruben Josefson, turned down the request, fearing complications with the émigré Latvian Lutheran church headquartered in Stockholm, sending instead retiring Bishop Sven Danell. The LWF sent Deputy General Secretary Carl Mau, but LWF General Secretary Appel and the point man for Eastern ties, Paul Hansen, did not attend.

84. LVA.1419.3.198, l. 123. Overriding the Church's recommendations, the commissioner promoted Mesters to serve as pastor at the Moscow Olympics in 1980, an indication of the favor with state officials that he enjoyed.

85. LVA.1419.3.281, l. 149–50. The Gustav-Adolf-Werk society of Germany was cited by the Latvian commissioner as speculating that Kiivit's support for the Soviet German Lutherans was the cause. Altnurme (*History*, 137) sees Kiivit's high international profile as the cause of his ouster. Viise ("Estonian Evangelical-Lutheran Church," 193) also argues that Kiivit's strong administrative organization helped struggling parishes, more than Turs in Latvia.

86. The attack of the Estonian KGB on Kiivit is found in ERA.R-1989.2.38, l. 120–21, and Commissioner Teder's concurrence in ERA.R-1989.2.38, l. 127. Finnish National Committee, LWF, 1 Nov. 1967. Kiivit would continue teaching theological courses until his death in 1971. Neumärker, "In Memoriam," 163–72; Altnurme, "Foreign Relations," 163–64.

87. ESSR Commissioner, Characteristika, Tooming. In the very early evaluation written by Commissioner Kivi in 1949, Tooming was already described as disciplined and loyal. He "proved his loyalty to Soviet power already in 1941 when he responded to the call for mobilization. It is necessary to describe his sermons in the church before believers and meetings of pastors as positive, since whenever possible, they draw patriotic conclusions." Interview, Toomas Paul, regarding views among the clergy of Tooming and Hark.

88. ERA.R-1989.2.12, l. 59–60, implies that the state blocked Hark's efforts at a secular career and directed him into a church career instead, with the idea of using him to infiltrate the Church. GARF.6991.3.1364, l. 25, indicates using Hark to connect with pro-regime clergy in the GDR. ERA.R-1989. 1.199, l. 123–25, reports on Hark's installation. High level representation from the LWF, Sweden, Finland, and other Baltic republics was present at this installation, lending it greater legitimacy than earlier ones.

89. Trups-Trops, "Römisch-Katholische Kirche," Teil 3, 77–78, 79–81.

90. LVA.1448.1.264, l. 69–84, contains the handwritten notes by Kaulins on the GDR church visit to Latvia. Kalnins's report on the visit of Professor Hans-Dieter Döppman of Humboldt University is found in LVA.1419.3.281, l. 157–58.

91. Based on Ozolins's "patriotic role" internationally, the commissioner lobbied for a private house and car for him in 1980, according to LVA.1419.3.196, l. 11–12, and LVA.1419.3.294, l. 70–71. But when the commissioner proposed a special medical group for key church leaders, he was refused by the Health Ministry, according to LVA.1419.3.194, l. 86–88.

92. LVA.1419.3.15.

93. RGANI.5.63.89, l. 1–17.

94. LVA.1419.3.287, l. 36–38.

95. "Documents from Estonia," 3–72.

96. ERA.R-1989.2.41, l. 115, 121–25. In order to "paralyze his effect," the state moved the pastor in question, Arder, from Rakvere, in heavily Russian eastern Estonia, to Suure-Jaani, in southwestern Estonia, which would again become a wellspring of Estonian national renaissance in the 1980s.

97. ERA.R-1989.2.60, l. 119. Baptist and Methodists hosted Jim Irwin and the Oral Roberts Ensemble at Oleviste Church in 1978.

98. LVA.1419.3.12, l. 56–59; LVA.1419.3.13, l. 5–6; LVA.1419.3.13, l. 115–16. Refusing registration, schismatic Baptists in Ogre, Riga, and Jelgava met in Lutheran churches until state officials forbade it. LVA.1419.3.292, l. 58–59.

99. ERA.R-1989.2.38, l. 14.

100. LVA.1419.3.283, l. 84–85. The Latvian commissioner complained that, unlike the Lutheran hosts, Baptist Bishop Peteris Egle did not "secure the work" during the visit of WCC leaders to Latvia in 1969, reported only generalities, and had unchecked contact with WCC delegates.

101. RGASPI.606.4.189, l. 98–106. Pilli ("Union," 39–42) hints at the greater tendency in Estonia of Russian Baptists to engage in illegal religious activities or for evangelistic services in Russian to produce state crackdowns.

102. LVA.1419.3.282, l. 60. "With time we will succeed in normalizing the situation of German colonists, include them in working religious parishes and end their illegal activity."

103. LVA.1419.3.284, l. 66.

104. ERA.R-1989.1.165, l. 188–89, in which Tooming argued that if we do not help the weak parishes with repairs and housing, "a number of churches would declare closing, and believers would move to the sects."

105. ERA.R-1989.2.56, l. 106–11.

106. ERA.R-1989.2.57a, l. 142–45. Pentecostals and tourists from Finland were affecting the Baptists and Methodists, as by the use of choirs and orchestras and the introduction of pop music. On increased use of music and youth evangelization after 1967, see Pilli, *Dance or Die*, 86–100.

107. ERA.R-1989.2.64, l. 113.

108. ERA.R-1989.2.56, l. 112.

109. ERA.R-1989.2.58, l. 143. The commissioner's analysis refers to the "negative activity" of young pastors, who were not in agreement with "those who stand with the established powers, conservative-minded clergy, pressing for wider activity of religious life." This was the first mention of a generational conflict in the Lutheran clergy. ERA.R-1989.2.60, l. 116–19. The commissioner indicated that Jürjo and Andres Põder complained of restrictions by the government, held nationalist meetings in apartments, and reproduced materials on state equipment. Jürjo's letter to Bishop Hark claimed that the new religion law violated the USSR

Constitution, the Helsinki Accord, and the UN Universal Declaration of Human Rights. Viise, "Estonian Evangelical-Lutheran Church," 209–15; *Kulturpolitische Korrespondenz*; interview, Villu Jürjo.

110. ERA.R-1989.2.58, l. 135–37; Salum, *Church and the People*.

111. ERA.R-1989.2.58, l. 143–44. Hammer formulated and circulated theses critical of the new religious law, but was "neutralized" at meetings on the constitution held by the commissioner for church officials; ERA.R-1989.2.62, l. 134. In 1979, Hallaste was expelled as a law student at Tartu "for behavior unworthy of a Soviet student," despite Bishop Hark's protest that it was due to religious conviction. This set him on the path toward theological studies and dissent.

112. ERA.R-1989.2.65, l. 90–91, 102. Jürjo lost his registration as a pastor for organizing youth camps. Another young pastor, Paul Luhamets of Kuresaare, criticized atheism, the materialist view of society, and the Communist party in his sermons and posted the schedule for the Voice of America's religious programming. Future Archbishop Põder emphasized elements of national culture, such as love of the native Estonian language, in his sermons. In response, the state cracked down more mildly—by warnings, fines, and "administrative measures"—on new activities of churches, especially focused on youth. Other dissenting pastors noted frequently included Tiit Salumäe and Peeter Kaldur. ERA.R-1989.2.64, l. 111–14.

113. ERA.R-1989.1.224, l. 151; ERA.R-1989.1.224, l. 150; *Kulturpolitische Korrespondenz* documents the 1980 arrest, confinement to a psychiatric institution, and decertification of Salum in 1982.

114. LVA.1419.3.291, l. 53–54. In particular, Pastor Kārlis Kalderovskis in Slokas heralded Lutheranism's historical role in education and spiritual renaissance and criticized the repression of religion. Bishop Matulis was warned about him.

115. LVA.1419.3.14, l. 136.

116. After Bishop Kiivit complained in 1963 of confiscation of an East German theological publication, CARC sought to devolve control over foreign mailings to the Estonian commissioner, but was rebuffed by Moscow officials. See GARF.6991.3.1421, l. 78–79, 83.

117. ERA.R-1989.1.177, l. 76; ERA.R-1989.2.57a, l. 155–56

118. ERA.R-1989.2.62, l. 130.

119. ERA.R-1989.1.188, l. 77f. Kuroedov endorsed Estonia's meetings by government officials with clergy. ERA.R-1989.1.212, l. 3–4. They were suspended "due to the conservative approach of some officials but quickly we realized that conservatism was damaging and contradicting the basic function of the commissioner." Also, Altnurme, *History*, 124–25; Rohtmets and Ringvee, "Religious Revival," 358. Remmel ("(Anti-)Religious Aspects,") sees these seminars primarily as preventive measures toward the Church, but the topics suggest some room for discussion of broader topics, beyond legal constraints.

120. LVA.1419.3.193, l. 90, 206–11. The Latvian government documented increased theft and vandalism against churches in that republic in 1978–1979.

121. ERA.R-1989.2.60, l. 127–28.

122. ERA.R-1989. 1.188, l. 4, 77. This seems at odds with Altnurme ("Foreign Relations," 164), who sees the international contacts as greatly attenuated after Kiivit's departure.

6 Perestroika and Religious Policy in the Baltics: Playing Harmony in the Singing Revolution, 1985–1991

Without a doubt, it is difficult to comprehend the revolutions of 1989, particularly those in Central Europe, without addressing the role of religion and the churches. In Poland, the Catholic Church sustained the nation during the dark days of martial law, bridged the gap between intelligentsia and workers, and helped deliver the electorate for Solidarity in the compromise election of 1989. In East Germany, activist clergy and laity, utilizing the social space of the Lutheran churches, mobilized to produce a "Protestant revolution" in a society otherwise notable for its lack of organized opposition to the Communist regime. Even in highly secular Czechoslovakia, the Catholic Church's successful petition for greater autonomy revealed the first cracks in Husák's façade of "normalization." In other cases—the negotiated revolution in Hungary or the palace coups in Romania and Bulgaria—the churches played a marginal role.

In contrast to the revolutions in Central Europe, the end of communism in the USSR coincided with a rupture in the political community, making comparison between the cases problematic. Still, several points of comparison remain valid. To what extent did the churches critique "stagnation" as part of nascent civil society? To what extent did the churches embody the national culture as part of a national renaissance? To what extent did the churches provide a source of leaders for the democratic movement? Finally, to what extent were the churches engines of the "singing revolution" versus passive beneficiaries of it?

"Mature Socialism" or Pre-Crisis Stagnation?

As discussed in the previous chapter, under Brezhnev the antireligious policy moderated after the era of repression under Khrushchev: crude atheistic efforts gave way to more nuanced, rational atheism; secular rites were promoted to replace religious ones; monitoring of churches and sermons became routine; and legal concerns were given more attention. Churches continued to be closed, especially Lutheran churches, and training of clergy stabilized, though at very low levels. At the same time, the regime accepted and even promoted international ties, particularly as a result of new visibility accorded the churches in the context of the inter-German tensions and the issue of Soviet German Lutherans, the East-West détente process, and Soviet peace campaigns. Localism was evident in the efforts by republic officials and commissioners to develop new instruments, such as commissions to monitor legality or the unsuccessful proposal to create a council of churches in Estonia. Overt religious dissent remained minimal, but advocates of religious-based national culture and energetic resistance to Lutheran passivity were becoming more visible in the churches, particularly among younger cohorts of clergy.

When Brezhnev died in 1982, the churches were extremely weak, as measured by church adherence. In 1981, the Estonian commissioner estimated that 85 percent of Estonians were indifferent to religion and Lutheran church membership was approximately 30,000 (of a population of 1.5 million).[1] Church attendance on a normal Sunday was 4,000 to 5,000; even at Christmas services no more than 100,000 attended. The statistics for Latvia were hardly much better. Religion was marginalized, even if the end result of thirty years of propaganda was indifference to religion more than avowed atheism.[2]

Institutionally, the churches were in desperate circumstances. The number of clergy had been reduced to 113 in Estonia, heavily skewed to older cohorts. Few students matriculated in theological study, portending a future crisis. Official Estonian reports heaped scorn on the efforts of the churches to recruit new theology students, suggesting most had "spoiled their lives" or were "psychologically sick."[3] Parishes continued to be deregistered. Latvia eliminated seventeen churches in between 1975 and 1985, including eight Lutheran churches.[4] Financially, the Estonian Lutherans were a shell of their former self: with only one-third the members, the ROC boasted 20 percent more income than the Lutheran churches.[5] The income of the Lutheran Church in Latvia only increased 3.2 percent during the decade preceding 1985.[6]

As shown in previous chapters, the church leadership in both Baltic republics was largely co-opted by and loyal to the Soviet regime. In the case of Estonia, Bishop Edgar Hark had been positioned for the role of bishop by the regime since the 1950s and was duly elected in 1978. In the state personnel file, he was described as "disciplined and accurate," and his public activities as "always having patriotic-educational character." A Red Army veteran, Hark indicated that "if again necessary, I would exchange my clerical collar for a military uniform."[7] Likewise, in Bishop Janis Matulis, the state had a reliable partner in Latvia.

Institutionally, the situation of the Latvian Catholic Church was substantially better. Financially, it enjoyed a 23 percent increase in income for the decade 1975–1985. The clergy shortage was less: 108 priests served 179 parishes, in contrast to the Lutheran Church, where 80 pastors served 203 parishes. Moreover, it boasted a younger, more highly educated profile than the Lutheran Church: 60 percent of priests were under age sixty, whereas 70 percent of Lutheran clergy were older than sixty.[8] But, until 1981, the Catholic seminary had been limited to only twenty students.[9]

Under politically loyal Archbishop Vaivods, the Catholic leadership had been largely passive and isolated. In his sermons, Vaivods criticized atheism, but he followed the tradition of Strods in his acceptance of Soviet authority. Although the regime permitted Vaivods more routine contact with the Vatican in the 1970s, it strictly limited his visits to his own parishes in Latvia.[10] Vatican II reforms, such as the use of Latvian in services, were not implemented until the late 1980s.[11] Vaivods criticized the extension of religious activity by the Lithuanian Catholics into Belorussia. Unlike his predecessors, Vaivods preached at ecumenical services to celebrate the anniversary of the end of WWII, although by the 1980s he had become very inactive.[12] Though elevated to cardinal by Pope John Paul II in 1983, he was quite skeptical of the Polish experience ("an impulsive nation that ... risks losing what they have gained") and objected to papal proposals to celebrate the 800th anniversary of the Christianization of Latvia in 1986.[13]

This pattern of leadership loyalty to the state was mirrored at the parish level as well. Both Estonian and Latvian commissioners reported few if any legal violations by clergy or parishes. To the extent any occurred, they involved primarily unregistered Pentecostal groups and Baptists meeting in apartments.[14] Indeed, it is striking that in a review of samizdat materials published since 1973 by Keston College in *Religion in Communist Lands*, there are virtually none from Latvia or Estonia until the mid-1980s.

Not surprisingly, Moscow praised the performance of the local officials in dealing with the churches. These republics were touted as the poster children for the USSR regarding the propagation of secular rites to supplant religious ones.[15] CRA Chair Kuroedov acknowledged them in 1977 for exemplary increases in registering parishes for the German population, implementing the 1974 CPSU decision to legally recognize the Soviet Germans in religious terms, in an effort to co-opt them politically.[16]

From such a position of strength, it is not surprising that the regime would engage in rather innovative strategies toward the church leadership. The Estonian commissioner began consultative seminars with church leaders involving high-level state officials, similar to those in the GDR.[17] On one hand, this suggested some political dialogue with the Lutheran Church; on the other, it confirmed how co-opted the church leadership was. Seminars for theology students by state officials increased, conferring legitimacy to such training, but simultaneously designed to influence clergy replacement.[18]

This context portended a limited potential for churches to be drivers of political change. But some factors militated in favor of such a role. First and foremost was Baltic national culture, with which Catholicism (in the Latgāle region of Latvia especially) and Lutheranism are closely identified. As earlier chapters showed, both religious repression and liberalization had carried national overtones. Any revival of national identity, even in the form of cultural preservation movements, could be expected to be closely connected with religious renaissance. Russification, particularly regarding the issue of language, was increasingly seen as undermining this culture.[19]

Second, the churches had attained considerable international visibility in the preceding twenty years. The fact that the LWF held a high-level meeting in Tallinn in 1980 suggests interaction with the ecumenical movement. In addition, the Baltic Lutherans enjoyed special gatekeeper status with the Western churches on the Soviet German issue. As the FRG increased in prominence in Soviet foreign policy in the early 1980s, the Baltic churches could derive benefit from this.

Third, relatedly, the shell of sovereignty had been penetrated far more than in other areas of the USSR. The reception of media broadcasts from Finland and Sweden and the advent of ferry tourists from Finland to Estonia compromised the ability of the regime to totally control access to the West. Comparisons with Western economic performance would increasingly take a toll on legitimacy.

Fourth, a generational change was imminent in the churches. In both republics, bishops were aged and state officials were nervous about who would succeed these "progressive" figures. Key support leaders in the church administrations were likewise superannuated. Young pastors had begun to show discontent with their compromised elders.

Finally, the local and republic officials had become somewhat complacent. Their major challenges came from the small number of dissident Baptists and Pentecostals, many of whom had immigrated to the Baltics recently and hoped to emigrate to the West. Atheistic work was apparently successful in reducing religiosity, and scientific atheism was increasingly sophisticated in method and ensconced in academic circles in the region. As in the GDR, such academic specialists focused on the residual psychological roots of religion, assuming the immutability of the trend toward continued marginalization of religion. Official Agitprop efforts could afford to target cultural and educational institutions more narrowly and eliminate religious content from culture.[20] Heightened interaction with Western church leaders seemed to serve Soviet foreign policy interests, and the trade-offs in terms of possible domestic enlivening of religion seemed minimal and manageable.

Harbingers of Change

Despite the grim picture for Lutheran churches by the end of the Brezhnev period, there were some less visible indications of potential change. One such indication was the subtle shift in religious adherence. In 1979, Estonian state officials noted a modest rise in Lutheran rites, such as baptisms, although the

ROC continued to outpace the Lutherans. Relatedly, participation in secular rites began to drop sharply. Between 1981 and 1983, participation in summer days of youth declined by almost 50 percent.²¹ By 1984, the state officials simply dropped reference to secular rite statistics in their reports. After receiving kudos from CRA as recently as 1980 for their success in inculcating these rites in the population, Estonia and Latvia found it expedient to leave such statistics completely unmentioned in their 1984 reports.²² Although it would be an exaggeration to label this a religious renaissance, it is clear that the precipitous decline in church adherence had halted by the early 1980s.

Another indication of potential social change was the growing interest in cultural religion and architectural preservation, until now ignored by the Soviets. As noted, the 500th anniversary of Luther's birth in 1983 was celebrated in a more high-profile manner than the 1967 anniversary of the Reformation, including high-level ecumenical visitors, publications on Luther, and well-attended events in churches across the two republics.²³ By the mid-1980s, in response to decisions by CRA, the republic commissioners began to highlight the sorry state of many church edifices, along with vandalism and theft from churches.²⁴ They criticized the indifference of local officials, failure to provide guards, and lack of alarm systems. The income of pensioners who worked as guards at churches was taxed, but that of guards at state museums was not. In 1985, the Latvian commissioner urged that the tax code be changed to provide greater incentive for guards at churches. The Latvian government acted on these recommendations in 1986, issuing a decree regarding the thefts in eastern Latvia, with recommendations for action.²⁵ State officials now approached the churches' dilemma sympathetically—churches also represented the "people's accomplishment"—in contrast to their earlier criticism of deterioration and theft to justify nationalizing church property. This shift reflected growing concerns among the intellectual and cultural establishment that an important part of Baltic national tradition was endangered. While hardly a religious resurgence, this undercurrent of nationalism nonetheless represented support for church institutional interests. State officials worried about cultural elites "playing with religion and mysticism," but some Baltic Communists undoubtedly shared this curiosity.²⁶ With considerable engagement from parish priests, a Society for Protection of National Heritage in Estonia was founded in 1987, an indication of growing civic nationalism.²⁷

The most important indicator of the potential for change was the advent of generational change in the clergy. Some younger pastors began to experiment with innovative methods of ministry, running summer camps for youth and engaging choirs and music groups in services. In the late 1970s, Villu Jürjo (Viru) held camps that became very popular with youth from eastern Estonia.²⁸ They tried to form a conference of young pastors that was critical of the Consistory and state policy on religion. Jürjo teamed up with Harri Hammer (Tarvastu), an older critic among the pastorate, to criticize the new Soviet law on religion as inconsistent with the Helsinki declaration and the UN Declaration of Human Rights.[29] In Latvia, in the early 1980s, a movement of young pastors under the leadership of Modris Plāte took a different approach, emphasizing a conservative, "Catholic" dimension (for example, reading scriptures in Latin and Greek) but also employing contemporary aspects, like rock music. The regime had long favored traditional services, with a liturgical emphasis and uninspiring, patriotic sermons; modernization of religion was not in its game plan. Whether innovative or conservative, both tendencies threatened to upset the regime's desired trend toward the dying out of religion and its anachronistic manifestation, the church.

State officials could not remain indifferent to these nominally internal church issues. In conjunction with the respective bishops, they engineered the transfer of such activist pastors to other regions in order to curtail their influence. In the case of Jürjo, the state canceled his registration as a pastor from 1981 to 1983. After being moved to Palamuse in 1982, Illar Hallaste was moved again from Palamuse to Torma in 1983.[30] Plāte was moved from Riga to remote Kuldīga.

Perhaps politically more dangerous than the new methods of ministry of these young Turks were manifestations of nationalist sentiment among older clergy, particularly in Estonia. Most prominent to the human rights community in the West was Harri Mõtsnik, who criticized the repression of religious freedom and Estonian identity. Stabilizing the ethnically Finnish Ingrian Lutheran parish outside Leningrad was the highest priority of the Finnish Church in the context of developing ties to Soviet churches in the 1960s. As a result, the regime permitted the Estonian Church to delegate a pastor to minister to this group in 1975. Mõtsnik himself had been designated for this position due to his fluency in Finnish. But Mõtsnik's high level of activism caused problems with the parish and the Estonian Consistory; Bishop Hark ordered him to return to Estonia in 1982. Ironically, when consulted by Estonian officials, the commissioner for religious affairs in the Leningrad Oblast lent his support to Mõtsnik, describing him as loyal and arguing that disgruntled parishioners were behind the pressure on Hark to recall Mõtsnik.[31] Despite this local political support, Mõtsnik was transferred to a rural church in Estonia where he continued to demand religious freedom and criticize Soviet policies of Russification and militarization. After his sermons were published in the West, he was fined and lost his registration as a pastor. Eventually he was arrested in 1984, released only after "confessing" a mental breakdown and resigning from the pastorate. Mõtsnik complained to the Finnish Church regarding Hark's treatment, but the Finnish Church refused to intervene on his behalf.[32]

Another prominent advocate of Estonian nationalism was Vello Salum, pastor in the southwestern Estonian parish of Ambla, long a repository of Estonian national sentiment. Salum's sermons regularly criticized Soviet policies for eroding the national consciousness of Estonians. As the number of activist parishes increased by the mid-1980s, transferring pastors as a strategy to marginalize them became more routine. It is striking that, with the exception of Plāte, in Latvia the evidence of innovative or nationalistic clergy is thinner than in the case of Estonia.

One should not exaggerate the phenomenon. In both Latvia and Estonia, the loyal bishops, Matulis and Hark, acted to discipline these few dissenters and earned the regime's regard as a result. Until 1985, they remained isolated. Secular dissident groups did develop, focused primarily on human rights, environmental decay, nuclear disarmament and peace, and nationalist youth; unlike in the GDR, however, the narrow religious dissent did not initially join forces with them.[33] But the older nationalist clergy and the younger activist clergy both represented significant disaffection with the existing modus vivendi between the church leadership and the regime and the potential for more radical action in a changing context of perestroika.

Ironically subtle forms of nationalism crept into policies of the republic-level commissioners themselves. They objected to migration into their respective republics from other areas of the USSR, arguing that this increased the numbers of unregistered parishes. Most of these were Russian, often of Baptist or Pentecostal persuasion, and state officials had long worried that they would interfere with the planned decline of religion in their republic. Now this argument was made more openly with Moscow.[34]

Adding to the potential for change was the growth of international contacts by the churches in the early 1980s. To be sure, the international ties of the Baltic churches had already expanded greatly in the 1970s, but the West European churches' interest in issues of peace and arms control produced an even more dramatic increase in visitors. Estonian officials sought to check the growth of religious tourists in 1982, but were resigned to their increase as the price to pay for the Soviet peace offensive. The Luther anniversary in 1983 permitted extensive bilateral exchanges, although Moscow continued to forbid invitations to the émigré churches.[35] Direct ties between German churches and the Baltic churches, no longer requiring the LWF as a vehicle, began in 1982. Despite Vaivods's objections and Communist propaganda against it, the 800th anniversary of the Christianization of Latvia in 1986 occasioned visits by a high-level German Catholic delegation and major pilgrimages to Aglona.[36] By 1985, the number of visitors skyrocketed, especially among Baptists and Methodists.[37] The state attributed this to the significance and success of glasnost.

Early Liberalization under Gorbachev

Given his priority on economic and political reform, the assumption of power by Gorbachev in February 1985 initially had little direct effect on Soviet religious policy. Indeed, the primary effect of Gorbachev in the Baltics was to open space for discussion and criticism of environmental dangers and historical grievances, such as annexation under the Molotov-Ribbentrop agreement and commemoration of those deported under Stalin.[38] But the atmospheric change due to glasnost led to liberalization in practice, as believers felt less constrained in their practice of religion and some local and republic authorities ceased enforcing legal restrictions. The replacement of Kuroedov by Konstantin Kharchev in January 1985 also signaled a potential change in policy. Kharchev's public support for and early deliberations regarding drafts of a new, more liberal law on religion brought perestroika into religious policy.[39] Finally, the planning for the 1000th anniversary of the baptism of Russia, and Gorbachev's embrace of the celebration, occasioned an opening to the ROC in 1988.

This pattern was replicated in the Baltics as well. The modest increase in religious adherence evident in the early 1980s continued in 1986 and 1987, even before the contours of political liberalization were clear. Citing statistics for 1975–1985, Latvian Commissioner Kokars-Trops sought to highlight the long-term trend downward, but could not hide the slight short-term increases.[40] Estonian Commissioner Piip attributed this uptick to "tradition and habit," but indicted the Communist Party's poor youth work and indifference to religion and indirectly criticized Gorbachev's anti-alcohol campaign ("religion is more dangerous than vodka").[41]

Another early indication of liberalization was the decline in the antireligious work of the party. Already growing complacent toward religion under Brezhnev, the local commissions set up to promote Soviet rites and check the legality of church activity started to break down.[42] Despite periodic platitudes by republic officials to "take measures to strengthen control of observance of legality in religious rites," these watchdog groups were officially disbanded by republic authorities by 1988. By 1987 or 1988 the agitation efforts by the party's specialists in scientific atheism had also begun to erode. The Estonian consultations with the church leaders tailed off in 1987, as did sociopolitical lectures at the Theological Institute.[43]

Given these negative trends on the atheistic front, it is logical that republic officials placed more emphasis on appeasing church institutional interests, in order to assure the churches' co-optation politically in this period of instability. An early olive branch toward the churches concerned church construction and repairs, long rejected by the state. Already in July 1985, CRA issued a new order giving commissioners greater latitude in approving construction projects.[44] After

1988, Estonian officials highlighted their pragmatic help with construction and repairs, facilitating allocation of funds and materials for such projects, even from abroad.[45] Such assistance dovetailed well with the regime's new priority on cultural preservation.

State officials also began to approve requests for registering new parishes, although this initially brought little benefit to the Lutherans, and there were complications for sects. The chronic question of registering underground Pentecostals produced division among state officials: the commissioners, following the policy line of CRA, advocated registration of these groups in order to reduce their underground activities, whereas the KGB opposed their registration until virtually the end of the USSR.[46] With increased international contacts, the Soviet regime encountered "new religious movements," such as Hare Krishnas, as well. Latvian authorities refused registration to this group in 1986, but by 1988 CRA overturned the decision.[47]

The state also became more accommodating on other church institutional interests. Financial interests of the churches were accorded more favorable treatment. The regime declared church expenses for international activities deductible from taxable income, giving a tax benefit to the churches. Taxes were eliminated on churches if they were categorized as architectural monuments.[48] Eventually taxes on individual clergy and insurance charges on church buildings were lowered.[49] Likewise, church publications were facilitated more liberally than in the past. State officials moved to approve the import of Bibles to meet the large shortfall in supply, especially by reaching agreements with the International Bible Society. A major breakthrough with distinctly national overtones occurred: a long-requested new translation of the New Testament into Estonian was approved, entailing collaboration with the Finnish Church regarding the academic and logistical aspects.[50] Not surprisingly, given how controversial they have proved since the end of communism in many settings, property issues were more difficult, as revealed in the rejection of the request by the Estonian Lutherans in 1987 for return of its Consistory building.[51]

The state had controlled the preparation of new clergy, including the number and selection of theological students, as well as any foreign study by them, another institutional interest of the churches. The churches had long sought to educate more students and train professors abroad. Now they were permitted to increase the contingent of students at their theological institutes, though these students were still vetted to exclude "undesirable persons." Remarkable by contrast with earlier periods was the 1986 declaration of the Latvian commissioner: "the right of free conduct of rites of cults cannot be realized without the right of preparation of certain persons—cult servants who perform these rites."[52] Lutheran enrollment rose dramatically, but the big winners were the Latvian Catholics, who were permitted to increase their contingent from twenty to sixty-five in 1986, and undertake long-forbidden contact with Lithuanian seminaries. The authorities also looked quite favorably on requests for foreign study by theology students seeking advanced degrees.[53] Earlier such opportunities had been severely circumscribed by the regime and often entailed a commitment to the KGB or CRA. The possibility for Baltic theology institutions, staffed with aged, overworked faculty, to avoid a personnel crisis and raise academic standards was enhanced.

During this early Gorbachev period, the motive for these measures by the Baltic officials was damage limitation. As Estonian Commissioner Piip put it, the goal was to deter the churches from aligning with "Western propaganda organizations which seek to link the situation of believers with nationalistic remnants and the desire to emigrate."[54] But regime officials viewed this linkage as less likely among Lutherans than among the "sects," such as Pentecostals and Baptists, who challenged the legitimacy of the Soviet system, refused registration, and could call upon foreign support and pressure.

At the same time, state officials were loath to raise the white flag with the churches and religion. They argued that cooperation with the churches on these institutional interests was expedient in terms of fostering "positive results in realizing the process of perestroika in the sphere of church-state relations in ESSR," but without producing renewed religious activism and undermining the ultimate goal of eliminating the roots of religion.[55] Like Gorbachev, they invoked the Leninist principle of freedom of conscience, but they worried that their policy focus was being overshadowed by his other priorities.

Internal Upheaval in the Church and the State

Initially the commissioners' reports wrapped their successes in the mantle of Gorbachev's policy of glasnost. As his initiatives became more radical and as the democratic popular movements arose in response, Moscow became more interested in the churches' political positions: how were they responding to Gorbachev's initiative to create the Congress of People's Deputies? What was their stance toward the new political formations?

For decades the Lutheran church leadership had been intimidated from expressing political criticism and had offered support for Soviet socialism. It was not surprising that it offered perfunctory rhetorical support for perestroika, but sought to avoid alienating conservatives and risking the benefits of the newfound cooperation. However, social organizations caught in the midst of broader societal liberalization often cannot insulate themselves from internal change.

In this respect, the years 1985 and 1986 were transitional ones for the churches' internal governance. Both the Estonian and Latvian churches had been headed by aging, politically loyal bishops. Given the generational change in the clergy, state officials expressed concern that "the politics of selection and placement is on fragile ground."⁵⁶ The stakes were even higher in Estonia, where August Leepin, the General Secretary of the Church and a secret police collaborator, was 78 years old. Tiit Pädam, considered his likely successor, was incarcerated for three months on charges of currency violations, despite international church intercession on his behalf.

The succession to the very-ill Archbishop Hark was likewise fraught. Efforts to unite behind a successor failed in 1985, and Hark agreed to serve longer. Fate forced a decision one year later, however, when Hark died; his successor was the state-approved candidate, Kuno Pajula. Though he had been mobilized by the Germans in WWII, Pajula had spent more than two years in a filtration camp of the Ministry of Internal Affairs and was recorded as an informant in KGB records. He had enjoyed state support for study in West Germany in the 1970s and was considered reliable in ecumenical settings and domestic decisions.⁵⁷ But his selection was not uncontroversial. In the context of perestroika, the young Turk pastors were unhappy with Pajula's passivity. At the synodal election, they proposed an alternative candidate, Jaan Kiivit Jr., son of the late Bishop Jaan Kiivit, but he withdrew from consideration.

In Latvia, the divisions were even more apparent than in Estonia. In August 1985, Bishop Matulis died, and the synod that selected his successor was divided. The regime promoted the candidacy of Eriks Mesters, a member of the church leadership who had fought in WWII in the Red Army and been awarded a medal by the state for that service; he had also been chosen to provide pastoral service at the 1980 Moscow Olympics. With a comparatively weak background in theology and languages, Mesters was known for his opposition to the Plāte faction and supported Matulis's transfer of Plāte to provincial Kuldīga, away from the capital Riga. But the disaffected pastors promoted an alternative candidate at the synod, Kārlis Gailītis, who while generationally not one of the young Turks, was sympathetic to their cause.⁵⁸ The split result—28 votes for Mesters, 15 for Gailītis—would hardly have been noteworthy in the West. But for Soviet Latvia, which had not had an open selection of a bishop since WWII, it was revolutionary. The regime secured its preferred candidate, but his authority was badly damaged.

The internal church opposition grew in both Estonia and Latvia after these bishop successions, but the outcomes would be different. In the case of Estonia, Kiivit and two other leaders demonstrated their opposition to Pajula by withdrawing from Consistory leadership in 1989.⁵⁹ But Pajula reached out to the reformist faction with personnel decisions: he named Toomas Paul, popular pastor and theology professor, as dean in Tallinn and a member of the three-member Consistory; after assuming the title of archbishop, he installed a younger reformist, Einar Soone, as bishop. As a result, his legitimacy as bishop was never openly challenged, although in 1990 the synod voted to replace the Soviet-era church constitution with that from 1919 and to elect a young, critical

Consistory. One-time critic Jaan Kiivit eventually succeeded Pajula, symbolizing an incremental perestroika in the Estonian case.

In Latvia, however, the internal church opposition never reconciled itself to the legitimacy of Mesters. Although informally active since 1984 and providing the base for Gailītis's unsuccessful candidacy for bishop in 1985, the opposition coalesced more openly in the context of perestroika in 1987, creating a movement called Rebirth and Renewal under the leadership of Plāte and other dissident young pastors, such as Juris Rubenis and future archbishop Jānis Vanags, as well as respected senior theology instructors, such as Roberts Akmentins, Jānis Feldmanis, and Aivars Beimanis. The group distributed its "Basic Principles of the Christian Movement 'Rebirth and Renewal,'" claiming to be only a "religious-ethical movement" and demanding changes in Soviet law to permit churches to prevent state interference in parish councils, provide religious instruction to children, and allow access to radio and TV, publication, and mission work.[60] In July 1987, the Latvian church leadership condemned the movement as schismatic and Bishop Mesters conveyed this decision in a circular sent to all clergy. Under regime pressure, Mesters had ordered Plāte removed from Kuldīga in March 1987, but he refused to move, supported by a petition signed by 350 parish supporters, numerous clergy, and some senior theology professors. The split escalated when Plāte was stripped of his office as pastor, dean, and theological instructor in August 1987, provoking petitions to CRA, threats of a strike by pastors supporting Plāte, and protests by a Latvian human rights group, Helsinki 86. The severe shortage of clergy constrained Mesters from disciplining the Rebirth and Renewal group. Mesters became increasingly dependent on the regime for his power, leaving him vulnerable to the polarization both in Latvian society and the Moscow leadership. After attacking Rebirth and Renewal as "schismatic, adventurist, and socially damaging" and threatening its leaders with lengthy deregistration in November 1987, Commissioner Kokars-Trops abruptly reversed course in February 1988, and Plāte was restored to his position as pastor.[61] As the Latvian movement for liberalization grew in 1988, Mesters' position became less tenable. Eventually, in April 1989, the opposition used the opportunity of the Latvian Synod to restore the 1928 church constitution and oust Mesters as bishop, replacing him with his erstwhile opponent, Gailītis. The state undertook no action to prevent this reversal of the earlier election.[62]

The timing of the twin successions, 1986–1987 in Estonia and 1985 in Latvia, may have produced the different outcomes. One might have actually expected less opposition in the Latvian case than in the Estonian case, because perestroika was relatively untested in 1985; by 1987, Estonians might have been emboldened by Gorbachev's widening reforms. But in the Latvian case, the bishop issue was the lightning rod for intense internal church conflict, whereas, in Estonia, rather than focus their opposition on Pajula and internal church reforms, dissident pastors took advantage of the broader political opportunity structure to focus on external sociopolitical organization.

Liberalization also had perverse effects on inter-confessional relations in the republics. Entirely new organizations were created, analogous to councils of churches in many Western countries, reflecting an ecumenical spirit and offering the prospect of a unified voice in pressing the regime for change.[63] But national and ethnic divisions began to arise, even within denominations. Lutheran parishes that had previously permitted Baptist or Pentecostal groups to use their churches now began to cancel such agreements.[64] Baptist and Pentecostal groups began to split into separate groups along ethno-linguistic lines (Latvian vs. non-Latvian). Latvian Baptists remained rather passive during this political mobilization, but many Russian Baptists feared the consequences of Latvian national revival.[65]

Though largely a homogeneous national church, the Lutheran Church was not immune from the new ethnic divisions. In the context of perestroika, the Soviet German Lutherans, till now administered by Harald Kalnins, sought to establish their own identity and church institutions. Kalnins planned to train pastors at the Lutheran seminary in Riga, which Catholics from other republics had been able to do at their Riga seminary since 1981, and to obtain a separate hard-currency account for the purpose of soliciting Western funds and making purchases. Already named a superintendent in 1983, Kalnins had long sought elevation to bishop, to officially establish the German Lutherans as a religious center with perquisites from the Moscow CRA, rather than an appendix of the Latvian Church. CRA approved this in 1988, along with the simultaneous formation of the German Evangelical Lutheran Church in the USSR; Germans were permitted to take theological training in Riga under Kalnins's tutelage. Yet the new opening under Gailītis did not reduce tensions with Kalnins, and the growing Latvian national movement heightened it: the Latvians resented Kalnins's support for Mesters during the Plāte affair and objected to the use of the Russian language in Kalnins's theological instruction.[66]

But Kalnins was to face his own schisms within the new German church, as the centrifugal forces at work in the last phase of the USSR produced challengers to his authority. Charging that Kalnins was compromised by his past and dependence on the liberal LWF and Germany, a young clergyman of Lithuanian background, Jonas Baronas, acted in 1991 to create a separate, conservative, multiethnic United Evangelical Lutheran Church in Russia. But he too relied on external support in this dispute, in this case from reformist and democratic groups in St. Petersburg and Moscow. Ousted Bishop Mesters, his presence in Latvia doubtless embarrassing to the new leadership, was delegated by Gailītis in February 1991 to minister to parishes in Leningrad. He proceeded to consecrate Baronas in March 1991 as head of the new church, exacting revenge on

Gailītis. Gailītis then rejected Mesters' function and legitimacy, contending that the Latvian Church would not be reintegrated into Baronas's project of a multi-ethnic Lutheran Church.[67] In the meantime, the German EKD was permitted its first direct delegation to the Soviet German congregations in 1989 and began to assume a higher profile in managing the fraught transition in the new German Evangelical Church in the USSR, from Riga and the leadership of Kalnins to St. Petersburg and the leadership of Georg Kretschmar, previously theology professor in Munich.[68]

Just as custom and internal divisions led the church leadership to be risk-averse and ambivalent about Gorbachev's liberalization, so, too, the republic commissioners were cross-pressured by the perestroika process. They were obviously expected to support perestroika in religious policy and felt constrained to express self-criticism for their role in the Brezhnev period of stagnation, but they were cautious about abandoning long-standing orthodoxy on scientific atheism and policy toward the churches. The Latvian commissioner, Kokars-Trops, known earlier as a hard-liner, acknowledged his mistakes, but he sought to deflect some of the responsibility by blaming other republics and immigrants into Latvia: "Interfering with our work is also that in our past emphasis on the development of the world-idea and relations to the future, we too often forgot about the concrete person, his personal interests, concerns and needs. We hurried as fast as possible to realize our intentions. In this we did not always consider the economic-technical and social-cultural possibilities, the real situations and processes taking place in society. That which we desired turned out to be beyond reality, and to our dismay, we became used to this."[69] Glowing reports to Moscow emphasized "correct and trusting relations" with the churches and the "patriotic mood, loyal and legally-conforming" in the religious population; Moscow, however, was interested in the extent of nationalist extremism in the churches.[70] The commissioners increasingly attributed the untenable situation with churches to the absence of clear legal guidelines. In January 1989, Kokars-Trops regretted to Moscow that "it is still not clear to us how to apply perestroika to our work locally, which criteria to use in this, so that the control of the observance of socialist legality is made more effective, to strengthen our influence on clergy and believers."[71]

Accelerating Liberalization

The years 1988–1990 revealed an accelerating process of change, parallel to that in the broader society. Caught up with societal changes, church leaderships pressed increasing demands on the state to revise the entire Stalinist/Khrushchev order in religious policy. Even leaders who had been co-opted and loyal to Soviet power, such as Latvian Catholic Cardinal Vaivods and Estonian Lutheran Bishop Pajula, now became more assertive in the context of the erosion of Moscow's control and rising social protest. Likewise, political authorities began to distance themselves from Moscow, reflected in policy and personnel changes.

The churches demanded the return of highly symbolic properties nationalized by the state. For example, Catholics requested the Aglona monastery, a major pilgrimage site; Lutherans and Orthodox demanded their symbol-rich cathedrals in Riga. By 1990, Bishop Gailītis held the first service in the Riga Cathedral since the seizure in 1959.[72] As noted earlier, many closed churches were in fact not being used or were being used for a purpose different than had been designated. This fact legitimized the claims of the church leaders for restitution.[73] Registration of new parishes surged, redounding now to benefit particularly Lutheran parishes, which had been eclipsed by the Orthodox and Baptists. In Latvia, ten formal requests were initiated in 1988 to reopen Lutheran churches closed since the 1960s.[74] Soviet policy in this regard shifted union-wide in August 1988 as CRA gave the green light to approve most requests for registration, overriding local rejections if necessary.[75] As a result, thirty-two new parishes were in fact registered in Latvia in 1989, including twenty-two Lutheran ones.[76]

Striking was the dramatic increase in religious rites during this period of late perestroika among all denominations, particularly Lutherans. Earlier they had shown modest increases, far outpaced by the ROC and Catholics. Now, however, ROC church adherence stagnated and Lutheran baptisms and confirmations skyrocketed, as pent-up demand for rites was accommodated.[77] In one year, from 1988 to 1989, Lutheran baptisms increased from 4,500 to 12,400. Despite this surge, regular attendance at services initially remained low among Lutherans, at roughly 10 percent of members; by 1989 even this measure of church adherence began to show dramatic increases.[78] Nonetheless, the decades of Lutheran losses left the Catholics as the leading confession in Latvia by 1990.[79]

By early 1988, the Catholic Church in Latvia was also raising its voice for greater privileges. Many clergy lobbied for the legalization of religious instruction for youth, long a source of tension with the state. Vaivods also demanded a new Catholic journal, as well as greater access to the state media. He conveyed Pope John Paul II's request to open theological seminaries in Ukraine and Belarus as part of the creation of independent religious centers in those republics.[80]

In this accelerating context, church leaders began to press for legal changes, including a new law on religion, in order to guarantee the churches more rights, such as conduct of charity, religious instruction of youth, and legal personality.[81] However, in the absence of such a law on religion at the union level—the subject of contentious and lengthy deliberations among interests in Moscow from 1988 to 1990—and with the indecision in Moscow, the Baltic republics found it expedient to instead concede ground regarding church institutional interests over which they had more room for maneuver. For example, in 1989, Latvia annulled the 1958 conviction of Cardinal Vaivods.[82] Some concessions represented a continuation of recent trends, such as the growing admissions to theology study and the return of previously nationalized buildings to accommodate the increased number of students.[83] Estonia eliminated the 50 percent tax rate on clergy and permitted the number of theology students to increase by 30 percent from 1988 to 1989.[84] But other concessions conferred new privileges on the churches.[85] Religious instruction was permitted in Latvian schools in 1988; the theological faculty, closed in 1944, was restored to the University of Latvia in April 1989. New church publications were approved, with publication runs that were unprecedented. After years of struggling to obtain 15,000 copies of its annual calendar, the Latvian Lutheran Church was awarded the right to publish a newspaper with a print run of 50,000. Similarly, 50,000 copies of a new Latvian Catholic monthly were approved.[86] Christmas was celebrated officially in 1988, and media coverage of church services, especially major holidays, was granted to the major confessions, even to the small, long-disfavored group of Seventh-Day Adventists. After earlier trying to break ties between secular cultural figures and the churches, Estonian authorities now promoted concerts by secular musicians in churches.[87] For their part, the commissioners tended to blame the local media and their "unfounded and exaggerated interest in religious activity" for this trend and worried about the ensuing pressure for recognition of religious holidays.[88] But the fact of the matter was that there was little they could do to halt this rediscovery of the link between cultural Lutheranism and the nation. The social presence of the churches was enhanced by their recruitment into quasi-official bodies formed to promote the process of perestroika. Bishop Pajula became a member of the Estonian Society for Foreign Friendships, and Erik Hiisjarv joined the leadership of the Estonian Culture Fund.

In the context of this legal limbo and accelerating liberalization, dissident groups in the churches also became bolder. After important signals in 1988 (the CPSU Party Conference, Gorbachev's proposal for parliamentary elections for a new Congress of People's Deputies, and the purge of the Estonian Communist leadership) some Estonian clergy became engaged openly in politics.[89] Most supported the Estonian Popular Front, seeing greater freedom of action for the churches in this movement of reform Communists supportive of perestroika. But several others, such as Vello Salum, cofounded the more radical Estonian National Independence Movement, a half-legal group that advocated independence from the USSR. In December 1988, ten pastors, under the leadership of long-time dissident Illar Hallaste, joined fifty-five others to found the Christian Democratic Union, which supported Christian values against Communism and developed ties with the Christian Democratic International to press for support for Baltic independence.[90] Justifying this direct role in politics, Hallaste maintained that "today it is very important that the church has its representatives in parliament and communal levels for this transition period."[91] Jaan Kiivit Jr.

associated with the Estonian Committee, which also sought to restore Estonian independence and eventually aligned more with the Popular Front under Edgar Savisaar. Sermons became more political, tackling subjects like economic and environmental problems that had long been taboo; many openly described the Lutheran Church as the national church. Disaffected younger pastors formed a Brotherhood of Pastors in 1988 to "protect against secular and clerical power," challenging the church leadership's relatively cautious stance. Having experienced decades of repression, the church leadership feared that the growing politicization by clergy might cause fragmentation in a church already weakened in terms of the number of pastors; some argued that politics was "not an issue for the church," and that "as a body we cannot afford to participate in the Popular Front, the Greens, or in the struggle of the Party for National Independence of Estonia."[92] But the leadership could no longer prevent it. For his part, the Estonian commissioner acknowledged that the heightened political activism of religious figures "paralleled the complex political struggle in the republic."[93]

In Latvia, the political response in the churches was equally bold, if less directly partisan. In November 1988, the Rebirth and Renewal movement petitioned the Chair of the Supreme Soviet, Andrei Gromyko, and Gorbachev, demanding legal changes and the right to join political organizations.[94] Some pastors joined Juris Rubenis in the Popular Front and were largely responsible for its official 1988 position in favor of greater religious and church freedoms and claiming use of the nationalized Riga Cathedral for its founding meeting.[95] For his part, newly elected Bishop Gailītis was active in the more nationalistic Latvian National Independence Movement. At its breakthrough 1989 synod, the Latvian Church also broached taboos, calling for merging with exile Latvians in a United Latvian Lutheran Church and for revocation of the Molotov-Ribbentrop secret protocols and independence for Latvia.[96] But, unlike Estonia, few pastors became involved in forming the Christian Democratic Party, and the Church distanced itself.[97] Nor did the Lutheran Church put forth its own candidates for the 1988 elections for the Congress of People's Deputies.[98] The Lutheran and Catholic leaderships focused their energies into forming nonpolitical organizations, such as the Bible Society, Mission Society, and Charity Society. Baptist clergy tended to avoid the new social movements and were cautious about political independence, though they did separate from the AUCECB in Moscow in December 1989.[99]

The erosion of the state's position did produce a backlash among some in the apparat. In early 1988, alarmed at the collapse of secular rites and rise of religious ones, the Council of Ministers in Latvia ordered republic officials to "take measures to strengthen Soviet traditions, holidays and rites, to strengthen control of the observance of legality in religious rites." But the Cultural Ministry dodged the criticism, replying that the commissions to promote the Soviet rites had been abolished in 1985, that local governments had assumed the role from the commissions and were pursuing divergent policies, and that greater attention to the issue at all levels was needed.[100] Return of high-profile churches sometimes met with opposition from the bureaucracy. The return of the Russian Orthodox cathedral in Riga was vetoed by the commissioner and the Council of Ministers in 1988, although by 1989 the decision had been reversed.[101]

The bureaucratic struggle between the KGB and CRA widened on the subject of registration of sects. The more liberal line of CRA after 1988 was opposed by the KGB in Estonia. The commissioner felt compelled to articulate a goal of "taking operative steps to end illegal actions of fanatics and sectarian extremists," even as he advocated registration of all Pentecostals by local governments.[102]

Meanwhile, the legal limbo due to the delay in implementing a new unionwide law on religion posed real problems for the state officials. The Estonian commissioner complained that there was no legal enforcement any more: the General Prosecutor refused to bring charges against illegal sects, such as the Word of Life, or extreme nationalists, such as Vello Salum.[103] Requests for deferments from the military service for theology students also challenged democratic centralism: Latvian authorities favored granting them, but temporized, awaiting authorization by the Soviet government and Defense Ministry.[104]

In October 1989, the Latvian commissioner sent a laundry list of requests for decisions that had gone unanswered by the CRA in Moscow (approval of new church publications, import of Bibles, etc.), contending that internal church matters should no longer require approval in Moscow.[105]

While the Baltic republics tended to defer to the center on the issue of a new religion law, they moved ahead in terms of bureaucratic personnel and restructuring. An early signal of independence from Moscow was the 1987 replacement of the deputy commissioner in Latvia, Sacharov. Normally this position was held by a Russian whose portfolio was the ROC, but Sacharov was replaced with an ethnic Latvian.[106] In April 1989, the long-time commissioner, Jānis Kokars-Trops, "retired" by decision of the Latvian Council of Ministers. CRA replaced him with his deputy, Alfreds Kublinskis. After declaring Latvian sovereignty in July 1989, the new Popular Front government passed a resolution in December 1989 creating a new Department of Religious Affairs, independent of Moscow and CRA. The official justification is illuminating: "This change allows a timely and operative decision-making that affects religious organizations in the republic, and avoids the goal of unnecessary and unproductive consensus with CRA of the USSR. The department rejected the strict control of activities of religious organizations; more attention is now being given to creating constructive mutual relations with the churches, demonstrating help in deciding organizational-economic questions. These changes were dictated by the real situation in the Republic and changes in its status, but also the processes of democratization of social life."[107]

The last commissioner, Kublinskis, remained nominally in charge of the new department, but official reporting to the CRA ceased as of January 1990. Consultation with CRA and Soviet authorities regarding the union-wide law ceased as well, and Latvia set up a commission including church leaders to promulgate a new republic law on religion.[108] Kublinskis matter-of-factly informed CRA of Latvia's declaration of sovereignty and the bureaucratic reorganization.

Similar political and bureaucratic maneuvering occurred in Estonia, with some nuances. The commissioner, Rein Ristlaan, remained in office until he was replaced in mid-1990 after the new Popular Front government took power. He continued to report to CRA until that point, later than in Latvia. But the Estonian context—the growing popularity of the Popular Front and the victory of reformers in the Estonian Communist Party after hard-liner First Secretary Karl Vaino was replaced by the more liberal Vaino Valjäs in 1988—and the growing paralysis of CRA in Moscow resulted in an eventual shift in policy and bureaucratic organization. By July 1989, the Estonian government had formed its own working group to review legal changes, giving up on the union-wide deliberations. By December 1989, Ristlaan and the working group came to the Estonian government with a proposal for an independent Department of Religious Affairs, similar to that in Latvia.[109]

In his final report for 1990, Ristlaan's shift to accommodate the new reality in church-state relations was clear. He described the resurgence of church adherence as a "normal situation" and the introduction of Sunday schools (i.e., the long-taboo religious instruction of youth) as "healthy for society." In his analysis, most clergy and believers supported economic and political autonomy for Estonia from Moscow, a stance he no longer disputed. Ristlaan credited perestroika that "religion now assumes the role corresponding to its position in the real life of society" and "believers now enjoy full rights as citizens and may confidently express their convictions on all questions of interest to them."[110] Despite this supportiveness for the churches in the final period of perestroika, he was replaced when the Popular Front government took over in 1990.

Summary and Conclusion

By 1990 the Baltic governments were in the hands of the Popular Front movements, but were being challenged by the growing polarization between nationalist movements and groups of Russians opposed to sovereignty and independence. The early consensus in favor of greater liberalization—whether in terms of economic policy, individual freedoms, or religious policy—was to be increasingly overshadowed by the question of the political community, that is, would Estonia and Latvia remain part of the USSR or not. The Popular Front governments of former Communists were inclined to incrementalism on all these issues. The Lutheran churches now became part of the official symbolism: joining in the

Song Festivals, holding summit meetings with the new leadership, celebrating Christian holidays as official holidays, and officiating at mass rallies for independence. Non-Lutheran churches also enjoyed greater freedoms, but did not benefit from the national spotlight. The ROC was, in fact, now on the defensive, as non-Orthodox churches questioned the triumphalism of the commemoration of the baptism of Russia in 1988.

In the context of increased social tensions and polarization, the churches were swept along by the tide of public opinion favoring independence. During the assaults by Soviet Black Berets in January 1991 in Riga and Vilnius, the churches appealed for peaceful passive resistance, seeking to avoid more bloodshed. But the Lutheran churches also claimed a new legitimacy as "the only champion of national consciousness during the era of Russification."[111] Ultimately of course the question would be decided in August 1991.

In terms of the factors utilized throughout this study, how can one analyze the church-state relationship during this final phase of Gorbachev's perestroika process? First, the national churches were very weak, but not irrelevant actors in terms of nascent civil society. They did serve as a locus on certain valence issues, like architectural preservation and cultural life. But the church leadership did not criticize Soviet policies on human rights, peace, or the environment and provided a very weak forum for organization of the informal sector so characteristic of the late Gorbachev period. For the most part, as they grew assertive toward the regime, the churches sought instead to reclaim the institutional interests they had lost in the 1940s and only partially and provisionally regained in later periods: registration of new churches, renovation of churches, relaxation of financial strictures, freedom of publication, and increased theological education. Estonian pastor Peeter Kaldur captured the churches' dilemma—"when there is no democratic society, there can also be no democracy in the church"—but also highlighted the contrast with cases in Central Europe.[112]

Second, perestroika permitted the mobilization of disaffected elements in the churches, particularly the Lutheran churches with their synodal system of church governance and leadership successions in this period. These small groups of young Turks and aging nationalists began to develop during the Brezhnev period, but the advent of broader liberalization after 1985 encouraged them to successfully mount challenges to the passive Lutheran church leaderships.

Third, the national churches, particularly the Lutheran ones, did in fact embody the revival of national culture in these republics, even if not a deep-seated religious one.[113] Dramatic increases in church adherence, restoration of official status for major Christian holidays, and return of major symbolic churches buildings, along with strong affinity with cultural traditions such as the song festivals and cemetery days, underscore the contribution of cultural Christianity to the national renaissance. The rapid collapse of participation in secular rites, as well as the atheistic apparatus, also suggests this process. The barely concealed tension with Russophone Baptists and Pentecostals, as well as with Soviet Germans, is further evidence. Religion is one marker of nationality. Despite their political caution, the Lutheran and Catholic Church leaderships could not avoid being viewed as national institutions.

Fourth, as in the 1949–1953 period, union-wide processes provided the context for these changes in religious policy, in this case perestroika and liberalization rather than repression. The opening to the ROC in 1988, CRA directives to liberalize registration of parishes, and promotion of increased international ties: all these were permissive causes for the commissioners at the republic level to be more forthcoming toward the churches. But the delay and deliberation regarding a new law on religious freedom in Moscow prompted the Baltic republics to pursue independent initiatives, legal and bureaucratic, parallel to those undertaken by the newly elected Popular Front governments. The republics took religious perestroika much farther than Moscow was ready for. The legal limbo at the union level fostered a national assertiveness by commissioners and republic officials, converging with the interests of the national churches more openly after forty years, but a convergence that previous chapters suggest was incipient long before perestroika.

Finally, the churches did not produce the revolutions in the Baltics, but rather were largely beneficiaries of broader political changes. The churches did not engage regarding the overriding dilemma driving politics during the denouement of the USSR: reform within a redefined Soviet federation versus independence based on illegitimate annexation.[114] As Ristlaan summarized, "the churches rode the wave." Leading Estonian theologian Toomas Paul put it differently: the popular trust in the churches did not derive from "a new stance of the church ... or a church strategy, but rather ... its previous position ... as the only organization not under the control of the party."[115] The churches certainly provided a moral guide and aided the national revival of these small, threatened nationalities. But despite the activism of some clergy and the formation of the CDU in Estonia, the churches did not provide the leadership cadre for the independence movements, unlike in the GDR. Nor did they provide an organizational and ideational framework for the opposition, as was the case in Poland. The churches played harmony rather than melody in the Singing Revolutions.

Notes

1. ERA.R-1989.2.64, l. 109.
2. Remmel, "Ambiguous Atheism," 241.
3. ERA.R-1989.2.65, l. 89–90.

4. LVA.1419.3.265, l. 71f. The Latvian commissioner did a major review of functioning churches in 1986 as part of the new approach under Kharchev.
5. ERA.R-1989.2.65, l. 89.
6. LVA.1419.3.276, l. 11.
7. Characteristika, Hark. ESSR Commissioner.
8. LVA.1419.3.276, l. 8, 13.
9. Commissioner Kokars-Trops's 1986 review of problems at the Riga Seminary, in LVA.1419.3.265, l. 94–97.
10. Trups-Trops, "Römisch-Katholische Kirche," Teil 3, 74–78, 98–99.
11. Benz, "Schwieriger Neubeginn," 128; LVA.1419.3.281, l. 96–97; LVA.1419.3.281, l. 70–71. At Aglona in 1967, Vaivods is quoted as saying that "the only ones who live better [in the West] are those with a thick wallet, but simple workers live worse."
12. LVA.1419.3.264, l. 6; LVA.1419.3.264, l. 23–25. Vaivods apparently only held five masses in 1985, one of which was to commemorate the end of WWII, and he ordered all churches to hold similar services; in the 1950s Bishop Strods had refused to participate in such propagandistic events. Heinrihs Strods ("Roman Catholic Church," 179–80) highlights his imprisonment in the 1950s and Vaivods' achievements as an historian of the Church.
13. "Interview with the New Latvian Cardinal," 207–9. Trups-Trops ("Römisch-Katholische Kirche," Teil 3, 81) indicates that Vaivods wished to celebrate the anniversary simultaneously with the 1,000th anniversary of Christianity in Russia in 1988.
14. LVA.1419.3.265, l. 2–3 and LVA.1419.3.265, l. 66, indicate that the Latvian Interior Ministry and Procurator office had found no violations of the criminal law by cult servants or believers that "would discredit Soviet Government and social construction by cult servants during occurrence of religious activities." In 1985, two cases of Catholic priests found using children in services were merely warned. Baptists meeting in apartments were given minimal fines. Previously these types of legal violations would have provoked harsh retaliation by the state. LVA.1419.3.276, l. 36.
15. ERA.R-1989.1.134, l. 17–18. CRA Chair Kuroedov hailed Estonia's success and cited it as a role model for other Soviet authorities and socialist states.
16. ERA.R-1989.1.188, l. 17, l. 77.
17. ERA.R-1989.1.212, l. 4–5. The rationale of Commissioner Piip ("due to the high level of education of church leaders … in order to give first-hand information from high-level state authorities and illuminate questions of domestic and foreign policy of our state at the necessary high level") suggests the qualitative opening to church elites, similar to the *Sachgespräche* with the Lutheran churches in the GDR. State participants included the ministries of Justice, Finance, Education, Construction, Chairs of friendship societies, the Peace Fund, and Kodumaa (Homeland).
18. ERA.R-1989.1.212, l. 9–10. Such lectures were to "inculcate a feeling of friendship of peoples and socialist internationalism and create an atmosphere of intolerance toward national organizations."
19. Gerhard Simon ("Nationalitätenprobleme," 759–68) presciently highlights the decreasing legitimacy of the USSR, particularly among Baltic elites, and the likelihood of a governability crisis before Gorbachev.
20. ERA.R-1989.1.199, l. 136. In the robust musical life in Estonia, the Estonian Commissioner targeted the composition and repertoire of music schools and choirs and ensembles, to "prohibit performance of compositions of religious content."

21. ERA.R-1989.2.66, l. 121.
22. ERA.R-1989.2.67, l. 17–46. The increased interest in religion was not limited to the Baltics, according to Gernot Seide, "Religiöse Renaissance," 910–20.
23. Rozitis, "Aus der Evangelisch-Lutherischen Kirche," 80–81; "Gesellschaftliche Entwicklung," 786. Luther oaks were planted across Latvia, a new Small Catechism was issued, and Luther's letters to Baltic contemporaries were publicized.
24. LVA.1419.3.264, l. 43–51. The CRA decision of 21 November 1985 prompted the oblast and republic commissioners to respond on this issue. To be sure, the problem of theft was apparently much greater among ROC and Old Believer churches, where icons and other valuables were at risk, as well as rural churches where services were infrequent. The Commissioner recommended recruiting younger members of the parish executive committee who might more carefully look after church valuables, but if necessary for the local officials to take a larger role and removal of objects to other, more active parishes. Viise ("Estonian Evangelical-Lutheran Church," 234) discusses the heritage societies' increased interest in national-church figures buried in cemeteries.
25. LVA.1419.3.265, l. 9–10; LVA.1419.3.276, l. 40–41.
26. ERAF.1.4.6048, l. 11, quoting A. Soidla, deputy head of Agitprop in the Estonian Communist leadership. Burchard Lieburg, "Aus dem Leben," 124–28.
27. Rohmets and Ringvee ("Religious Revival," 362–69) discuss the formation and development of the Estonian Heritage Society, along with other social movements during perestroika.
28. ERA.R-1989.2.60, l. 116–17. Commissioner Piip reported that this group was holding meetings with nationalist content in apartments, using clothing from "bourgeois Estonia" at its meetings, and distributing printed materials with religious propaganda content.
29. Ibid., l. 120.
30. ERA.R-1989.2.67, l. 22. Another young activist pastor, Andres Põder, was moved from the nationalistic parish of Suure-Jaani to Rapina.
31. ERA.R-1989.1.224, l. 151, l. 150. This suggests that this unorthodox arrangement between an oblast and a republic carried potential for bureaucratic differences and politics. Also, Mõtsnik insisted on being on the parish executive committee, contrary to the Soviet law since Khrushchev, but apparently not implemented in Estonia.
32. ERA.R-1989.2.68, l. 23. Radio Free Europe/Radio Liberty, "Situation Report," 13–14 (1985) and 7–8 (1985), report Mõtsnik's sermon content, his recantation, and his reduced sentence in 1985. Mõtsnik's criticism and fate engendered support in the North Elbian Church, German partner church of the Estonian Church. But the Finnish church official in charge of foreign relations, Jaakko Launikari, saw it as "personally difficult to demand solidarity of any church towards a person so double-folded as in the case of Mõtsnik." Finnish National Committee, LWF, 25 Oct. 1985.
33. Regarding the increased criticism, including by scientists, of environmental problems in Estonia, see Radio Free Europe/Radio Liberty, "Situation Report," 9–23 (1985) and 5–6 (1986). There is no reference to church dissenters in Taagepera, "Citizens' Peace Movement," 183–92; Misiunas and Taagepera, "Baltic States: Years of Dependence, 1980–1986," 83–85. Remmel ("(Anti-)Religious Aspects," 379) indicates some in the Estonian Lutheran Church today see it as having been an oppositional organization. He and other scholars discount this claim, citing for example that in 1986 only one registered clergyman received an

administrative penalty. But the cultural argument I make does not rest solely on such quantifiable measures of dissent.

34. ERA.R-1989.2.66, l. 123–24. Commissioner Piip argued that the growth of unregistered immigrant groups of believers was demoralizing the legally registered groups.

35. ERA.R-1989.1.264, l. 13–14. The Estonian commissioner supported this overture to the émigré church, but was vetoed by Moscow.

36. Sapiets, "Anniversaries," 200–3; Trups-Trops, "Römisch-Katholische Kirche," Teil 3, 81–84. No Latvian Catholic leaders were permitted to travel to the Vatican's colloquium on the anniversary; state officials pressured Vaivods not to attend the celebratory events in Riga and state protocol was kept very low level.

37. ERA.R-1989.2.69, l. 67–68; interview with Siegfried Markert, August 1990.

38. Levits, "Politische Aufbruch," 403–12. There is no mention of the churches or religion in the analysis. Vardys, "Role of the Churches," 287–300.

39. In his interview in *Ogonyek* in 1988, Kharchev called for greater legal rights for churches and believers. See Ellis, "New Soviet Thinking," 100–111. For a treatment from a Western specialist on religious liberty, see Bourdeaux, *Gospel's Triumph*, especially 132–58.

40. LVA.1419.3.276, l. 3-7

41. Piip wrote, "We campaigned against alcoholism, but forgot that religion is more dangerous than vodka." ERA.R-1989.2.69, l. 46–47.

42. LVA.1419.3.276, l. 37–39, indicating the commissions were deteriorating in 1985; LVA.1419.3.267, l. 20–21, confirms that they were abolished officially in 1985 and monitoring functions subsumed under local governments and the Ministry of Culture, replacing the commissions but in effect deemphasizing this task. Viise, "Estonian Evangelical-Lutheran Church," 234.

43. ERA.R-1989.2.70, l. 49–50. Piip blamed Znanie for the fact that only one seminar was held with church leaders in 1986.

44. LVA.1419.3.264, l. 37–39. This order replaced a more restrictive 1967 decree of the USSR Council of Ministers. Viise, "Estonian Evangelical-Lutheran Church," 242.

45. ERA.R-1989.1.328, l. 2–4; ERA.R-1989.2.72, l. 26–30. The new commissioner, Rein Ristlaan, indicated a priority in his work-plan for 1988 on helping churches acquire scarce building materials and approved 35,000 rubles for repair of the fourteenth-century church in Kohlta-Järve on grounds of its architectural significance, despite the fact that its pastor, Peeter Kaldur, had long been considered an oppositional activist in the church.

46. ERA.R-1989.1.328, l. 13–15.

47. LVA.1419.3.265, l. 39, and "Conclusions" of Kokars-Trops, l. 36–38, rejecting this group as composed of "inactive, introverted" individuals and "outside the framework of cult activities and the principles of freedom of conscience." The CRA reversal is found in LVA.1419.3.267, l. 24.

48. ERA.R-1989.2.73, l. 6.

49. LVA.1419.3.296, l. 2, documents Latvia's dramatic lowering of insurance rates for churches and lower income tax on clergy in 1989.

50. ERA.R-1989.2.73, l. 6; Trups-Trops, "Römisch-Katholische Kirche," Teil 3, 93–95. That the new publication occurred on the 250th anniversary of the first Bible in the Estonian language was not lost on the commissioner.

51. Confiscated in the 1940s, the building would eventually be returned to the Church by the new government in 1990.

52. LVA.1419.3.265, l. 94–97. Trups-Trops, "Römisch-Katholische Kirche," Teil 2, 125.
53. LVA.1419.3.267, l. 64, indicates approval for Uldis Savelev, age thirty-one, to attend the theological seminary in Chicago.
54. ERA.R-1989.2.71, l. 165.
55. Estonian Commissioner Ristlaan, quoted in January 1989, in ERA.R-1989.2.73, l. 8.
56. ERA.R-1989.2.67, l. 19. Regarding Finnish and LWF intercession on behalf of Pädam: Finnish National Committee, LWF, 9 Dec. 1985; 7 Oct. 1985.
57. ESSR Commissioner, Charakteristika, Kuno Pajula. Official preference for Pajula as bishop, "for whom work is being conducted with the appropriate organs," was noted in ERA.R-1989.2.70, l. 33–34. Hark was hailed as a "patriot" and "politically-convinced person"; noting the battle in the Church over the succession, Commissioner Piip opined that getting an equal to him would be difficult. Lieberg, "Aus der Evangelisch-Lutherischen Kirche," 61 (1987) and 87 (1988). Viise, "Estonian Evangelical-Lutheran Church," 232–33.
58. The commissioner's report on the synod is found in LVA.1419.3.265, l. 47–48. The regime blocked Western church leaders from attending Matulis's funeral, an indication of the impact of the controversy. Rozitis, "Aus der Evangelisch-Lutherischen Kirche," 88–89 (1988).
59. Kiivit's blunt critique of Pajula and past church leadership was evident in his 1989 article, "Ruckkehr aus dem Schweigen," 104: "The church leadership, which ruled according to the demands of state power was not up to the challenges. Its main focus was increasingly aimed at maintaining foreign ties and needs of representation." Lieberg, "Aus dem Leben," 101–5.
60. Kokars-Trops was more descriptive than policy focused in his August 1987 report, in LVA.1419.3.266, l. 40–48. Three hundred parishioners in Kuldīga signed a petition objecting to Archbishop Mesters's attempt to move Plāte. State officials pressured many Lutheran leaders to distance themselves from the movement. Radio Free Europe/Radio Liberty, "Situation Report," 9–10 (1987). Keston News Service (1987) and (1987); "Latvians Defend Dismissed Pastor," 340–45; Sapiets, "Rebirth and Renewal," 237–49.
61. Rozitis, "Aus der Evangelisch-Lutherischen Kirche," 125 (1989).
62. Benz, "Lage der Kirchen," 25–26; Rozitis, "Aus der Evangelisch-Lutherischen Kirche," 122–27 (1989) and 128–33 (1990).
63. ERA.R-1989.2.74, l. 18–19, and Rohtmets and Ringvee ("Religious Revival," 372–75) on formation of the Estonian Council of Churches (ECC) and its official registration in November 1989. The goal of the ECC was initially to promote inter-confessional dialogue, but soon became "an organ to consolidate all Christian churches," based on consensus. The commissioner indicated that all its suggestions were accepted by the government and the ECC represented "a positive influence on religious affairs in Estonia." The Latvian commission of churches to propose a new law on religion was formed in September 1989 and is discussed in LVA.1419.3.296, l. 13.
64. LVA.1419.3.267, l. 48–49. In Latvia, the Baptists were demanding the return of churches that had been converted by the state. State officials hoped to arrange for Baptists and Pentecostals to use Lutheran facilities at St. Paul's in Riga, but were rebuffed by the Lutherans, who planned to use it for the theological seminary.
65. LVA.1419.3.279, l. 10–12. Though some Baptist clergy, such as Jānis Rozkalns, were close to and supportive of the Rebirth and Renewal movement, as a whole the Baptist leadership avoided politics and limited its role to contributions to the Culture Fund and charity.

66. Interviews, Elmars Rozitis and Johannes Baumann, August 1990; Stricker, "Visit to German Congregations," 19-21.
67. Iozef Baron, *Rossiiskoe Liuteranstvo*, 58-59, 256-57, 284-93.
68. Interviews, Georg Kretschmar and Siegfried Markert, August 1990.
69. LVA.1419.3.266, l. 59-60.
70. ERA.R-1989.2.70, l. 28.
71. LVA.1419.3.279, l. 15.
72. LVA.1419.3.279, l. 2-3; Radio Free Europe/Radio Liberty, "Situation Report," 3 (1990).
73. LVA.1419.3.279, l. 16. In his 1988 report, the Latvian commissioner indicated that 107 of 118 nonworking churches were in fact not used as planned.
74. LVA.1419.3.279, l. 15.
75. The CRA order is documented in ERA.R-1989.1.327, l. 5-7. With this order, CRA criticized local authorities' rejection of registering parishes as "grounded in old stereotypes of relations with believers."
76. LVA.1419.3.279, l. 4.
77. ERA.R-1989.2.71, l. 140-43. Lutheran baptisms increased by 20 percent, but ROC baptisms actually declined. LVA.1419.3.296, l. 4-8. Viise, "Estonian Evangelical-Lutheran Church," 243-45.
78. ERA.R-1989.2.73, l. 12; ERA.R-1989.2.74, l. 22. Despite the sharp increase in its social activity, church attendance remained the same as in 1987, a paltry 4,000 communicants on a regular basis, only 50,000 at major holidays. By 1989, however, officials were reporting significant increases to 5,000 to 6,000 communicants weekly, and 100,000 for major holidays.
79. Benz, "Schwieriger Neubeginn," 123-25.
80. LVA.1419.3.279, l. 7. Of the sixty-five attending the seminary, twenty-five were from Ukraine and seventeen from Belarus, forming an absolute majority of students, according to LVA.1419.3.267, l. 15-18. The Pope's proposal would mean fewer students at the Riga Seminary and less clout for Vaivods in those republics; it is questionable whether this reflected Vaivods's personal position. "Students at Riga Seminary," 358-59.
81. Viise, "Estonian Evangelical-Lutheran Church," 236-38.
82. Trups-Trops, "Römisch-Katholische Kirche," Teil 3, 85.
83. Lutheran World Federation, *Informationsdienst*, 12-13 for the return of premises for the Latvian theological institute and Estonian consistory.
84. ERA.R-1989.2.74, l. 21; *Glaube in der 2. Welt* (1989), 5.
85. ERA.R-1989.2.73, l. 5-10.
86. LVA.1419.3.296, l. 3. The state even permitted importation of newsprint for the new Lutheran biweekly newspaper, for 50,000 copies. Archbishop Gailītis informed (rather than requested) Commissioner Kublinskis, as documented in LVA.1419.3.268, n. 437, no list number.
87. ERA.R-1989.2.73, l. 7.
88. ERA.R-1989.2.73, l. 5, 9. Commissioner Ristlaan also reported high-level meetings of church leaders with the new reformist First Secretary of the CP Estonia, Vaino Väljäs, in 1988.
89. ERA.R-1989.2.73, l. 8-9. Viise, "Estonian Evangelical-Lutheran Church," 239.
90. Radio Free Europe/Radio Liberty, "Daily Report," 3 (1990).
91. Interview, Illar Hallaste, 21 Jan. 1991.
92. Kalle Kasemaa, head of the Theological Institute, quoted in Lutheran World Federation, *Informationsdienst*, 14-16 (1989); Bourdeaux, *Gospel's Triumph*, 150.

93. ERA.R-1989.2.74, l. 20.

94. LVA.1419.3.267, l. 2–9, documents the demands of an interdenominational group for wide-reaching legal changes in the rights of churches, particularly non-Orthodox churches, signed by most leading figures of Rebirth and Renewal.

95. Radio Free Europe/Radio Liberty, "Situation Report," 27–28 (1988); Rubenis, "Which Way?" 81–86; Rozitis, "Aus der Evangelisch-Lutherischen Kirche," 129 (1989).

96. The Latvian Church in Exile reciprocated by agreeing in September 1989 that Bishop Gailitis "legally and morally represents the true interests of the church of Latvia and the Latvian people." See *Glaube in der 2. Welt* (1989), 7.

97. Interviews, Johannes Baumann and Siegfried Markert, August 1990.

98. LVA.1419.3.296, l. 5–9. Radio Free Europe/Radio Liberty, "Situation Report," 15–18 (1989).

99. Pilli, *Dance or Die*, 111–12, 129–30.

100. LVA.1419.3.267, l. 20–21.

101. LVA.1419.3.267, l. 82. The commissioner rejects repatriation, but supports removal of the atheistic exhibits in the Cathedral. Reversal of this decision is documented in LVA.1419.3.296, l. 10.

102. ERA.R-1989.1.328, l. 13–15. The head of the Estonian KGB calls for "active measures" against underground sects, including fines and penalties at places of work and study; ERA.R-1989.1.328, l. 2–4, quoting commissioner's office.

103. ERA.R-1989.2.73, l. 10. Salum apparently experienced a nervous illness or schizophrenia in the midst of the ENIP controversy, according to the state.

104. The memo of 18 Dec. 1989 from the Latvian military commissar to the commissioner and main churches, in LVA.1419.3.268, l. 71–72, indicates the catch-22 situation for the churches resulting from the decision by the Presidium of the USSR Supreme Soviet (10 Oct. 1989) to defer students in higher education: due to the fact that theological seminaries were not state institutions, the decision did not apply to theology students. As a result, theology students in Latvia were deferred on an ad hoc basis. Commissioner Kublinskis favored a broader application of conscientious objector status, not limited to theology students, according to his November 1989 memo, in LVA.1419.3.268, l. 67.

105. LVA.1419.3.268, n. 307, no list number.

106. LVA.1419.3.266, l. 30. Juris Kublinskis, local CP secretary in Dobele, was named as new deputy commissioner.

107. LVA.1419.3.296, l. 1.

108. LVA.1419.3.268, "Resolution, Presidium of Supreme Soviet LSSR" created a commission to draft a new law on religion. Three months later the commissioner's office was reorganized, ending subordination to CRA.

109. ERA.R-1989.2.74, l. 18, 21. Ristlaan indicated it used "Leninist principles as the basis" for its deliberations, but also studied Scandinavian laws, in particular those of Finland. In an interview on 21 Jan. 1991, Illar Hallaste indicated that the Estonian Church lobbied in December 1990 for replacing the ESSR commissioner with an office filled by a Christian and directly accountable to the prime minister, objecting to the Popular Front government's decision to create a subordinate office in the Ministry of Culture. See also Rohtmets and Ringvee ("Religious Revival," 369–75) on Ristlaan's shift in stance and eventual abolishment of the CRA commissioner function.

110. ERA.R-1989.2.74, l. 16.

111. Salumäe (press spokesman for the Estonian Church), "Comment: The Estonian Church," 15–16. On the churches' role in the January 1991 crisis, Lutheran World Federation, *Informationsdienst*, 3–5.

112. Interview, Peeter Kaldur, February 1991.

113. Noted scholar of Lutheran church history in Russia, Wilhelm Kahle ("Orthodoxie im Baltischen Raum," 100) argues that "For Estonians, Latvians, and Lithuanians, Orthodoxy contributes to a loss of independence, whereby Lutheran and Catholic churches help to develop and sustain Estonian, Latvian, and Lithuanian self-awareness." Viise ("Estonian Evangelical-Lutheran Church," 263) also draws this conclusion regarding the Estonian case. Vardys, "Role of the Churches," 287–300.

114. Taagepera, "Estonia in September 1988," 174–90.

115. Interview, Rein Ristlaan, March 11, 1991; Paul, "Begegnung der Evangelisch-Lutherischen Kirche," 207. Some, such as Strods ("Roman Catholic Church," 181), exaggeratedly see the Catholic Church as a "rock that could not be shaken by atheist power, having helped in the collapse of the power of the Communist Party in Latvia." Strods, 181. Similarly, Catholic theologian Henriks Trups-Trops ("Römisch-Katholische Kirche," Teil 3, 85) hailed Vaivods as "a courageous leader of the Latvian church through difficult and threatening years of religious persecution."

Conclusion: The Contours of Baltic Exceptionalism in Soviet Religious Policy—and Its Limits

THIS STUDY OF religious policy in Estonia and Latvia during the postwar period confirms the broad periodization often used by scholars to analyze Soviet religious policy generally. But the in-depth description of these two republics also reveals nuances and anomalies in the general policy toward church-state relations.

In the 1944–1949 period, the Soviets undertook to implement control over the churches using the legal, political, and coercive tactics that they had employed earlier in Soviet Russia: extension of the bureaucratic apparatus of the Councils of Religious Affairs, nationalization of churches and property agreements with individual parishes, elimination of religious instruction and curtailment of confirmations of youth, and limits on the theological education of clergy. But they were initially relatively accommodating toward the national denominations, Catholic and Lutheran: religious practice surged after the end of the war and Soviet authorities had scant experience with these Western versions of Christianity; in any case, pacifying the resistance and establishing political order took precedence. After achieving this, however, the regime forced acquiescence by the churches. Targeted by the KGB, growing numbers of clergy were arrested and church leaders were purged in favor of pro-Soviet ones; international ecumenical ties were ruptured, especially with the Vatican and the émigré Lutheran churches; and the regime sought to play off Protestant churches against each other and briefly attempted a Renovationist-like schism in the Lutheran and Catholic churches. Despite the familiar Stalinist strategy, the study of this period reveals differences in tempo and tactics both between Moscow and the republics (the republics pressed harder than Moscow) and between denominations (the Catholic Church fared better than the Lutherans).

By mid-1948, the outlines of the shift to a harsher line were evident, manifested initially in growing criticism by the Central Committee of the CPSU of the soft line of CARC and republic authorities. A main focus of this assault on the churches was church closures, using coercion and various pretenses, and conversion to secular uses. In some cases mergers of parishes were forced.

Accompanying this repression was an aggressive atheistic campaign using media and schools. The churches were pressured to parrot the regime's peace pronouncements and diatribes against the West and the émigré churches. Catholic ties with the Vatican virtually ceased; synodal structures of governance in the Lutheran churches were subverted and KGB penetration of church bureaucracies deprived the leadership of what little autonomy remained. Naturally, religious practice plummeted as a result of this repressive policy.

With the death of Stalin, some liberalization in policy occurred, though not immediately. Local and republic officials continued their hard line, but their decisions began to be overturned by Moscow. Eventually, by 1955, directives from Moscow (CPSU and CARC) made this line more systematic, even extending to the approval to build new churches. The churches found more openness regarding other institutional interests, such as theological education, publications, and even religious services outside church buildings. The post-Stalin period initially brought a heightened atheistic campaign—couched as a liberal alternative to coercive administrative measures—which was quickly reversed by late 1954 as a result of negative feedback from churches and pressure from state officials in religious affairs. Finally, even foreign contacts began anew, particularly with the German Lutherans, though these remained ad hoc and under the watchful auspices of the ROC.

Predictably, this less restrictive context significantly facilitated increased church adherence, producing a backlash under Khrushchev after 1958. The crackdown took a variety of forms. Most visible was the renewed drive to close churches and to reject requests to open new ones. Newly tightened legal requirements governing parish administration sought to limit the power of the clergy. In addition, state officials curtailed access to theological study, though it was not prohibited entirely. Monasteries were closed and pilgrimages were made all but impossible. Paradoxically, the Khrushchev period saw increased international activity by Lutheran and other Protestant churches, now permitted to join ecumenical and confessional organizations; but this was a defensive move driven by the regime, whose long-standing suspicion of the Catholic Church was now heightened by its fears of the Second Vatican Council. Pride of place in international ties remained with the religious peace fronts, such as the Christian Peace Conference. Accompanying this repression was a renewed atheistic campaign using crude propaganda and exposés of allegedly depraved clergy and converts to atheism; secular rites-of-passage were promoted to substitute for religious rites. The archival record attests that this reversal produced considerable bureaucratic friction between CARC officials and CPSU officials, occasioning purges of those CARC officials too vested in the status quo with church leaders.

As in so many policy areas, the Brezhnev years brought stability and complacency in religious policy. There was no rebound of religious practice after

Khrushchev, as had occurred after Stalin. Church closures tapered off, but few new churches were opened. Clergy and theological education continued a slow decline. Atheistic propaganda and monitoring of religious activity became routinized, with most church leaders co-opted by the regime. Dissent began to grow, but was limited primarily to dissident Baptists and Pentecostals, Soviet Germans hoping to emigrate to Germany from the Baltics, and a few younger Lutheran pastors. However, the détente policy of the Brezhnev period did bring considerable change for the churches' international ties: alongside the peace fronts, the Lutheran churches engaged particularly with the LWF and German Lutheran churches, which in turn used the Baltic churches as a bridge to their co-confessionals in Central Asia and Siberia.

Perestroika under Gorbachev would lead to general liberalization, including religious policy. In the early 1980s some signs of reawakening in the Baltic churches could be detected, with modest rises in church adherence, growing interest in architectural and cultural preservation, and small groups of young Turk clergy critical of co-opted church leaders and promoting modern forms of religious expression. However, the primary impetus for liberalization of religious policy came from Moscow authorities, especially after 1988. The churches sought to reclaim their institutional interests as part of this broader Soviet liberalization: high-profile churches were reopened and/or converted back to religious use; religious literature was imported freely; censorship was lifted; and theological faculties were reconstituted at the state universities. But in the context of the intensified crisis and growing demands for independence, the cultural affinity of the Lutheran and Catholic Churches with each nation meant that they could not focus solely on their institutional interests. A number of individual leaders of the independence movements in Latvia and Estonia came from clergy backgrounds. The co-opted Latvian church leadership was ousted in the process of perestroika. But, unlike in other east European settings, the churches were more passive beneficiaries of liberalization than engines of it. Culturally, religion was crucial to the failure of the Soviet experiment in these republics, but the churches sang harmony rather than melody in their singing revolutions.

One conclusion, obvious yet worth underscoring, is the importance of geography. Due to their western position, the Baltic republics were exposed to greater Western influences than other parts of the USSR. Finnish radio broadcasts had early penetrated Estonia with religious ideas, undermining antireligious propaganda. After 1959 this was complemented by growing numbers of short-term tourists from Finland, including those with religious motives, who brought literature and information from the West. The concern of the regime regarding these influences is widely documented in archival records. The special relationship with the Finnish Lutheran Church, blossoming especially after membership in the LWF and WCC, benefited the Estonian Church over time, in the form of material assistance and indirect leverage.

Latvia was less vulnerable to such foreign influences, due to geography and language. As a result, Latvia never developed the special relationship with the Swedish Lutheran Church that the Estonians had with the Finnish Church. Indeed, the Latvian Lutherans initially were cautious about such contacts due to the fact that the headquarters of the Latvian exile church was in Stockholm, unlike the Estonians, whose exile church was located in West Germany.

A second conclusion that can be drawn regards the role of leadership. Other cases, such as the GDR and Poland, have demonstrated the remarkable influence of church leaders with strong character and vision. In the cases under study, church leaders did not have a significant impact on the church-state relationship, with a few exceptions. Suborned by the regime during the Stalinization process, most of the Lutheran leaders after 1948 were in fact weak and without profile. The regime exploited the personal weaknesses of leaders, most obviously in the case of the heavy-drinking Bishop Turs of Latvia, and expended great efforts to "recruit" politically acquiescent church leaders, as in the cases of Bishops Hark and Pajula in Estonia and Bishops Matulis and Mesters in Latvia. To a certain extent, Archbishop Jaan Kiivit in Estonia defied this pattern in the mid-1960s and managed to widen somewhat the profile of the Church; but his unceremonious ouster as head of the Church in 1967 suggests that ultimately there was little room for bold leadership. On the Latvian Catholic side, leadership did play a larger role, with Archbishop Antonijs Springovičs cutting a larger figure in the relationship and demonstrating significant autonomy in the 1940s. Yet the selection of Julijans Vaivods as leading prelate in a brokered settlement with the state would leave even the more robust Catholic Church with weak, compromised leadership until the end of perestroika. Needless to say, small denominations concentrated on their "cultic functions" in hopes of sheer survival.

Another explanation of the church-state relationship must also be rejected, namely theological approaches regarding the churches' relation to society. In the case of the GDR, homeland of Luther and strong national churches, the regime was forced to grapple and react to theological schools of thought regarding the proper relationship to state power, a particularly acute debate after the Nazi period. The traditional Lutheran doctrine of the two kingdoms contended with the Barthian school of the Lordship of Christ in formulating the churches' stance toward the GDR. The notion of a "symphony" of church and state offered a theological fig leaf for Russian Orthodox compromise with Soviet power, as did the theology of service for Hungarian Lutherans. But the institutional weakness of the Baltic churches left them too weak to formulate a fig leaf, much less engage in theological discourse. Early notions of the Christian roots of socialism (e.g., Turs in Latvia) never gained traction in the churches, and the theological case for supporting Soviet peace campaigns remained superficial. Pragmatism and accommodation trumped theology.

The study provides intriguing evidence of the impact of scientific atheism and atheistic propaganda. Under Stalin and later during the Khrushchev campaign, it was utilized quite consciously to undermine popular support for the churches and religion, with considerable success. Religiosity plummeted, especially among Lutherans. The regime managed to recruit atheist specialists even among the clergy; the Institute for Scientific Atheism of the Academy of Social Science of the CPSU established active branches in all three Baltic republics. Baltic researchers on atheism were role models for other parts of the USSR, employing social science techniques such as survey research and focus groups and maintaining an active exchange with researchers in Eastern Europe and Moscow. Analyzing the remaining psychological and sociological roots of residual religious motivation and practice, they confidently anticipated the end of religion as a result of the construction of socialism. Unlike in the GDR, where scientific atheistic researchers were marginalized to the provinces and forced to publish in Soviet journals to avoid endangering the official modus vivendi with the church leadership after 1969, Baltic atheists remained active and prominent until the end of the USSR.

Yet the study also highlights the implementation problems of this atheistic effort. Early propaganda was quite crude and counterproductive to the official efforts to co-opt church leaders and mobilize the churches on behalf of regime policy, such as for disarmament and peace in the 1950s, and to deflect foreign criticism of religious policy in the 1960s and 1970s. Even the more sophisticated antireligious propaganda of the later Soviet period proved inadequate: it became harder to motivate party and state cadres to monitor and control religious activity at the republic level; religion became a novelty for growing numbers in the late Brezhnev period; and Protestant cult activity remained largely impervious to the propaganda while underground religious activity was even encouraged by it.

However, despite these problems, it is untenable to argue that the atheistic policies left no trace. The widespread dechristianization of contemporary Estonia and Latvia, in the absence of coercion and ideological pressure since 1991, contrasts starkly with former Communist settings such as Lithuania and Poland, but reflects a similar pattern found in eastern Germany and the Czech Republic. It would seem that, at least in Lutheran or mixed Protestant-Catholic settings, the success of atheistic agitation was ironically demonstrated after the *end* of communism.

In addition to the impact of atheistic policy, the current study sheds light on the impact of church institutional interests. As indicated in the early chapters, the institutional interests of the Catholic and Lutheran Churches—conduct of rites and religious instruction, clergy recruitment and training, maintenance of church infrastructure, contact with co-confessionals internationally, and internal autonomy of church governance—left them vulnerable to state pressure in the early Stalinization process in Estonia and Latvia, by comparison with Protestant sects and Orthodox Church. In an effort to defend these interests, both the Lutheran Churches and to a lesser extent the Catholic Church were eventually co-opted in the Stalinist period. By the same token, during periods of liberalization, such as from 1954 to 1958 and in the 1980s, the institutional interests of the church facilitated concessions by the regime to the churches, such as registration and construction of churches, new opportunities for theological education, and more publications. The small Protestant sects, on the other hand, stood to benefit less from such liberalization. Such concessions risked criticism from conservatives, especially in the Agitprop apparatus of the Communist Party, but could be monitored using leverage over co-opted church leaders and rescinded if expedient, as happened during the Khrushchev repression of 1958 to 1964.

By the early 1980s, the churches' institutional interests had been severely curtailed but at a stable level. Training and recruitment of clergy was possible at seminaries, but the curriculum had been modified to conform to state dictates and clergy shortages were dire. Sacramental rites were held, but religious instruction was illegal and practice of confirmation and first communion was significantly curtailed. Mechanisms of church governance, such as synods, were intact but penetrated by informants and substantial interference of state officials, leaving the church leadership with little autonomy.[1] The state ceased an active effort to close churches and monasteries, but took minimal steps to maintain existing churches. International contacts had increased significantly due to détente, but were closely monitored.

This low level of church institutional strength left the churches ill-prepared to provide the social space for dissent, unlike in the GDR and Poland. When perestroika and glasnost arrived under Gorbachev, it was in fact elements of the republic communist parties that pressed for greater autonomy and liberalization. However, this study does indicate that the Lutheran churches were not unaffected by perestroika. As revealed in chapter 6, internal dissent arose in the early 1980s (the Renaissance and Renewal Movement in Latvia, various national- and modernizing-minded pastors in Estonia), but it was repressed and failed to spark a broad social movement. Eventually, key individual leaders in the drive for sovereignty and independence did come from these pastors. But they channeled their activism through the broader national movements rather than using the official Church as a vehicle. As elements of civil society the churches were too weak and their leaderships too compromised, yet their modest institutional base did facilitate the articulation of long-taboo national goals.

This study also illuminates the impact of the churches as transnational actors and permits one to draw conclusions about the effect of such foreign ties on the regime's relations with the churches. Both the Catholic and Lutheran

Churches enjoyed strong international ties before the communist period; transnational actors value access and autonomy in their international activities, eroding sovereignty to a certain extent. In these Baltic cases, the transnational ties provided little respite from the Stalinist policies after 1944; indeed the ties to the Vatican and the German- and American-dominated ecumenical organizations made the churches more suspect than the Orthodox and other churches. As chapter 2 indicated, international ties were severely curtailed under Stalin. The post-Stalin foreign policy of greater openness offered possibilities for greater international contact, albeit on an ad hoc basis and under the auspices of the ROC. In the late Khrushchev era and throughout the period of Brezhnev's détente policy, the transnational ties were allowed to assume more regularized, institutional form (as, for instance, with the WCC and LWF).

The findings of this study confirm that the churches' transnational status positioned them for new opportunities when shifts in Soviet foreign policy occurred. The USSR's more active diplomacy in international organizations and the Third World after 1955, designed to increase the Soviets' image during the Cold War, entailed permitting Soviet churches to engage internationally as well. The interest in legitimizing the GDR translated into state support for exchanges with the East German churches. Likewise, the special political relationship with Finland engendered its own religious counterpart between Estonian and Finnish Lutheran churches. Compared with most Soviet churches, including the ROC, the Estonian and Latvian churches were in this way far less isolated and became engaged in global religious deliberations.

But the churches gained comparatively little domestic leverage from this transnational activity. The regime's penetration of the church leadership limited contacts to compromised church leaders; concessions were restricted to narrow institutional perquisites, such as publications and theological education, certainly not a broader liberalization. Only under Gorbachev did broader benefits accrue to the churches, such as opening of churches and lifting of censorship, and it is hard to attribute these concessions primarily to international leverage: even those churches with less transnational activity benefited from perestroika.

The strategy of Western church organizations was crucial to this transnational influence. West German Lutherans spearheaded the initial ad hoc contacts in the 1950s, motivated in part by a German hybrid of Realpolitik and Ostpolitik with the USSR. In the 1960s, particular interest in the fate of Soviet Germans motivated the LWF and German Lutherans to engage in bridge building with East bloc partners in Estonia and Latvia. Without this confessional and national priority of the West German Lutherans, the Baltic churches would not have been positioned to take advantage of the shift in Soviet foreign policy. The German churches became crucial to the Brezhnev détente strategy in the 1970s, enabling them to extract concessions from the regime regarding transnational access to Soviet Germans.

On balance the transnational ties represented a net gain for the churches, especially after Stalin. To be sure the gains were accrued largely by the church leadership and in the later period by Soviet German Lutherans; the transnational ties did little to enliven church adherence, much less political dissent. The regime sought to encourage envy of church leaders with Western church contacts in leaders and laity lacking them. Moreover, the loss of sovereignty for the regime was limited, particularly compared with other East European regimes such as Poland or the GDR. But Western transnational attention did encourage Soviet German identity and strengthen the European cultural identity of the Baltics.

The current study allows one to draw conclusions regarding the impact of bureaucratic actors in the formulation and implementation of religious policy. This study yields strong evidence that the monolithic Communist regime suffered from bureaucratic tensions along center-regional lines, as well as party-state lines. As found in chapter 1, republic officials, usually drawn from KGB backgrounds, were initially inclined to extend Soviet religious policy to the Baltics faster than those in Moscow, which was interested in securing political control before challenging the churches. Likewise, during implementation of nationalizations in the 1946–1948 period, central authorities insisted on delaying pressure on the Catholic Church. Localism was apparent in application of salami tactics: on the Herrnhuter question, for example, Baltic officials disagreed with central authorities who simply had little understanding of this pietistic group and its limited potential. To make the policy shift to high Stalinism in 1948 and 1949, cautious republic commissioners had to be replaced by hard-liners. The bureaucratic alignments reversed during the liberalization after Stalin, with republic officials continuing the crackdown while central officials sent mixed signals of moderation during 1953 and 1954, as described in chapter 3. The return to a hard-line policy under Khrushchev, analyzed in chapter 4, found Central Committee officials attacking the ideological laxness of CARC and promoting atheistic indoctrination, as well as running bureaucratic disputes between CARC and CROC over responsibility for foreign relations.

Localism also showed up in the implementation of policy. Republic commissioners often overturned local officials regarding nationalizations and closing of churches, seeking to avoid conflict with church leaders. Republic officials skewed the implementation of the Khrushchev campaign by closing disproportionately fewer Lutheran churches than sect and Orthodox churches. Follow-up studies later found that many allegedly closed churches had never actually been converted to secular purposes.

In the Brezhnev years, bureaucratic differences and immobilism widened further. Republic commissioners, often viewed by the churches as demoted from more powerful positions, developed clientele relations with the church leaders, seeking to avoid destabilizing the status quo: they lobbied against migration from other republics as destabilizing the religious situation in their respective republics and opposed contacts between Baltic and Soviet German Lutherans, both positions out of sync with Moscow. Similarly, republic officials often were resistant to the increased foreign contacts in the late Brezhnev period, but were usually overruled by central party and state officials interested in using the transnational ties for Soviet foreign purposes. With the advent of underground religious groups, the KGB tended to favor their legal registration in order to increase surveillance and control; republic officials usually opposed registration to avoid giving the appearance of an increase in religion. Enthusiasm for atheistic indoctrination waned in the party; scientific atheism became routinized and of interest only to party academics. By the 1980s, the distinctiveness at the republic-level is evident (as in the surge in support for cultural and architectural preservation of churches), even a certain assertiveness (with Estonian proposals for limited decentralization of decision-making, creation of a council of churches, and public policy forums with church officials). Of course, with the advent of perestroika, even these manifestations of exceptionalism paled as officials rushed to embrace the churches or risk being identified with stagnation and replaced by advocates of perestroika.

This study argues that policy was largely set by doctrinaire CPSU central authorities and followed uniform approaches, but met with resistance at certain points from the state officials of CARC. In turn, shortfalls in implementation at the republic level suggest significant localism.[2] The focus of the bureaucratic tensions shifted from early differences over the tempo and process of legal and political subordination of the churches to later divergences over how to manage the institutional relationship and the international and domestic trade-offs. The resulting distinctiveness of religious policy in Latvia and Estonia greatly facilitated the resurgence of national identity and movement for independence.

Of course localist tendencies might be responding to another explanatory factor, namely the distinctive national culture of these republics as manifested in the Western-based religions of Lutheranism and Catholicism. The structure, organization, and faith practices of these Western religions differ from Russian Orthodoxy: setting them apart were the historical connection with Western Europe, the role and training of clergy, Christian education and the role of laity, parish and church governance, and social infrastructure.

The regime was acutely aware of their significance in Baltic national culture, as well as the historical confessional differences between them. The early effort to woo Latvian Catholics coincided with the purge of the Latvian Lutheran leadership, as the state sought to exploit the Catholics' greater resistance to Hitler for advantage over the Lutherans. The more hierarchical structure of the Catholic

Church also led the regime to initiate its crackdown on confirmation with the less-cohesive Lutherans. Early policy sought to curtail the extensive seminary training for clergy, assuming that fewer and less-educated clergy would reduce the influence of the churches. Any sign of the churches invoking national symbols provoked consternation by the state.

The nominal success of regime efforts to curtail church adherence attenuated the state's anxiety over the national significance of these churches. Since they were "dying institutions" with co-opted leaderships under political control, the regime accepted the distinctive Western aspects. Moreover, the rising threat of dissident Baptists, Pentecostals, and Jews—often not ethnic Balts—made the Catholics and Lutherans seem politically loyal by comparison. Features that had earlier been seen as impeding control, such as their highly educated clergy, became preferable to the less-educated but oppositional Baptist clergy. Their rational leaders were manageable compared with the unpredictable, leaderless Pentecostals. Both the regime and the churches had adapted to each other. Though this adaptation did not lead to a general moderation of Soviet religious policy, it did produce a notably nuanced model in Estonia and Latvia.

But it would be going too far to argue that the cultural Lutheranism or Catholicism engendered the dissent that challenged the regime. Latvian Catholics were not to be confused with Lithuanian ones. Unlike in the GDR, the Lutheran cultural legacy in these two republics produced more accommodation than opposition. Yet the Western religious legacy, though emasculated in terms of religious practice, did provide the symbols and cultural trappings to embolden the national movement when perestroika eventually changed the opportunity-cost context for political action. When the Spiritual Administration of Moslems in Central Asia and Kazakhstan appealed to Estonian authorities in June 1989 to "avoid breaking the cultural, economic and spiritual ties created during the period of Soviet power," it woefully underestimated the influence of Western religious culture as a permissive factor for political change.[3]

Notes

1. This study does not support Chadwick (*Christian Church*, 33), who claims that in selecting bishops "in Estonia and Latvia there was frequent deadlock—the church refusing to have the person the state wanted, the state refusing to have the person the church electors wanted." The bishop selections from 1946 until 1989 were determined by the regime.

2. Remmel ("Believers, Human Rights") also finds that local officials in Estonia retained some agency in the religious policy, making Estonian policy more lenient than in the USSR as a whole.

3. ESSR Commissioner of CRA, Toimik 328, "Telegram."

Glossary

Bratsvo	brotherhood
Bruderschaften	brotherhood (Confessing Church groups opposed to Hitler)
Dvatsatka	group of twenty parisioners necessary to petition to register a parish and who assumed responsibility for the parish, under Soviet law
Gleichschaltung	co-optation and suborning of societal groups into the political system
Herrnhuter	Bohemian Brethren, pietistic group
Initsiativniki	dissident group which rejected legal registration and split with AUCECB
Ispolkom	executive committee (state body)
Ispolorgan	executive council, responsible for church parish decision-making
Jugendweihe	youth consecration ceremony (GDR)
Oblast	region
Raiispolkom	executive committee of local government
Raion	local district
Sovnarkom	Council of People's Commissars

Bibliography

Archival References
Estonian State Archive (ERA)
ERA.R-1989.1.2, "Appeal of the Church Assembly of the EELK to Members of the EELK," l. 31.
ERA.R-1989.1.4, n. 3 "Address of Estonian Commissioner Kivi at Meeting of CARC, 16 Jan. 1947," l. 4-7.
ERA.R-1989.1.134, n. 150c (9 Aug. 1972), "On Contemporary Condition of Religion in the Tasks to Strengthen Control of Observance of Legality on Religious Cults," cover (l. 44) and speech, CRA Chair Kuroedov (25 Apr. 1972), l. 1-40.
ERA.R-1989.1.155, n. 180c (4 Sept. 1974), Postanovlenie CRA of 28 Aug. 1974, "On Measures of Systemizing the Network of Religious Organizations of Citizens of German Nationality and Strengthening the Control of their Activity," l. 54.
ERA.R-1989.1.155, Spravka "On the Citizens of German nationality living on the territory of the ESSR, their inclinations regarding religious organizations and the situation of maintaining legality of religious cults," (17 Dec. 1974), Piip—CRA, l. 123-27.
ERA.R-1989.1.165, "On Systematizing Soviet Law on Religious Cults," Speech, CRA Chair Kuroedev (10 Jul. 1975), Zhiguleva (CRA), l. 50-57.
ERA.R-1989.1.165, no date, no number, KGB ESSR—Piip, l. 103.
ERA.R-1989.1.165, no title, no date (1975), Report by L.A. Tsibulski, Senior Inspector, CRA, l. 185, 187-89.
ERA.R-1989.1.177, Postanovlenie, Buro CC CP Estonia (14 Jun. 1976), Protocol N. 14, "On Perspective Plan of Ideological Work of CC CP Estonia in Implementation of Decisions of the 25th Congress of CPSU, 1976-1980," l. 18-20.
ERA.R-1989.1.177, n. 22c (23 Aug. 1976), Piip—Kuroedov, CM ESSR, CC -CP Estonia, and "administrative organs," l. 76.
ERA.R-1989. 1.188, n. 175c (4 Jul. 1977), Barmenkov (Deputy Chair, CRA)—all Commissioners, cover letter and speech by CRA Chair Kuroedov (29 Mar. 1977), l. 77f.
ERA.R-1989.1.199, n. 28c (5 Oct. 1978), Piip—Rakhmankulov (Deputy Chair, CRA), l. 105.
ERA.R-1989.1.199, n. 310c (9 Oct. 1978) Tarasov—Piip, with "Report regarding Investigative Visit to ESSR May 1978," L.A. Tsibulskii (CRA), l. 121.
ERA.R-1989. 1.199, n. 31c (4 Sept. 1978), Piip—Kuroedov, l. 123-25.
ERA.R-1989.1.199, n. 34c (6 Dec. 1978), Piip—Kuroedev, l. 136.
ERA.R-1989.1.212, n. 10c (20 Apr. 1979), "Overview of Prophylactic Work with Clergy and Activists," Piip—Kuroedov, l. 3-11.
ERA.R-1989.1.224, n. 172c (30 Aug. 1980), Makartsev—Piip, l. 27-29.
ERA.R-1989.1.224, no date, "Report on 1980 LWF Conference in Tallinn," Piip, l. 107-13.
ERA.R-1989.1.224, n. 2c (7 Jan. 1980), Zharinov (Commissioner, Leningrad Oblast)—Piip, l. 150.

ERA.R-1989.1.224, n. 25c (24 Dec. 1979), Piip—Zharinov (Commissioner, Leningrad Oblast), l. 151.
ERA.R-1989.1.264, "Excerpts from CRA Protocol N. 5 (30 May 1983), 'On the Conduct of the 500th Anniversary of Luther,'" l. 12.
ERA.R-1989.1.264, n. 4/94 (28 Mar. 1983), Piip—Kuroedov, l. 13–14.
ERA.R-1989.1.327, CRA Resolution N. 2 (28 Aug. 1988), "On Facts of Violations of Approved Order of Consideration of Requests for Registration by Religious Groups," l. 5–7.
ERA.R-1989.1.328, no date, no number, "Plan of Work of Commissioner's Apparat for 1988," Ristlaan—Kharchev (Chair, CRA), l. 2–4.
ERA.R-1989.1.328, n. 292 (16 Mar. 1988), K.E. Kortelainen (Chair of KGB ESSR),—Bruno Saul (Chair of Council of Ministers, ESSR), l. 13–15.
ERA.R-1989.2.1, n. 347 (27 Mar. 1945), Dep. Chair CARC, Sadovski—Kivi, l. 4.
ERA.R-1989.2.1, n. 232–101c, "Circular Letter, Sovnarkom USSR," l. 25–26.
ERA.R-1989.2.1, n. 582c (6 Aug. 1947), Polyanski—Kivi, l. 79.
ERA.R-1989.2.2, n. 403c (24 Dec. 1945), Sadovski—Kivi, l. 47.
ERA R-1989.2.3, n. 387c (10 Dec. 1945), Polyanski—Kivi, l. 43.
ERA.R-1989.2.3, n. 53 (23 Jan. 1946), Kivi—Polyanski, l. 46–47.
ERA.R-1989.2.3, no author, no date, l. 72–73.
ERA.R-1989.2.3, "Informational Report 3rd Qtr. 1946," Kivi—Polyanski, l. 83, 89
ERA.R-1989.2.4, no number (14 Jan. 1946), Kivi—Sadovski, l. 1–3.
ERA.R-1989.2.4, no number (31 Jan. 1946), Kivi—Polyanski, l. 10–12.
ERA.R-1989.2.4, n. 159c (21 Mar. 1946), Polyanski—Kivi, l. 27.
ERA.R-1989.2.4, n. 205 (24 Apr. 1946), Kivi—Polyanski, l. 39–42.
ERA.R-1989.2.4, n. 215 (30 Apr. 1946), Kivi—Polyanski, l. 47–51.
ERA.R-1989.2.4, n. 139 (25 May 1946), Kivi—Polyanski, l. 53–54.
ERA.R-1989.2.4, "The Estonian Church and the German Fascist Occupation of Estonia, 1941–1944," l. 71–74.
ERA.R-1989.2.4, n. 390c (2 Jul. 1946), Polyanski—Kivi, l. 75.
ERA.R-1989.2.5, n. 124c (8 Feb. 1947), Sadovski—Kivi, l. 9–10.
ERA.R-1989.2.5, n. 295 (13 Mar. 1947), Kivi—Dep Chair CM ESSR Pusepp and 1. Sec CPE Karotamm, l. 42–44.
ERA.R-1989.2.5, n. 418 (29 Apr. 1947), Kivi—Sadovski, l. 45–48.
ERA.R-1989.2.5, n. 448 (13 May 1947), Kivi—Sadovski, l. 60–64, 67–69.
ERA.R-1989.2.5, n. 339 (2 Apr. 1947), Kivi—Pusepp, l. 72–78, 83.
ERA.R-1989.2.5, no number, no date, "Outstanding Tasks," Kivi—Pusepp/Karotamm, l. 79, 82, 85.
ERA.R-1989.2.5, n. 504 (29 May 1947), Kivi—Polyanski, l. 86–89.
ERA.R-1989.2.5, "Proposed By-Laws, Theological Institute," May 1947, l. 91–94.
ERA.R-1989.2.5, n. 414c (6 Jun. 1947), Sadovski—Kivi, l. 95.
ERA.R-1989.2.5, n. 628 (19 Jun. 1947), Kivi—Polyanski, l. 108.
ERA.R-1989.2.5, n. 633 (20 Jun. 1947), Kivi—Deputy Minister, KGB, USSR, l. 118.
ERA.R-1989.2.5, n. 323 (18 May 1947), Deputy Bishop Pahn—Kivi, l. 119.
ERA.R-1989.2.6, n. 1032 (5 Jun. 1947), Kivi—Polyanski, l. 45–52.
ERA.R-1989.2.6, no date, "Overview of Herrnhuter Parishes in the Baltic States," Kivi, l. 59–69.
ERA.R-1989.2.6, n. 713c (13 Oct. 1947), Polyanski—Kivi, l. 110–11.
ERA.R-1989.2.6, n. 1271 (20 Oct. 1947), Kivi—Polyanski, with attached Letter (29 Aug. 1947) Saag—Kivi, l. 112.

ERA.R-1989.2.6, n. 760c (4 Nov. 1947), Polyanski—Kivi, l. 113.
ERA.R-1989.2.6, n. 1312 (17 Nov. 1947), Kivi—Polyanski, l. 126–29.
ERA.R-1989.2.7, no number (8 May 1947) "Informational Report 1st Qtr 1947," Kivi—Polyanski, l. 24, 29.
ERA.R-1989.2.7, no number (14 Oct. 1947), "Informational Report 3rd Qtr 1947," Kivi—Polyanski, l. 54–67.
ERA.R-1989.2.7, n. 785c (22 Nov. 1947), Polyanski—Kivi, l. 79.
ERA.R-1989.2.7, no number (19 Jan. 1948), "Informational Report 4th Qtr 1947," Kivi—Polyanski, Karotamm, Pusepp, Kumm, l. 85–105.
ERA.R-1989.2.7, n. 627 -K1 (18 Nov. 1947), Kivi—All Chairs of Executive Committees of Counties and Republic-level Cities, l. 113–15.
ERA.R-1989.2.7, n. 67c (17 Feb. 1948), Polyanski—Kivi, l. 120–120r.
ERA.R-1989.2.7, no number (9 Apr. 1948) "Informational Report 1st Qtr. 1948," Kivi—Polyanski, l. 121–70.
ERA.R-1989.2.7, no number, no date, "Spravka, Changes in List of Registered Cult Servants in First Quarter, 1948," l. 171, 171r.
ERA.R-1989.2.7, "Circular Letter of Consistory, EELK," n. 1 (14 Jan. 1948), Kivi—Polyanski, l. 173.
ERA.R-1989.2.7, n. 74c (16 Jul. 1948), "Informational Report 1st Half 1948," Kivi—Polyanski, l. 182–205.
ERA.R-1989.2.7, no number (9 Oct. 1948) "Informational Report 3rd Qtr 1948," Kivi—Polyanski, l. 222–54.
ERA.R-1989.2.7, no number (12 Jan. 1949) "Informational Report 4th Qtr. 1948," Kivi—Polyanski, l. 261–78.
ERA.R-1989.2.8, n. 8c (28 Feb. 1948), Kivi—Pusepp, l. 18–19.
ERA.R-1989.2.8, n. 14c (6 Mar. 1948), Kivi—Polyanski, l. 30.
ERA.R-1989.2.8, n. 21c (9 Mar. 1948), Kivi—Polyanski, l. 45.
ERA.R-1989.2.8, n. 387 (30 Mar. 1948), Polyanski—Kivi, l. 46.
ERA.R-1989.2.8, n. 3/106 (8 May 1948), Polyanski—Kivi, l. 50, 50r.
ERA.R-1989.2.8, n. 186c (16 Apr. 1948), Polyanski—Kivi, l. 65, 65r.
ERA.R-1989.2.8, n. 30c (16 Mar. 1948), Kivi—Polyanski, l. 66.
ERA.R-1989.2.8, n. 166c (9 Apr. 1948), Polyanski—Kivi, l. 71.
ERA.R-1989.2.8, n. 60c (2 Jun. 1948), Kivi—Polyanski, l. 97–101.
ERA.R-1989.2.8, n. 79c (27 Aug. 1948), Kivi—Polyanski, l. 141–42.
ERA.R-1989.2.8, n. 84c (30 Aug. 1948), Kivi—Polyanski, l. 149–53.
ERA.R-1989.2.8, n. 100c (19 Oct. 1948), Kivi—Polyanski, l. 167.
ERA.R-1989.2.8, n. 14/107c (28 Oct. 1948) Polyanski—Kivi, l. 168, 168r.
ERA.R-1989.2.9, no number (31 Jan. 1953) "Informational Report 4th Quarter 1952," Kivi—Polyanski, l. 18, 19–27, 29–30, 34.
ERA.R-1989.2.9, no number, no date, "Informational Report 1st Quarter 1953," Kivi—Polyanski, l. 61.
ERA.R-1989.2.9, no number (14 Jul. 1953), "Informational Report 2nd Quarter 1953," Kivi—Polyanski, l. 83–84, 93–94.
ERA.R-1989.2.9, no number, no date, "Informational Report 3rd Quarter 1953," Kivi—Polyanski, l. 134.
ERA.R-1989.2.10, n. 44 (14 Jul. 1953), Kivi—Polyanski, 1. 67–69.
ERA.R-1989.2.10, n. 8-85c (5 Aug. 1953), Polyanski—Kivi, l. 185.
ERA.R-1989.2.10, n. 63 (1 Dec. 1953), Kivi—Polyanski, l. 246–47.

ERA.R-1989.2.11, n. 1 (16 Jan. 1954), Kivi—Green (Dep Chair, CM ESSR), l. 10–11.
ERA.R-1989.2.11, n. 25 (27 Feb. 1954), Kivi—Polyanski, l. 50.
ERA.R-1989.2.11, n. 30 (16 Mar. 1954), Spravka, Kivi, l. 58.
ERA.R-1989.2.11, n. 35 (8 Apr. 1954), Kivi—Polyanski, l. 77–78.
ERA.R-1989.2.11, n. 44 (8 May 1954), Kivi—Polyanski, l. 104–5.
ERA.R-1989.2.11, n. 54 (16 Jun. 1954), "Report on Condition and Activity of Branches of Lutheran Churches—Former Prayer Houses of Herrnhuters," Kivi—Polyanski, l. 130–34.
ERA.R-1989.2.11, n. 55 (16 Jun. 1954), Kivi—Green (Dep Chair CM ESSR), l. 135–36.
ERA.R-1989.2.11, n. 58 (25 Jun. 1954), Kivi—Polyanski, Green (Dep Chair CM ESSR) and Merimaa (Sec, CC CP ESSR), l. 145–46.
ERA.R-1989.2.11, n. 10-85c (4 Aug. 1954), Polyanski—Kivi, l. 152.
ERA.R-1989.2.11. n. 68 (17 Sept. 1954), Kivi—Muresepp (Chair CM ESSR), l. 158.
ERA.R-1989.2.11, n. 72 (6 Oct. 1954), Kivi—Polyanski, l. 169–77.
ERA.R-1989.2.11, n. 78 (12 Oct. 1954), Kivi—Polyanski, l. 202.
ERA.R-1989.2.11, n. 84 (25 Oct. 1954), Kivi—Polyanski, l. 217–20.
ERA.R-1989.2.11, n. 94 (25 Dec. 1954), Kivi—Polyanski, l. 279.
ERA.R-1989.2.11, no number (27 Dec. 1954), l. 286.
ERA.R-1989.2.12, n. 22 (7 Apr. 1949), "Informational Report 1st Qtr. 1949," Kivi—Polyanski, l. 57–64.
ERA.R-1989.2.14, n. 1 (23 Feb. 1955), Veiderpass—Karpov (Chair, KGB ESSR), 7–9.
ERA.R-1989.2.14, n. 7-81c (3 Aug. 1955), Polyanski—Veiderpass, l. 14.
ERA.R-1989.2.14, n. 7 (14 Mar. 1955), Veiderpass—Polyanski, l. 31–41.
ERA.R-1989.2.14, n. 10 (17 Mar. 1955), Veiderpass—Käbin (Secretary, CC CP ESSR) and Green (Dep Chr, CM ESSR), l. 42.
ERA.R-1989.2.14, n. 14 (27 Apr. 1955), Veiderpass—Murrisepp (Chr CM ESSR), l. 49.
ERA.R-1989.2.14, n. 15 (4 May 1955), "Informational Report...1954," Veiderpass—Polyanski, l. 50–90.
ERA.R-1989.2.14, n. 390 (5 May 1955), Bishop Kiivit—Veiderpass, l. 102–3.
ERA.R-1989.2.14, n. 30 (27 May 1955), Veiderpass—Polyanski, l. 122.
ERA.R-1989.2.14, n. 31 (3 Jun. 1955), Veiderpass—Green/Lentsman, l. 123–25.
ERA.R-1989.2.14, "Informational Report 1st Half 1955," Kivi—Polyanski, l. 175–76.
ERA.R-1989.2.14, no number (20 Dec. 1955), "Work Plan for 1st Half 1956," l. 249–51.
ERA.R-1989.2.14, n. 55 (28 Dec. 1955), Veiderpass—Polyanski, l. 256.
ERA.R-1989.2.17, n. 34 (24 Jul. 1956), "Informational Report 1st Half 1956," l. 116–18, 122–25, 128.
ERA.R-1989.2.17, n. 38 (31 Jul. 1956), Veiderpass—Polyanski, l. 146.
ERA.R-1989.2.17, n. 42 (13 Oct. 1956), Veiderpass—Polyanski, l. 169, 171.
ERA.R-1989.2.17, n. 45 (12 Nov. 1956), Veiderpass—Gostev (Dep Chair, CARC), l. 176–81.
ERA.R-1989.2.17, n. 46 (22 Nov. 1956), Veiderpass—Gostev, l. 182–83.
ERA.R-1989.2.17, n. 47 (28 Nov. 1956), Veiderpass—Gostev, l. 185–87.
ERA.R-1989.2.18, n. 9-76c (19 Aug. 1957), Puzin—Veiderpass, with attachments, l. 34, 39, 40.
ERA.R-1989.2.18, n. 10-78c (23 Aug. 1957), Puzin—Veiderpass, l. 36–37
ERA.R-1989.2.19, n. 2 (11 Jan. 1957), l. 7–10.
ERA.R-1989.2.19, n. 3 (16 Jan. 1957), "Informational Report 1956," Veiderpass—CARC, l. 14–15, 27–32.
ERA.R-1989.2.19, n. 4 (21 Jan. 1957), Veiderpass—Gostev (CARC), l. 53–54.
ERA.R-1989.2.19, n. 6 (2 Feb. 1957), Veiderpass—Gostev, l. 55–60.

ERA.R-1989.2.19, n. 10 (6 Mar. 1957), Veiderpass—Lentsman (Sec., CC CPSU), l. 71–72.
ERA.R-1989.2.20, n. 30 (10 Sept. 1957), Veiderpass—Puzin, l. 53.
ERA.R-1989.2.20, n. 34 (14 Oct. 1957), Veiderpass—Puzin, l. 67–71.
ERA.R-1989.2.21, n. 2-71c (17 Jan. 1958), Puzin—Veiderpass, l. 2.
ERA.R-1989.2.21, n. 1–105c (25 Sept. 1956), Ryazanov/CARC—Veiderpass, l. 27.
ERA.R-1989.2.22, no number, no date, "Informational Report 1957," Veiderpass—Puzin, l. 7–11, 26.
ERA.R-1989.2.22, n. 13 (9 May 1958), Veiderpass—Puzin, l. 112–18.
ERA.R-1989.2.22, n. 16 (14 Jul. 1958), "Information Report 1st Half 1958," Veiderpass—Puzin, l. 143–45.
ERA.R-1989.2.22, n. 23 (2 Oct. 1958), Veiderpass—Puzin, l. 182.
ERA.R-1989.2.23, n. 3–72c (3 Aug. 1959), Puzin—Veiderpass, l. 24.
ERA.R-1989.2.24, no number, no date, "Information Report 2nd Half 1958," Veiderpass—Puzin, l. 28–30.
ERA.R-1989.2.24, n. 10 (3 May 1959) Veiderpass—Puzin—Lentsman—Murrisepp, l. 105–8.
ERA.R-1989.2.24, no number, no date, "Information Report 1st Half 1959," Veiderpass—Puzin, l. 172–74.
ERA.R-1989.2.26, n. 1 (21 Jan. 1960), "Information Report 1959," Veiderpass—Puzin, l. 7, 26–28.
ERA.R-1989.2.26, n. 14 (9 Aug. 1960) Veiderpass—Lentsman/CPE-Muurisepp/CM ESSR, l. 104–6.
ERA.R-1989.2.26, n. 11–83c (6 Sept. 1960) Puzin—Veiderpass, l. 118.
ERA.R-1989.2.26, n. 17–83c (19 Dec. 1960), Puzin—Commissioners, l. 131–33.
ERA.R-1989.2.27, Protocol N. 5, Meeting of CARC (31 Jan. 1961), l. 16–17.
ERA.R-1989.2.27, Protocol N. 15, Meeting of CARC (27 Mar. 1961), l. 32.
ERA.R-1989.2.28, n. 2 (24 Jan. 1961), "Information Report 1960," Veiderpass—Puzin, l. 24–25, 34–46.
ERA.R-1989.2.28, n. 4 (3 Mar. 1961), Veiderpass—Käbin/CPE, l. 68–70.
ERA.R-1989.2.30, n. 1 (25 Jan. 1962), "Information Report 1961," Veiderpass—Puzin, l. 8–9, 38–39.
ERA.R-1989.2.30, n. 9 (25 May 1962), Veiderpass—CM ESSR-Puzin-CPE, l. 81–83.
ERA.R-1989.2.30, n. 17 (15 Nov. 1962), Veiderpass—Puzin, l. 103.
ERA.R-1989.2.32, n. 1 (21 Jan. 1963), "Information Report 1962," Veiderpass—Puzin, l. 10.
ERA.R-1989.2.34, n. 1 (3 Jan. 1964), Veiderpass—Puzin, Klauson (Chair, CM ESSR), Lentsman (CC-CPE), l. 1–2.
ERA.R-1989.2.34, n. 3 (17 Jan. 1964), "Information Report 1963," Veiderpass—Puzin, l. 14.
ERA.R-1989.2.36, n. 1 (16 Jan. 1965), "Informational Report 1964," Veiderpass—Puzin, l. 22–25, 33–37.
ERA.R-1989.2.37a, n. 1 (20 Jan. 1966), "Informational Report 1965," Andrusov—Kuroedov, l. 32f.
ERA.R-1989.2.38, n. 3c (29 Jan. 1967), "Informational Report 1966," Teder—Kuroedov, l. 14, 24–26, 40–43.
ERA.R-1989.2.38, no number (21 Feb. 1967) "Spravka on Jaan Kiivit," V. Naidenkov, deputy head, KGB ESSR, l. 120–21.
ERA.R-1989.2.38, n. 6c (15 Mar. 1967), Teder—Kuroedev, l. 127.
ERA.R-1989.2.39, no number, no date, likely Informational Report 1967, l. 76–81.
ERA.R-1989.2.41, n. 3c (13 Feb. 1969), "Informational Report 1968," Teder—Kuroedov, l. 83–84, 115, 121–25, 178–215, 222–40.
ERA.R-1989.2.43, no number, no date, "Informational Report 1970," Teder—Kuroedov, l. 114.
ERA.R-1989.2.48, no number, no date, "Informational Report 1971," l. 20.

ERA.R-1989.2.50, no number, no date, "Informational Report 1972," l. 82, 125–27, 131.
ERA.R-1989.2.52, no number, no date, "Informational Report 1973," Piip—Kuroedov, l. 161–62.
ERA.R-1989.2.54, no number, no date, "Informational Report 1974," Piip—Kuroedov, l. 121.
ERA.R-1989.2.56, no number, no date, "Informational Report 1975," Piip—Kuroedov, l. 106–12.
ERA.R-1989.2.57a, no number, no date, "Informational Report 1976," Piip—Kuroedov, l. 142–45, 155–56.
ERA.R-1989.2.58, no number, no date, "Informational Report 1977," Piip—Kuroedev, l. 135–38, 143–44, 165.
ERA.R-1989.2.60, no number, no date, "Informational Report 1978," Piip—Kuroedov, l. 116–20, 127–28.
ERA.R-1989.2.62, no number, no date, "Informational Report 1979," Piip—Kuroedov, l. 130, 134.
ERA.R-1989.2.64, n. 3c (16 Feb. 1981), "Informational Report 1980," Piip—Kuroedov, l. 109, 111–14.
ERA.R-1989.2.65, n. 2c (11 Feb. 1982), "Report on Status of Religion in ESSR," l. 89–91, 102.
ERA.R-1989.2.66, n. 2c (15 Feb. 1983), "Informational Report 1982," Piip—Kuroedov, l. 121–24.
ERA.R-1989.2.67, n. 1c (14 Feb. 1984), "Informational Report 1983," Piip—Kuroedov, l. 17–46.
ERA.R-1989.2.68, no number, no date, "Informational Report 1984," Piip—CRA, l. 23.
ERA.R-1989.2.69, n. 2c (30 Jan. 1986), "Informational Report 1985," Piip—CRA, l. 46–47, 67–68.
ERA.R-1989.2.70, n. 2c (29 Jan. 1987), "Informational Report 1986," Pipp—Kharchev (Chair, CRA), l. 28, 33–34, 49–50.
ERA.R-1989.2.71, n. 2c (22 Jan. 1988), "Informational Report 1987," Deputy Commissioner Oya –CRA, l. 140–43.
ERA.R-1989.2.71, no number (28 Nov. 1988), "Distribution of religious views and moods in the republic," Ristlaan, l. 165.
ERA.R-1989.2.72, n. 43 (14 Dec. 1988), "Information on Activity of Religious Organizations in the City of Kohlte-Järve in 1988," Ristlaan—Kharchev (Chair, CRA), l. 26–30.
ERA.R-1989.2.73, no number (3 Jan. 1989), "Informational Report 1988," Ristlaan—CRA, l. 5–10, 12.
ERA.R-1989.2.74, no number (13 Feb. 1990), "Informational Report 1989," Ristlaan—CRA, l. 16–22.

Communist Party of Estonia Archive (ERAF)

ERAF.1.4.6048, Material and Protocol N. 28 (3 Mar. 1982), A. Soidla, "Notes on Strengthening Atheistic Upbringing of the Population of the Republic," l. 11.
ERAF.1.14a.37, n. 38/0527 (6 Aug. 1949), "Informational Report 2nd Quarter 1949," Kivi—Polyanski, l. 122–24, 136–37.
ERAF.1.14a.37, n.59/0613 (21 Oct. 1949), "Informational Report 3rd Quarter 1949," Kivi—Polyanski, l 162–64.
ERAF.1.14a.37, n. 63 (26 Oct. 1949), Kivi—Polyanski, l. 200–2.
ERAF.1.14a.37, n. 2 (14 Jan. 1950), "Informational Report 4th Quarter 1949," Kivi—Polyanski, l. 220.
ERAF.1.72.26, n. 2 (16 Jan. 1951), "Informational Report 4th Quarter 1950," Kivi—Polyanski, l. 16–21.
ERAF.1.72.26, n. 46 (11 Dec. 1951), "Informational Report 3rd Quarter 1951," Kivi—Polyanski, l. 167, 192, 196, 206.
ERAF.1.72.26, n. 52 (26 Dec. 1951) Kivi—Kabin (Secretariat, CC CPE) and Muurisepp (CM ESSR), l. 221–22.
ERAF.1.72.26, n. 3 (10 Jan. 1952), Kivi—Gostev (dep Chair, CARC) l. 231–35.
ERAF.1.72.26, n. 5 (11 Jan. 1952), Kivi—Gostev, l. 236.

ERAF.1.72.26, "Note to Files," Lentsman (CC-CPE) (26 Apr. 1952), l. 239
ERAF.1.72.26, n. 2/011 (6 Apr. 1952), "Informational Report 4th Quarter 1951," Kivi—Polyanski, l. 246, 247–50, 253–54, 260.
ERAF.1.143.25, n. 66 (17 Sept. 1954), Kivi—Murresepp and Kabin, l. 160.
ERAF.1.216.23, n. 6 (30 Apr. 1960), Veiderpass—Puzin, l. 13–16.
ERAF.129SM.1.25217, Alfred Tooming, "Accusation Findings based on Investigation n. 7466" (21 Jan. 1946), Sverdlovsk Oblast NKVD and Protocol n. 1 (4 Jan. 1947) Special Commission, KGB.

ESSR Commissioner of CARC/CRA, Personnel Files

Charakteristika, Edgar Hark, no date, Kivi.
Charakteristika, Jaan Kiivit, Sr., no date, Kivi.
Characteristika, Kuno Pajula, no date.
Characteristika, Alfred Tooming (12 Aug. 1949), Kivi.
Toimik 328, Telegram (31 June 1989), Spiritual Administration of Moslems of Central Asia and Kazakhstan—Chair of Council of Ministers, ESSR, l. 79–80.

Latvian State Archive (LVA)

LVA.270.2.5716, n. 8/110 (30 Apr. 1949), Restberg—Ostrov (dep Chair, CM LSSR), l. 27.
LVA.678.1.69, Directive Order N. 979 (14 Oct. 1954), Pavele (LSSR Ministry of Culture), l. 87–95.
LVA.938.6.91a, n. 4/32 (5 Oct. 1961), J. Fredrickson, Chair of Juridical Commission of CM LSSR, l. 105–8.
LVA.1419.3.1, n. 47 (29 Jan. 1966), Postanovlenie CM LSSR N. 565 (13 Nov. 1965), l. 1.
LVA.1419.3.1, n.28–416 (20 Sept. 1966) Ministry of Finance, LSSR, l. 39–41.
LVA.1419.3.3, n. 118 (6 May 1967), Liepa—Kuroedov, l. 26.
LVA.1419.3.3, n. 202 (30 Aug. 1967), Liepa—Kuroedov, l. 52.
LVA.1419.3.3, n. 219 (4 Oct. 1967), Liepa—CC CPL, l. 53–54.
LVA.1419.3.4, n. 64 (27 Mar. 1968), Liepa—Tarasov, l. 25–26.
LVA.1419.3.4, n. 170 (6 Sept. 1968), Liepa—Kuroedov, l. 133, 163.
LVA.1419.3.5, n. 212 (5 Nov. 1969), Liepa—Kuroedov, l. 174–79.
LVA.1419.3.6, n. 386 (31 Dec. 1970), Sacharov—Makartsev, cover to Matulis letter to WCC General Secretary Eugene Carson Blake (31 Dec. 1970), l. 241–42.
LVA.1419.3.7, n. 107 (23 Apr. 1971), Liepa—Kuroedov, l. 25–30.
LVA.1419.3.7, Letter, WCC General Secretary Blake to Matulis (2 Apr. 1971), l. 36.
LVA.1419.3.7, Letter, Consistory of ELC Latvia to WCC General Secretary Eugene Blake (4 Apr. 1971), l. 37.
LVA.1419.3.9, n. 518 (27 Dec. 1973), Liepa—Tarasov, l. 71–74.
LVA.1419.3.12, n. 345 (11 May 1976), Liepa—Kuroedov, l. 56–59.
LVA.1419.3.12, n. 374 (7 Jun. 1976), Liepa—Makartsev, l. 76–77.
LVA.1419.3.13, n. 274 (12 May 1977), Liepa—Kuroedov, l. 5–6.
LVA.1419.3.13, n. 401 (21 Jul. 1977), Liepa—Ispolkom, Liepaja, l. 115–16.
LVA.1419.3.14, n. 1774 (12 Jun. 1978), Makartsev—Raman (Chair, Gosplan LSSR), l. 136.
LVA.1419.3.15, n. 74 (13 Jan. 1969), "CRA Overview Finding on Practice of Application of the Directive of Presidium of SS, 'On Administrative Responsibility for Violations of Law on Religious Cults'," unpaginated.

LVA.1419.3.17, n. 2/169 (1 Mar. 1977), Liepa—Titov (CRA), l. 142-44.
LVA.1419.3.193, n. 326 (27 Feb. 1979), Kokars-Trops—Kuroedov, with Appeal of Latvian Evangelical Lutheran Church of 19 Feb. 1979," l. 11-12.
LVA.1419.3.193, n. 18-3450k (3 Aug. 1978), Krūminš—All Ispolkoms, LSSR, l. 90.
LVA.1419.3.193, n. 993 (25 Dec. 1979), "Spravka," l. 206-11.
LVA.1419.3.194, n. 893 (24 Mar. 1980), Kokars-Trops—V. V. Kanep (Ministry of Health LSSR), l. 86-88.
LVA.1419.3.196, n. 557 (28 Dec. 1981), Kokars-Trops—Praude (Dep Chair CM LSSR), l. 11-12.
LVA.1419.3.196, (22 Dec. 1982), "Spravka," Sakharov, l. 89-92.
LVA.1419.3.196, n. 446 (28 Dec. 1982), Kokars-Trops—Tarasov, l. 102-3.
LVA.1419.3.198, n. 585 (5 Jul. 1979), Sacharov—Fitsev (Dep Chair CRA), l. 86, 98.
LVA.1419.3.198, n. 618 (23 Aug. 1979), Sacharov—Fitsev, l. 123.
LVA.1419.3.198, n. 902 (14 Nov. 1979), Kokars-Trops—Fitsev, l. 145-47.
LVA.1419.3.200, n. 203 (13 May 1981), Kokars-Trops—Tarasov, l. 24-26.
LVA.1419.3.262, n. 437 (29 Oct. 1973), Liepa—CM LSSR, l. 170-76.
LVA.1419.3.262, n. 1010 (11 Jun. 1980), Kokars-Trops, l. 177.
LVA.1419.3.264, n. 114 (6 Mar. 1985), Kokars-Trops—CRA, "Spravka …," l. 6.
LVA.1419.3.264, n. 225 (6 Jun. 1985), Kokars-Trops—CRA, "Information on the 40th Anniversary of the End of WWII," l. 23-25.
LVA.1419.3.264, n. 320 (10 Sept. 1985), Kokars-Trops—Local Executive Committees, l. 37-39.
LVA.1419.3.264, n. 450 (17 Dec. 1985), Kokars-Trops—CRA, "Spravka on Condition of Maintaining Cultural Valuables," l. 43-51.
LVA.1419.3.265, no number (11 Aug. 1986), Kokars-Trops—CRA, Spravka…, l. 94-97.
LVA.1419.3.265, n. 25 (13 Jan. 1986), Kokars-Trops—CRA, l. 2-3.
LVA.1419.3.265, n. 18-20/240 (7 Jan. 1986), Decree, Council of Ministers LSSR to raions/cities, l. 9-10.
LVA.1419.3.265, n. 1059 (25 Mar. 1986) CRA—Kokars-Trops, l. 39 and "Conclusions" of Kokars-Trops, l. 36-38
LVA.1419.3.265, n. 137 (18 Apr. 1986), Kokars-Trops—CRA, "Information on the Course of the Extraordinary General Synod of the Ev. Lutheran Church of Latvia," l. 47-49.
LVA.1419.3.265, n. 173 (26 Jun. 1986), Kokars-Trops—CRA, l. 66.
LVA.1419.3.265, n. 275 (1 Sept. 1986), Kokars-Trops—CRA, "Spravka on Condition of Control of Observance of Law on Religious Cults and Activity of Religious Organizations in LSSR," l. 71f.
LVA.1419.3.265, no number (11 Aug. 1986), Kokars-Trops—CRA, "Spravka on Problems Arising in Case of Increasing the Number and Change in Contingent of Students at Riga Catholic Seminary," l. 94-97.
LVA.1419.3.266, n. 33 (22 Jan. 1987), Kokars-Trops—CRA, l. 1-6.
LVA.1419.3.266, n. 206 (16 Jun. 1987), Kokars-Trops—CRA, l. 30.
LVA.1419.3.266, n. 282 (12 Aug. 1987), Kokars-Trops—CRA, "Information on the Formation and Activity of the Group 'Rebirth and Renewal' among Ev. Lutheran Cult Servants in LSSR," l. 40-50.
LVA.1419.3.266, n. 305 (4 Sept. 1987), Kokars-Trops—Agitprop Department, CC- CPL, l. 59-60.
LVA.1419.3.267, n. 4064 (19 Nov. 1987), Michailov/CRA—Kokars-Trops, l. 2-9.
LVA.1419.3.267, n. 43 (3 Feb. 1988), Kokars-Trops—CRA, l. 15-18.

LVA.1419.3.267, no number (15 Feb. 1988), Bluka (Cultural-Social Development Department)—Dep. Chair Bartkevich, CM LSSR, l. 20–21.
LVA.1419.3.267, Telefonogramma, Kharchev—Commissioner LSSR, l. 24.
LVA.1419.3.267, n. 233 (18 Jun. 1988), Kublinskis—CM LSSR, l. 48–49.
LVA.1419.3.267, no date or number, Ishchenko (deputy Commissioner)—CRA, l. 64.
LVA.1419.3.267, n. 396 (6 Dec. 1988), Ishchenko (deputy Commissioner)—Bartkevich (deputy Chair, CM LSSR), l. 82.
LVA.1419.3.268, n. 437 (9 May 1989), Gailītis and Predele—Commissioner Kublinskis, no list number.
LVA.1419.3.268, "Resolution, Presidium of Supreme Soviet LSSR (24 August 1989)" no list number.
LVA.1419.3.268, n. 307 (11 Oct. 1989), Kublinskis—CRA, no list number.
LVA.1419.3.268, n. 375 (24 Nov. 1989), Kublinskis—CRA, l. 67.
LVA.1419.3.268, n. 2/4659 (18 Dec. 1989), Major General J. Duda (Military Commissar LSSR)—Commissioner, Catholic Curia, and Lutheran Consistory, l. 71–72.
LVA.1419.3.276, n. 4c (31 Jan. 1986), "Informational Report 1985," Kokars-Trops—CRA, l. 3–7, 8, 11, 13, 36, 37–39, 40–41.
LVA.1419.3.279, no number (31 Jan. 1989), Kokars-Trops—CRA, "Informational Report 1988," l. 2–3, 4, 7, 10–12, 15, 16.
LVA.1419.3.280, n. 1c (23 Feb. 1966), Liepa to Kuroedov, l. 6–7.
LVA.1419.3.280, n. 3c (7 Jun. 1966), Liepa—Krūmiņš and Ruben, l. 30–34.
LVA.1419.3.280, n.4c (22 Jul. 1966), Liepa—Kuroedov, l. 35, with Letter, Turs-Appel (LWF) (16 Jun. 1966), l. 36–37.
LVA.1419.3.280, n. 9c (5 Oct. 1966), Liepa—Kuroedov, l. 43–55.
LVA.1419.3.281, n. 8c (14 Mar. 1967), Liepa—V.P. Ruben (Chair of CM LSSR), l. 59–65.
LVA.1419.3.281, n. 9c (21 Mar. 1967), Liepa—Kuroedev, l. 70–71.
LVA.1419.3.281, n. 11c (8 Apr. 1967), Liepa—Kuroedov, l. 93–94, 96–97.
LVA.1419.3.281, n. 25c (6 Jul. 1967), Liepa—Kuroedov, Krūmiņš (Chair, CM LSSR), Ruben (CC CPLatvia), l. 149–50.
LVA.1419.3.281, n. 26c (16 Aug. 1967), Sacharov—Kuroedov, with attached "Information" by Harald Kalnins, l. 157–58.
LVA.1419.3.282, n. 7c (7 Mar. 1968), "Informational Report 1967," Liepa—Kuroedov, l. 32–35, 60.
LVA.1419.3.282, "Characteristika Petr E. Kleperis," (18 Mar. 1968), l. 78–79.
LVA.1419.3.282, A. Freijs and H. Kalnins—Liepa (4 May 1968), l. 136–38.
LVA.1419.3.282, n. 25c (12 Jul. 1968), Liepa—Kuroedev, l. 196.
LVA.1419.3.282, n. 28c (6 Aug. 1968), Sakharov—Makartsev, l. 222–27.
LVA.1419.3.283, n. 6c (10 Mar. 1969), "Informational Report 1968," l. 26–27, 30, 37–38.
LVA.1419.3.283, n. 18c (22 May 1969), Liepa—Makartsev, l. 84–85.
LVA.1419.3.283, n. 47c (4 Sept 1969), Liepa—Kuroedov, l. 202–4
LVA.1419.3.283, "Report by Matulis" (22 Sept 1969) and "Report by Ozolins" (25 Sept 1969), l. 209–13.
LVA.1419.3.284, n. 3c (27 Feb. 1970), "Informational Report 1969," Liepa—Kuroedov, l. 29, 66.
LVA.1419.3.284, n. 15c (8 Sept. 1970), Liepa—Makartsev, with attachment of Bishop Matulis' report "V. Assembly of LWF in Evian," l. 87–102.

LVA.1419.3.284, n. 21c (23 Oct. 1970), Liepa—Kuroedov, with Matulis Report on September 1970 delegation to Hungary and Romania (LWF Minority Churches in Europe), l. 113-21.
LVA.1419.3.284, no date, "Spravka on Émigré Churches," l. 138-58.
LVA.1419.3.286, n. 12c (23 Jun. 1971), l. 64.
LVA.1419.3.287, n. 1c (18 Jan. 1973), l. 20.
LVA.1419.3.287, n. 5c (5 Feb. 1973), Liepa—Kuroedov, with "Work Plan 1973," l. 36-38.
LVA.1419.3.287, n. 6c (16 Feb. 1973) "Informational Report 1972," Liepa—Kuroedov, l. 42-44.
LVA.1419.3.291, n. 2c (21 Feb. 1977), "Informational Report 1976," Liepa—Kuroedov, l. 53-54.
LVA.1419.3.291, n. 8c (19 Sept. 1977), Sakharov—Kuroedov, l. 71-72.
LVA.1419.3.292, n. 2c "Informational Report 1977," Liepa—Kuroedov, l. 58-59.
LVA.1419.3.292, n. 8c (15 Sept. 1978), with handwritten decision (20 Nov. 1978) of V.I. Krūmiņš (Chair CM LSSR), l. 84.
LVA.1419.3.294, n. 8c (3 Sept. 1980) Kokars-Trops—I.J. Krastins (Chair, Ispolkom, Jelgava Gorsoviet), l. 70-71.
LVA.1419.3.296, no number or date, "Information Report 1989," l. 1, 2, 3, 4-9, 10, 13.
LVA.1432.6.242, Letter, Cathedral Organist Nikolai Kachalov (20 Oct. 1958) to Lācis, CM LSSR; Letters, Kachalov (18 Feb. 1959 and 13 Feb. 1959) to Riga City Executive Committee; Petition (10 Jan. 1959), l. 13-16, 30-31, 33-34, and 37.
LVA.1448.1.1, n. 8-66 (4 Mar. 1949), Restberg—Polyanski, l. 2.
LVA.1448.1.1, n. 8/43(19 Feb. 1949), Restberg—Polyanski, l. 4.
LVA.1448.1.1, n. 8/56 (1 Mar. 1949), Restberg—Polyanski, l. 10.
LVA.1448.1.1, n. 6-106 (18 Mar. 1949), Polyanski—Restberg, l. 13.
LVA.1448.1.1, n. 9-104 (21 Mar. 1949), Polyanski—Restberg, l. 15.
LVA.1448.1.1, n. 10-104 (21 Mar. 1949), Polyanski—Restberg, l. 16.
LVA.1448.1.1, n. 8/83 (22 Mar. 1949), Restberg—Tsimdins (CM LSSR), l. 18.
LVA.1448.1.1, n. 9/107 (28 Apr. 1949), Restberg—Ostrov (CM LSSR), l. 19.
LVA.1448.1.1, n. 8/204 (26 Jun. 1949), Restberg—Ostrov (CM LSSR) and Pelše (CC CP LSSR), l. 21.
LVA 1448.1.1, n. 17-104 (18 Jun. 1949), CARC—Restberg, l. 30.
LVA.1448.1.1, n. 8/135 (18 May 1949), Restberg—Polyanski, l. 31.
LVA.1448.1.1, n. 8/227 (3 Aug. 1949), Restberg—Polyanski, l. 43-47.
LVA.1448.1.1, n. 8/270 (5 Sept. 1949), Restberg—Polyanski, l. 50-51.
LVA.1448.1.1, n. 21-104 (9 Sept. 1949), Sadovski—Restberg, l. 52.
LVA.1448.1.1, n. 8/335 (22 Nov. 1949), Acting Commissioner Veinar—Polyanski, l. 65-71.
LVA.1448.1.2, n. 2-102 (1 Jan. 1950), Polyanski—Restberg, l. 7.
LVA.1448.1.2, n.8/21 (7 Feb. 1950), Restberg—Polyanski, l. 14.
LVA.1448.1.2, n. 8/89 (16 Mar. 1950), "Zakluchenie," Restberg and Sacharov, l. 22.
LVA.1448.1.2, n. 11-104 (24 Mar. 1949), Polyanski—Restberg, l. 25.
LVA.1448.1.2, Decree n. 552 (6 May 1950), "On the Confirmation of the Status of Cemeteries in Cities and Villages LSSR," l. 27-34.
LVA.1448.1.2, n. 19-102 (15 Aug. 1950), Polyanski—Restberg, l. 41.
LVA.1448.1.2, n. 8/267 (18 Nov. 1950), Restberg—Polyanski, l. 62.
LVA 1448.1.3, n. 6/73 (6 Feb. 1951), Restberg—Tsimdin, Deputy Chief of Staff, CM LSSR, l. 5.
LVA.1448.1.3, n. 1346 (15 Jun. 1951), Turs—CARC Chair Polyanski, l. 5-6.
LVA.1448.1.3, n. 6/146 (25 Jun. 1951) Restberg—Polyanski, l. 6.

LVA.1448.1.3, n. 1060 (6 Jun. 1951), "Spravka," Head of Architectural Administration, CM LSSR Kishe, l. 17.
LVA.1448.1.3, n. 8/189 (10 Sept. 1951), Restberg—Pusinis (Commissioner, LithuaniaSSR), l. 18.
LVA.1448.1.3, n. 496 (24 Feb. 1951), G. Stolbov (CP Secretariat Moscow Raion, Riga) and A. Straums (Chair, Ispolkom Moscow Raisoviet, Riga)—Lācis (Chair, CM LSSR), l. 26.
LVA.1448.1.3, n. 6/106 (26 Mar. 1951), Restberg—Polyanski, l. 31 and 34.
LVA.1448.1.3, n. 22/9/656 (13 Mar. 1951), Tabolin (Ministry of State Security LSSR)—Restberg, l. 38.
LVA.1448.1.3, n. 6-167 (21 Apr. 1951) Polyanski—Restberg, l. 46.
LVA.1448.1.3, n. 8/140 (6 Jun. 1951), Notes and Report, Restberg—Lācis (Chair, CM LSSR), l. 54–63.
LVA .1448.1.3, n. 8/124 (30 Apr. 1951), Restberg—Polyanski, l. 51–54.
LVA.1448.1.3, n. 6-166 (9 Jun. 1951) Restberg—Polyanski, l. 66–67.
LVA.1448.1.3, n. 6/178 (1 Sept. 1951), Ostrov—Rezekne Ispolkom, l. 73.
LVA.1448.1.3, n. 6/179 (1 Sept 1951), Ostrov—Preili Ispolkom, l. 74.
LVA.1448.1.3, "Notes on Meeting, Chair CARC Polyanski with Archbishop Turs (25 Oct. 1951)," l. 83–84.
LVA.1448.1.3, Strods Address to All-Union Conference of Supporters of Peace (27 Nov. 1951), l. 95–100.
LVA.1448.1.4, n. 8/40 (22 Mar. 1952), Restberg—Polyanski, l. 5–7.
LVA.1448.1.4, n. 9-118 (17 Jul. 1953), Polyanski—all commissioners, l. 30–31.
LVA.1448.1.4, n.8/103 (24 Aug. 1953), Restberg—Lācis (Chair, CM LSSR), l. 38–39.
LVA.1448.1.4, n. 10/122 (29 Sept. 1953), Restberg—Lācis (Chair, CM LSSR), l. 59.
LVA.1448.1.4, n. 8/100 (8 Jul. 1952), Restberg—Gostev (CARC), l. 63–64.
LVA.1448.1.6, n. 8/162 (28 Nov. 1953), Restberg—Pludon (Dep Chair, CM LSSR), l. 3–4.
LVA.1448.1.6, n. 99/139 (15 Jun. 1954), Restberg—Polyanski, l. 36–37.
LVA.1448 1.6, no number, no date, "Report on Condition and Activity of the Lutheran Cult in Latvia as of 1 Nov. 1954," l. 85–91.
LVA.1448.1.7, n. 7 (14 Jan. 1955), Vereshagin—Polyanski, l. 6.
LVA.1448.1.7, n. 5-109 (22 Mar. 1955) Polyanski—all commissioners, l. 17–18.
LVA.1448.1.7, no number (14 May 1955), Memorandum of Meeting (Turs-Polyanski), l. 64–65.
LVA.1448.1.7, n. 25-78 (3 Aug. 1955), Gostev—Restberg, l. 76–77.
LVA.1448.1.7, no number (3 Oct. 1955), Report, Restberg—E.K. Berklavs (dep Chr, CM LSSR), l. 93–98.
LVA.1448.1.8, n. 120-80 (11 Jun. 1956), Weinberg (Ministry of Justice, LSSR)—Restberg, l. 47–48.
LVA.1448.1.8, n. 170 (2 Nov. 1955), Restberg—Pelše and Berklavs, l. 111–17.
LVA.1448.1.10, n. 20 (20 Feb. 1958), Restberg-CM LSSR, l. 24.
LVA.1448.1.10, n. 56 (3 Mar. 1958), Restberg—Prikhodko (CARC), l. 30–31.
LVA.1448.1.10, Letter, Turs—CARC (January 1958), l. 33, 33r.
LVA.1448.1.10, n. 4-83c (26 Jun. 1958) Puzin-commissioners, l. 77.
LVA.1448.1.10, n. 199 (11 Nov. 1958), Restberg—Puzin, with Strods' text (7 Nov. 1958), l. 141–46.
LVA.1448.1.11, n. 20 (11 Feb. 1959), Restberg—CARC, with attachment, Bishop Turs, "What has the Evangelical Lutheran Church of Latvian SSR Done to Promote Peace in the World and for Friendship among Peoples and How Has it Maintained Relations with Christian Churches Abroad?" l. 30–35.
LVA.1448.1.11, n. 65 (15 Apr. 1959), Restberg-CM LSSR, l. 46.

LVA.1448.1.11, n. 315 (30 Apr. 1959) Turs-Restberg, l. 63–64.
LVA.1448.1.11, n. 60 (7 May 1959), Restberg-Puzin, l. 76.
LVA.1448.1.11, n. 83 (7 May 1959) Restberg-Puzin, l. 82.
LVA.1448.1.11, Order N. 400 (8 May 1959), Riga City Executive Committee, "On Repair and Exploitation of the Building Riga Cathedral Church," l. 92–93.
LVA.1448.1.49, n. 3431 (28 Mar. 1946), Turs—Šeškens, l. 56.
LVA.1448.1.53, n. 16 (21 Jan. 1952), Boshkina (Head of Agitprop Department, Kirov Raion, CPL)—Restberg, l. 19.
LVA.1448.1.58, n. 140 (29 Sept. 1954), Restberg—Head of Letters Editorial Dept., *Cīna*, l. 77.
LVA.1448.1.155, n. 20 (11 Feb. 1960), Restberg—Puzin, l. 7.
LVA.1448.1.155, n. 111 (2 Jul. 1960), Pizāns—Puzin, l. 19–23.
LVA.1448.1.156, n. 356 (29 Apr. 1961), Puzin—Pizāns, l. 15.
LVA.1448.1.156, n. 123 (18 Jul. 1961), Sakharov—Iesmina (Valmiera raiispolkom chair), l. 38–39.
LVA.1448.1.156, n. 212 (25 Sept 1961), Sakharov—CM LSSR, Agitprop Dept. CC-CPL, l. 56–57.
LVA.1448.1.156, n. 1025 (26 Oct. 1961), Ryazanov/CARC—Sakharov, l. 68.
LVA.1448.1.158, n. 133 (27 Jul. 1960), Pizāns—CPL/CM LSSR, l. 34–35.
LVA.1448.1.183, n. 4514 (4 Nov. 1946), Turs and Schlossberg—Šeškens, l. 24–25.
LVA.1448.1.185, "Report on Trip of Janis Vegers to Estonia," (16 Feb. 1948), l. 22–24.
LVA.1448.1.186, "Protocol Synods of Church Districts Ev.-Lutheran Church LSSR May-August 1951," l. 19, 40.
LVA.1448.1.187, "Protocol n. 75, Meeting of Presidium of Evangelical Lutheran Church of Latvia HCA (18 May 1951), l. 28–30.
LVA 1448.1.187, n. 1288 (19 May 1951), Turs—CARC, l. 31–33.
LVA.1448.1.187, "Protocol, X. General Synod Evangelical Lutheran Church LSSR," l. 75–99.
LVA 1448.1.188, n. 290 (22 Nov. 1944) Taiwans—A. Kirchenšteins (Chair, Supreme Soviet LSSR), l. 1.
LVA.1448.1.188, n. 1970 (23 Nov. 1944), Irbe—Šeškens, l. 2.
LVA.1448.1.188 no number (29 Nov. 1944), Lācis (Chair, Council of People's Commissars, LSSR)—Kirchenšteins, l. 6.
LVA.1448.1.189, n. 2435 (12 May 1945), Archbishop Irbe—Šeškens, l. 18.
LVA.1448.1.189, no date, no author, l. 33–38.
LVA.1448.1.189, "Appeal to the Latvian People of Lutheran Faith, 6 Dec. 1945," l. 65–66
LVA.1448.1. 237, "Resolution on Additional Convention to the Concordat between Holy See and Government of Bourgeois Latvia 1938" and "Concordat between Holy See and Latvian Government 1922," l. 1–5.
LVA.1448.1.238, n. 398 (15 Dec. 1945), Sadovski—Šeškens, l. 1
LVA.1448.1.239, n. 13 (4 May 1945), Šeškens—Polyanski, l. 7.
LVA.1448.1.239, n. 18 (15 Jun. 1945), Šeškens—Polyanski, l. 25–28.
LVA.1448.1.239, n. 24 (24 Aug. 1945) Šeškens—Polyanski, l. 38.
LVA.1448.1.239, n. 34 (7 Oct. 1945), Šeškens—Polyanski, l. 39.
LVA.1448.1.239, n. 35 (20 Oct. 1945), Šeškens—Polyanski, l. 42.
LVA.1448.1.239, n. 38 (11 Nov. 1945), Šeškens—Polyanski, l. 44.
LVA.1448.1.239, n. 41 (31 Dec. 1945), "Informational Report 1945," Šeškens—Polyanski, l. 50–52.
LVA.1448.1.239, n.23c (22 Jan. 1946), Sadovski—Šeškens, l. 55.
LVA.1448.1.239, n. 42 (31 Dec. 1945), Šeškens—Polyanski, l. 57–58.

LVA.1448.1.242, n. 5 (5 May 1947), "Informational Report 1st Quarter 1947," Šeškens—Polyanski, l. 4–6.
LVA.1448.1.242, n. 17 (28 Oct. 1947), "Informational Report 3rd Quarter 1947," Šeškens—Polyanski, l. 12.
LVA.1448.1.244, n. 5c (21 Apr. 1948), Šeškens—Polyanski, l. 6–11, 14–19.
LVA.1448.1.244, n. 9c (26 Jun. 1948), "Informational Report 2nd Quarter 1948," Šeškens—Polyanski, l. 26–34.
LVA.1448.1.244, n. 13c (12 Oct. 1948), "Informational Report 3rd Quarter 1948," Šeškens—Polyanski, l. 36–41.
LVA.1448.1.244, n. 1c (15 Jan. 1949), "Informational Report 4th Quarter 1948" Restberg—Polyanski, l. 46–58.
LVA.1448.1.244, n. 4c (26 Feb. 1949), Restberg—Polyanski, l. 64–65.
LVA.1448.1.246, n. 9 (15 Apr. 1949), "Informational Report 1st Quarter 1949," Restberg—Polyanski, l. 23–38.
LVA.1448.1.246, n. 15c (18 Jul. 1949), "Informational Report 1st Half 1949," Restberg—Polyanski, l. 45–57.
LVA.1448.1.246, n. 20c (25 Jul. 1949), Restberg—Lācis (Chair, CM LSSR), with "Notes of July 21, 1949 meeting with Springovičs and Strods," l. 64–66.
LVA.1448.1.246, n. 25c (15 Oct. 1949), "Informational Report 3rd Quarter 1949," Restberg—Polyanski, l. 73–92.
LVA.1448.1.246, n. 1–102c (25 Jan. 1950), Polyanski—Restberg, l. 96–97.
LVA.1448.1.246, n. 29c (14 Nov. 1949), Restberg—Polyanski, l. 101–2.
LVA.1448.1.246, n.1c (1 Feb. 1950) "Informational Report 4th Quarter 1949," Restberg—Polyanski, l. 105–15.
LVA.1448.1.247, n. 6c (14 Apr. 1950), Informational Report 1st Quarter 1950," Restberg—Polyanski, l. 4–7, 9, 11, 12, 14, 17, 18, and 20.
LVA.1448.1.247, n. 18c (13 Jul. 1950), "Informational Report 2nd Quarter 1950," Restberg—Polyanski, l. 33–37.
LVA.1448.1.247, n. 23c (12 Aug. 1950), Restberg—Polyanski, l. 45–46.
LVA.1448.1.247, n 31c (12 Oct. 1950),"Informational Report 3rd Quarter 1950," Restberg—Polyanski, l. 50–57, 59–60.
LVA.1448.1.247, n. 1c (13 Jan. 1951), "Informational Report 4th Quarter 1950," Restberg—Polyanski, l. 66–67, 72–81.
LVA.1448.1.249, n. 2c (15 Jan. 1951), Restberg—Polyanski, l. 1–2.
LVA.1448.1.249, n. 5c (26 Jan. 1951), Restberg—Polyanski, l. 3–6.
LVA.1448.1.249, n. 7c (31 Jan. 1951), Restberg—Polyanski, l. 10–11.
LVA.1448.1.249, n. 15c (14 Apr. 1951), "Informational Report 1st Quarter 1951," Restberg—Polyanski, l. 13–30.
LVA.1448.1.249, n. 17c (10 May 1951), "Report on Activity of Religious Organizations in 1950 and Plan of Work of Commissioner for 1951," Restberg—Polyanski, l. 57–66.
LVA.1448.1.249, n. 8–102c (6 Jul. 1951), Polyanski—Restberg, l. 70, 72.
LVA.1448.1.249, n. 22c (23 Jul. 1951), Lācis and Kalnberzins—K.E. Voroshilov (deputy chair, CM USSR), l. 78.
LVA.1448.1.249, n. 26c (10 Oct. 1951), "Informational Report 3rd Quarter 1951," Restberg—Polyanski, l. 80–106.

LVA.1448.1.249, n. 12–102c (16 Nov. 1951), Polyanski—Restberg, l. 113.
LVA.1448.1.249, n. 2c (6 Jan. 1952), "Informational Report 4th Quarter 1951," Restberg—Polyanski, l. 120–21.
LVA.1448.1.250, n. 7c (27 Feb. 1952), Restberg—Polyanski, l. 3.
LVA.1448.1.250, n.11c (10 Apr. 1952), "Informational Report 1st Quarter 1952," Restberg—Polyanski, l. 6–7, 11, 14–15, 17.
LVA.1448.1.250, n. 20c (3 Jun. 1952), Restberg—Polyanski, l. 36–37.
LVA.1448.1.250, n. 23c (5 Jul. 1952), "Informational Report 2nd Quarter 1952," Restberg—Polyanski, l. 45, 48, 49, 50, 53–55, 57.
LVA.1448.1.250, n. 26c (2 Aug. 1952), Restberg—Polyanski, l. 60–61.
LVA.1448.1.250, n. 31c (11 Oct. 1952), "Informational Report 3rd Quarter 1952," Restberg—Polyanski, l. 72, 73, 75, 81, 90–91, 93–96.
LVA.1448.1.250, n. 8/142 (18 Oct. 1952), Restberg—Polyanski, l. 88–89.
LVA.1448.1.250, n. 2c (10 Jan. 1953), "Informational Report 4th Quarter 1952," Restberg—Polyanski, l. 130–33, 137–39.
LVA.1448.1.251, n. 16–76c (9 Oct. 1952), Polyanski—Restberg, l. 3.
LVA.1448.1.252, n. 11c (9 Apr. 1953), Restberg—Polyanski, l. 21–25.
LVA.1448.1.252, n. 13c (14 Apr. 1953), "Informational Report 1st Quarter 1953," Restberg—Polyanski, l. 32–47.
LVA.1448.1.252, n.21c (10 Jul. 1953), Informational Report 1st Half 1953," Restberg—Polyanski, l. 59.
LVA.1448.1.252, n. 25c (21 Aug. 1953), Restberg—Lācis (Chair, CM LSSR), l. 79–81.
LVA.1448.1.252, n. 33c (16 Oct. 1953), "Informational Report 3rd Quarter. 1953," Restberg—Polyanski, l. 97–98.
LVA.1448.1.252, n. 1c (15 Jan. 1954), "Informational Report 4th Quarter 1953," Restberg—Polyanski, l. 115, 118, 124–25.
LVA.1448.1.253, n. 32c (13 Jul. 1954), "Informational Report 1st Half 1954," l. 29–30, 35–36.
LVA.1448.1.253, n. 34c (26 Jul. 1954), Restberg—Polyanski, l. 60–61.
LVA.1448.1.253, no date, Strods—Polyanski and Strods—Malenkov, l. 90–92.
LVA.1448.1.253, n.18–78c (8 Dec 1954), Polyanski—Vereshagin, l. 93.
LVA.1448.1.253, n. 64c (16 Oct. 1954), Restberg—Polyanski, l. 116–17.
LVA.1448.1.253, n. 74c (13 Nov. 1954), Restberg—Polyanski, l. 138–39.
LVA.1448.1.253, no number, "Informational Report 2nd Half 1954," Vereshagin—Polyanski, l. 157–59, 162.
LVA.1448.1.254, n. 2c (5 Jan. 1955), Vereshagin—Polyanski, l. 1–3.
LVA.1448.1.254, n. 26c (5 Apr. 1955), Restberg—Polyanski, l. 20–25.
LVA.1448.1.254, n. 47c (22 Jul. 1955), "Informational Report 1st Half 1955," Restberg—Polyanski, l. 72, 76–81.
LVA.1448.1.254, n. 54c (6 Sept. 1955), Restberg—Polyanski, l. 111–16.
LVA.1448.1.254, n. 69c (30 Oct. 1954), Restberg—Polyanski, l. 123.
LVA.1448.1.254, n. 67c (1 Dec. 1955), Restberg—Polyanski, l. 133–36.
LVA.1448.1.254, n. 4c (19 Jan. 1956), "Informational Report 2nd Half 1955," Restberg—Polyanski, l. 152, 155–60, 162.
LVA.1448.1.255, n. 26c (7 Jul. 1956), Restberg—Polyanski, l. 35–38.
LVA.1448.1.255, n. 28c (14 Jul. 1956), "Informational Report 1st Half 1956," Restberg—Polyanski, l. 42–45, 52.
LVA.1448.1.255, n. 31c (10 Aug. 1956), Vereshagin—Gostev, l. 60–63.

LVA.1448.1.255, n. 35c (24 Aug. 1956), Restberg—Polyanski, l. 65.
LVA.1448.1.255, n. 47c (1 Oct. 1956), Restberg—Polyanski, l. 79–82.
LVA.1448.1.255, n. 49c (17 Aug. 1957), "Report on Religious Activity of the Roman Catholic Church in LSSR," Vereshagin (Commissioner, LSSR) and Chelnikov (Sr. Inspector, CARC)—Puzin, l. 134–46.
LVA.1448.1.256, n. 18c (2 Mar. 1957), Restberg—Gostev, l. 46–48.
LVA.1448.1.256, n. 31 (4 May 1957), Restberg—Gostev, l. 67.
LVA.1448.1.256, n. 45c (17 Jul. 1957), "Informational Report 1st Half 1957," Restberg—Puzin, l. 102–3, 108–9, 111–13.
LVA.1448.1.256, n. 41c (24 Oct. 1959), Restberg—Puzin and Excerpt from Protocol N. 16, Meeting of CARC, 6 July 1959, l. 116–19.
LVA.1448.1.256, n. 53c (13 Sept. 1957), Restberg-Puzin, l. 158.
LVA.1448.1.256, n. 1c (10 Jan. 1958), Informational Report 2nd Half 1957," Restberg—Puzin, l. 176, 178–80, 193, 196.
LVA.1448.1.257, n. 24c (15 Jul. 1958), "Informational Report 1st Half 1958," Restberg—Puzin, l. 24, 29–31, 33–34, 36, 47.
LVA.1448.1.257, n. 25c (18 Jul. 1958), Restberg-Pelše-Berklavs (CPL and CM LSSR), l. 56–57.
LVA.1448.1.257, n. 33c (8.8.58), Egerman-Puzin, l. 73–77.
LVA.1448.1.257, n. 46c (11 Oct. 1958), Restberg—Puzin, l. 92–96.
LVA.1448.1.257, n. 48c (17 Nov. 1958), Restberg—Puzin, l. 98–102, 104–7, 110.
LVA.1448.1.257, n. 49c (8 Dec. 1958), Restberg—Puzin, l. 113–21.
LVA.1448.1.257, n. 3c (23 Jan. 1959), Informational Report 2nd Half 1958," Restberg—Puzin, l. 135–40, 142–44, 147, 149, 151–54.
LVA.1448.1.257, n. 53c (13 Sept 1957), Restberg—Puzin, l. 158.
LVA.1448.1.258, n. 12c (11 Mar. 1959), Restberg—CM LSSR, l. 2–7.
LVA.1448.1.258, n. 16c (20 Mar. 1959), Restberg—Puzin, l. 8.
LVA.1448.1.258, n. 18c (25 Mar. 1959) Restberg/Sakharov—CM LSSR, l. 37–38.
LVA.1448.1.258, n. 20c (7 Apr. 1959), Restberg—Puzin, l. 46–53.
LVA.1448.1.258, n. 27c (23 May 1959), Restberg—Puzin, l. 60–62.
LVA.1448.1.258, n. 32c (14 Jul. 1959), "Informational Report 1st Half 1959," Restberg—Puzin, l. 73–80, 82–84, 93–94.
LVA.1448.1.258, n. 36c (21 Jun. 1959), Restberg—Puzin, l. 107–9.
LVA.1448.1.258, n. 46c (17 Dec. 1959), Restberg—Puzin, l. 126.
LVA.1448.1.258, n. 2c (6 Feb. 1960), "Information Report 1959," Restberg—Puzin, l. 135, 136, 142, 151.
LVA.1448.1.259, n. 3c (Mar. 1960), Pizāns—Puzin, l. 3–4.
LVA.1448.1.259, n. 4c (3 May 1960), "Information Report," Pizāns—Puzin, l. 6.
LVA.1448.1.259, n. 7c (21 May 1960), Pizāns—Puzin, l. 19–21.
LVA.1448.1.259, n. 8c (20 Aug. 1960), Pizāns—Puzin, l. 23–25.
LVA.1448.1.259, n. 10c (22 Oct. 1960), Pizāns—Puzin, l. 30.
LVA.1448.1.259, n. 11c (26 Oct. 1960), Pizāns—Puzin, l. 35–37.
LVA.1448.1.259, n. 13c (13 Dec. 1960), Pizāns—Puzin, and n. 18–68 (17 Nov. 1960), Ryaznov/CARC—Pizāns, l. 41–45.
LVA.1448.1.259, n. 14c (Dec. 1960), Pizāns—Secretary Voss, CPL, l. 48–49.
LVA.1448.1.260, n. 16c (30 Jan. 1961), "Information Report 1960," Pizāns—Puzin, l. 1–3, 5, 8, 10–12, 18, 25, 26.

LVA.1448.1.260, n. 18c (17 Feb. 1961), Pizāns and Sakharov—CM/LSSR, l. 46–47, 49.
LVA.1448.1.260, n. 18c (28 Mar. 1961), Pizāns—Puzin, l. 61–62.
LVA.1448.1.261, no number (Feb. 1962), Krūminš/CM LSSR—Prokofiev/Talsi Raiispolkom, l. 1–5.
LVA.1448.1.261, n. 2c (20 Feb. 1962), Liepa/Sakharov—CM LSSR, l. 11–16.
LVA.1448.1.261, Directive N. 393–317 (21 Jun. 1962), CM LSSR, "On the Liquidation of the Representative of Non-Existing All-Union Center of Seventh-Day Adventists in the Latvian SSR" l. 32–33.
LVA.1448.1.261, n. 20c (21 Jul. 1962), Liepa—Puzin, l. 59–60.
LVA.1448.1.261, n. 20c-11c (18 May 1962), Liepa/Sakharov-Raion Executive Committees, "On Monitoring and Submission of Overviews of Composition and Use of Monetary Funds in Religious Organizations," l. 61–65.
LVA.1448.1.261, n. 29c (24 Oct. 1962), Liepa—Puzin, l. 85–95.
LVA.1448.1.261, n. 31c (14 Dec. 1962) Liepa—Puzin, l. 103–5.
LVA.1448.1.262, n. 4c (19 Feb. 1963), "Information Report 1962," Liepa—Puzin, l. 13, 16–17.
LVA.1448.1.262, n. 7c (6 Apr. 1963), Liepa—Puzin, l. 32–36.
LVA.1448.1.264, n. 1c (26 Jan. 1965), Krūminš—Raiispolkom, l. 1.
LVA.1448.1.264, n 4c (15 Jul. 1965), Liepa—Puzin, l. 25–27.
LVA.1448.1.264, n. 7c (29 Jul. 1965) Liepa—Puzin, l. 30–34.
LVA.1448.1.264, n. 10c (15 Sept. 1965), Liepa—Puzin, l. 49–68, 69–84.
LVA.1448.1.268, n. 661c (6 Jun. 1962), Krūminš—Ispolkom chairs, l. 27–29.

Lithuanian Central State Archive (LCVA)

LCVA.181.3.19, n. 602 (15 Nov. 1949), Pusinis (Commissioner, Lithuania)—Polyanski (Chair, CARC), l. 26.
LCVA.181.3.29, no number (25 Jan. 1952), "Informational Report 4th Quarter 1951," Pusinis—Polyanski, l. 136.
LCVA.181.3.44, n. 25s (14 Jun. 1956), Pusinis—Polyanski, l. 39.
LCVA.181.3.46, n. 27c (7 Jul. 1956), "Informational Report 1st Half 1956," l. 27.
LCVA.181.3.46, n. 7c (15 Jan. 1957), "Informational Report 2nd Half 1956," Pushinis—Gostev, l. 42–43.
LCVA.181.3.49, n. 23c (6 Jul. 1957) "Information Report 1st Half 1957," Rugenis—Puzin, l. 5.
LCVA.181.3.53, n. 1–70c (31 Mar. 1959), Puzin—Rugenis, l. 35–36.
LCVA.181.3.53, no number (31 Aug. 1959), Burkevicius (Chair of Evangelical Lutheran Consistory)—Puzin, l. 41.
LCVA.181.3.59, Protocol N. 7 CARC (9 Feb. 1961) and CARC Resolution on the Report of Comrade Rugenis on Lithuanian SSR, l. 50–51.
LCVA.181.3.60, n. 3c (15 Jan. 1961), Rugenis—Barkauskas (CP Lithuania), l. 1–2.
LCVA.181.3.61, n. 8c (Jan. 1962) "Information Report," Rugenis—Puzin, l. 29.
LCVA.181.3.128, no number, no date, "Informational Report 1987," l. 1–26.
LCVA.181.3.135, no number, no date, "Informational Report 1988," l. 2–24.

State Archive of the Russian Federation (GARF)

GARF.6991.3.3, n. 153c (7 Sept. 1944), Gedvilas, Chair Sovnarkom, LithSSR,—Polyanski, l. 31.
GARF.6991.3.3, n. 24c (28 Aug. 1944), Polyanski—Lācis, Chair Sovnarkom, LSSR, l. 32.
GARF.6991.3.3, n. 75c (10 Nov. 1944), Polyanski—Weimer, Chair Sovnarkom, ESSR, l. 48.

GARF.6991.3.4, no number (25 Sept. 1944), Polyanski—RSFSR Commissioners, l. 31.
GARF.6991.3.4, n. 50 (27 Sept 1944), Polyanski—Commissioners of Lithuania, Latvia and Armenia, l. 52.
GARF.6991.3.5, n. 1 (3 Oct. 1944), "Informational Letter," Šeškens—Polyanski, l. 19-24.
GARF.6991.3.5, no number (21 Nov. 1944), Polyanski—Šeškens, l. 32.
GARF.6991.3.5, no number (20 Nov. 1944), Šeškens—Polyanski, l. 34-35r, 37-38, 40-41.
GARF.6991.3.8, no number (4 Jan. 1947), "Reception by Comrade K.E. Voroshilov," l. 98-108.
GARF.6991.3.8, no number (15 Jun. 1948), Memo of Voroshilov-Polyanski Meeting in Cultural Buro of CM USSR on the Work of CARC for 1947 and 1st Quarter of 1948," Sadovski, l. 153-55.
GARF.6991.3.8, no number (12 Feb. 1949), "Memo of Reception by K.E. Voroshilov," Polyanski, l. 175-77.
GARF.6991.3.8, Notes on Meeting (21.2.51), Voroshilov—Polyanski, l. 229-30.
GARF.6991.3.8, no number, "Memo of Conversation (5 Jan. 1952) Niemöller," Polyanski, l. 265-68.
GARF.6991.3.10, n. 42 (15 Feb. 1945), Polyanski—Molotov, Sovnarkom, l. 5-7.
GARF.6991.3.10, n. 383c (7 Dec. 1945), Polyanski—Molotov, Sovnarkom, l. 95, 98-105.
GARF.6991.3.10, n. 409c (21 Dec. 1945), Polyanski—Molotov, Sovnarkom, l. 123-24.
GARF.6991.3.10, "Appeal of Turs to the Latvian People, 6 April 1946," l. 154-57.
GARF.6991.3.11, n. 38c (14 Feb. 1945), Polyanski—all commissioners, l. 1.
GARF.6991.3.11, n. 43c (16 Feb. 1945), Polyanski—all Baltic commissioners, l. 5.
GARF.6991.3.17, n. 17 (13 Jun. 1945), Šeškens—Polyanski, l. 1-2.
GARF.6991.3.17, n. 191c (19 Jul. 1945), Polyanski—Šeškens, l. 4.
GARF.6991.3.22, n. 20 (17 Jul. 1945), Šeškens—Polyanski, l. 16-17.
GARF.6991.3.46, n. 731c (28 Jul. 1953), Dep Chair Belishev (CROC)—Polyanski, l. 154.
GARF.6991.3.53, n. 8 (8 Jun. 1948), Report on Work of the CARC 1947, Polyanski, l. 42-45.
GARF.6991.3.58, n. 41 (31 May 1949), Peregud (Chair, Pskov Oblast Soviet)—Polyanski (CARC), l. 117.
GARF.6991.3.58, no date, no number, "Telegram," Turs—Commissioner, Pskov Oblast, l. 118.
GARF.6991.3.61, n. 6/168c (22 Mar. 1949), Polyanski—Voroshilov, l. 14.
GARF.6991.3.61, n. 11/168c (23 Apr. 1949), "Dokladnaya Zapiska" Polyanski—Voroshilov (CM-USSR) and Malenkov (CC-CPSU), l. 59-60.
GARF.6991.3.61, n. 11/168 (23 Apr. 1949), Polyanski—Voroshilov, l. 61.
GARF.6991.3.61, n. 19-168c (29 Jun. 1949), Sadovski—Voroshilov (CM USSR), l. 80.
GARF.6991.3.61, n. 25-168c (22 Jul. 1949), Polyanski—Voroshilov, l. 90-92.
GARF.6991.3.61, n. 31-168c (17 Sept 1949), Sadovski—Kaftanov (Buro of Culture, CM-USSR), l. 112.
GARF.6991.3.61, n. 4-179c (18 Sept. 1949), Polyanski—Burdzhalov (CC CPSU), l. 133-37.
GARF.6991.3.66, n. 3978 (30 Sept. 1949), Lavrentiev (Dep Minister, MFA)—Polyanski, l. 46-50.
GARF.6991.3.66, n. 1-154c (2 Jan. 1950), Polyanski—Lavrentiev (Dep Minister, MFA), l. 51.
GARF.6991.3.66, Protocol n. 12 (20 Sept. 1950), l. 80-81.
GARF.6991.3.68, n. 4-158c (9 Feb. 1950), Polyanski—Voroshilov, l. 7-8.
GARF.6991.3.68, n. 7-158c (10 Mar. 1950), Polyanski—Voroshilov (CM USSR), l. 15-20.
GARF.6991.3.68, n. 17-158c (14 Jun. 1950), Polyanski—Molotov and Voroshilov (CM USSR), l. 54-67.
GARF.6991.3.68, n. 25-158c (11 Aug. 1950), Polyanski—Molotov and Voroshilov, l. 137.

GARF.6991.3.68, n.29–158c (5 Sept. 1950), "CARC Report for 1949 and 1st Quarter 1950," Polyanski—Suslov (CC-CPSU) and Sinetskom (Deputy Chair, Buro of Culture, CM-USSR), l. 168, 171, 176.
GARF.6991.3.68, n. 9–162c (9 Sept. 1950), Polyanski—Grigoryan (CC-CPSU), l. 202–6.
GARF.6991.3.68, n. 11–162c (13 Sept 1950), Polyanski—Grigoryan and Sinetskom (Buro of Culture, CM USSR), l. 219–20.
GARF.6991.3.68, n. 39–158c (27 Oct. 1950), Polyanski—Molotov and Voroshilov, l. 262–65.
GARF.6991.3.68, n. 41–158c (5 Nov. 1950), Polyanski—Molotov and Voroshilov, l. 269–70.
GARF.6991.3.71, n. 39–154c (9 Sept. 1950), Polyanski—Lavrentiev (Dep Minister, MFA), l. 16–17.
GARF.6991.3.71, n. 1–160c (13 Sept. 1950), Polyanski—Karpov (CROC), l. 25–28.
GARF.6991.3.76, n. 4–161c (17 Mar. 1951), Polyanski—CM USSR (Voroshilov, Malenkov), CC CPSU (Suslov), and KGB (Abakumov), l. 31–36.
GARF.6991.3.76, n. 8–161c (30 Jun. 1951) "Informational Report 1950," Polyanski—Malenkov (CM USSR), Suslov (CC-CPSU), and Abakumov (KGB), l. 83.
GARF.6991.3.76, n.9–161c (10 Aug. 1951), Polyanski—Pomaznev (CM USSR), l. 123–24.
GARF.6991.3.76, n. 2–162c (23 Nov. 1951), Polyanski—Buro Presidium, CM USSR, l. 171–74.
GARF.6991.3.76, n. 21–165c (21 Dec. 1951), Order n. 24120-pc (17 Dec. 51) of CM USSR, signed Stalin, l. 176.
GARF.6991.3.80, n. 1972 (23 Dec. 1952), Savchenko (Info Buro, MFA)—Polyanski, l. 96–98.
GARF.6991.3.88, n. 19–116c (23 May 1952), Polyanski—Bazikin (MFA), l. 182.
GARF.6991.3.88, n. 2148 (26 Aug. 1952), Pushkin (dep Minister, MFA)—Polyanski, l. 50, 50r.
GARF.6991.3.88, n. 38–116 (4 Sept 1952), Polyanski—Pushkin (MFA), l. 51.
GARF.6991.3.93, n. 23–124c (7 Aug. 1953), Polyanski—Pospelov (CC CPSU), l. 175.
GARF.6991.3.97, n. 1/16–358 (30 Jan. 1958), Mortin—Puzin, l. 1–2.
GARF.6991.3.97, n. 7–125 (3 Mar. 1953), Polyanski—Goglidze (Dep Minister, MGB), l. 23–24.
GARF.6991.3.102, n.1–121c (5 May 1954) Gostev—CC CPSU, Dept of Science and Culture, l. 65–69.
GARF.6991.3.102, n. 13–78c (6 Oct. 1954), Polyanski—CM USSR, l. 326–27.
GARF.6991.3.106, "Spravka on Addresses of Heads of Eparchies to the Holy Synod on Condition of Sects" (2 Mar. 1954), l. 13–20.
GARF.6991.3.113, n. 110c-2/11c (5 Feb. 1955), Polyanski and Karpov—CM USSR, l. 110–11.
GARF.6991.3.113, n. 265c and 25–115c (16 Apr. 1955), Karpov and Polyanski—CC CPSU, l. 131–33.
GARF.6991.3.114, n. 512 (28 Jun. 1955), "Notes for Report 1955," Polyanski—CC CPSU, l. 59–62, 73–80.
GARF.6991.3.115, no number (28 Dec. 1955), "Memorandum of Conversation," Mikoyan and Reding, l. 78–83.
GARF.6991.3.117, n. 27–113c (10 Aug. 1955), Polyanski—Zorin (Dep Minister, MFA), l. 151–56.
GARF.6991.3.125, n. 1/9–1518 (19 Jul. 1961), A. Krokin—Puzin, l. 5–7.
GARF.6991.3.129, n. 7–110c (7 Feb. 1956), Polyanski—CC CPSU, l. 27–29.
GARF.6991.3.129, n. 10–110c (27 Feb. 1956), Polyanski—Mikoyan (Chair CM USSR), l. 40–46.
GARF.6991.3.129, n. 19–110c (4 Apr. 1956), Polyanski—CC CPSU, l. 87–91.
GARF.6991.3.130, n. 47–110c (10 Sept. 1956), Gostev—CC CPSU, l. 51–52.
GARF.6991.3.130, n. 57–110c (26 Nov. 1956), Gostev—Agitprop Dept, CC CPSU, l. 78–79.
GARF.6991.3.135, n. 31–121c (28 Apr. 1956), Spravka, Archbishop Turs, l. 68–71.
GARF.6991.3.135, n. 45 (12 Nov. 1956), Veiderpass—Polyanski, l. 103–9.

GARF.6991.3.135, n. 57–121 (24 Dec. 1956), Gostev—Zorin (Dep Min, MFA), l. 110.
GARF.6991.3.135, n. 27c (4 Jul. 1956), Restberg—Polyanski, l. 200–5.
GARF.6991.3.143, n. 1c/16/2625 (12 Jun. 1956), Sakharovskii (Head, Main Directorate, KGB)—Polyanski, l. 16.
GARF.6991.3.143, n. 1c /3/3023 (4 May 1956), Sakharovskii (Head, Main Directorate, KGB)—Polyanski, l. 22–25.
GARF.6991.3.143, n. 1c/16/4695 (8 Oct. 1956), Sakharovskii (Head, Main Directorate, KGB)—Polyanski, l. 42–43.
GARF.6991.3.143, n. 8–115c (22 Nov. 1956), Klopichev (head secretary, CARC)—Cadre Dept., KGB, l. 89.
GARF.6991.3.146, n. 15–113c (31 May 1957), Spravka, Gostev—Konstantinov (CC, Dept of Agitprop), l. 102–3.
GARF.6991.3.146, n. 17–113c (4 Jul. 1957), Puzin—CC CPSU, l. 108–9.
GARF.6991.3.146, Evaluation of LWF, Prikhodko (CARC), l. 110.
GARF.6991.3.146, n. 27–113c (20 Sept. 1957), Puzin-Andropov (KGB), l. 162–81.
GARF.6991.3.147, n. 15–113c (31 May 1957), Gostev—Konstantinov (CC CPSU Agitprop Dept.), l. 90–91.
GARF.6991.3.148, n. 10–84c (2 Jun. 1958), Puzin—CC, l. 76–77.
GARF.6991.3.163, n.1Kr/16/4549 (23 Aug. 1957), Krokhin (KGB)—Puzin, l. 52.
GARF.6991.3.166, n. 35–84c (1 Dec. 1958), Puzin—CC/CPSU, l. 58–60.
GARF.6991.3.166, n. 11–84c (2 Jun. 1958) Puzin—CC/CPSU and Spravka "On International Relations of the Religious Organizations of the USSR," l. 78–79 and l. 80–83.
GARF.6991.3.166, n. 8–85c (16 May 1958), "Note on Facts of Activation of Religious Organizations," Puzin—CC/CPSU, l. 87–91.
GARF.6991.3.166, n. 7–85 (11 Jun. 1958), Puzin—CC/CPSU, l. 110.
GARF.6991.3.166, n. 289c-13/84c (14 Jun. 1958), Puzin and Cherednyak—CC/CPSU, l. 111–13.
GARF.6991.3.166, n. 16–84c/316c (3 Jul. 1958), Puzin/Cherednyak—CC/CPSU, l. 127–28.
GARF.6991.3.166, n. 22–84c (13 Aug. 1958), Puzin (CARC Chair)—CC/CPSU, l. 198.
GARF.6991.3.167, n. 23–84c (3 Sept. 1958), Puzin—CC/CPSU, l. 8.
GARF.6991.3.167, n. 27–84c (25 Sept. 1958), Report, "On Facts of Charlatanism and Use of Superstition of Believers by Clergy of Muslim Confession, Armenian and Catholic Churches," Ryazanov—CC/CPSU, l. 13–26.
GARF.6991.3.167, n. 31–84c (22 Oct. 1958), l. 40–42.
GARF.6991.3.167, n. 34–84c (14 Nov. 1958), Puzin—CC/CPSU, l. 43–47, 55–56.
GARF.6991.3.171, n. 241 (17 May 1958), Arutiniyan MFA—Puzin, l. 44–46.
GARF.6991.3.172, n. 148–89c (10 Oct. 1958), Puzin—MFA, l. 7–8.
GARF.6991.3.172, n. 511 (22 Dec. 1958), Medvedovskii—Puzin, l. 97–100.
GARF.6991.3.188, n. 5–85c/42c (19 Feb. 1959), Karpov (CROC) and Puzin (CARC)—CC/CPSU, l. 22–25.
GARF.6991.3.188, n. 1–90c (23 Feb. 1959), Puzin—Shelepin (Chair, KGB), cover to draft "On Measures Directed to Weaken the Influence on Believing Citizens of USSR of anti-Soviet Elements of Catholic Clergy and the Vatican," l. 26–42.
GARF.6991.3.188, n. 8–85c (13 Mar. 1959), Puzin—CC, CPSU, Final version "On Measures Directed ... Vatican," l. 47–56.
GARF.6991.3.188, n. 18–85c (14 May 1959), Note on Work of the CARC, Oct. 1958-May 1959, l. 82–92.

GARF.6991.3.188, n. 19–85c (23 May 1959), Puzin—CC/CPSU, l. 93–94.
GARF.6991.3.188, n. 29–58c (28 Aug. 1959), Puzin—CC/CPSU, l. 134.
GARF.6991.3.188, no number (24 Dec. 1959), Puzin—CC/CPSU, l. 190–93.
GARF.6991.3.189, n. 21–89c (20 Mar. 1959), Puzin—MFA, l. 28.
GARF.6991.3.189, n. 38–89c (8 May 1959), Puzin—MFA, l. 53–65.
GARF.6991.3.189, n. 61–89c (29 Jun. 1959), Puzin—MFA, l. 108.
GARF.6991.3.189, n. 87–89c (2 Oct. 1959), Ryazin—Zorin (MFA), l. 172–73.
GARF.6991.3.190, n. 722 (14 Oct. 1959), Puzhin (Dep Minister, MFA)—Puzin, l. 75.
GARF.6991.3.197, n. 1/16/77g (27 Feb. 1959), Makarev—Puzin, l. 2–3.
GARF.6991.3.197, n. 1/16/3942 (17 Aug. 1959), Kotov—Puzin, l. 27–29.
GARF.6991.3.197, n. 1/16/1644 (6 Apr. 1959), Sakharovskii (KGB)—Puzin, cover to "New Tendencies in Policy of Vatican," Vidyasov (6 Apr. 1959), l. 34–47.
GARF.6991.3.209, n. 12–84c (13 May 1960), Puzin—CC/CPSU, l. 46.
GARF.6991.3.209, n. 6–84c (18 May 1960), "Spravka," Baranova—CC/CPSU, l. 79.
GARF.6991.3.209, n. 26–84c (22 Sept 1960), Puzin—CC/CPSU, l. 134 and Spravka, "On Utilization of Foreign Activities of Religious Organizations of the USSR in the Interests of the Soviet State," l. 135–255.
GARF.6991.3.210, n. 32–84c (5 Dec. 1960), Puzin—CC/CPSU, l. 57–61.
GARF.6991.3.210, n. 34–84c (15 Dec. 1960), Ryazanov—Ilichev, l. 65–66.
GARF.6991.3.471, n. 13 (10 Mar. 1946), Šeškens—Polyanski, l. 4–6. "Spravka on Turs" (7 Mar. 1946), l. 12; "Autobiography of Šlosbergs," l. 13.
GARF.6991.3.471, n. 16 (5 Apr. 1946), "Informational Report 1st Quarter 1946," l. 30–33.
GARF.6991.3.471, no number (21 Jun. 1946), "On the Condition and Activity of Religious Confessions in Latvian SSR (August 1944–June 1946)," l. 158–71.
GARF.6991.3.471, n. 42c (15 Jan. 1947), Sadovski—Šeškens, l. 207–8.
GARF.6991.3.471, n. 482c (8 Jul. 1947), Polyanski—Šeškens, l. 233.
GARF.6991.3.471, no number (6 Nov. 1947) and (29 Mar. 1947), Springovičs—Šeškens, l. 243, 244.
GARF.6991.3.471, n. 6 (16 May 1947), Šeškens—Polyanski, l. 248.
GARF.6991.3.471, n. 8 (26 May 1947), Šeškens—Polyanski, l. 249.
GARF.6991.3.471, n. 636c (29 Aug. 1947), Polyanski—Šeškens, l. 264.
GARF.6991.3.472, no date, no number, Sadovski—Šeškens, l. 1.
GARF.6991.3.472, n. 105 (5 Jul. 1948), Polyanski—Šeškens, l. 121, 121r.
GARF.6991.3.472, n. 8c (10 Jun. 1948), Šeškens—Polyanski, l. 124–25.
GARF.6991.3.473, n. 283c (31 Mar. 1949), CM LSSR—Chairs, Executive Committees, l. 48.
GARF.6991.3.473, n. 12c (6 May 1949), Restberg—Polyanski, l. 59–60.
GARF.6991.3.473, n. 11–105c (29 Jul. 1949), Polyanski—Restberg, l. 67–68.
GARF.6991.3.473, n. 14–105c (16 Sept. 1949), Polyanski—Restberg, l. 96.
GARF.6991.3.473, n. 18c (19 Jul. 1949), l. 97–153.
GARF.6991.3.473, n. 19c (19 Jul. 1949), Restberg—Polyanski, l. 155–93.
GARF.6991.3. 473, no number (18 Apr. 1950), Karpov (CARC)—Polyanski, l. 268–69.
GARF.6991.3.473, "Report of Karpov (CARC) to Polyanski (18 Apr. 1950), with Notes of April 1, 1950 Meeting with Springovičs and Strods," l. 274–77.
GARF.6991.3.473, no number (24 Mar. 1950), "Short Overview of the Activity of Catholic Metropolitan Antonijs Springovičs," Restberg, l. 282–84.
GARF.6991.3.473, n. 11c (25 Apr. 1950), Restberg—Polyanski, l. 292–95.

GARF.6991.3.474, n. 5–102c (2 Mar. 1951), Polyanski—Restberg, l. 342.
GARF.6991.3.475, n. 12c (11 Apr. 1952), Restberg—Polyanski, l. 61–62.
GARF.6991.3.475, n. 13c (24 Apr. 1952), Restberg—Polyanski, l. 64–65.
GARF.6991.3.476, n. 5c (3 Feb. 1952), Restberg—Polyanski, l. 33.
GARF.6991.3.476, n. 10–118c (13 Mar. 1952), Polyanski—General Shtemenko (General Staff, Soviet Army), l. 42–43.
GARF.6991.3.476, n. YYCV/2/108983 (4 Apr. 1952), Shtemenko—Polyanski, l. 56.
GARF.6991.3.476, n. 1c (2 Jan. 1952), Restberg—Polyanski, l. 109–10.
GARF.6991.3.476, n. 1c Karpov (CARC) "On the Question of the Riga Seminary Raised by Met. Springovičs" (21 Feb. 1952), l. 115–16.
GARF.6991.3.476, n. 24c (23 Jul. 1952), Restberg—Polyanski, l. 143–44.
GARF.6991.3.476, n. 18–78c (22 Nov. 1952), Polyanski—Restberg, l. 187.
GARF.6991.3.476, n. 33c (24 Nov. 1952), Restberg—Polyanski, l. 194–95.
GARF.6991.3.476, n. 19–78c (16 Dec. 1952), Polyanski—Restberg, l. 269.
GARF.6991.3.478, n. 7c (19 Mar. 1954), Restberg—Polyanski, l. 212.
GARF.6991.3.479, no number (24 Aug. 1954), "Notes for Report on Business Trip to Riga," Koltsev (Dep. Dept. Head, CARC), l. 127–29.
GARF.6991.3.479, n. 12–78c (4 Sept. 1954), Polyanski—Restberg, l. 136.
GARF.6991.3.479, n. 20–78c (4 Sept. 1954), Polyanski—Kruzhkov (Head, Agitprop, CC CPSU), l. 140.
GARF.6991.3.479, n. 53c (9 Sept. 1954), Restberg—CARC, l. 166.
GARF.6991.3.479, n. 57c (24 Sept 1954), Restberg—Polyanski, l. 198.
GARF.6991.3.479, n. 73c (12 Nov. 1954), Restberg—Polyanski, l. 282–83.
GARF.6991.3.479, n. 79c (11 Dec. 1954), Vereshagin—Polyanski, l. 315–16.
GARF.6991.3.479, n. 80c (17 Dec. 1954), Vereshagin—Polyanski, l. 322–23.
GARF.6991.3.480, n. 3 (8 Jan. 1955), Vereshagin—Polyanski, l. 6, 11.
GARF.6991.3.480, n. 6 (15 Jan. 1955), Vereshagin—Polyanski, l. 18.
GARF.6991.3.480, n. 5–78c (13 Jan. 1955), Report Notes, Rumyantsev, l. 54–62.
GARF.6991.3.480, n. 10c (29 Jan. 1955), Vereshagin—Polyanski, l. 96.
GARF.6991.3.480, n. 2–78c (16 Feb. 1955), Gostev—Vereshagin, l. 112–13.
GARF.6991.3.481, n. 41c (17 Jun. 1955), Restberg—Polyanski, l. 115–18.
GARF.6991.3.482, n. 60c (7 Oct. 1955), Restberg—Polyanski, l. 12–14.
GARF.6991.3.482, n. 62c (18 Oct. 1955), Restberg—Polyanski, l. 15–18.
GARF.6991.3.483, n. 68c (6 Dec. 1955), Restberg—Polyanski, l. 50–54.
GARF.6991.3.484, n. 38c (29 Aug. 1956), Restberg—Polyanski, 30–38.
GARF.6991.3.484, n. 20 (8 Mar. 1957), Restberg—Gostev, l. 110.
GARF.6991.3.484, n. 22 (22 Mar. 1957), Restberg—Gostev, l. 133–39.
GARF.6991.3.486, n. 54 (Sept. 1957), Restberg—Puzin, l. 95–98.
GARF.6991.3.486, n. 63c (12 Nov. 1957), Restberg—Puzin, cover for Springovičs—Puzin (10 Nov. 1957), l. 144–48.
GARF.6991.3.1364, n. 11c (16 Jan. 1961), Puzin—CC/CPSU, l. 7.
GARF.6991.3.1364, n. 34 (14 Feb. 1961) Puzin—CC/CPSU, l. 25.
GARF.6991.3.1375, n. 1/9–1671 (9 Aug. 1961), Kotov-Puzin, l. 8–10.
GARF.6991.3.1389, n. 23–113c (8 Aug. 1957), Puzin—Lunev (Dep Chair, KGB), l. 153.
GARF.6991.3.1389, n. 27–113c (20 Sept. 1957), Puzin—Andropov (Head of Dept, CC/CPSU), l. 162–81.

GARF.6991.3.1394, n. 185c (20 Nov. 1962), Ryazanov—MFA, l. 73.
GARF.6991.3.1421, n. 197c (28 Sept. 1963), Ryazanov—State Committee on Publications, l. 78–79.
GARF.6991.3.1421, n. 1225c (5 Oct. 1963), Okhotnikov (State Committee on Publications)—Ryazanov, l. 83.
GARF.6991.3.1426, no number (21 Aug. 1962) Spravka, "On Process of Implementation," Rumyantsev, l. 100–2.
GARF.6991.3.1434, n. 15c (30 Jan. 1963), Notes, Puzin—Semichastny (Chair, KGB), l. 1–4.
GARF.6991.3.1577, no number, no date, Baranova (inspector, CARC)—Ryazanov, l. 4–8.

Russian State Archive of Socio-Political History (RGASPI)

RGASPI.17.117.449, Protocol N. 175 (27 Sept. 1944), "On the Organization of Mass Scientific-Enlightening Propaganda," Aleksandrov—Zhdanov and Malenkov, Central Committee Secretaries, l. 53–55, 60–62.
RGASPI.17.125.93. Agitprop 1942.
RGASPI.17.125.106, n. 5884 (4 Nov. 1942), I. Varbarus-Vares (Chair, Orgburo Union of Soviet Writers of Estonia)—Stalin, l. 109–10.
RGASPI.17.125.136, n. 9/491b (24 Nov. 1943), Secretaries Snieckius (Lithuania), Kalnberzins (Latvia), and Karotamm (Estonia)—Lozovskii (Sovinformburo), l. 146–49.
RGASPI.17.125.136, n. 24/359c (26 Nov. 1943), Karotamm (Estonia)—Lozovskii (Sovinformburo), l. 153–56.
RGASPI.17.125.235, n. 0310 (8 Sept. 1944), A. Lobachev (Head, Political Administration of Baltic Front)—Colonel Shcherbakov (Head, Main Political Administration, Red Army), l. 137–42.
RGASPI.17.125.407, Shepilov—Suslov (CC Secretariat), l. 134–35.
RGASPI.17.125.506, n. 458 (1 Jul. 1947), Polyanski—Aleksandrov, CC, l. 122.
RGASPI.17.125.506, Resolution of CM USSR, "On Directions to CARC regarding its Work in 1947," Attachment n. 1, l. 183.
RGASPI.17.132.109, n. 274c (18 Mar. 1949), Karpov—Shepilov (Agitprop CC/CPSU), l. 51–54.
RGASPI.17.132.109, n. 6/168c (8 Apr. 1949), Polyanski—Shepilov (Agitprop CC/CPSU), l. 57–58, 66.
RGASPI.17.132.110, no number, no date, "Proposed Resolution" and" Memo to Stalin," Agitprop Dept, CC/CPSU, l. 28, 30–31 and 35–36.
RGASPI.17.132.111, n. 11/168c (23 Apr. 1949), "Presentation Points," Polyanski—Malenkov (CC-CPSU), l. 54–55.
RGASPI.17.132.111, n. 243c (Mar. 1949), Karpov CROC—Voroshilov, l. 146–48.
RGASPI.17.132.285 (29 Dec. 1949), "Notes," Inspector Markov (CC/CPSU)—Suslov (CC/CPSU), l. 1–3.
RGASPI.17.132.285, n. 1–162c (14 Jan. 1950), Polyanski—Popov (Agitprop Dept, CC/CPSU), l. 5–6, with text of petition and signatures, l. 15–17.
RGASPI.17.132.285, n. 33–158c (7 Oct. 1950), Polyanski—Molotov (CM USSR), l. 188–89.
RGASPI.17.132.285, "Spravka, 24 Nov. 1950," Popov and Pokrovskii (Agitprop Department, CPSU), l. 190.
RGASPI.17.132.497, n.14–114c (24 Jun. 1952), "Report on Condition and Activity of Religious Cults in USSR in 1951," Polyanski—Suslov (CC/CPSU), l. 45–46.
RGASPI.17.132.497, n. 425c (6 Jun. 1951), Karpov (Chair, CROC)—Stalin, l. 113–19.

Bibliography | 235

RGASPI.17.132.509, n. 7c (3 Jan. 1952), Karpov (CROC)—Agitprop Dept, CC/CPSU, "Spravka on Pastor Martin Niemöller, Evangelical Lutheran Church of West Germany" l. 2–10.
RGASPI.17.132.509, n. 8–114c (5 Apr. 1952), Polyanski—Suslov, l. 88–94.
RGASPI.17.132.509, n. 738c (19 Jul. 1952), Karpov—Buro, Presidium CM USSR, l. 187–88.
RGASPI.17.132.509, n. 16–114c (24 Jun. 1952) Gostev (Dep Chair, CARC)—Bureau, Presidium, CM USSR, l. 213.
RGASPI.17.132.509, n. 817c (9 Aug. 1952), Karpov—Malenkov and Suslov, l. 214–18.
RGASPI.17.132, 509, "Memo," Furov (Dep. Dept Head, Agitprop)—Prokofiev (Controller, Party Control Commission), l. 219–23.
RGASPI.17.138.496, no number (23 Mar. 1951), D. Popov—Suslov (Secretariat, CC), l. 4.
RGASPI.606.4.16, Stenograph of Meeting-Seminar of Atheists in Baltics, 8–10 Sept. 1964, Address by K. Vimmsaare, l. 45–68.
RGASPI.606.4.189, "Preparation and Conduct of Holidays of Coming of Age, based on Experience in Kohle-Järve," Znanie, LSSR, Republic Council of Atheists (1965), l. 8–35.
RGASPI.606.4.189, "On the Work of Methods Council and the Model Case of Kohlte-Järve...1968," Soop, l. 98–106.
RGASPI.606.4.200.

Russian State Archive of Social-Political History (RGANI), former CPSU Central Committee Archive

RGANI.5.16.554, no number, Ilichev/Chernenko (Agitprop, CC)—CC/CPSU (16 Jun. 1959), l. 42.
RGANI.5.16.642, "Analytical Notes," Georgi Utkin (CROC) (24 Aug. 1955), with "Memo to the Files," V. Kruzhkov—CC/CPSU (Jun. 1954), l. 120–26.
RGANI.5.16.642, (19 Aug. 1953) "Analytical Notes," Georgi Utkin (CROC)—N.S. Khrushchev, CC CPSU, l. 140–41.
RGANI.5.16.642, (28 Aug. 1953), Tarasov and Furov—Khrushchev, l. 142.
RGANI.5.16.650, "On Major Inadequacy in the Condition of Scientific-Antireligious Propaganda," (27 Mar. 1954), V. Kruzhkov and A. Rumyantsev (Agitprop Dept.)—N.S. Khrushchev, l. 18–24.
RGANI.5.16.669, n. 339c (6 Mar. 1954), Karpov—CC/CPSU, l. 3–24.
RGANI.5.16.669, n. 708c, "Comments and Additions to the Draft Resolution of the Central Committee 'On Mistakes in the Conduct of Scientific-Atheistic Propaganda among the Population'," Karpov and Polyanski, l. 164–68.
RGANI.5.16.669, Memo, V. Kruzhkov and B. Pokrovskii—CC/CPSU, l. 215–18.
RGANI.5.16.705, n. 7–115c (11 Jan. 1955), Polyanski—CC/CPSU, l. 22–25.
RGANI.5.16.705, n. 45–115c (13 Aug. 1955), Polyanski—CC/CPSU and CC CP Byelorussia SSR, l. 89–91.
RGANI.5.16.705, n. 640/0c (16 Nov. 1955), CC-CP Byelorussia SSR—CC CPSU, l. 94–98.
RGANI.5.16.755, n. 248c (2 Jan. 1956), Bissenek CP LSSR—CC CPSU, l. 6–7.
RGANI.5.33.22, n. 1896c (1 Aug. 1956), I. Serov (Chair, KGB), l. 62–63.
RGANI.5.33.22, Resolution N. 44.1, Bureau CC CP Latvia (29 Oct. 1956), "On Measures to Improve Scientific-Atheistic Propaganda in the Republic," l. 64–68.
RGANI.5.33.23, no number (29 Sept. 1956), V. Snastin (Deputy Head of Agitprop) and K. Chernenko (Head of sector, Agitmass Work), l. 19–20.

RGANI.5.33.23, n. 1896c (1 Aug. 1956), Serov (Chair, KGB)—CC/CPSU, l. 62–63.
RGANI.5.33.53, n 109c (7 Feb. 1957), Karpov (Chair, CROC)—CC/CPSU, l. 16–20.
RGANI.5.33.53, "Memo to the Files" (15 Mar. 1957), V. Snastin and K. Chernenko (CC/CPSU), l. 22.
RGANI.5.33.54, "Memo," Koltsov (CARC Party Bureau)—CC/CPSU, l. 11–12.
RGANI.5.33.55, n. 475 (18 May 1957), "On Facts of Activization of Religious Organizations and Unregistered Groups of Believers," Prikhodko—CC/CPSU, l. 38–51.
RGANI.5.33.55, Resolution No. 9, Protocol n. 88 (5 Aug. 1957) of the Central Committee, CP Lithuania, l. 60.
RGANI.5.33.59, n. 149 (23 May 1958), Mitin/Znanie—CC/CPSU, l. 27–28.
RGANI.5.33.59, Snastin and Ilichev—CC/CPSU (17 Jun. 1958), l. 29.
RGANI.5.33.88, n. 2086c (12 Nov. 1958), Romanov/Glavlit—CC/CPSU, l. 73–84.
RGANI.5.33.90, n. 113 (25 Nov. 1957), Puzin—Chernenko, l. 103–4.
RGANI.5.33.91, n. 203c (23 Apr. 1958), Karpov—CC/CPSU, l. 32–34.
RGANI.5.33.91, n. 35–84c (1 Dec. 1958), Puzin—CC/CPSU, l. 161–63.
RGANI.5.33.92, n. 5–85c (19 Feb. 1959), Puzin and Karpov—CC/CPSU, l. 76–79.
RGANI.5.33.121, n. 1703 (14 Aug. 1959), Naidanov/Glavlit, "Note on Procedures for Control by Organs of Censorship of Literature Imported from Capitalist States," l. 122–30.
RGANI.5.33.126, n. 60c (21 Feb. 1959), Karpov—CC/CPSU, l. 22–24.
RGANI.5.33.126, n. 157 (7 Apr. 1959), Karpov—CC/CPSU, "Memorandum of Conversation, Patriarch Aleksei and Metropolitan Nikolai of 2 April 1959," l. 74–84.
RGANI.5.33.126, n. 1025 (18 Apr. 1959), Shelepin/KGB—CC/CPSU, l. 85–87.
RGANI.5.33.126, no number (12 Jun. 1959) "Spravka," Ilichev—CC/CPSU, l. 134.
RGANI.5.33.126, no number (31 Jul.1959) Snastin/Agitprop Dept.—Central Committee, l. 146–47.
RGANI.5.33.126, n. 372c (29 Jul. 1959), Cherednak/CROC—CC/CPSU, l. 187–91.
RGANI.5.33.126, n. 472c (29 Sept. 1959), Vasiliev/CROC—CC/CPSU, l. 223–26.
RGANI.5.33.162, n. 1c (3 Jan. 1960), Karpov—CC/CPSU, l. 1–4.
RGANI.5.33.162, n. 21–84c (2 Aug. 1960), Puzin—CC/CPSU and Spravka (30 Dec. 1960), Snastin/Morozov—CC/CPSU, l. 32–39.
RGANI.5.33.162, n. 571 (8 Jul. 1960), Ambassador Pervukhin—Andropov/CC/CPSU, l. 40–41.
RGANI.5.33.162, n. 26–84c (22 Sept. 1960), Spravka, "On Utilization of Foreign Activities of Religious Organizations of the USSR in the Interests of the Soviet State," Puzin—CC/CPSU, l. 51–80.
RGANI.5.33.190, n. 34c (20 Feb. 1961), Puzin—CC/CPSU and Snastin/Morozov, l. 48–51.
RGANI.5.33.190, n. 133c (3 Mar. 1961), Pelše/CPL—CC/CPSU, l. 71–74.
RGANI.5.33.190, n. 7c (21 Apr. 1961), Pelše—CC/CPSU, l. 105–7 and (15 Aug. 1961), Snastin/Morozov (Agitprop, CC CPSU), Note to the Files, l. 108.
RGANI.5.33.190, n. 85c (7 Jun. 1961), Kuroedov and Puzin—CC/CPSU, l. 112–16.
RGANI.5.33.215, n. 1380c (4 Jun. 1962), Semichastny (Chair, KGB)—CC/CPSU, l. 78–80.
RGANI.5.33.233, n. 197c (28 Jan. 1966), "Spravka on Foreign Religious Activities versus the USSR," Bannikov (Head, 2nd Main Administration, KGB)—CC/CPSU, l. 20–30.
RGANI.5.59.24, n. 836 (29 Dec. 1967), I. Sekin (Secretary of Karelia Obkom)—CC/CPSU, l. 147–48.
RGANI.5.60.24, n. 3004 (26 Dec. 1968), Kuroedov—CC/CPSU, l. 178–80.

RGANI.5.62.38, "Informational Report ...based on Materials of the CRA for 1969," Agitprop Dept., CC/CPSU, l. 118–20.
RGANI.5.63.89, n. 127ch (18 Jan. 1971), Chebrikov (KGB)—CC/CPSU, with attached "Spravka on Religious Conditions in the State," 5th Directorate, Seregin, l. 1–17.
RGANI.5.63.89, n. 91c (27 Apr. 1971), l. 99.
RGANI.5.80.24, n. 193ts (14 Aug. 1968), Tsvigun (Dep Chair, KGB)—CC/CPSU, l. 136–39.
RGANI.5.80.24, n. 169c (12 Nov. 1968), Kuroedov—CC/CPSU, l. 151–56.
RGANI.5.80.24, n. 2840 (28 Nov. 1968), Kuroedov—CC/CPSU, l. 173–74.
RGANI.5.80.24, n. 10912 (5 Mar. 1969), Tolstikov (Secretary, Lenobkom), l. 175–77.

Archive, Finnish National Committee of the LWF, Helsinki

WS/III. 2a, Letter, Bishop Aarre Lauha, Helsinki to LWF World Service Dept. (24 Aug. 1967).
GS III.1, Letter, Hark and Leepin (Consistory EELK) to Dr. Andre Appel, General Secretary LWF (1 Nov. 1967).
Letter, Launikari (Finnish Committee, LWF) to Karlheinz Schmale (25 Oct. 1985).
Letter, Launikari (Finnish Committee, LWF) to Theo Tschuy (WCC, Human Rights Program) (9 Dec. 1985).
Letter, Paul Wee (LWF) to Estonian CRA Commissioner Piip (7 Oct. 1985).

Published References

Altnurme, Riho. "Die Estnische Evangelisch-Lutherische Kirche in der Sowjetunion bis 1964." In *Estland, Lettland und Westliches Christentum*, 233–46. Edited by Siret Rutiku and Reinhart Staats. Kiel: Friedrich Wittig Verlag, 1998.
Altnurme, Riho. "Foreign Relations of the Estonian Evangelical Lutheran Church as a Means of Maintaining Contact with the Western World." *Kirchliche Zeitgeschichte* 19, no. 1 (2006): 159–65.
Altnurme, Riho. "The Form of Piety, the Theology and the Political Attitudes of the Clergy of the Estonian Evangelical Lutheran Church in the 1940s." In *Estonian Church History in the Past Millennium*, 157–65. Edited by Riho Altnurme. Kiel: Friedrich Wittig Verlag, 2001.
Altnurme, Riho. "Die Herrnhuter als Präger des Estnischen Kultur und ihr Schicksal im 20. Jahrhundert." In *Beiträge zur Ostdeutschen Kirchengeschichte* no. 8, 11–23. Edited by Peter Maser and Christian-Erdmann Schott. Münster: Ostkirchen Institut, 2007.
Altnurme, Riho, ed. *History of Estonian Ecumenism*. Tartu/Tallinn: Estonian Council of Churches, 2009.
Altnurme, Riho. "Die Lutherische Kirche Estlands 1945." In *Beiträge zur Ostdeutsche Kirchengeschichte* no. 8, 119–29. Edited by Peter Maser and Christian-Erdmann Schott. Muenster: Ostkirchen Institut, 2007.
Anderson, John. "The Archives of the Council of Religious Affairs." *Religion, State and Society* 20, no. 3-4 (1992): 399–404.
Anderson, John. "The Council for Religious Affairs and the Shaping of Soviet Religious Policy." *Soviet Studies* 43, no. 4 (1991): 689–710.
Anderson, John. *Religion, State and Politics in the Soviet Union and Successor States*. Cambridge: Cambridge University Press, 1994.

Anderson, John. "Soviet Religious Policy under Brezhnev and After." *Religion in Communist Lands* 11, no. 1 (1983): 25-30.
Anderson, John. "Twenty-Five Years of Science and Religion." *Religion in Communist Lands* 13, no. 1 (1985): 28-32.
Anusauskas, Arvydas, ed. *The Anti-Soviet Resistance in the Baltic States*. Vilnius: Akreta, 2001.
Aunver, Jakob. "Estlands Christliche Kirche der Gegenwart." *Acta Baltica* 1 (1960-1961): 75-92.
Aunver, Jakob. *Religious Life and the Church in Estonia*. Stockholm: Consistory of Estonian Ev.-Lutheran Church, 1961.
Aunver, Jakob. "Religious Life and the Church." In *Aspects of Estonian Culture*, 66-83. Edited by Evald Uustalu. London: Boreas, 1961.
Baron, Iozef. *Rossiiskoe Liuteranstvo. Istoriia, Teologiia, Aktual'nost*. St Petersburg: Aleteiia, 2011.
Benz, Ernst. "Schwieriger Neubeginn. Die Kirchen in den Baltischen Ländern nach der Wiederherstellung der Unabhängigkeit." *Acta Baltica* 33 (1995): 107-68.
Benz, Ernst. "Zur Lage der Kirchen in den Baltischen Ländern." *Kirche im Not* 37 (1989). Reprinted in *EPD Dokumentation* no. 22 (1990): 25-26.
Berzins, Janis. "Das Glaubenserbe für die Zukunft Bewahren." *Glaube in der 2. Welt* 16, no. 2 (1988): 16-17.
Bilmanis, Alfred. *Baltic Essays*. Washington, DC.: Latvian Legation, 1945.
Bilmanis, Alfred. *A History of Latvia*. Princeton: Princeton University Press, 1951.
Bilmanis, Alfred. *Latvia between Anvil and Hammer*. Washington, DC.: Latvian Legation, 1945.
Binns, Christopher. "Soviet Secular Ritual: Atheist Propaganda or Spiritual Consumerism?" *Religion in Communist Lands* 10, no. 3 (1982): 298-309.
Binns, Christopher. "Sowjetische Feste und Rituale." *Osteuropa* 29, no. 2 (February 1979): 110-21.
Bociurkiw, Bohdan. "Soviet Research on Religion and Atheism since 1945." *Religion in Communist Lands* 2, no. 1 (1974): 11-16.
Bourdeaux, Michael. *The Gospel's Triumph over Communism*. Minneapolis, MN: Bethany House, 1991.
Bourdeaux, Michael. *Land of Crosses. The Struggle for Religious Freedom in Lithuania, 1939-1978*. Chulmleigh, England: Augustine Press, 1979.
Bourdeaux, Michael. *Opium of the People*. New York: Bobbs-Merrill, 1966.
Central Committee of the Communist Party of Estonia, Department of Propaganda and Agitation. *Ideologiia i Praktika Sovremennogo Liuteranstva*. Tallinn: Znanie ESSR, 1987.
Chadwick, Owen. *The Christian Church in the Cold War*. London: Penguin, 1992.
Chumachenko, Tatiana. *Church and State in Soviet Russia: Russian Orthodoxy from World War II to the Khrushchev Years*. Edited and translated by Edward E. Roslof. Armonk, NY: M.E. Sharpe, 2002.
Corley, Felix. *Religion in the Soviet Union: An Archival Reader*. New York: New York University Press, 1996.
Cuibe, Leons. *The Lutheran Church of Latvia in Chains*. Stockholm: Oskars Sakarnis Latvian Reporter, 1963.

"Documents from Estonia on the Violation of Human Rights." In *Problems of the Baltic IV*, 3–72. Stockholm: Estonian Information Center, 1977.
Documents and Materials. Conference in Defence of Peace of All Churches and Religious Associations in the U.S.S.R., Troitse-Sergiyeva Monastery, Zagorsk, May 9–12, 1952. Moscow: Moscow Patriarchate, 1952.
Dubnaitis, Evalds. "Der totale Kampf gegen Religion und Geistlichkeit in den besetzten Baltischen Ländern." *Acta Baltica* 5 (1965): 127–99.
Duin, Edgar. *Lutheranism under the Tsars and the Soviets*. Ann Arbor, MI: University Microfilms, 1975.
Duin, Edgar. "Soviet Lutheranism after the Second World War." *Religion in Communist Lands* 8, no. 2 (1980): 11–18.
Dunn, Dennis. *The Catholic Church and Russia: Popes, Patriarchs, Tsars and Commissars*. Burlington, VT: Ashgate, 2004.
Durasoff, Steve. *The Russian Protestants*. Rutherford, NJ: Fairleigh Dickinson Press, 1969.
Elliott, Mark. "Methodism in the Soviet Union since World War II." In *Methodism in Russia and the Baltic States*, 151–66. Edited by S.T. Kimbrough. Nashville: Abingdon Press, 1995.
Elliott, Mark, and Sharyl Corrado. "The Protestant Missionary Presence in the former Soviet Union." *Religion, State and Society* 25, no. 4 (1997): 333–51.
Ellis, Jane. "New Soviet Thinking on Religion." *Religion in Communist Lands* 17, no. 2 (1989), 100–111.
Ellis, Jane. *The Russian Orthodox Church: A Contemporary History*. Bloomington: Indiana University Press, 1986.
"Fakten und Zahlen aus der Estnischen SSR." *Osteuropa* 21, no. 3 (1971), 196.
Felmy, Karl-Christian, et al. "Chronik." *Kirche im Osten* 11 (1968): 134.
Fletcher, William C. *Religion and Soviet Foreign Policy 1945–1970*. London: Oxford University Press, 1973.
Fletcher, William C., and D. A. Lawrie. "Khrushchev's Religious Policy, 1959–1964." In *Aspects of Religion in the Soviet Union, 1917–1967*, 131–56. Edited by Richard H. Marshall et al. Chicago: University of Chicago Press, 1971.
Fortin, Robert J. *The Catholic Chaplaincy in Moscow: A Short History, 1934–1999*. Brighton, MA: Augustinians of the Assumption, 2004. http://assumption.us/about-us/47-virtuallibrary/552-the-catholic-chaplaincy-in-moscow.
Freeze, Gregory. "Counter-Reformation in Russian Orthodoxy: Popular Response to Religious Innovation, 1922–1925." *Slavic Review* 54, no. 2: 305–39.
Glaube in der 2. Welt v. 17, n. 10 (1989): 7.
Glaube in der 2. Welt v. 17, n. 11 (1989): 5.
Grassman, Walter. "Geschichte der Evangelisch-Lutherischen Rußlanddeutschen in der Sowjetunion, der GUS und in Deutschland in der Zweiten Hälfte des 20. Jahrhunderts. Gemeinde, Kirche, Sprache und Tradition." PhD diss., Universität München, 2006.
Hark, Edgar. *The Estonian Evangelical Lutheran Church Today*. Tallinn: Perioodika, 1982.
Hart, Andrew. "Role of the Lutheran Church in Estonian Nationalism." *Religion in Eastern Europe* 13, no. 3 (June 1993): 6–13.
Hebly, J. A. *The Russians and the World Council of Churches: Documentary Survey of the Accession of the Russian Orthodox Church to the World Council of Churches*. Belfast: Christian Journals, 1978.

Hebly, J. A. "The State, the Church and the Oikumene: The Russian Orthodox Church and the World Council of Churches, 1948–1985." In *Religious Policy in the Soviet Union*, 105-24. Edited by Sabrina Ramet. New York: Cambridge University Press, 1993.
Hoffmann, Martin, et al. "Chronik." *Kirche im Osten* 12 (1969): 123.
Husband, William. *Godless Communists: Atheism and Society in Soviet Russia, 1917–1932*. DeKalb: Northern Illinois Press, 2000.
"An Interview with the New Latvian Cardinal." *Religion in Communist Lands* 11, no. 2 (1983): 207-9.
Jürjo, Indrek. *Pagulus ja Noukogude Eesti: Vaateid KGB, EKP za VEKSA arhiividokumentide pohjal*. Tallinn: Umara, 1996.
Johnston, Hank. "Religion and Nationalist Subcultures in the Baltics." *Journal of Baltic Studies* 23, no. 2 (1992): 133-48.
Kahle, Wilhelm. "Baltic Protestantism." *Religion in Communist Lands* 7, no. 4 (1979): 220-25.
Kahle, Wilhelm. "Die Orthodoxie im Baltischen Raum." *Kirche im Osten* 21-22 (1978-79): 78-107.
Keston News Service n. 284 (24 Sept. 1987) and n. 288 (19 Nov. 1987).
Ketola, Mikko. *The Nationality Question in the Estonian Evangelical-Lutheran Church, 1918–1939*. Helsinki: Kirkkohistorallinen Seura, 2000.
Ketola, Mikko. "Relations between the Estonian and the Finnish Lutheran Churches in the 20th Century." In *Estonian Church History in the Past Millennium*, 138-42. Edited by Riho Altnurme. Kiel: Wittig Verlag, 2001.
Ketola, Mikko. "Some Aspects of the Nationality Question in the Lutheran Church of Estonia, 1918–1939." *Religion, State and Society* 27, no. 2 (June 1999): 239-44.
Kiivit, Jaan. "Ruckkehr aus dem Schweigen." In *Lutherische Kirche in der Welt: Jahrbuch des Martin-Luther-Bundes* 38 (1991): 99-118.
Kimbrough, S. T., ed. *Methodism in Russia and the Baltic States*. Nashville: Abingdon, 1995.
Kiviorg, Merilin. *Religion and Law in Estonia*. Alphen aan den Rijn, The Netherlands: Kluwer, 2011.
Kowalewski, David. "Dissent in the Baltic Republics: Characteristics and Consequences." *Journal of Baltic Studies* 10, no. 4 (1979): 309-19.
Krumina-Konkova, Solveiga. "Collaboration between the LSSR KGB and the Representative of the Council for the Affairs of Religious Cults of the USSR in the LSSR (1944–1954)." In *Totalitārisma Sabiedrības Kontrole un Represijas. VDK Zinātniskās Izpētes Komisijas Raksti. 1. Sējums*. Rīga: LPSR Valsts drošības komitejas zinātniskās izpētes komisija, Latvijas Universitātes Latvijas vēstures institūts, 2015.
Kulturpolitische Korrespondenz no. 488 (September 5, 1982).
Laar, Mart. *War in the Woods: Estonia's Struggle for Survival, 1944–1956*. Washington: The Compass Press, 1992.
Lane, Christel. *Christian Religion in the Soviet Union: A Sociological Study*. London: Allen, Unwin, 1978.
"Latvians Defend Dismissed Pastor," *Religion in Communist Lands* 15, no. 3 (1987): 340-45.
Levits, Egil. "Der politische Aufbruch in den Baltischen Staaten." *Europa-Archiv* 13 (1989): 403-12.
Lieburg, Burchard. "Aus dem Leben der Evangelisch-Lutherischen Kirche Estlands." *Kirche im Osten* 33 (1990): 124-28.
Lieburg, Burchard. "Aus dem Leben der Evangelisch-Lutherischen Kirche Estlands." *Kirche im Osten* 34 (1991): 101-5.

Lieberg, Burchard. "Aus der Estnischen Evangelisch-Lutherischen Kirche." *Kirche im Osten* 24 (1981): 106-8.
Lieberg, Burchard. "Aus der Evangelisch-Lutherischen Kirche Estlands." *Kirche im Osten* 30 (1987): 61-63 and 31 (1988): 86-88.
Liemets, Ants. "Propovednichestkaia Deiatel'nost Kak Osnovnoe Stredstvo Religioznogo Vozdeistviia." In *Ideologiia i Praktika Sovremennogo L'iuteranstva*, 33-37. Edited by G. Girich. Tallinn: Znanie ESSR, 1987.
Loeber, Dietrich. "Administration of Culture in Soviet Latvia." In *Res Baltica*, 133-45. Edited by Adolf Spruds and Armins Rusis. Leyden: A.W. Sijthoff, 1968.
Luchterhandt, Otto. "The Council on Religious Affairs." In *Religious Policy in the Soviet Union*, 55-83. Edited by Sabrina Ramet. New York: Cambridge University Press, 1993.
Luchterhandt, Otto. *Die Religionsgesetzgebung der Sowjetunion*. Berlin: Berlin Verlag, 1978.
Lutheran World Federation. *Informationsdienst für Lutherische Minderheitskirche* n. 6/7 (1988): 12-13.
Lutheran World Federation, *Informationsdienst für Lutherische Minderheitskirchen* n. 5 (1989): 14-16.
Lutheran World Federation, *Informationsdienst für Lutherische Minderheitskirchen* n. 1 (1991): 3-5.
"Lutheraner in der Sowjetunion." *Glaube in der 2. Welt* 9, no. 7/8 (1981): 255-326.
Luukkanen, Arto. *The Religious Policy of the Stalinist State: A Case Study, the Central Standing Commission on Religious Questions, 1929-1938*. Helsinki: Finnish Historical Society, 1997.
Malkavarra, Mikko. "The Dispute between the Estonian Evangelical Lutheran Church and the Estonian Lutheran Church in Exile Concerning Lutheran World Federation Membership 1947-1963." In *Estonian Church History in the Past Millennium*, 166-86. Edited by Riho Altnurme. Kiel: Wittig Verlag, 2001.
Mankusa, Zanda. "Over the Iron Curtain: The Evangelical Lutheran Church of Latvia Meets the West." *Journal of Baltic Studies* 37, no. 3 (2006): 313-35.
Markert, Siegfried. *Die Evangelische Kirchen Osteuropas: Wende in der Gesellschaft. Wende für die Kirchen?* Erlangen: Martin-Luther-Bund, 1989.
Martin, Terry. *The Affirmative Action Empire: Nations and Nationalism in the Soviet Union, 1923-1939*. Ithaca: Cornell University Press, 2001.
Matchett, Kathleen. "German Lutherans in the Soviet Union." *Religion in Communist Lands* 1, no. 6 (1973): 13-17.
Melton, J. Gordon. *Encyclopedia of Protestantism*. New York: Facts on File, 2005.
Melton, J. Gordon, and Martin Bauman, eds. *Religions of the World: A Comprehensive Encyclopedia of Beliefs and Practices*. 2nd ed. Santa Barbara, CA: ABC-CLIO, 2010.
Misiunas, Ronald J., and Rein Taagepera. *The Baltic States: Years of Dependence, 1940-1980*. Berkeley: University of California Press, 1983.
Misiunas, Ronald J., and Rein Taagepera. "The Baltic States: Years of Dependence, 1980-1986." *Journal of Baltic Studies* 20, no. 1 (1989): 65-88.
National Committee for a Free Europe. *Religious Persecution in the Baltic Countries, 1940-1952*. New York: National Committee for a Free Europe, 1952.
Neumärker, Dorothea. "In Memoriam Jaan Kiivit." *Kirche im Osten* 15 (1972): 163-72.
Oras, Ants. *Baltic Eclipse*. London: Victor Gollancz Ltd, 1948.

Pähn, Elmar. "Martyrdom of the Churches under the Soviet Regime." In *Estonia Christiana*, 287–301. Wetteren, Belgium: Cultura Press, 1965.
Pajasoo, Toomas, ed. *Heroes of the Cross: Twentieth Century Men of Faith of the Methodist Church in Estonia*. Tallinn: Estonian Methodist Church, 2007.
Paul, Toomas. "Die Begegnung der Evangelisch-Lutherischen Kirche Estland mit dem neuen Zeitalter." In *Lutherische Kirche in der Welt. Jahrbuch des Martin-Luther-Bundes* 41 (1994): 206–14.
"Perestrojka in der Lutherische Kirche (Lettland)." *Glaube in der 2. Welt* 17, no. 5 (1989): 11.
Peris, Daniel. *Storming the Heavens: The Soviet League of Militant Godless*. Ithaca: Cornell University Press, 1998.
Perlitz, H. "The Fate of Religion and Church under Soviet Rule in Estonia in 1940–1941." In *The Church in Estonia*, 29–56. Edited by August Torma. New York: World Association of Estonians, 1944.
Pilli, Toivo. *Dance or Die: The Shaping of Estonian Baptist Identity under Communism*. Milton Keynes, U.K.: Paternoster, 2008.
Pilli, Toivo. "Union of Evangelical Christians and Baptists of Estonia, 1945–1989." *Journal of European Baptist Studies* 1, no. 2 (January 2001): 31–50.
Plaat, Jaanus. "Religious Change in Estonia and the Baltic States during the Soviet Period in Comparative Perspective." *Journal of Baltic Studies* 31, n. 4 (2003): 52–73.
Plakans, Andrejs. "Democratization and Political Participation in Post-Communist Societies: The Case of Latvia." In *The Consolidation of Democracy in East Central Europe*, 245–89. Edited by Karen Dawisha and Bruce Parrott. New York: Cambridge University Press, 1997.
Plakans, Andrejs. *The Latvians: A Short History*. Stanford: Hoover Institution Press, 1995.
Pospielovsky, Dimitry. "The 'Best Years' of Stalin's Church Policy (1942–1948) in the Light of Archival Documents." *Religion, State and Society* 25, no. 2 (1997): 139–62.
Pospielovsky, Dimitry. *A History of Marxist-Leninist Atheism and Soviet Antireligious Policies*. New York: St. Martin's Press, 1987.
Pospielovsky, Dimitry. *The Russian Church under the Soviet Regime, 1917–1982*. Crestwood, NY: St. Vladimir's Seminary Press, 1984.
Pospielovsky, Dimitry. *Soviet Antireligious Campaigns and Persecutions*. New York: St. Martin's Press, 1988.
Powell, David. *Antireligious Propaganda in the Soviet Union*. Cambridge, MA: MIT Press, 1975.
Prigge, William D. "The Strange Death of Latvian National Communism." In *From Recognition to Restoration. Latvia's History as a Nation-State*, 77–98. Edited by David J. Smith et al. Amsterdam: Rodopi, 2010.
Radio Free Europe/Radio Liberty. "Situation Report" no. 4 (23 April 1985): 13–14, n. 6 (26 July 1985): 9–23, and no. 9 (27 Nov. 1985): 7–8.
Radio Free Europe/Radio Liberty. "Situation Report" no. 4 (18 July 1986): 5–6.
Radio Free Europe/Radio Liberty. "Situation Report" no. 5 (17 July 1987): 9–10.
Radio Free Europe/Radio Liberty. "Situation Report" no. 13 (22 Nov. 1988): 27–28.
Radio Free Europe/Radio Liberty. "Situation Report" no. 4 (21 April 1989): 15–18.
Radio Free Europe/Radio Liberty. "Daily Report" n. 106 (5 June 1990): 3, and n. 125 (3 July 1990): 3.
Ramet, Sabrina. *Religious Policy in the Soviet Union*. New York: Cambridge University Press, 1993.

Raud, Villem. *Developments in Estonia, 1939–1941.* 2nd ed. Tallinn: Perioodika, 1987.
Raun, Toivo. "Democratization and Political Development in Estonia, 1987–1996." In *The Consolidation of Democracy in East Central Europe,* 344–74. Edited by Karen Dawisha and Bruce Parrott. New York: Cambridge University Press, 1997.
Remmel, Atko. "Ambiguous Atheism: The Impact of Political Changes on the Meaning and Reception of Atheism in Estonia." In *Annual Review of the Sociology of Religion: Sociology of Atheism* 7, 233–50. Leiden: Brill, 2016.
Remmel, Atko. "(Anti)-Religious Aspects of the Cold War: Soviet Religious Policy as Applied in the Estonian SSR." In *Behind the Iron Curtain. Soviet Estonia in the Era of the Cold War,* 359–92. Edited by Tõnu Tannberg. Frankfurt: Peter Lang, 2015.
Remmel, Atko. "Believers, Human Rights, and Freedom of Speech in Soviet Estonia." *Tuna* 3 (2013): 65–81.
Remmel, Atko. "Religioonivastane Võitlus Eesti NSV-s aastail 1957–1990: Tähtsamad Institutsioonid ja nende Tegevus" [Antireligious Struggle in Estonian SSR in 1957–1990: Main Institutions and their Activities]. Diss., University of Tartu, 2011.
Remmel, Atko, and Marko Uibu, "Outside Conventional Forms: Religion and Non-Religion in Estonia," *Religion and Society in Central and Eastern Europe* 8, no. 1 (2015): 5–20.
Report of the Sufferings of the Christian Churches in Latvia during 1940–1943. New York: Drauga Vests, 1944.
Ritsbek, Heigo. "Methodism in Estonia under Communism." In *Methodism in Russia and the Baltic States,* 145–50. Edited by S. T. Kimbrough. Nashville: Abingdon, 1995.
Rohtmets, Priit, and Ringo Ringvee. "Religious Revival and the Political Activity of Religious Communities in Estonia during the Process of Liberation and the Collapse of the Soviet Union, 1985–1991." *Religion, State and Society* 41, no. 4 (December 2013): 355–93.
Roslof, Edward. *Red Priests: Renovationism, Russian Orthodoxy, and Revolution, 1905–1946.* Bloomington: Indiana University Press, 2002.
Rozitis, Elmars. "Aus der Evangelisch-Lutherischen Kirche Lettlands." *Kirche im Osten* 28 (1985): 80–81; 31 (1988): 88–89; 32 (1989): 122–27; 33 (1990): 128–33.
Rozitis, Elmars. "Die Evangelisch-Lutherische Kirche Lettlands unter der Herrschaft der bolschewistischen Okkupationsmacht." *Acta Baltica* 1 (1960–1961): 110–19.
Rozitis, Elmars. "Die gesellschaftliche Entwicklung der Sowjetunion." *Osteuropa* 34, no. 10 (October 1984): 786.
Rozkalns, Janis. "Perestrojka in der Evangelischen Kirche Lettlands? Zur Amtsenthebung von Propst Modris Plate." *Glaube in der 2. Welt* 15, no. 7/8 (1987): 16–17.
Rubenis, Juris. "Which Way to Church?" *Religion in Communist Lands* 17, no. 1 (1989): 81–86.
Rukis, Karlis. "Die Verfolgung der Katholischen Kirche in Sowjetlettland." *Acta Baltica* 1 (1960–1961): 93–109.
Salo, Vello. "Antireligious Rites in Estonia." *Religion in Communist Lands* 1, no. 4–5 (1973): 28–33.
Salo, Vello. "The Catholic Church in Estonia, 1918–2001." *Catholic Historical Review* 88, no. 2 (April 2002): 281–92.
Salo, Vello. "The Struggle between the State and the Churches." In *A Case Study of a Soviet Republic: the Estonian SSR,* 191–222. Edited by Tonu Parming and Elmar Järvesoo. Boulder, CO: Westview, 1978.
Salum, Vello. *The Church and the People.* Stockholm: Repro Print AB, 1981.

Salumäe, Tiit. "Comment: The Estonian Church as Champion of National Consciousness." In Lutheran World Federation, *Lutheran World Information* no. 10/91 (21 March 1991): 15–16.
Sapiets, Marite. "The Anniversaries of Christianity in the Baltic Republics." *Religion in Communist Lands* 15, no. 2 (1987): 200–3.
Sapiets, Marite. "Monasticism in the Soviet Union." *Religion in Communist Lands* 4, no. 1 (1976): 28–34.
Sapiets, Marite. "Rebirth and Renewal in the Latvian Lutheran Church." *Religion in Communist Lands* 16, no. 3 (1988): 237–49.
Sawatsky, Walter. *Soviet Evangelicals since World War II*. Eugene, OR: Wipf and Stock, 2007.
"Secret Instructions on the Supervision of Parish Life." *Religion in Communist Lands* 1, no. 1 (1973): 30–33.
Seide, Gernot. "Religiöse Renaissance in der Sowjetunion—Mythos oder Wirklichkeit?" *Osteuropa* 34, no. 111/112 (Nov/Dec 1984): 910–20.
Shkarovski, Mikhail V. "The Russian Orthodox Church in 1958–1964." *Russian Studies in History* 50, no. 3: 71–95.
Shkarovski, Mikhail V. "The Russian Orthodox Church versus the State: the Josephite Movement, 1927–1940." *Slavic Review* 54, no. 2 (Summer 1995): 365–84.
Silde, Adolfs. *Resistance Movement in Latvia*. Stockholm: Latvian National Foundation, 1972.
Simon, Gerhard. *Church, State and Opposition in the USSR*. Translated by Kathleen Matchett. London: C. Hurst, 1974.
Simon, Gerhard. "Nationalitätenprobleme und die Regierbarkeit der Sowjetunion." *Osteuropa* 34, no.10 (Oct. 1984): 759–68.
Simons, Greg, and David Westerlund. *Religion, Politics and Nation-Building in Post-Communist Countries*. London: Routledge, 2015.
Solchanyk, Roman, and Ivan Hvit. "Catholicism in the Soviet Union." In *Catholicism and Politics in Communist Societies*, 49–92. Edited by Sabrina Ramet. Durham, NC: Duke University Press, 1990.
Soloviev, Erikh. *Nepobezhdennii eretik: Martin L'iuter i ego vremiia*. [An Invincible Heretic: Martin Luther and His Epoch]. Moscow: Molodaya Guardiya, 1984.
Sõtšov, Andrei. "The Ecumenical and Patriotic Activity of the Estonian Eparchy in the Context of Soviet Politics of Religion in 1954–1964." *Politics and Religion* 5, no. 1 (2011): 36–52.
Staffa, Ernst. "Religion im historischen Materialismus in Sowjetrussland und in den Baltischen Laendern." *Acta Baltica* 10 (1970): 9–120.
Stehle, Hansjakob. *The Eastern Politics of the Vatican, 1917–1979*. Athens, OH: Ohio University Press, 1981.
Stricker, Gerd. "German Protestants in Tsarist Russia and the Soviet Union." *Religion in Communist Lands* 15, no. 1 (1987): 30–53.
Stricker, Gerd. "A Visit to German Congregations in Central Asia." *Religion in Communist Lands* 17, no. 1 (1989): 19–33.
Strods, Heinrihs. "The Roman Catholic Church of Latvia and the Resistance Movement (1944–1990)." In *The Anti-Soviet Resistance in the Baltic States*, 174–81. 3rd ed. Edited by Arvydas Anusauskas. Vilnius: Akreta, 2001.
"Students at Riga Seminary." *Religion in Communist Lands* 16, no. 4 (1988): 358–59.
Taagepera, Rein. "Citizens' Peace Movement in the Soviet Baltic Republics." *Journal of Peace Research* 23, no. 2 (1986): 183–92.

Taagepera, Rein. "Estonia in September 1988: Stalinists, Centrists and Restorationists." *Journal of Baltic Studies* 20, no. 2 (1989): 175–90.
Taivans, Leons G. "Reflections in the 'Invisible' Religion of Youth: The Case of Latvia." *Occasional Papers on Religion in Eastern Europe* 17, no. 6 (1997), Article 3. http://digitalcommons.georgefox.edu/ree/vol17/iss6/3.
Talonen, Jouko. *Church under the Pressure of Stalinism: The Development of the Status and Activities of the Soviet Latvian Evangelical-Lutheran Church during 1944–1950.* Oulu, Finland: Historical Society of Northern Finland, 1997.
Talonen, Jouko. "Herrnhut and the Baltic Countries from 1730 to the Present: Cultural Perspectives." In *Estonian Church History in the Past Millennium*, 98–109. Edited by Riho Altnurme. Kiel: Friedrich Wittig Verlag, 2001.
Torma, A., and H. Perlitz. *The Church in Estonia*. New York: World Association of Estonians, 1944.
Trups-Trops, Heinrich. "Die Römisch-Katholische Kirche Lettlands in den Jahren des Kommunismus (1940–1990)," Teil 1. *Acta Baltica* 29/30 (1991/92): 75–97.
Trups-Trops, Heinrich. "Die Römisch-Katholische Kirche Lettlands in den Jahren des Kommunismus (1940–1990)," Teil 2. *Acta Baltica* 31 (1993): 77–131.
Trups-Trops, Heinrich. "Die Römisch-Katholische Kirche Lettlands in den Jahren des Kommunismus (1940–1990)," Teil 3. *Acta Baltica* 32 (1994): 51–109.
Urdze, Andrejs. "Nationalism and Internationalism: Ideological Background and Concrete Forms of Expression in the Latvian SSR." *Journal of Baltic Studies* 19, no. 3 (1988): 185–96.
Vahter, Leonhard. "Aspects of Life in Estonia (3): Religious Persecution." *Baltic Review* no. 28 (December 1964): 44–45.
Vardys, V. Stanley. *The Catholic Church, Dissent, and Nationality in Soviet Lithuania.* New York: Columbia University Press, 1978.
Vardys, V. Stanley. "The Role of the Churches in the Maintenance of Regional and National Identity in the Baltic Republics." *Journal of Baltic Studies* 18, no. 3 (1987): 287–300.
Veem, Konrad. "Estnische Evangelisch-Lutherische Kirche." *Acta Baltica* 17 (1977): 92–113.
Veinbergs, Alexander. "Lutheranism and other Denominations in the Baltic Republics." In *Aspects of Religion in the Soviet Union, 1917–1967*, 405–20. Edited by Richard H. Marshall et al. Chicago: University of Chicago Press, 1971.
Viise, Michael Gustav. "The Estonian Evangelical-Lutheran Church during the Soviet Period, 1940–1991." PhD diss., University of Virginia, 1995.
Vimmsaare, Kuulo. *Luterlus enne ja Nuud.* Tallinn: Eesti Raamat, 1969.
Vimmsaare, Kuulo. "O Religioznoi Ideologii sovremennoi L'iuteranskoi Tserkvi." In *Kritika religioznoi Ideologii.* Edited by Pavel N. Gapochka. Moscow: Academiia Obshchestvennikh Nauk, 1961.
Vimmsaare, Kuulo. *Religioon ja Kirik Eestis.* Tallinn: Eesti Raamat, 1978.
Vimmsaare, Kuulo. *Sovremennoe L'iuteranstvo.* Tallinn: Znanie, 1985.
Vimmsaare, Kuulo. "Sovremennoe Sostoianie Evangelichestko-L'iuteranskoi Tserkvi v Estonskoi SSR." In *Ideologiia I Praktika Sovremennogo L'iuteranstva*, 5–11. Edited by G. Girich. Tallinn: Znanie ESSR, 1987.
Voobus, Arthur. *The Department of Theology at the University of Tartu.* Stockholm: Estonian Theological Society in Exile, 1963.
Voobus, Arthur. *Studies in the History of the Estonian People.* Vol. 7. Stockholm: Estonian Theological Society in Exile, 1978.

Walters, Phillip, ed. *World Christianity: Eastern Europe*. Monrovia, CA: Missions Advanced Research and Communication Center, 1988.
Warhola, James. "Central vs. Local Authority in Soviet Religious Affairs, 1964–1989." *Journal of Church and State* 34, no. 1 (Winter 1992): 15–38.
Weiss, Helmut. "Die Baltische Staaten." In *Die Sowjetisierung Ost-Mitteleuropas*, 21–64. Edited by Ernst Birke et al. Frankfurt: Alfred Metzner, 1959.
Young, Glennys. *Power and the Sacred in Revolutionary Russia*. University Park, PA: Penn State University Press, 1997.
Zagaris, E. *Socialist Transformations in Latvia, 1940–1941*. Riga: Zinatne, 1978.

Interviews

Johannes Baumann, Evangelical Church in Germany, Aug. 1990.
Willi Ehotamm, former director, AgitProp, CPE, Feb. 1991.
Robert Feldmanis, theology professor, Latvia, April 1991.
Karlis Gailitis, late Archbishop, ELCL, April 1991.
Illar Hallaste, pastor EELC, and Estonian CDU leader, 21 Jan. 1991.
Voldear Ilja, pastor EELC, and church historian, Feb. 1991
Villo Jürjo, pastor EELC, and Estonian CDU leader, Feb. 1991.
Peeter Kaldur, pastor EELC, and theology professor, 29 Jan. 1991.
Harald Kalnins, late Bishop of ELKRAS, Latvia, April 1991.
Jaan Kiivit, Jr., late Archbishop EELC, 7 Feb. 1991.
Riina Kionka, RFE/RL, 30 Aug. 1990.
Visvaldis Klive, theology professor, Latvia, April 1991.
Georg Kretschmar, theology professor, Archbishop of ELKRAS, Aug. 1990.
Alfreds Kublinskis, former director, Department of Religious Affairs, Latvia, April 1991.
George Landberg, pastor, Estonian Methodist Church, Mar. 1991.
Siegfried Markert, referent, EKD, Aug. 1990.
Eriks Mesters, former Archbishop, ELCL, Riga, April 1991.
Tiit Pädam, former General Secretary, Consistory, EELC, Feb. 1991.
Kuno Pajula, late Archbishop EELC, 31 Jan. 1991.
Toomas Paul, pastor EELC, and theology professor, 26 Jan. 1991.
Modris Plāte, pastor ELCL, and theology professor, April 1991.
Rein Ristlaan, former CRA Commissioner, ESSR, 11 Mar. 1991.
Elmars Rozitis, Bishop emeritus, Latvian Evangelical Lutheran Church Abroad, 31 Aug. 1990.
Juris Rubenis, pastor ELCL, and theology professor, April 1991.
Leons Taiwans, pastor ELCL, and theology professor, 15 Oct. 1990.
Janis Timpa, former deputy director, Department of Religious Affairs, Latvia, April 1991.
Andra Veideman, former director, Office of Religious Affairs, Estonia, Feb. 1991.
Janis Vejs, Institute of Philosophy and Sociology, researcher in scientific atheism, Latvia, April 1991.
Kuulo Vimmsaare, professor, former member of Institute of Atheism, Academy of Social Sciences of CPSU (Vilnius branch) and researcher in scientific atheism, Estonia, 30 Jan. 1991.

Index

Adenauer, Konrad, 92, 123
Aizsargov, 55
Akmentins, Roberts, 183
Aleksei I, Patriarch, 60, 61, 97, 133n47
antireligious campaign, 2, 3, 34, 78, 79, 129, 130, 160, 179, 201–202; administrative measures, 56–57, 66, 105n99, 118; atheistic propaganda, 9, 21, 24, 28, 35, 37n29, 49, 67, 84, 90–91, 98, 106n105, 106n106, 109, 110, 120, 147–148, 162, 165n30, 172, 173, 175, 201, 202, 204; church response to, 42n126, 59, 91, 99, 105nn100–103, 106n103, 121, 137n98; monitoring sermons and legality, 128, 143, 144, 145, 158, 161, 164nn13–15, 172, 179, 195n42; press attacks on religion, 28, 73n107, 91, 105n102, 119–120, 137n93; scientific atheism research, 148–149, 165n39, 175, 204. *See also* secular (ersatz) rites
Appel, Andre, 151, 166n54, 169n83
Armenian Church, 22, 46, 61, 70n31, 74n126, 76n157, 86, 117
atheism. *See* antireligious campaign
Austria, 93, 169n80

baptisms. *See* church rites and adherence: baptism
Baptists, 15, 20, 21, 34, 55, 56, 63, 65, 67, 69n29, 70n31, 73n90, 77n175, 79, 81, 83–85, 86, 89, 90, 92, 93, 94, 99, 107n128, 115, 130, 134n49, 145, 149–150, 157, 161, 170n100, 178, 184, 186, 188, 192; All-Union Council of Evangelical Christians and Baptists, 11, 15, 23, 31, 54, 92; Estonia, 4, 15, 23, 39n77, 42n126, 43n147, 44n154, 47–48, 69n14, 69n15, 103n63, 116, 119, 164n18, 170n96, 170n97, 170n101, 170n106; Latvia, 50, 105n100, 114, 133n44, 170n98, 170n100, 184, 196n64, 196n65; unregistered (initsiativniki), 142, 154, 156, 157, 161–162, 170n98, 174, 175, 178, 181, 193n14, 202, 209
Baronas, Jonas, 184–185
bells, 78, 95, 105n98, 106n103, 118, 136n80
Belorussia SSR, 49, 52, 82, 90, 104n78, 105n93, 127, 140n156, 146
Berklavs, Eduards, 88, 97, 104n81, 128, 129
Berlin Conference of European Catholics, 125, 139n142
Bible studies, 55, 164n14
Blumbergs, Oskars, 54
Braecklein, Bishop Ingo, 123, 166n51
Brezhnev, Leonid, 5, 142, 143, 144–47, 149, 156, 157, 159–163, 172, 173, 175, 179, 185, 191, 201, 202, 204, 206
Buddhists, 22, 121
bureaucratic politics, 5–6, 10, 35n6, 58, 64–66, 67, 79, 85, 95–99, 108nn, 136–150, 111, 125–126, 128–129, 141n168, 141n172, 142, 159–160, 163, 194n31, 200–202, 207–208
burials. *See* church rites and adherence: burial
Butirovicz, Jazeps, 110, 131n7

Catholic Church: arrests of clergy, 17, 52, 71n60, 88, 110, 118; children's role in services, 58, 118, 136n78, 146, 193n14; Czechoslovak, 64; dissent, 12, 89–90, 105n92, 105n93, 156; excommunication of Communists, 46, 49; German, 64; international ties, 93–94, 99, 124–125, 153, 178; Latvian, 49–52, 80; leadership, 14, 52–53, 76n148, 88, 127–128, 203; Lithuanian (*see* Lithuania SSR: Catholic Church); Moscow Catholic chaplaincy, 131n7; Polish, 105n93, 110, 128 (*see also* Poland); Second Vatican Council, 112, 122, 201; state policy toward, 18, 19–20, 45, 48, 49–52, 67, 85–86, 88, 93–94, 103n67, 107n120,

247

107n123, 107n124, 109–110, 124–125, 127–128, 140nn156–160, 140n164, 146, 156, 162, 174, 200–202, 207, 208–209; Uniates, 110; visitation/census by clergy, 82, 98, 102n38. *See also* confirmation and first communion; monasteries; pilgrimages; religious instruction; theological education; Vatican; *see also names of individual church leaders and popes*

cemeteries: cemetery days traditions, 16, 57, 66, 68, 73n104, 74n119, 81, 84, 95, 102n52, 103n53, 118, 136n79; ownership and nationalization, 12, 55, 72n89, 84, 96, 103n54

Christian Democrats, 18, 123; Estonian: 187, 188

Christian Peace Conference (CPC), 111, 117, 118, 122, 138n108, 138n109, 155

church buildings, 10, 204–205; architectural preservation, 160, 163, 175, 176, 180, 191, 194n24, 202, 208; repair and construction, 11, 17, 38n55, 64, 71n56, 80, 101n19, 107n120, 112, 134n48, 157, 179–180, 195n45; vandalism, 55, 56, 72n89, 73n98, 90, 105n98, 144, 160, 171n20, 176, 194n24

church charity work, 55, 73n92, 186

church closures. *See* church legal status

church finances, 59, 60, 68n9, 121, 160–161; contributions as measure of church adherence, 16, 66, 74n122, 81, 145, 164n18, 173–174; taxation and insurance costs of churches, 18, 47, 69n10, 84, 96, 102n51, 108n137, 115–116, 145, 164nn16–20, 180, 187

church governance, 200–202, 204–205; church constitutions (Estonia Lutheran, Latvia Lutheran, Baptist, Methodist), 26–27, 52, 59, 116, 134n58, 146, 164n22, 182, 183; inter-confessional relations, 159, 184, 196n63; parish councils and laity, 29, 86, 103n70, 116, 134nn56–58, 145–146, 157, 183; parish *dvatsatka*, 22, 24, 47, 79–80, 100n11, 112; synods, 27, 52, 53, 61, 62, 191, 205

church international ties, 10, 63–66, 68, 76n154, 83, 86, 87, 91–95, 98, 99, 106n106, 106n112, 117, 121–124, 129, 142, 152–154, 157, 162, 172–173, 178, 200–202,

204–05. *See also individual countries and international organizations*

church leadership (Lutheran), 203; ecclesiastical legitimization of, 36n11, 63–64, 92, 155; ousters and changes in, 10–11, 18–19, 33, 39n62, 39n64, 39n67, 53, 154–156, 161, 169nn80–88, 175, 181–183, 196n58, 200–202, 208; recruitment and cooptation of, 29, 41n123, 44n159, 45, 52–54, 66, 72nn74–75, 86, 156, 159–160, 171n119, 174, 193n17, 195n43, 201–202, 204–206; state evaluation of, 13–15, 18, 44n160, 54, 72n85, 86–88, 104n74, 104n77, 127, 140n154, 154–155, 168n79, 169n87, 173, 181–183, 196n57. *See also names of individual church leaders*

church legal status, 96, 98, 161, 162, 186, 200–202, 204–205; nationalization and property issues, 17, 22–25, 34, 40nn90–99, 41nn100–105, 47, 49, 112–115, 132nn25–34, 133nn35–47, 134nn48–53, 144, 180, 186, 187, 189, 196n64, 198n101; registration and closure of parishes, 11, 22, 29–32, 34, 38n48, 46–50, 62, 66, 67, 68nn2–9, 69nn10–19, 69n29, 71n55–56, 78–81, 90, 100n3, 100nn5–13, 101n17, 101n19, 101n21, 115, 143, 149–150, 163n6, 173, 180, 186, 206, 208

church music, 55, 72n71, 81–82, 87, 100n10, 113–14, 136n80, 148, 157, 158, 170n106, 176, 177, 187, 193n20

church publications and media access: censorship, 116, 134nn60–61, 206; state approval and circulation, 12, 19, 36n22, 56, 58, 62, 74n117, 84–85, 93, 97, 103nn59–67, 107n120, 116–117, 125, 135nn62–66, 180, 186, 187, 197n86, 200–202, 204–206

church rites and adherence, 15–16, 45, 58–60, 67, 81, 101n26, 111, 129, 131n3, 131n13, 141n170, 143, 149, 160, 173, 179, 186, 197n78, 200–202, 207, 209; baptism, 59, 74n118, 81, 175, 197n77; burial, 54, 58, 59, 60, 66, 121, 143, 165n27; marriage, 16, 58–60, 74n117, 74n118, 131n13, 143, 149, 165n27. *See also* confirmation and first communion; religious instruction

church statistics, membership, 81, 138n120; number of parishes, 77n161, 77n175. *See also* church rites and adherence; clergy
civil society and churches, 5, 172, 191, 205
clergy, 204–205; arrests and imprisonment, 32, 43n151, 43n152, 47, 52, 56, 57, 68n6, 70n35, 73nn100–103, 177, 200; certification and decertification, 50, 79, 98, 137n95, 144, 177; generational change in, 176–177; informants (*see* KGB/NKVD); moral compromising of, 56, 87, 120; number of, 25, 65, 66, 82, 89, 143, 160, 173–174; recruitment of pro-regime priests, 29, 42n132; returning from gulag, 82, 87, 89–90, 97–99, 104n89, 118–119; serving outside Baltic republics, 49, 55, 73nn93–94, 82. *See also* religious instruction; theological education
Cold War, 35, 42n139, 45, 60, 67, 78, 206
collectivization, 9, 45, 49, 54, 66, 73n103
Commissioners of Religious Affairs, 9–10, 90, 91, 95–96, 103n70, 160, 162, 178, 207–208; Estonia, 11, 12, 13, 16, 20, 22, 23, 24, 25, 26, 27, 28, 30, 33, 34, 4n78, 40n83, 40n90, 40n96, 42n128, 42n141, 43n146, 43n147, 46, 47, 48, 57, 58, 61, 65, 69n14, 69n15, 69n19, 72n74, 77n168, 79, 85, 86, 100n6, 100n9, 100n11, 103n60, 105n95, 106n116, 125, 158–160, 174, 181, 188, 195n34; Latvia, 12, 14, 17, 18, 19, 24, 26, 31, 46–47, 49, 51, 52, 54, 55, 57, 62–64, 65, 68nn3–6, 69n10, 69n18, 69n29, 70n30, 72n86, 74n117, 74n121, 77n167, 77n169, 77n170, 79, 87–88, 89, 101n17, 115, 128, 152, 153, 166n58, 183, 185; Lithuania, 8n22, 55, 65, 75n138, 77n170, 117; Leningrad Oblast, 158, 167n65, 177. *See also* perestroika
Communist Party of the Soviet Union, 5–6, 45; Agitprop Department, 10, 20, 49, 64–65, 74n126, 86, 91, 129, 131n16, 133n47, 205; Central Committee, 61, 75n131, 97, 98, 121–122, 126, 128, 167n65, 207, 208; Estonian, 26; Lithuania, 7, 86, 110, 131n8
Conference of European Churches (CEC), 94, 99, 123, 124, 151, 169n80
confession/denomination, 2, 3, 67, 99, 162–163, 208–209

confirmation and first communion, 12, 20–21, 74n120s, 81, 118, 125, 205, 209; measure of church adherence, 16, 21, 36n19, 39n77, 58–59, 66, 101n30; state policy on, 11–12, 20–22, 34, 39nn74–83, 57, 58, 67, 74n116, 74n121, 98
Council for the Affairs of Religious Cults (CARC), 6, 11, 12, 14, 15, 16, 17, 18, 19–20, 21, 22, 24, 25, 26, 27, 29, 30, 32, 40n80, 40n83, 44n156, 45, 46, 47, 49, 50, 51, 52, 53, 58, 62, 63, 64–66, 67–68, 68nn1–5, 69n12, 69n21, 69n24, 69n29, 70n46, 70n48, 71n53, 71n65, 72n89, 74n116, 74n123, 75n137, 76n154, 76n157, 77n165, 77n166, 79, 80, 83, 84, 85–86, 87, 91, 93, 94, 95, 96, 97, 98, 100n6, 100n10, 100n12, 102n46, 104n77, 106n108, 111, 126, 128–129, 132n21, 135n75, 207, 208. *See also* Polyansky, Ivan; Puzin, Aleksei
Council for the Affairs of the Russian Orthodox Church (CROC), 6, 17, 61, 64–66, 68, 72n89, 77n162, 80, 91, 97–99, 108n149, 108n150, 111, 114, 116, 122, 126, 129, 132n20, 133n47, 134n61, 138n108, 138n110, 141n172, 207. *See also* Karpov, Georgi
Council for Religious Affairs (CRA) 6, 152, 153, 159, 166n58, 174, 176, 179, 180, 189, 192, 194n24, 197n75. *See also* Kuroedov, Vladimir; Kharchev; Konstantin
Czechoslovakia, ix, 29, 86, 118, 122, 142, 154

Daugavpils, 78, 80, 105n93, 114–115, 132n31, 134n48
Denmark, 65, 87, 104n90, 151
de-Stalinization, 78, 99, 109
détente, 5, 108n42, 142, 149, 151–153, 161, 163, 173, 202, 205, 206
Dibelius, Bishop Otto, 64, 76n159, 138n122, 139n125
dissent in churches, 3, 80–81, 89, 104n91, 107n134, 128, 142, 156–159, 161–62, 171nn111–14, 173, 176–178, 182–183, 187–188, 194n33, 202, 205, 207, 209. *See also* Catholic Church; Rebirth and Renewal
Döppmann, Hans-Dieter, 166n49, 169n90
Dukalski, Michael, 52

250 | Index

Dulbinskis, Bishop Kazimirs, 18, 52, 71n61, 82, 84, 88, 90, 98, 104n78, 127, 128, 131n5

Eastern Europe, ix, 64, 66, 69n24, 94, 122, 123, 125, 154, 204; 1989 revolutions, ix, 5, 172, 202
elections, 12, 18, 19, 33, 39n64, 44n160, 54, 68n3, 158
emigration, 10, 17, 27, 37n32, 119
emigré churches, 9, 19, 85, 92, 94–95, 107n129, 107n131, 107n133, 110, 116, 122, 127, 134n60, 151–152, 161, 167nn60–64, 168n66, 178, 195n35, 200, 201, 203; Estonian, 25, 85, 138nn114–116, 152, 153, 195n35; Latvian, 152, 167n60, 167n63, 167n64, 169n83, 188, 198n96
Estonian Christian Democratic Party. See Christian Democrats
Estonian Committee, 188
Estonian National Independence Movement, 187
Estonian Orthodox Church. See Orthodox Church: Estonian
Estonian SSR government. See republic governments
Evangelical Church in Germany (EKD). See Germany, West

Feldmanis, Roberts, 56, 73n101, 73n102, 89, 183
Finland: church contacts/communications with Estonia, 63, 122, 123, 138n117, 146, 152, 161, 164n23, 177, 180, 194n32, 202, 203, 206; Ingrian Finns, 21, 122, 167n65, 177
first communion. See confirmation and first communion
foreign policy. See Union of Soviet Socialist Republics; *specific international organizations; and individual countries*
forest brothers. See World War II: guerrilla resistance in Baltics after
Freijs, Alberts, 41n123, 56, 73n101, 169n80, 169n82

Gailitis, Bishop Kārlis, 182–186, 188, 197n86, 198n96
Germans: historical legacy in Baltics, 13, 15, 18, 36n32, 36n33, 150–151; prisoners of war (*see* World War II). *See also* Soviet Germans
Germany, division of and the German question, 66, 92, 123
Germany, East (German Democratic Republic), 1, 76n158, 76n160, 77n173, 83, 124–126, 133n41, 138n109, 139n125, 150, 151, 153–155, 169n90; Christian Democratic Union (East), 123, 124, 126; Communist Party, 64, 122, 123, 126; Evangelical-Lutheran Churches in, 83, 116, 119, 138n122, 139n126, 140n151, 140n152, 150, 161, 166n49, 169n88, 171n116; as case of religious policy and change, ix, 1, 5, 70n48, 96, 108n142, 120, 147–149, 153, 160, 165n39, 168n73, 169n80, 172, 174–175, 178, 192, 193n17, 203–207, 209
Germany, West (Federal Republic of Germany), 5, 118, 119, 150, 153, 175, 182, 206; Bruderschaften, 124, 125; EKD/ Evangelical-Lutheran Churches, 63–64, 77n173, 92, 95, 99, 106n111, 107n134, 124–126, 138n122, 150–151, 161, 178, 185, 206
Gorbachev, Mikhail, 179, 181, 183, 185, 187, 188, 191, 193n19, 202, 205, 206. *See also* perestroika
Great Britain, 32, 85, 92, 94, 119, 136n84; Archbishop of Canterbury, 87, 92; Anglican Church, 36n11
Grinbergs, Bishop Theodore, 11, 18, 39n64

Hallaste, Illar, 158, 171n111, 177, 187, 198n109
Hammer, Harri, 32, 43n152, 44n155, 146, 158, 171n111, 177
Hansen, Paul, 151, 153, 166n50, 166n54, 169n83
Hare Krishna, 180, 195n47
Hark, Archbishop Edgar, 37n35, 53, 72n74, 75n140, 124, 139n124, 154, 155, 158, 159, 164n23, 169n87, 169n88, 170n109, 171n111, 173, 177, 178, 182, 196n57, 203
Herrnhuters (Bohemian Brethren), 15, 29–32, 33, 34, 37n31, 38n46, 42n136–141, 43nn142–148, 44n159, 48, 66, 79, 100n9, 100n10, 113, 125, 132n34, 133n35, 207; Eugene Tanner faction of, 15, 29, 30, 37n31, 38n46, 42n138, 42n139; Juri Leidtorf faction of, 29, 43n145

Hiiuma, 14, 32, 39n77, 44n154, 47, 69n14, 79, 98, 100n6
Horn, Adolph, 32, 33, 42n141, 43n152, 44n155
Hromadka, Josef, 122
human rights, 176–177
Hungary ix, 66, 85, 94, 95, 99, 107n129, 125, 147, 172, 203

Ilves, Peter, 57
informants. *See* clergy; KGB/NKVD
interwar history, 13, 18, 29, 36n30, 36n31. *See also* Päts, Konstantin; Ulmanis, Kārlis; Germans
Irbe, Acting Bishop Kārlis, 11, 12, 14, 18, 19, 25, 26, 32, 37n37, 38n55, 39n64, 42n132, 43n153
Islam. *See* Moslems

Jacob, Günter, 166n51
Jänicke, Bishop Johannes, 166n51
Jehovah's Witnesses, 111, 156
Jews, 8n22, 11, 15, 78, 81, 101n26, 115, 154, 167n52, 209
John XXIII, Pope, 111, 122, 129, 142
John Paul II, Pope, 156, 174, 186
Jürjo, Villu, 158, 170n109, 171n112, 176–177
Juva, Bishop Mikko, 153

Käbin, Johannes, 100n6
Kalderovski, Kārlis, 171n114
Kaldur, Peeter, 171n112, 191, 195n45
Kalnberzins, Jānis, 68n5, 69n21
Kalnins, Bishop Harald, 43n148, 75n140, 89, 150, 151, 153, 156, 166n49, 166n50, 167n58, 169n82, 169n90, 184–185
Karpov, Georgi, 65–66, 69n21, 76n159, 77n162, 77n172, 97, 98, 108n150, 111, 129, 131n16, 141n167
Kaulins, Arvids, 39n67, 87, 156, 164n19
KGB/NKVD, 6, 9, 18, 96, 105n92, 105n95, 107n133, 115, 145, 169n86, 207; arrests and coercion of clergy, 10, 32–33, 44nn154–157, 47, 50, 53, 56, 71n59, 78, 105n95, 131n5, 155, 158, 200; dual roles of state religious officials, 33, 44n158, 96, 108n140, 108n141, 207; informants, 42n138, 43n153, 44n158, 53, 72n72, 72n73, 73n101, 73n102, 74n122, 87, 90, 99, 104n73, 104n76, 119, 131n7, 136n84, 140n149, 155, 156, 161, 166n49, 181, 182, 201, 205; policy positions, 35, 49, 65, 67, 70n41, 74n117, 79, 82, 86, 87, 90, 93, 94, 100n6, 107n123, 107n126, 110–111, 122, 131n15, 138n111, 140n152, 149–152, 159, 160, 165n41, 167n60, 180, 189, 198n102, 208
Kharchev, Konstantin, 179, 195n39
Khrushchev, Nikita, 3, 5, 63, 78, 79, 88, 91, 93, 97, 99, 104n81, 109, 113, 114, 116, 117, 119, 121, 123, 128, 129, 134n49, 142–147, 157, 160–162, 163n6, 164n22, 172, 185, 194n31, 201, 202, 204–207
Kiivit, Archbishop Jaan, 29, 33, 43n152, 44n156, 53–55, 58, 61–65, 72n86, 73n93, 74n122, 74n123, 75n130, 75n132, 75n137, 75n139, 79, 86, 87, 89, 92, 95, 100n9, 101n23, 104n89, 106n110, 106n115, 107n131, 112, 113, 119, 121–124, 127, 129, 138n116, 139n146, 151, 154, 155, 169n85, 169n86, 171n116, 171n122, 182, 203
Kiivit Jr., Archbishop Jaan, 164n23, 182, 183, 187, 196n59
Kleperis, Peteris, 39n67, 72n85, 87, 90, 104n73, 104n76, 104n90, 107n134, 108n143, 155–156, 164n19, 166n52, 169n81
Kohtla-Järve, 149, 165n39, 195n45
Kokars-Trops, Jānis, 179, 183, 185, 189, 195n47, 196n60
Komsomol, 28, 51, 57, 59, 67, 68n3, 73n102, 74n113, 74n121, 90, 98, 105n97, 105n98, 120, 121, 137n93, 137n101
Kopp, Bishop Johan, 10
Korean War, 45, 61
Krummacher, Bishop Friedrich-Wilhelm, 126, 140n151, 166n51
Kublinskis, Alfreds, 189–90, 197n86, 198n104, 198n106
Kuroedov, Vladimir, 147, 149, 150, 157, 165n26, 166n48, 171n119, 174, 179, 193n15

Latgāle, 9, 46, 48, 52, 69n18, 71n56, 82, 107n123, 110, 113, 114, 127, 156, 174
Lācis, Vilas, 11, 68n5, 69n21, 101n17
Latvian Orthodox Church. *See* Orthodox Churches: Latvian

Latvian Popular Front. *See* Popular Front
Latvian SSR government. *See* republic governments
Leepins, August, 53, 90, 156, 182
Leningrad, 89, 90, 95, 105n93, 122, 158, 167n65, 177, 184
Lentsman, Leonid, 74n123, 77n168, 103n60, 106n115
Levindanto, Nikolai, 54
Liepaja, 47, 52, 53, 80, 112, 120
Lithuania SSR, 1, 3, 6, 7, 10, 25, 37n27, 49, 52, 75n138, 86, 110, 135n67, 161, 167n58, 204; Catholic church, 3, 6, 8n22, 12, 13, 14, 17, 37n27, 70n46, 85, 86, 93, 103n65, 103n67, 106n118, 107n120, 110, 128, 131n3, 131n7, 134n57, 139n143, 142, 158, 174, 181, 209; Lutheran church, 55, 56, 62, 65, 75n138, 87, 97, 108n143, 117, 135n66, 140n154, 152, 167n59; Reformed church, 55, 97, 108n143, 140n154
local governments, 11, 23, 24, 38n76, 43n146, 46, 50, 55, 57, 65, 68n4, 68n6, 80, 84, 91, 95, 100n6, 112–115, 125, 145, 162, 188, 207. *See also* republic governments
Luhamets, Joel, 158, 171n112
Lusis, Bishop Arnold, 167n62, 167n63
Luther, Martin, 150—151, 153–154, 163, 166n52, 176, 178
Lutheran Church. *See all entries under* church; *see names of individual church leaders*
Lutheran World Federation, 46, 76n159, 76n160, 94–95, 99, 107n129, 111, 114, 122–124, 126–127, 129, 138n116, 138n117, 150–155, 161, 166n50, 166n54, 167n58, 167n59, 167n62, 169n80, 169n83, 169n88, 175, 178, 184, 196n56, 202, 203, 206; Conference of Lutheran Minority Churches, 94, 95, 123, 139n127, 151, 153, 168n66, 168n68, 168n75. *See also* Soviet Germans; Hansen, Paul

Malenkov, Georgi, 74n124, 83
marriages. *See* church rites: marriages
Matulis, Archbishop Janis, 150, 152, 154, 155, 166n52, 167n58, 167n62, 167n64, 169n83, 171n114, 173, 178, 182, 196n58, 203

Mau, Carl, 151, 166n50
Mennonites, 149, 150
Mesters, Archbishop Eriks, 155, 159, 169n84, 182–185, 196n60, 203
Methodists, 15, 66, 92, 99, 157, 178; Estonia, 4, 15, 23, 32, 24, 38n45, 44n154, 48, 94, 106n108, 107n128, 113, 116, 133n35, 164n18, 170n97, 170n106; Latvia, 15, 48
Migla, Wilhelm, 72n85
migration, 45, 59, 79, 104n81, 110, 149, 150, 157, 161, 166n45, 178, 208. *See also* emigration
Mikoyan, Anastas, 93, 103n65
military service. *See* theological education
Ministry of Foreign Affairs (MFA). *See* Union of Soviet Socialist Republics
Mitzenheim, Bishop Moritz, 123
Molotov, Vyacheslav, 14
monasteries, 9, 50, 67, 68n8, 114, 116–118, 130, 133n47, 135nn67–74, 142, 210, 205; Aglona, 12, 17, 50, 51, 84, 88, 90, 95, 102n37, 103n58, 117, 118, 127, 135n67, 135n71, 135n72, 135n73, 178, 186; Kannepene, 117, 135n67; Kraslava, 84, 102n37, 103n56; Riga, 26, 70n37. *See also* pilgrimages
Moscow Catholic Chaplaincy. *See* Catholic Church: Moscow Catholic chaplaincy
Moslems, 22, 46, 65, 70n31, 76n157, 86, 93, 111, 115, 117, 121, 209
Mõtsnik, Harri, 158, 177, 194n31, 194n32

Narva, 100n11
nationalism, 1
national identity and religion, 1–2, 68, 81, 82, 129, 141n171, 149, 157–159, 163, 170n109, 171n114, 172, 174–178, 180, 181, 184, 190–191, 194n28, 195n50, 199n113, 202, 208, 209
nationalization of churches. *See* church legal status
NATO, 1, 64, 92
Niemöller, Church President Martin, 64, 66, 75n137, 76n159, 77n173, 92, 93, 106n110
nuclear weapons, 45, 61, 153, 178

Old Believers, 15, 23, 44n154, 46, 65, 70n31, 75n138, 76n157, 77n165, 77n170, 79, 97, 100n5, 115, 194n24

Orthodox Churches, ix, 2, 4, 34, 61, 65, 75n128, 76n144, 114, 122, 129, 138n111, 148, 156, 198n94, 199n13; autocephalous, 61; Estonian, 37n29, 113, 149; Georgian, 61; Latvian, 114, 118, 132n30, 132n32, 186, 198n101; Serbian, 132n18. *See also* Russian Orthodox Church

Ozolins, Viktor, 139n124, 155, 167n60, 169n83, 170n91

Pähn, Bishop August, 10, 12, 24, 33, 41n100, 43n152, 44n160, 53, 54

Pajula, Archbishop Kuno, 53, 119, 136n85, 166n52, 182, 183, 185, 187, 196n57, 196n59, 203

parishes. *See* church legal status; Tallinn; Tartu; Riga

Päts, Konstantin, 13

Paul VI, Pope, 163

peace issue, 201; Estonian Lutheran Church regarding, 61–62, 75n132, 75n139, 92, 106n115, 154; Latvian Catholic Church regarding, 63, 67, 75n144, 76n147, 93–94; Latvian Lutheran Church regarding, 55, 61–63, 75nn135–138, 133n43, 154; regime evaluation of churches' stance, 56, 62, 62–63, 75n131, 75n135, 75n140, 75n141, 178; Soviet conferences on, 61, 63, 75n138; Soviet Peace Fund, 125, 133n42, 139n143, 155; Stockholm Appeal, 61, 63, 75n128, 75n144. *See also* Christian Peace Conference (CPC)

Pelše, Arvids, 69n21, 100n3, 103n58, 104n81, 115, 129, 135n65, 137n102

Pentecostals, 54, 70, 90, 98, 111, 158, 161, 162, 170n106, 174, 175, 178, 180, 181, 184, 189, 192, 196n64, 202, 209

perestroika, 179, 205; Baltic autonomy, sovereignty, political community, 190–192; Baltic officials' response, 181, 185, 189–190, 208; churches' response, 181, 185, 186, 187–188, 196n65, 199n115; Congress of People's Deputies, 181, 187, 188; law on freedom of religion, 186, 190, 192, 198n94; reorganization and autonomy of Baltic commissioners, 189–90, 198n109

pilgrimages, 49–51, 67, 69n21, 70nn40–41, 82, 84, 88, 90, 94, 98, 99, 102n37, 103nn56–58, 117–118, 127, 129, 130, 135n71, 178, 186. *See also* monasteries

Pius XII, Pope, 14, 46, 49, 111, 125, 132n17

Plāte, Modris, 177–178, 182–184, 196n60

Pöder, Andres, 170n109, 171n112, 194n30

Poland, ix, 29, 85, 94, 99, 124, 142, 160, 172, 174, 192, 203, 204, 205, 207; Lutheran Church, 124

Polyansky, Ivan, 20, 35n4, 40n79, 53, 56, 65, 69n23, 71n56, 71n65, 73n93, 75n135, 75n137, 76n158, 77n161, 77n165, 77n173, 83, 94, 96, 97, 98, 100n13, 102n43, 102n44, 102n45, 105n92, 107n120, 108n140, 111

Popular Front, 1, 192; in Estonia, 187, 188, 190, 198n109; in Latvia, 188, 189, 190, 192

Priede, Roberts, 155, 169n80

Pugo, Kārlis, 26, 47

Puzin, Aleksei, 111, 121, 128, 131n3, 141n168

Rätsep, Kaide, 119, 136n84

Rebirth and Renewal, 159, 183, 188, 196n65, 198n94, 205. *See also* dissent in churches

Reding, Marcel, 93

Red Army, 9–10, 13, 15, 19, 22, 29, 37n35, 38n44, 53, 57, 70n48, 81, 96, 114, 156, 169n81, 173, 182. *See also* theological education: military service obligation

Reformed Church, 36n11, 66, 114, 124, 133n45

Reformed World Alliance, 124

registration of churches. *See* church legal status

religious centers in Moscow, 11, 15, 54, 65, 77n165, 77n170, 85, 97, 131n15, 153, 159, 167n58, 184

religious holidays, 9, 57, 73n110, 121, 129, 131n3, 137n101, 137n102, 187, 191, 197n78; Christmas, 12, 28, 57, 81, 101n29, 102n36, 105n98, 105n100, 143, 173, 187; Easter, 65, 81, 82

religious instruction, 16, 17, 19, 20, 51–52, 67, 82, 86, 89, 118, 146, 183, 186, 200, 205. *See also* confirmation and first communion

republic governments, 62, 93, 95–97, 100n12, 125–126, 159, 175, 207, 208; Estonia, 11, 23, 24, 40n99, 69n15, 74n123, 79, 82–83, 85,

86, 103n60, 106n115; Latvia, 23, 41n118, 46, 50, 68n4–6, 69n12, 80, 82–83, 86, 101n17, 102n46, 115, 128, 152, 166n58, 188
revolutions of 1989. *See* Eastern Europe: 1989 revolutions
Riga: Lutheran Cathedral, 37n32, 82, 113–114, 133nn38–44, 186, 188; New Gertrude Parish, 89, 114, 133n45; Orthodox Cathedral, 189; Reformed Parish, 114, 133n45
Ristlaan, Rein, 190, 192, 195n45, 197n88, 198n109
Rozenbergs, Pauls, 18, 39n64, 43n153
Rubenis, Juris, 183, 188
Russian Orthodox Church, 2–4, 11, 12, 18, 23, 27, 29, 30, 32, 37n29, 42n148, 47, 54, 55, 57, 59, 60, 61, 63, 64–67, 74n124, 77n162, 80, 82, 85, 86, 92–94, 98, 101n21, 108n150, 111, 113, 114, 116, 122–124, 131n16, 132n21, 134n49, 134n61, 135n68, 135n71, 138n110, 138n111, 138n112, 138n113, 138n122, 139n124, 142, 143, 156, 159, 161, 163n6, 167n62, 173, 176, 186, 189, 194n24, 197n77, 201, 203, 205, 206, 207, 208; 1000th anniversary, 179, 191, 193n13

Saag, Evald, 25, 26, 29, 57, 73n104, 96
Saarema, 14, 32, 38n45, 39n77, 44n154
Salum, Vello, 158, 171n113, 178, 187, 189, 198n103
Salumae, Tiit, 158, 171n112
Savisaar, Edgar, 188
Scandinavia, 36n11, 61, 62, 75n131, 92, 148, 162, 198n109
Scharf, Bishop Kurt, 126, 140n152
Schönherr, Bishop Albrecht, 166n51
sects, 4, 14, 21, 22, 25, 38n46, 42n141, 48, 49, 54, 58, 59, 74n124, 80, 84, 90–91, 96–99, 101n21, 108n150, 111, 145–148, 157, 161, 162, 163n2, 163n3, 164n16, 170n104, 180, 181, 189, 198n102, 205, 207. *See also* Baptists; Herrnhuters (Bohemian Brethren); Jehovah's Witnesses; Mennonites; Pentecostals; Seventh-Day Adventist Church
secular (ersatz) rites, 59–60, 147, 160, 162, 174, 176, 188, 191–192; burials, 121; folk holidays and, 121, 137n101, 137n102; name-giving ceremonies, 165n27; Summer Days of Youth (coming-of-age ceremony), 120–121, 147, 165n27, 165n39, 176; weddings, 165n27. *See also* antireligious campaign
secularization, 1
Seigewasser, Hans, 126, 140n151
Seventh-Day Adventist Church, 11, 47, 50, 54, 56, 57, 65, 68n4, 70n31, 73n102, 89, 104n91, 111, 131n15, 156, 157, 164n18, 187
Shaurums, Gustav, 54
Simojoki, Bishop Maarti, 127
Šlosbergs, Krišjānis, 28, 54
Soone, Bishop Einar, 182
Soviet Germans, 89, 125, 139n146, 149, 175, 202, 206–207; Baltic church responses, 150–153, 166n50, 184–185; German Evangelical Lutheran Church in the USSR, 184–185; LWF and, 150–151, 153, 184; state policy, 3, 149–152, 157, 161, 166n45, 166n50, 166n57, 174, 184, 208
Springovičs, Archbishop Antonijs, 10, 12, 14, 17–19, 24–26, 35, 37n27, 38n39, 39n58, 41n105, 49, 51, 52, 54, 63, 65, 67, 69n25, 75n144, 76n148, 77n169, 82, 88, 94, 110, 120, 127, 128, 131n7, 203
Stalin, Joseph, 3, 4, 12, 17, 20, 21, 26, 37n29, 46, 51, 54, 63, 64, 76n157, 76n158, 77n162, 77n172, 78–79, 84, 89, 91, 92, 98, 117, 129, 149, 179, 201, 204
stalinization, 26, 29, 34, 45, 102n45, 203, 205
Strods, Bishop Peteris, 18, 26, 51, 52, 63, 64, 69n24, 71n59, 72n79, 76n147, 82, 83, 88–91, 94, 102n41, 103n58, 104n83, 105n93, 105n95, 105n100, 106n103, 107n133, 115, 118, 120, 124, 127, 128, 134n51, 135n71, 136n76, 136n78, 136n92, 137n93, 139n138, 140n156, 140n159, 140n164, 174, 193n12
synods. *See* church governance
Sweden, 10, 14, 63, 64, 76n151, 92, 94, 95, 107n128, 152, 155, 166n54, 169n83, 169n88, 175, 203

Taiwans, Leons, 11, 73n93, 75n140, 89, 95, 104n90, 107n134
Tallinn, 18, 32, 44n158, 53, 59, 69n15, 75n139, 83, 107n128, 113, 153, 158, 175, 182; Holy

Ghost Parish, 74n122; Jaani Parish, 33, 43n152, 44n156, 68n5, 74n118; Kaarli Parish, 44n156, 48, 74n118; Oleviste Parish, 48, 69n15, 170n97; Peeteli Parish, 43n152, 113; Toom-Nikuliste Parish, 43n152 Tartu, 9, 17, 18, 19, 35n1, 44n159, 119, 171n111; Paulus Parish, 43n152, 80, 112; Peetri Parish, 89

Tedder, Lembit, 57, 62

theological education, 200–202, 204–206, 209; Baptists, 83–84; Catholic seminaries in Lithuania, 51, 70n46, 181; Catholic seminary in Belarus and Ukraine, 186; Catholic seminary in Riga, 12, 14, 17, 26, 41n117, 50, 51, 56, 69n21, 70nn45–48, 71n52, 71n59, 72n79, 83, 102nn41–43, 146, 174, 180–81, 197n80; Lutheran institute in Estonia, 17–18, 25–26, 174, 187; Lutheran institute in Latvia, 17–18, 102n45, 136n83; Lutheran institutes, 41n116, 41n120, 42n133, 55–56, 83, 119, 146, 180; military service obligation, 17, 38n57, 51, 70n48, 83, 102n44, 189, 198n104; general state policy regarding, 12, 17, 25—26, 34, 67, 83, 119, 146–147, 165n26, 180

theology, 203–204

Tooming, Archbishop Alfred, 37n35, 53, 72n75, 75n140, 155, 157, 166n52, 169n87, 170n104

totalitarian model, 2–3, 34, 67

transnational actors, 5, 205–207

Trops, Henrik, 88

Turs, Archbishop Gustav, 12, 18–19, 21, 22, 25–27, 39n64, 39n66, 39n68, 40n80, 41n120, 41n123, 45–47, 52–56, 61–64, 66, 68n3, 71n65, 72n71, 72nn84–86, 72n88, 73n93, 74n117, 74n120, 75n130, 75n135, 75n137, 75n138, 75n141, 76n160, 77n173, 81–83, 86–89, 91, 92, 95, 97, 101n19, 101n31, 102n45, 103n68, 104n73, 104n74, 104n77, 105n100, 105n101, 106n103, 107n133, 108n143, 112–114, 117, 118, 124, 127, 129, 133nn41–43, 135n65, 136n77, 137n100, 138n120, 139n129, 139n136, 140n149, 140n154, 151, 154, 155, 164n19, 167n59, 168n79, 169n80, 169n82, 169n85, 203

Ukrainian SSR, 1, 49, 55, 73n94, 77n175, 82, 97, 102n41, 110, 146, 167n58, 186, 197n80; Reformed churches, 124

Ulmanis, Kārlis, 14, 82

Union of Soviet Socialist Republics: Council of Ministers, 20, 22, 23, 26, 31, 77n162, 117; foreign policy of, 5, 45, 46, 64, 76n158, 91, 99, 111–112, 121, 123–124, 129, 142, 153, 163, 175, 206; Ministry of Culture, 56, 63; Ministry of Foreign Affairs (MFA), 6, 66, 68, 76n154, 76n160, 77n173, 93, 94, 107n129, 126–127, 132n17. *See also* Council for Affairs of Religious Cults (CARC); Council for Affairs of the Russian Orthodox Church (CROC); Council for Religious Affairs (CRA); détente; KGB/NKVD; peace issue

United States: Lutheran Church, 64; National Council of Churches, 92

unregistered groups. *See* Baptists: unregistered (initsiativniki); church legal status

Unt, Henn, 44n157, 56, 73n103

Urbšs, Bishop Antonijs, 53

Vaikuls, Stanislav, 12, 18, 37n27, 52

Vaivods, Julijans Cardinal, 53, 63, 76n148, 88, 104n80, 128, 140n160, 156, 163, 174, 178, 185, 186, 193nn11–13, 195n36, 197n80, 199n115, 203

Vanags, Archbishop Jānis, 183

Vatican, 8n22, 14, 49, 61, 63, 67, 68, 69n23, 69n24, 85, 88, 93–95, 98, 99, 102n39, 103n67, 107n126, 110–112, 122–125, 127, 130, 131n5, 132n18, 132n20, 138nn110–12, 139n127, 140n156, 140n159, 142, 156, 163, 168n66, 174, 195n36, 200, 201, 206

Vejs, Andris, 119, 136n84, 148

Vetsmanis, Alfons, 72n85

Vimmsaare, Kuulo, 148, 163n3

Virbulus, Alberts, 18, 19, 39n64

Vitols, Alberts, 54

Voroshilov, Klement, 19, 20, 22, 56, 63, 65, 68n1, 74n124, 76n152, 77n165, 77n166

weddings. *See* church rites and adherence: marriages

Wilm, Ernst, 124
World Council of Churches (WCC), 46, 92, 94, 106n115, 111, 122–124, 129, 132n20, 138nn110–114, 138n120, 151, 152, 154, 167n60, 167n64, 168n74, 170n100, 203, 206
World Peace Council, 122
World War II, 3; destruction from, 9–10, 17; German occupation of Baltics during, 9, 13, 36n29; German POWs, 64, 77n161, 150; guerrilla resistance in Baltics after, 9–10, 12, 13, 14, 36n27, 43n151

Zachests, Julijans, 127, 140n159, 140n160
Zhdanov, Andrei, 10, 20, 65, 77n166
Zhidkov, Yakov, 54
Znanie, 120, 137n95, 165n39, 195n43
Zondaks, Bishop Valerian, 52, 63, 73, 83, 88, 98, 131n5, 131n7, 139n142, 156

ROBERT F. GOECKEL is Professor of Political Science and International Relations at the State University of New York at Geneseo. He is author of *The Lutheran Church and the East German State: Political Conflict and Change under Ulbricht and Honecker,* and its German edition, *Die Evangelische Kirche und die DDR. Konflikte, Gespraeche, Vereinbarungen unter Ulbricht und Honecker.*